50% OFF Online ISEE Upper Level Prep Course!

Dear Customer,

We consider it an honor and a privilege that you chose our ISEE Upper Level Study Guide. As a way of showing our appreciation and to help us better serve you, we have partnered with Mometrix Test Preparation to offer you **50% off their online ISEE Upper Level Prep Course**. Many ISEE Upper Level courses are needlessly expensive and don't deliver enough value. With their course, you get access to the best ISEE Upper Level prep material, and **you only pay half price**.

Mometrix has structured their online course to perfectly complement your printed study guide. The ISEE Upper Level Prep Course contains **in-depth lessons** that cover all the most important topics, over **450 practice questions** to ensure you feel prepared, and more than **350 digital flashcards**, so you can study while you're on the go.

Online ISEE Upper Level Prep Course

Topics Included:
- Verbal Reasoning
    - Agreement and Sentence Structure
    - Nuance and Word Meanings
- Quantitative Reasoning and Mathematics Achievement
    - Geometry and Measurement
    - Data Analysis and Probability
- Reading Comprehension
    - Author's Purpose
    - Persuasion and Rhetoric
- Essay
    - The Writing Process
    - Coherence in Writing

Course Features:
- ISEE Upper Level Study Guide
    - Get content that complements our best-selling study guide.
- Full-Length Practice Tests
    - With over 450 practice questions, you can test yourself again and again.
- Mobile Friendly
    - If you need to study on the go, the course is easily accessible from your mobile device.
- ISEE Upper Level Flashcards
    - Our course includes a flashcard mode with over 350 content cards to help you study.

To receive this discount, visit them at mometrix.com/university/isee-upper or simply scan this QR code with your smartphone. At the checkout page, enter the discount code: **ISEEU50TPB**

If you have any questions or concerns, please contact them at support@mometrix.com.

Sincerely,

 partnership with

Online Resources & Audiobook Access

Included with your purchase are multiple online resources. This includes the practice tests in an interactive format and a convenient study timer to help you manage your time.

Instructions for accessing these resources can be found on the last page of this book.

ISEE® Upper Level Prep Book 2025-2026
4 ISEE Practice Tests and Study Guide [Includes Detailed Answer Explanations]

Lydia Morrison

Copyright © 2025 by TPB Publishing

All rights reserved. No part of this publication may be reproduced, distributed, or transmitted in any form or by any means, including photocopying, recording, or other electronic or mechanical methods, without the prior written permission of the publisher, except in the case of brief quotations embodied in critical reviews and certain other noncommercial uses permitted by copyright law.

Written and edited by TPB Publishing.

TPB Publishing is not associated with or endorsed by any official testing organization. TPB Publishing is a publisher of unofficial educational products. All test and organization names are trademarks of their respective owners. Content in this book is included for utilitarian purposes only and does not constitute an endorsement by TPB Publishing of any particular point of view.

ISBN 13: 9781637753378

Table of Contents

Welcome 1

Quick Overview 2

Test-Taking Strategies 3

Study Prep Plan for the ISEE Upper Test 7

Introduction to the ISEE Upper Level Exam 10

Verbal Reasoning 13

Sentence Completion 20

Practice Quiz 24

Answer Explanations 25

Quantitative Reasoning and Mathematics Achievement 26

Numbers and Operations 27

Algebra 68

Geometry/Measurement 89

Data Analysis/Probability 125

Practice Quiz 136

Answer Explanations 137

Reading Comprehension 138

Main Idea 138

Supporting Ideas 140

Inference 141

Vocabulary 143

Organization/Logic 145

Tone/Style/Figurative Language 148

Practice Quiz 154

Answer Explanations 156

Essay 157
Practice Essay 163

Practice Test #1 164
Verbal Reasoning 164
Quantitative Reasoning 169
Reading Comprehension 177
Mathematics Achievement 185
Essay 197

Answer Explanations #1 198
Quantitative Reasoning 202
Reading Comprehension 207
Mathematics Achievement 209

Practice Test #2 217
Verbal Reasoning 217
Quantitative Reasoning 222
Reading Comprehension 230
Mathematics Achievement 239
Essay 249

Answer Explanations #2 250
Verbal Reasoning 250
Quantitative Reasoning 255
Reading Comprehension 258
Mathematics Achievement 263

ISEE Upper Practice Tests #3 & #4 273
Online Resources 275

Welcome

Dear Reader,

Welcome to your new Test Prep Books study guide! We are pleased that you chose us to help you prepare for your exam. There are many study options to choose from, and we appreciate you choosing us. Studying can be a daunting task, but we have designed a smart, effective study guide to help prepare you for what lies ahead.

Whether you're a parent helping your child learn and grow, a high school student working hard to get into your dream college, or a nursing student studying for a complex exam, we want to help give you the tools you need to succeed. We hope this study guide gives you the skills and the confidence to thrive, and we can't thank you enough for allowing us to be part of your journey.

In an effort to continue to improve our products, we welcome feedback from our customers. We look forward to hearing from you. Suggestions, success stories, and criticisms can all be communicated by emailing us at support@testprepbooks.com.

Sincerely,
Test Prep Books Team

Quick Overview

As you draw closer to taking your exam, effective preparation becomes more and more important. Thankfully, you have this study guide to help you get ready. Use this guide to help keep your studying on track and refer to it often.

This study guide contains several key sections that will help you be successful on your exam. The guide contains tips for what you should do the night before and the day of the test. Also included are test-taking tips. Knowing the right information is not always enough. Many well-prepared test takers struggle with exams. These tips will help equip you to accurately read, assess, and answer test questions.

A large part of the guide is devoted to showing you what content to expect on the exam and to helping you better understand that content. In this guide are practice test questions so that you can see how well you have grasped the content. Then, answer explanations are provided so that you can understand why you missed certain questions.

Don't try to cram the night before you take your exam. This is not a wise strategy for a few reasons. First, your retention of the information will be low. Your time would be better used by reviewing information you already know rather than trying to learn a lot of new information. Second, you will likely become stressed as you try to gain a large amount of knowledge in a short amount of time. Third, you will be depriving yourself of sleep. So be sure to go to bed at a reasonable time the night before. Being well-rested helps you focus and remain calm.

Be sure to eat a substantial breakfast the morning of the exam. If you are taking the exam in the afternoon, be sure to have a good lunch as well. Being hungry is distracting and can make it difficult to focus. You have hopefully spent lots of time preparing for the exam. Don't let an empty stomach get in the way of success!

When travelling to the testing center, leave earlier than needed. That way, you have a buffer in case you experience any delays. This will help you remain calm and will keep you from missing your appointment time at the testing center.

Be sure to pace yourself during the exam. Don't try to rush through the exam. There is no need to risk performing poorly on the exam just so you can leave the testing center early. Allow yourself to use all of the allotted time if needed.

Remain positive while taking the exam even if you feel like you are performing poorly. Thinking about the content you should have mastered will not help you perform better on the exam.

Once the exam is complete, take some time to relax. Even if you feel that you need to take the exam again, you will be well served by some down time before you begin studying again. It's often easier to convince yourself to study if you know that it will come with a reward!

Test-Taking Strategies

1. Predicting the Answer

When you feel confident in your preparation for a multiple-choice test, try predicting the answer before reading the answer choices. This is especially useful on questions that test objective factual knowledge. By predicting the answer before reading the available choices, you eliminate the possibility that you will be distracted or led astray by an incorrect answer choice. You will feel more confident in your selection if you read the question, predict the answer, and then find your prediction among the answer choices. After using this strategy, be sure to still read all of the answer choices carefully and completely. If you feel unprepared, you should not attempt to predict the answers. This would be a waste of time and an opportunity for your mind to wander in the wrong direction.

2. Reading the Whole Question

Too often, test takers scan a multiple-choice question, recognize a few familiar words, and immediately jump to the answer choices. Test authors are aware of this common impatience, and they will sometimes prey upon it. For instance, a test author might subtly turn the question into a negative, or he or she might redirect the focus of the question right at the end. The only way to avoid falling into these traps is to read the entirety of the question carefully before reading the answer choices.

3. Looking for Wrong Answers

Long and complicated multiple-choice questions can be intimidating. One way to simplify a difficult multiple-choice question is to eliminate all of the answer choices that are clearly wrong. In most sets of answers, there will be at least one selection that can be dismissed right away. If the test is administered on paper, the test taker could draw a line through it to indicate that it may be ignored; otherwise, the test taker will have to perform this operation mentally or on scratch paper. In either case, once the obviously incorrect answers have been eliminated, the remaining choices may be considered. Sometimes identifying the clearly wrong answers will give the test taker some information about the correct answer. For instance, if one of the remaining answer choices is a direct opposite of one of the eliminated answer choices, it may well be the correct answer. The opposite of obviously wrong is obviously right! Of course, this is not always the case. Some answers are obviously incorrect simply because they are irrelevant to the question being asked. Still, identifying and eliminating some incorrect answer choices is a good way to simplify a multiple-choice question.

4. Don't Overanalyze

Anxious test takers often overanalyze questions. When you are nervous, your brain will often run wild, causing you to make associations and discover clues that don't actually exist. If you feel that this may be a problem for you, do whatever you can to slow down during the test. Try taking a deep breath or counting to ten. As you read and consider the question, restrict yourself to the particular words used by the author. Avoid thought tangents about what the author *really* meant, or what he or she was *trying* to say. The only things that matter on a multiple-choice test are the words that are actually in the question. You must avoid reading too much into a multiple-choice question, or supposing that the writer meant something other than what he or she wrote.

5. No Need for Panic

It is wise to learn as many strategies as possible before taking a multiple-choice test, but it is likely that you will come across a few questions for which you simply don't know the answer. In this situation, avoid panicking. Because

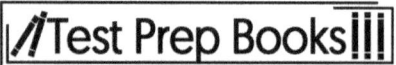

most multiple-choice tests include dozens of questions, the relative value of a single wrong answer is small. As much as possible, you should compartmentalize each question on a multiple-choice test. In other words, you should not allow your feelings about one question to affect your success on the others. When you find a question that you either don't understand or don't know how to answer, just take a deep breath and do your best. Read the entire question slowly and carefully. Try rephrasing the question a couple of different ways. Then, read all of the answer choices carefully. After eliminating obviously wrong answers, make a selection and move on to the next question.

6. Confusing Answer Choices

When working on a difficult multiple-choice question, there may be a tendency to focus on the answer choices that are the easiest to understand. Many people, whether consciously or not, gravitate to the answer choices that require the least concentration, knowledge, and memory. This is a mistake. When you come across an answer choice that is confusing, you should give it extra attention. A question might be confusing because you do not know

the subject matter to which it refers. If this is the case, don't eliminate the answer before you have affirmatively settled on another. When you come across an answer choice of this type, set it aside as you look at the remaining choices. If you can confidently assert that one of the other choices is correct, you can leave the confusing answer aside. Otherwise, you will need to take a moment to try to better understand the confusing answer choice. Rephrasing is one way to tease out the sense of a confusing answer choice.

7. Your First Instinct

Many people struggle with multiple-choice tests because they overthink the questions. If you have studied sufficiently for the test, you should be prepared to trust your first instinct once you have carefully and completely read the question and all of the answer choices. There is a great deal of research suggesting that the mind can come to the correct conclusion very quickly once it has obtained all of the relevant information. At times, it may seem to you as if your intuition is working faster even than your reasoning mind. This may in fact be true. The knowledge you obtain while studying may be retrieved from your subconscious before you have a chance to work out the associations that support it. Verify your instinct by working out the reasons that it should be trusted.

8. Key Words

Many test takers struggle with multiple-choice questions because they have poor reading comprehension skills. Quickly reading and understanding a multiple-choice question requires a mixture of skill and experience. To help with this, try jotting down a few key words and phrases on a piece of scrap paper. Doing this concentrates the process of reading and forces the mind to weigh the relative importance of the question's parts. In selecting words and phrases to write down, the test taker thinks about the question more deeply and carefully. This is especially true for multiple-choice questions that are preceded by a long prompt.

9. Subtle Negatives

One of the oldest tricks in the multiple-choice test writer's book is to subtly reverse the meaning of a question with a word like *not* or *except*. If you are not paying attention to each word in the question, you can easily be led astray by this trick. For instance, a common question format is, "Which of the following is...?" Obviously, if the question instead is, "Which of the following is not...?," then the answer will be quite different. Even worse, the test makers are aware of the potential for this mistake and will include one answer choice that would be correct if the question were not negated or reversed. A test taker who misses the reversal will find what he or she believes to be a correct answer and will be so confident that he or she will fail to reread the question and discover the original error. The only way to avoid this is to practice a wide variety of multiple-choice questions and to pay close attention to each and every word.

10. Reading Every Answer Choice

It may seem obvious, but you should always read every one of the answer choices! Too many test takers fall into the habit of scanning the question and assuming that they understand the question because they recognize a few key words. From there, they pick the first answer choice that answers the question they believe they have read. Test takers who read all of the answer choices might discover that one of the latter answer choices is actually *more* correct. Moreover, reading all of the answer choices can remind you of facts related to the question that can help you arrive at the correct answer. Sometimes, a misstatement or incorrect detail in one of the latter answer choices will trigger your memory of the subject and will enable you to find the right answer. Failing to read all of the answer choices is like not reading all of the items on a restaurant menu: you might miss out on the perfect choice.

11. Spot the Hedges

One of the keys to success on multiple-choice tests is paying close attention to every word. This is never truer than with words like *almost*, *most*, *some*, and *sometimes*. These words are called "hedges" because they indicate that a statement is not totally true or not true in every place and time. An absolute statement will contain no hedges, but in many subjects, the answers are not always straightforward or absolute. There are always exceptions to the rules in these subjects. For this reason, you should favor those multiple-choice questions that contain hedging language. The presence of qualifying words indicates that the author is taking special care with his or her words, which is certainly important when composing the right answer. After all, there are many ways to be wrong, but there is only one way to be right! For this reason, it is wise to avoid answers that are absolute when taking a multiple-choice test. An absolute answer is one that says things are either all one way or all another. They often include words like *every*, *always*, *best*, and *never*. If you are taking a multiple-choice test in a subject that doesn't lend itself to absolute answers, be on your guard if you see any of these words.

12. Long Answers

 In many subject areas, the answers are not simple. As already mentioned, the right answer often requires hedges. Another common feature of the answers to a complex or subjective question are qualifying clauses, which are groups of words that subtly modify the meaning of the sentence. If the question or answer choice describes a rule to which there are exceptions or the subject matter is complicated, ambiguous, or confusing, the correct answer will require many words in order to be expressed clearly and accurately. In essence, you should not be deterred by answer choices that seem excessively long. Oftentimes, the author of the text will not be able to write the correct answer without offering some qualifications and modifications. Your job is to read the answer choices thoroughly and completely and to select the one that most accurately and precisely answers the question.

13. Restating to Understand

Sometimes, a question on a multiple-choice test is difficult not because of what it asks but because of how it is written. If this is the case, restate the question or answer choice in different words. This process serves a couple of important purposes. First, it forces you to concentrate on the core of the question. In order to rephrase the

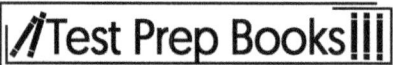

question accurately, you have to understand it well. Rephrasing the question will concentrate your mind on the key words and ideas. Second, it will present the information to your mind in a fresh way. This process may trigger your memory and render some useful scrap of information picked up while studying.

14. True Statements

Sometimes an answer choice will be true in itself, but it does not answer the question. This is one of the main reasons why it is essential to read the question carefully and completely before proceeding to the answer choices. Too often, test takers skip ahead to the answer choices and look for true statements. Having found one of these, they are content to select it without reference to the question above. The savvy test taker will always read the entire question before turning to the answer choices. Then, having settled on a correct answer choice, he or she will refer to the original question and ensure that the selected answer is relevant. The mistake of choosing a correct-but-irrelevant answer choice is especially common on questions related to specific pieces of objective knowledge.

15. No Patterns

One of the more dangerous ideas that circulates about multiple-choice tests is that the correct answers tend to fall into patterns. These erroneous ideas range from a belief that B and C are the most common right answers, to the idea that an unprepared test-taker should answer "A-B-A-C-A-D-A-B-A." It cannot be emphasized enough that pattern-seeking of this type is exactly the WRONG way to approach a multiple-choice test. To begin with, it is highly unlikely that the test maker will plot the correct answers according to some predetermined pattern. The questions are scrambled and delivered in a random order. Furthermore, even if the test maker was following a pattern in the assignation of correct answers, there is no reason why the test taker would know which pattern he or she was using. Any attempt to discern a pattern in the answer choices is a waste of time and a distraction from the real work of taking the test. A test taker would be much better served by extra preparation before the test than by reliance on a pattern in the answers.

Study Prep Plan for the ISEE Upper Test

1 **Schedule** - Use one of our study schedules below or come up with one of your own.

2 **Relax** - Test anxiety can hurt even the best students. There are many ways to reduce stress. Find the one that works best for you.

3 **Execute** - Once you have a good plan in place, be sure to stick to it.

One Week Study Schedule

Day 1	Verbal Reasoning
Day 2	Algebra
Day 3	Geometry/Measurement
Day 4	Data Analysis/Probability
Day 5	Organization/Logic
Day 6	Practice Test #1
Day 7	Take Your Exam!

Two Week Study Schedule

Day 1	Verbal Reasoning	Day 8	Data Analysis/Probability
Day 2	Quantitative Reasoning and Mathematics...	Day 9	Practice Quiz
Day 3	Percents	Day 10	Organization/Logic
Day 4	Algebra	Day 11	Practice Test #1
Day 5	Systems of Linear Inequalities	Day 12	Practice Test #2
Day 6	Perimeter and Area of Geometric Shapes	Day 13	Practice Test #3
Day 7	Locating Ordered Pairs in All Four Quadrants...	Day 14	Take Your Exam!

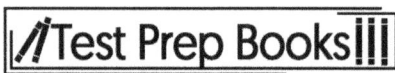

Study Prep Plan for the ISEE Upper Test

One Month Study Schedule

Day 1	Verbal Reasoning	Day 11	Zeros of Polynomials	Day 21	Essay
Day 2	Synonyms	Day 12	Geometry/Measurement	Day 22	Practice Test #1
Day 3	Quantitative Reasoning and...	Day 13	Perimeter and Area of Geometric Shapes	Day 23	Answer Explanations #1
Day 4	Estimation and Rounding	Day 14	Surface Area	Day 24	Practice Test #2
Day 5	Percents	Day 15	Points, Lines, and Angles	Day 25	Answer Explanations #2
Day 6	Sequences and Series	Day 16	Locating Ordered Pairs in All Four Quadrants...	Day 26	Practice Test #3
Day 7	Determinants	Day 17	Data Analysis/Probability	Day 27	Answer Explanations #3
Day 8	Algebra	Day 18	Practice Quiz	Day 28	Practice Test #4
Day 9	Distributive Property	Day 19	Organization/Logic	Day 29	Answer Explanations #4
Day 10	Systems of Linear Inequalities	Day 20	Tone/Style/Figurative Language	Day 30	Take Your Exam!

Build your own prep plan by visiting:

testprepbooks.com/prep

As you study for your test, we'd like to take the opportunity to remind you that you are capable of great things! With the right tools and dedication, you truly can do anything you set your mind to. The fact that you are holding this book right now shows how committed you are. In case no one has told you lately, you've got this! Our intention behind including this coloring page is to give you the chance to take some time to engage your creative side when you need a little brain-break from studying. As a company, we want to encourage people like you to achieve their dreams by providing good quality study materials for the tests and certifications that improve careers and change lives. As individuals, many of us have taken such tests in our careers, and we know how challenging this process can be. While we can't come alongside you and cheer you on personally, we can offer you the space to recall your purpose, reconnect with your passion, and refresh your brain through an artistic practice. We wish you every success, and happy studying!

Introduction to the ISEE Upper Level Exam

Function of the Test

The Independent School Entrance Exam (ISEE) Upper Level is an entrance exam for grades 9–12 for independent schools across the U.S and abroad, developed and facilitated by the Educational Records Bureau (ERB). Complete scores are sent to the school of choice for application review. Although schools take the score into consideration, the score is not the only criteria for acceptance.

Test Administration

The ISEE is offered during three separate testing seasons throughout the year: Fall (August through November), Winter (December through March), and Spring/Summer (April through July). Students must register well before the test date, as registration closes two weeks before the test is given. Testing is offered online at Prometric testing centers, approved ERB member school test sites, ISEE testing offices, or at home. The option to take the test by paper is offered at school test sites and ISEE testing offices. For retesting, students may retake the ISEE up to three times in a twelve-month admission period, but only once per testing season.

Students must arrive at the testing center 15–30 minutes before the test begins. The verification letter provides the check-in time that the student must arrive by. Those who arrive late are not permitted into the testing room and must reschedule their exam. Personal items are not allowed in the exam room, including cell phones, paper, rulers, watches, compasses, etc. Paper testing permits students to bring four #2 pencils, two pens with either blue or black ink, and four erasers if the pencils do not have erasers. Two five- to ten-minute breaks are given during the exam. The first break is after the Quantitative Reasoning section. The second break is after the Mathematics Achievement section.

Introduction to the ISEE Upper Level Exam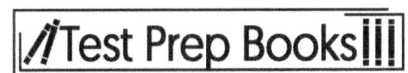

Test Format

The ISEE Upper Level exam includes Verbal Reasoning, Quantitative Reasoning, Reading Comprehension, Mathematics Achievement, and an essay, in that order. Below is a table with more details on each section:

Section	Questions	Time
Verbal Reasoning	40 (35 scored, 5 unscored)	20 minutes
Quantitative Reasoning	37 (32 scored, 5 unscored)	35 minutes
Reading Comprehension	36 (30 scored, 6 unscored)	35 minutes
Mathematics Achievement	47 (42 scored, 5 unscored)	40 minutes
Essay	1 prompt	30 minutes
Total	160 questions + 1 essay	160 minutes

Test takers encounter two parts in the Verbal Reasoning section of the Upper Level ISEE. In the first part, the synonym section, questions address the test taker's understanding of language and the meanings of different words. The second part is the sentence completion section, which assesses the test taker's knowledge of words along with their ability to create logical sentences by filling in one or two blanks using context clues to choose the most appropriate word or words. Of the thirty-five scored questions in the Verbal Reasoning section, seventeen will be synonym questions and eighteen will be sentence completion questions. For sentence completion, ten questions will have one blank to fill in and eight questions will have two blanks to fill in.

The vocabulary words are pulled from all areas of study and are of age-appropriate difficulty. Successful test takers should think about the parts of a word and the structure of the English language, including things like:

- Word origins
- Root words
- Prefixes
- Suffixes
- Words with multiple meanings

The Quantitative Reasoning section of the exam consists of two types of questions: word problems and quantitative comparison questions. Of the thirty-two scored questions, eighteen will be word problems and fourteen will be quantitative comparison.

The Reading Comprehension section of the test consists of thirty scored questions that accompany passages of varying lengths. Skill that are assessed in this section are broken down into six ISEE strands: main idea, supporting ideas, inference, vocabulary, organization/logic, and tone/style/figurative language.

The Mathematics Achievement section of the exam consists of forty-two scored questions that do require calculation.

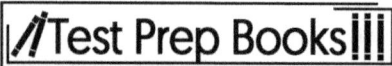

Scoring

Students should try to narrow down correct answers, as scores are determined by the number of questions answered correctly. There is no penalty for guessing incorrectly since there is no score difference between an omitted answer and an incorrect answer. Not all questions on the test will be scored. The unscored questions are experimental for the creation of future test questions. Additionally, the essay will not be scored. The school will receive the essay to assess the student's skills in writing. For the scored sections of the exam, students are compared to fellow students by grade within the previous three years by a percentile ranking on the score report. Scores for paper tests are sent to the Individual Student Report (ISR) and an email will be sent when scores are ready. Score reports for online tests will post three to five days after the test.

Scoring comes with a raw score and a scaled score. Raw scores might be something like 35/40 for the Verbal Reasoning section, showing the number of questions guessed correctly. Scaled scores have been converted to a higher number and show a range from 760 to 940.

Verbal Reasoning

This Verbal Reasoning portion of the exam is specifically constructed to test vocabulary skills and the ability to discern the best answer that matches the provided word or completes the sentence. The synonym questions chiefly test vocabulary knowledge by asking test takers to select the best synonym for the provided word. Prior knowledge of what the words mean is helpful in order to answer correctly. If the meaning of a word is unknown, there are some strategies that can be used to rule out false answers and choose the correct ones.

The sentence completion portion of the test goes beyond simply testing for knowledge of definitions. Test takers must be able to choose the word that functions best to complete the sentence based on context clues. Some questions will have a sentence with two blanks that need to be filled in with the correct words. The correct choice will be the set of words that together complete the sentence. The tips for the synonym portion of the test apply for this section as well, but there are additional things to consider for the sentence completion section.

Format of the Questions

The synonym questions are very simple in construction, providing just a single word. There are no special directions, alternate meanings, or analogies to work with. The objective is to analyze the given word and then choose the answer that means the same thing as or is closest in meaning to the given word. Note the example below:

BLUSTERY

a. Hard
b. Windy
c. Mythical
d. Stoney

All of the questions in this section will appear exactly like the above sample. This is generally the standard layout throughout other exams, so some test-takers may already be familiar with the structure. The principle remains the same. At the top of the section, clear directions will be given to choose the answer that most precisely defines the given word. In this case, the answer is *windy* (B), since *windy* and *blustery* are synonymous.

Sentence completion questions are simply sentences with one or two missing words. Four answer choices are given, and for the sentences that have two blanks, the order of the words in the answer choices coincides with the order of the blanks in the sentence. Here's an example:

> The clever girl, desperate to make a batch of chocolate chip cookies, charmed her mother into letting her take over the kitchen by writing a(n) _____ poem about the _____ treat.

a. brief; dessert
b. sad; elusive
c. delectable; persuasive
d. eloquent; desired

The answer for this sentence completion question would be Choice *D*. Choice *A* is incorrect because a brief poem probably wouldn't be enough to charm the mother unless it was extra witty and impressive in its conciseness. Also, *dessert* makes the phrase "dessert treat" redundant, and it doesn't make sense. Choice *B* is incorrect because a sad poem about an elusive, or difficult to find, treat might be cute, but the sentence is about the girl wanting to make cookies, not find them. Therefore, it's narrowed down to the last two choices. Both choices have words that could logically complete the sentence, but Choice *C* is not in the correct order. The first word in the pair must be able to

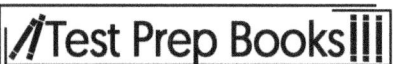

Verbal Reasoning

go in the first blank and the second word must make sense in the second blank. A delectable poem about the persuasive treat is incorrect. Choice *D* is the perfect choice since eloquent means articulate and persuasive, which would be perfect for a poem that's created to charm a mother into letting her daughter make cookies. Of course, the cookies are what the girl desires, so *desired* is the best word for the second blank.

Preparation

In truth, there is no set way to prepare for this portion of the exam that will guarantee a perfect score since the words used on the test are unpredictable. There is no set list provided to study from. The definition of the provided word needs to be determined on the spot. This sounds challenging, but there are still ways to prepare mentally for the test. It may help to expand your vocabulary a little each day. Several resources are available, in books and online, that collect words and definitions that tend to show up frequently on standardized tests. Knowledge of a variety words can increase the strength of your vocabulary.

Mindset is key. The meanings of challenging words can often be found by relying on the past experiences of the test-taker. How? Well, test-takers have been talking their entire lives—knowing words and how words work. It helps to have a positive mindset from the start, understanding that the answer can still be found even if the definition of a word is not immediately known. There are aspects of words that are recognizable and can help discern the correct answers and eliminate the incorrect ones.

Word Origins and Word Parts

Studying a foreign language in school, particularly Latin or any of the romance languages (Latin-influenced), is advantageous. English is a language that is highly influenced by Latin and Greek words. The **roots** of much of the English vocabulary have Latin origins; these roots can bind many words together and often allude to a shared definition.

A word can consist of the following combinations:

- root
- root + suffix
- prefix + root
- prefix + root + suffix

If someone is unfamiliar with the word *submarine* they could break the word into its parts.

    prefix + root

    sub + marine

It can be determined that *sub* means *below* as in *subway* and *subpar*. Additionally, one can determine that *marine* refers to *the sea* as in *marine life*. Thus, it can be figured that *submarine* refers to something below the water.

Roots

Roots are the basic components of words. Many roots can stand alone as individual words, but others must be combined with a prefix or suffix to be a word. For example, *calc* is a root but it needs a suffix to be an actual word (*calcium*).

Verbal Reasoning

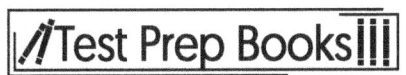

Here's an example synonym question:

FERVENT

    a. Lame
    b. Joyful
    c. Thorough
    d. Boiling

Fervent descends from the Latin word, *fervere*, which means "to boil or glow" and figuratively means "impassioned." The Latin root present in the word is *ferv*, which is what gives *fervent* the definition: showing great warmth and spirit or spirited, hot, glowing. This provides a link to *boiling* (D) just by root word association, but there's more to analyze. Among the other choices, none relate to *fervent*. The word *lame* (A) means "crippled, disabled, weak, or inadequate." None of these words share the same meaning as or define the word *fervent*. While being fervent can reflect joy, *joyful* (B) directly describes "a great state of happiness," while *fervent* is simply expressing the idea of having very strong feelings—not necessarily joy. *Thorough* (C) means "complete, perfect, painstaking, or with mastery;" while something can be done thoroughly and fervently, none of these words match *fervent* as closely as *boiling* does. Not only does *boiling* connect in a linguistic way, it also connects in the way it is used in our language. While *boiling* can express being physically hot and undergoing a change, *boiling* is also used to reflect emotional states. People say they are "boiling over" when in heightened emotional states; "boiling mad" is another expression. *Boiling*, like *fervent*, also embodies a sense of heightened intensity. This makes *boiling* the best choice!

The Latin root *ferv* is seen in other words such as *fervor*, *fervid*, and even *ferment*. Each of these words are connected to and can be described by "boil" or "glow," whether it is in a physical sense or in a metaphorical one. Such a pattern can be seen in other word sets. Here's another example:

GRACIOUS

    a. Fruitful
    b. Angry
    c. Grateful
    d. Understood

This one is a little easier; the answer is *grateful* (C) because both words mean "thankful." Even if the meanings of both words are not known, there's a connection found by looking at the beginnings of both words: *gra/grat*. Once again, there is a root that stretches back to classical language. Both terms come from the Latin, *gratis*, which literally means "thanks."

Understanding root words can help identify the meaning in a lot of word choices as well as help the test-taker grasp the nature of the given word. Many dictionaries, both in book form and online, offer information on the origins of words, highlighting these roots. When studying for the test, it helps to look up an unfamiliar word for its definition and then to check whether it has a root that can be connected to any of the other terms.

Prefixes
The **prefix** of a word can actually reveal a lot about its definition. Many prefixes are actually Greco-Roman roots as well—but these are more familiar and a lot easier to recognize! When encountering any unfamiliar words, try

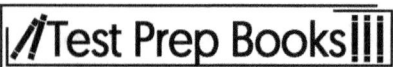

Verbal Reasoning

looking at prefixes to discern the definition and then compare that with the choices. The prefix should be determined in order to help find the word's meaning. Some of the most common prefixes are the following:

Prefix	Meaning	Example
a-	not	amoral, asymptomatic
anti-	against	antidote, antifreeze
auto-	self	automobile, automatic
circum-	around	circumference, circumspect
co-, com-, con-	together	coworker, companion
contra-	against	contradict, contrary
de-	negation or reversal	deflate, deodorant
extra-	outside, beyond	extraterrestrial, extracurricular
in-, im-, il-, ir-	not	impossible, irregular
inter-	between	international, intervene
intra-	within	intramural, intranet
mis-	wrongly	mistake, misunderstand
mono-	one	monolith, monopoly
non-	not	nonpartisan, nonsense
pre-	before	preview, prediction
re-	again	review, renew
semi-	half	semicircle, semicolon
sub-	under	subway, submarine
super-	above	superhuman, superintendent
trans-	across, beyond, through	trans-Siberian, transform
un-	not	unwelcome, unfriendly

Here's an example synonym question:

PREMEDITATE

a. Sporadic
b. Calculated
c. Interfere
d. Determined

With *premeditate*, there's the common prefix *pre*. This helps draw connections to other words like *prepare* or *preassemble*. *Pre* refers to "before, already being, or having already." *Meditate* means "to think or plan." Therefore, *premeditate* means "to think or plan beforehand with intent." Therefore, it makes sense to look for a term that deals with thinking or planning in preparation of something. *Sporadic* (A) refers to events happening in irregular patterns, which is quite the opposite of premeditated. *Interfere* (C) also has nothing to do with premeditate; the prefix *inter* mean "between" and the word means to "obstruct" or "intrude." *Determined* (D) is an adjective with no hint of being related to something done before or in preparation of something, so this choice is incorrect. However, *calculated* (B) does share a similar meaning with the word *premeditate*. *Calculated* refers to acting with a full awareness of consequences, so inherently, planning beforehand is involved. A route or the cost of starting a plan

Verbal Reasoning

are things that can be calculated. Just by paying attention to a prefix, the doors to a meaning can open to help easily figure out which word would be the best choice. Here's another example.

REGAIN

    a. Erupt
    b. Ponder
    c. Seek
    d. Recoup

Recoup (D) is the right answer. The prefix *re* often appears in front of words to give them the meaning of occurring again. *Regain* means "to repossess something that was lost." *Recoup*, which also has the *re* prefix, literally means "to regain." In this example, both the given word and the correct answer share the *re* prefix, which makes the pair easy to connect. However, do not rely only on prefixes to choose an answer. Make sure to analyze all options before marking an answer. Going through the other words in this sample, none of them come close to meaning "regain" except *recoup*.

Suffixes

A **suffix** is a letter or group of letters added at the end of a word to form another word. When written alone, suffixes are preceded by a dash to indicate that the root word comes before. While the addition of a prefix alters the meaning of the base word, the addition of a **suffix** may also affect a word's part of speech. It is often very helpful to determine the **part of speech** of a word when choosing an answer for the sentence completion questions. Should it be an adjective, adverb, noun, verb, etc.? Notice how suffixes change the form of a word: adding a suffix can change the noun *material* into the verb *materialize* and back to a noun again in *materialization*. For synonym questions, often the correct answer will also be the same part of speech as the given word. Isolate the part of speech and what it describes and look for an answer choice that also describes the same part of speech. For example, if the given word is an adverb describing an action word, then look for another adverb describing an action word:

SWIFTLY

    a. Fast
    b. Quietly
    c. Sudden
    d. Quickly

Swiftly is an adverb that describes the speed of an action. *Fast* (A) and *sudden* (C) can be eliminated because they are not adverbs, and *quietly* (B) can be eliminated because it does not describe speed. This leaves *quickly* (D), which is the correct answer. *Fast* and *sudden* may throw off some test-takers because they both describe speed, but *quickly* matches more closely because it is an adverb, as is swiftly.

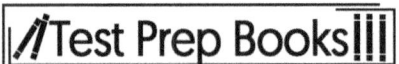

Verbal Reasoning

The following are some common suffixes:

Suffix	Part of Speech	Meaning	Example
-able, -ible	adjective	having the ability to	honorable, flexible
-acy, -cy	noun	state or quality	intimacy, dependency
-al, -ical	adjective	having the quality of	historical, tribal
-en	verb	to cause to become	strengthen, embolden
-er, -ier	adjective	comparative	happier, longer
-est, -iest	adjective	superlative	sunniest, hottest
-ess	noun	female	waitress, actress
-ful	adjective	full of, characterized by	beautiful, thankful
-fy, -ify	verb	to cause, to come to be	liquefy, intensify
-ism	noun	doctrine, belief, action	Communism, Buddhism
-ive, -ative, -itive	adjective	having the quality of	creative, innovative
-ize	verb	to convert into, to subject to	Americanize, dramatize
-less	adjective	without, missing	emotionless, hopeless
-ly	adverb	in the manner of	quickly, energetically
-ness	noun	quality or state	goodness, darkness
-ous, -ious, -eous	adjective	having the quality of	spontaneous, pious
-ship	noun	status or condition	partnership, ownership
-tion	noun	action or state	renovation, promotion
-y	adjective	characterized by	smoky, dreamy

Positive Versus Negative Sounding Words

Another tool for the mental toolbox is simply distinguishing whether a word has a positive or negative **connotation**. Like electrical wires, words carry energy; they are crafted to draw certain attention and to have certain strength to them. Words can be described as positive and uplifting (a stronger word) or they can be negative and scathing (a stronger word). Sometimes they are neutral—having no particular connotation. Distinguishing how a word is supposed to be interpreted will help with learning its definition as well as help with drawing parallels between word choices. While it is true that words must usually be taken in the context of how they are used, word definitions have inherent meanings as well. They have a distinct vibe to pick up on. Here is an example:

EXCELLENT

a. Fair
b. Optimum
c. Reasonable
d. Negative

As you know, *excellent* is a very positive word. It refers to something being better than good—above average. In this sample, *negative* (D) can easily be eliminated. *Reasonable* (C) is more or less a neutral word: it's not bad but it doesn't communicate the higher quality that excellent represents. It's just, well, reasonable. This leaves the possible choices of fair (A) and optimum (B). Or does it? *Fair* is a positive word; it is used to describe things that are good, even beautiful. But in the modern context, *fair* is defined as "good, but somewhat average or just decent": "You did a fairly good job." or, "That was fair." On the other hand, *optimum* is positive and is a stronger word. *Optimum* describes the most favorable outcome. This makes *optimum* the best word choice that matches *excellent* in both

Verbal Reasoning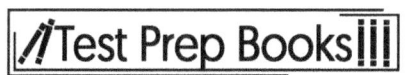

strength and connotation. Not only are the two words positive, but they also express the same level of positivity. Here is another example:

REPULSE

   a. Draw
   b. Encumber
   c. Force
   d. Disgust

Repulse sounds strongly negative when said. It is commonly used in the context of something being repulsive, disgusting, or distasteful. It's also defined as "an attack that drives people away." This means that a synonym is needed that also carries a negative meaning. *Draw* (A) and *force* (C) are both neutral. *Encumber* (B) and *disgust* (D) are negative. *Disgust* is a stronger negative than *encumber*. Of all the words given, only *disgust* directly defines a feeling of distaste and aversion that is synonymous with *repulse* while also matching in both negativity and strength.

Placing the Word in a Sentence

Often it is easier to discern the meaning of a word if it is used in a sentence. If the given word can be used in a sentence, then try replacing it with some of the answer choices to see which words seem to make sense in the same sentence. Here's an example:

REMARKABLE

   a. Often
   b. Capable
   c. Outstanding
   d. Shining

A sentence can be formed with the word *remarkable*. "My grade point average is remarkable." None of the examples make sense when replacing the word *remarkable* in the sentence other than the word *outstanding* (C), so *outstanding* is the obvious answer. *Shining* (D) is also a word with a positive connotation, but *outstanding* fits better in the sentence.

Picking the Closest Answer

As the answer choices are reviewed, two scenarios might stand out. An exact definition match might not be found for the given word among the choices, or there might be several word choices that could be considered synonymous with the given word. This is intentionally done to test the ability to draw parallels between the words to produce an answer that best fits the prompt word. Again, the closest fitting word will be the answer. Even when facing these two circumstances, finding the one word that fits best is the proper strategy. Here's an example:

INSUBORDINATION

   a. Cooperative
   b. Disciplined
   c. Rebel
   d. Contagious

Insubordination refers to a defiance or utter refusal of authority. Looking over the choices, none of these terms provide definite matches to *insubordination* like *insolence*, *mutiny*, or *misconduct* would. This is fine; the answer doesn't have to be a perfect synonym. The choices don't reflect *insubordination* in any way, except *rebel* (C). After

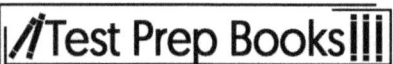

all, when *rebel* is used as a verb, it means "to act against authority." It's also used as a noun: someone who goes against authority. Therefore, *rebel* is the best choice.

In this section of the test, being a detective is a good course to take. Two or even three choices might be encountered that could be the answer. However, the answer that most perfectly fits the prompt word's meaning is the best answer. Choices should be narrowed one word at a time. The least-connected word should be eliminated first and then proceed until one word is left that is the closest synonym. Here is an example:

SEQUENCE

- a. List
- b. Range
- c. Series
- d. Replicate

A sequence reflects a particular order in which events or objects follow. The two closest options are *list* (A) and *series* (C). Both involve grouping things together, but which fits better? Consider each word more carefully. A list is comprised of items that fit in the same category, but that's really it. A list doesn't have to follow any particular order; it's just a list. On the other hand, a series is defined by events happening in a set order. A series relies on sequence, and a sequence can be described as a series. Thus, *series* is the correct answer!

For both portions of the Verbal Section in the Upper Level ISEE, the following information about vocabulary can provide helpful background knowledge to successfully answer questions. While some of this information has previously been touched upon, test takers can benefit from further explanation for several of these concepts.

Sentence Completion

Synonyms

When reading the sentence for the first time, a particular word might come to mind that would complete the sentence, but that word might not be an answer choice for the question. Recall that **synonyms** are words that mean the same or nearly the same thing in the same language. When presented with different options than the word that automatically comes to mind, consider that more than one word may be similar. Synonyms should always share the same part of speech. For instance, *shy* and *timid* are both adjectives and hold similar meanings. The words *shy* and *loner* are similar, but *shy* is an adjective while *loner* is a noun. Another way to test for the best synonym is to reread the sentence with each possible word and determine which one makes the most sense. Consider the following sentence: *He will love you forever.*

Now consider the words: *adore, sweet, kind*, and *nice*. They seem similar, but when used in the following applications with the initial sentence, not all of them are synonyms for *love*.

He will *adore* you forever.

He will *sweet* you forever.

He will *kind* you forever.

He will *nice* you forever.

In the first sentence, the word *love* is used as a verb. The best synonym from the list that shares the same part of speech is *adore*. *Adore* is a verb, and when substituted in the sentence, it is the only substitution that makes grammatical and semantic sense.

Synonyms can be found for nouns, adjectives, verbs, adverbs, and prepositions. Here are some examples of synonyms from different parts of speech:

- **Nouns**: clothes, wardrobe, attire, apparel
- **Verbs**: run, sprint, dash
- **Adjectives**: fast, quick, rapid, swift
- **Adverbs**: slowly, nonchalantly, leisurely
- **Prepositions**: near, proximal, neighboring, close

Here are several more examples of synonyms in the English language:

Word	Synonym	Meaning
smart	intelligent	having or showing a high level of intelligence
exact	specific	clearly identified
almost	nearly	not quite but very close
to annoy	to bother	to irritate
to answer	to reply	to form a written or verbal response
building	edifice	a structure that stands on its own with a roof and four walls
business	commerce	the act of purchasing, negotiating, trading, and selling
defective	faulty	when a device is not working or not working well

Conjunctions

For the sentence completion questions, one must have the ability to pick up on context clues. Conjunctions can be great clues. Words such as *but*, *however*, and *although* could mean that things, ideas, or actions are being contrasted. The correct answer might be the opposite of another word that appears in the sentence. Antonyms are words that are complete opposites. When choosing an antonym, one should choose the word that represents as close to the exact opposite in meaning as the given word and ensure that it shares the same part of speech.

Here are some examples of antonyms:

- Nouns: predator – prey
- Verbs: love – hate
- Adjectives: good – bad
- Adverbs: slowly – swiftly
- Prepositions: above – below

Sometimes the correct answer will not be an exact opposite of another word in the sentence, so it's crucial to understand the turn that the sentence is making based on words like *although*, *while*, or *however* along with other words in the sentence and choose the option that best reflects the change. For example, consider the following sentence:

> Allie had a wonderful time during her family's visit, showing them around her new town, making them a lovely dinner at home, and ending the weekend with a day full of _____ games for the entire family, but when everyone left, the _____ set in and she immediately passed out on the couch.

- a. boring; excitement
- b. childish; sadness
- c. quiet; rejuvenation
- d. lively; exhaustion

For this sentence, it's clear that the first part conveys positive ideas due to the use of words like *wonderful* and *lovely*; however, the conjunction *but* indicates that the sentence will end on a different note. This doesn't necessarily mean that it will be terribly negative, but somehow the energy of the sentence will change. The first choice doesn't make sense. Although the words convey opposite tones, *boring* would be part of the positive side of the sentence and *excitement* would be part of the more negative side, which doesn't work to complete the sentence properly. The second choice is a possibility because games are typically thought of in the context of children, and it's reasonable to think that Allie would be sad after her family left. Looking at the third option, a day full of quiet games would not automatically be unreasonable, but to say that Allie was rejuvenated and immediately fell asleep doesn't make sense. However, the words given in the last choice do make sense. Even if it's not clear that the games were lively, the word *lively* still gives that part of the sentence a positive feeling and it also helps to contribute to Allie immediately falling asleep on the couch, which would be due to exhaustion. *Exhaustion* is the word that really makes the last choice stand out as correct because it fits perfectly with Allie falling asleep. Knowing that the goal is to look for opposites in the set of words—indicated by the conjunction *but*—, pairing lively with exhaustion is the obvious choice over pairing childish with sadness.

As mentioned, some conjunctions introduce an opposing opinion, thought, fact, feeling, action, etc. They can also reinforce an opinion, introduce an explanation, reinforce cause and effect, or indicate time. For example:

> She wishes to go to the movies, *but* she doesn't have the money. (Opposition)

> The professor became ill, *so* the class was postponed. (Cause and effect)

> They visited Europe *before* winter came. (Time)

Each conjunction serves a specific purpose in uniting two separate ideas. Below are common conjunctions in the English language:

Opposition	Cause & Effect	Reinforcement	Time	Explanation
however	therefore	besides	afterward	for example
nevertheless	as a result	anyway	before	in other words
but	because of this	after all	firstly	for instance
although	consequently	furthermore	next	such as

Practice Quiz

Synonyms

1. GARISH
    a. Drab
    b. Flashy
    c. Gait
    d. Hardy

2. INANE
    a. Illicit
    b. Ratify
    c. Senseless
    d. Uncouth

3. SOLACE
    a. Comfort
    b. Depose
    c. Induce
    d. Marred

Sentence Completion

4. The new antique mall in town has _____ booths with a wide range of vintage items from small trinkets to large pieces of furniture.
    a. identical
    b. copious
    c. dreadful
    d. unkempt

5. The _____ teens would not make room for the new student in the cafeteria; _____, a few kindhearted girls asked her to join them outside.
    a. supercilious; fortunately
    b. older; likewise
    c. fickle; foolishly
    d. obnoxious; reluctantly

See answers on the next page.

Answer Explanations

1. B: The word *garish* means excessively ornate or elaborate, which is most closely related to the word *flashy*.

2. C: The word *inane* means senseless or absurd.

3. A: The word *solace* most closely resembles the word *comfort*.

4. B: *Copious* means an abundance, and this fits best since the sentence mentions the wide range of items. The range wouldn't be quite so wide if the booths were identical (Choice *A*). There is nothing in the sentence to make one think that the booths are dreadful (Choice *C*). Choice *D* is incorrect because *unkempt* means disordered or messy, and the sentence does not indicate that the booths are messy.

5. A: Choice *A* is correct. *Supercilious* means arrogant, so it makes sense that arrogant teens would not make room for the new student. *Fortunately* means luckily, which works for the second blank. Another choice that might stand out for the first blank is *obnoxious*, but *reluctantly* doesn't work well in the second blank. Since the girls are described as kindhearted, it is not likely that they made this gesture to the new student reluctantly. Choice *B* can be eliminated because the word *likewise* would mean that the kindhearted girls acted similarly to the teens in the cafeteria, and this is not the case. The words in Choice *C* do not logically complete the sentence either, especially the word *foolishly* since there is nothing foolish about asking the new student to join them.

Quantitative Reasoning and Mathematics Achievement

Both math sections of the ISEE Upper exam, Quantitative Reasoning and Mathematics Achievement, test the student's ability to answer questions regarding numbers and operations, algebraic concepts, measurement, geometry, and data analysis and probability. Test takers will encounter three types of questions: calculations, quantitative comparison, and word problems.

Format of the Questions

The Quantitative Reasoning section has two types of questions: quantitative comparison and word problems. Quantitative comparison questions give two quantities that the student will need to compare. Some questions may have additional information that can be used to help solve the problem. The same four answer choices are provided for each question: that one quantity is greater than the other (A greater than B, or B greater than A), that the quantities are equal to each other, or that no determination can be made based on the information provided. Calculations may need to be performed in order to compare the quantities. Here's an example:

Quantity A	Quantity B
16%	$\frac{8}{50}$

   a. Quantity A is greater.
   b. Quantity B is greater.
   c. The two quantities are equal.
   d. The relationship cannot be determined from the information given.

The answer to this question is that the two quantities are equal, Choice *C*. To find out what $8/50$ is as a percent, divide 8 by 50 to get 0.16. Move the decimal place to the right two places to convert the number to a percent: 16%.

The word problems will require simple calculations or no calculation at all, with the focus being on the ability to understand the rules of math. There will be four answer choices to choose from. Here's an example:

If square A and square B are similar squares and the scale factor is 3, what is the length of the side of square B if the side of square A is 12?
   a. 4
   b. 6
   c. 15
   d. 36

The answer is Choice *D*, 36. A scale factor of 3 means that the amount triples from the first object to the second object. $12 \times 3 = 36$.

The questions in the Mathematics Achievement section will be more like the word problems, but these questions will involve calculations.

Numbers and Operations

Basic Concepts of Number Theory

Prime and Composite Numbers

Whole numbers are classified as either prime or composite. A **prime number** can only be divided evenly by itself and 1. For example, the number 11 can only be divided evenly by 11 and 1; therefore, 11 is a prime number. A helpful way to visualize a prime number is to use concrete objects and try to divide them into equal piles. If dividing 11 coins, the only way to divide them into equal piles is to create 1 pile of 11 coins or to create 11 piles of 1 coin each. Other examples of prime numbers include 2, 3, 5, 7, 13, 17, and 19.

A **composite number** is any whole number that is not a prime number. A composite number is a number that can be divided evenly by one or more numbers other than itself and one. For example, the number 6 can be divided evenly by 2 and 3. Therefore, 6 is a composite number. If dividing 6 coins into equal piles, the possibilities are 1 pile of 6 coins, 2 piles of 3 coins, 3 piles of 2 coins, or 6 piles of 1 coin. Other examples of composite numbers include 4, 8, 9, 10, 12, 14, 15, 16, 18, and 20.

To determine whether a number is a prime or composite number, the number is divided by every whole number greater than one and less than its own value. If it divides evenly by any of these numbers, then the number is composite. If it does not divide evenly by any of these numbers, then the number is prime. For example, when attempting to divide the number 5 by 2, 3, and 4, none of these numbers divide evenly. Therefore, 5 must be a prime number.

Odd and Even Numbers

Even numbers are all divisible by the number 2. **Odd numbers** are not divisible by 2; an odd quantity of items cannot be paired up into groups of 2 without having 1 item leftover. Examples of even numbers are 2, 4, 6, 20, 100, and 242. Examples of odd numbers are 1, 3, 5, 27, 99, and 333.

Factors, Multiples, and Divisibility

The **Fundamental Theorem of Arithmetic** states that any integer greater than 1 is either a prime number or can be written as a unique product of prime numbers. Factors can be used to find the combination of numbers to multiply to produce an integer that is not prime. The factors of a number are all integers that can be multiplied by another integer to produce the given number. For example, 2 is multiplied by 3 to produce 6. Therefore, 2 and 3 are both factors of 6. Similarly:

$$1 \times 6 = 6$$

and

$$2 \times 3 = 6$$

So 1, 2, 3, and 6 are all factors of 6. Another way to explain a factor is to say that a given number divides evenly by each of its factors to produce an integer. For example, 6 does not divide evenly by 5. Therefore, 5 is not a factor of 6.

Essentially, **factors** are the numbers multiplied to achieve a product. Thus, every product in a multiplication equation has, at minimum, two factors. Of course, some products will have more than two factors. For the sake of most discussions, assume that factors are positive integers.

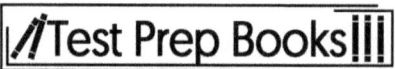

To find a number's factors, start with 1 and the number itself. Then divide the number by 2, 3, 4, and so on, seeing if any divisors can divide the number without a remainder, keeping a list of those that do. Stop upon reaching either the number itself or another factor.

Let's find the factors of 45. Start with 1 and 45. Then try to divide 45 by 2, which fails. Now divide 45 by 3. The answer is 15, so 3 and 15 are now factors. Dividing by 4 doesn't work and dividing by 5 leaves 9. Lastly, dividing 45 by 6, 7, and 8 all don't work. The next integer to try is 9, but this is already known to be a factor, so the factorization is complete. The factors of 45 are 1, 3, 5, 9, 15 and 45.

A **common factor** is a factor shared by two numbers. Let's take 45 and 30 and find the common factors:

The factors of 45 are: 1, 3, 5, 9, 15, and 45.

The factors of 30 are: 1, 2, 3, 5, 6, 10, 15, and 30.

The common factors are 1, 3, 5, and 15.

The **greatest common factor** is the largest number among the shared, common factors. From the factors of 45 and 30, the common factors are 3, 5, and 15. Thus, 15 is the greatest common factor, as it's the largest number.

Multiples of a given number are found by taking that number and multiplying it by any other whole number. For example, 3 is a factor of 6, 9, and 12. Therefore, 6, 9, and 12 are multiples of 3. The multiples of any number are an infinite list. For example, the multiples of 5 are 5, 10, 15, 20, and so on. This list continues without end. A list of multiples is used in finding the **least common multiple**, or **LCM,** for fractions when a common denominator is needed. The denominators are written down and their multiples listed until a common number is found in both lists. This common number is the LCM.

If two numbers share no factors besides 1 in common, then their least common multiple will be simply their product. If two numbers have common factors, then their least common multiple will be their product divided by their greatest common factor. This can be visualized by the formula:

$$LCM = \frac{x \times y}{GCF}$$

Here, x and y are some integers, and LCM and GCF are their least common multiple and greatest common factor, respectively.

Prime factorization breaks down each factor of a whole number until only prime numbers remain. All composite numbers can be factored into prime numbers. For example, the prime factors of 12 are 2, 2, and 3 ($2 \times 2 \times 3 = 12$). To produce the prime factors of a number, the number is factored, and any composite numbers are

Quantitative Reasoning and Mathematics Achievement

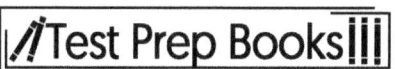

continuously factored until the result is the product of prime factors only. A factor tree, such as the one below, is helpful when exploring this concept.

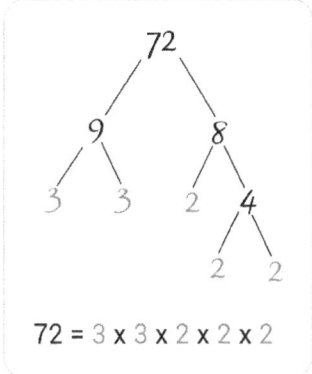

Let's break 129 down into its prime factors. First, the factors are 3 and 43. Both 3 and 43 are prime numbers, so we're done. But if 43 was not a prime number, then it would also need to be factorized until all of the factors are expressed as prime numbers.

Real and Complex Numbers

The mathematical number system is made up of two general types of numbers: real and complex. **Real numbers** are both irrational and rational numbers, while **complex numbers** are those composed of both a real number and an imaginary one. Imaginary numbers are the result of taking the square root of -1, and $\sqrt{-1} = i$.

The real number system is often explained using a Venn diagram. Consider the diagram below:

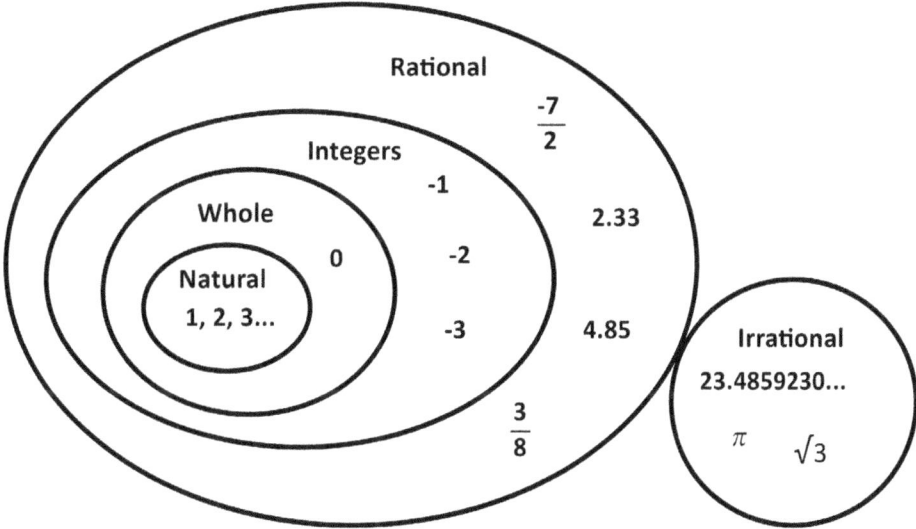

After a number has been labeled as a real number, further classification occurs when considering the other groups in this diagram. If a number is a never-ending, non-repeating decimal, it falls in the irrational category. Otherwise, it is rational. Furthermore, if a number does not have a fractional part, it is classified as an integer, such as -2, 75, or 0. Whole numbers are an even smaller group that only includes positive integers and 0. The last group of natural numbers is made up of only positive integers, such as 2, 56, or 12.

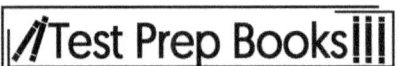

Quantitative Reasoning and Mathematics Achievement

Real numbers can be compared and ordered using the number line. If a number falls to the left on the real number line, it is less than a number on the right. For example, $-2 < 5$ because -2 falls to the left of 0, and 5 falls to the right.

Complex numbers are made up of the sum of a real number and an imaginary number. Some examples of complex numbers include $6 + 2i$, $5 - 7i$, and $-3 + 12i$. Adding and subtracting complex numbers is similar to collecting like terms. The real numbers are added together, and the imaginary numbers are added together. For example, if the problem asks to simplify the given expression $6 + 2i - 3 + 7i$, the 6 and -3 would combine to make 3, and the $2i$ and $7i$ combine to make $9i$. Multiplying and dividing complex numbers is similar to working with exponents. One rule to remember when multiplying is that $i \times i = -1$. For example, if a problem asks to simplify the expression $4i(3 + 7i)$, the $4i$ should be distributed throughout the 3 and the $7i$. This leaves the final expression $12i - 28$. The 28 is negative because $i \times i$ results in a negative number. The last type of operation to consider with complex numbers is the conjugate. The **conjugate** of a complex number is a technique used to change the complex number into a real number. For example, the conjugate of $4 - 3i$ is $4 + 3i$. Multiplying $(4 - 3i)(4 + 3i)$ results in $16 + 12i - 12i + 9$, which has a final answer of $16 + 9 = 25$.

Integers are any whole number, both positive and negative. They include numbers like 5, 24, 0, -6, and 15. They do not include fractions or numbers that have digits after the decimal point.

Rational numbers are all numbers that can be written as a fraction using integers. A **fraction** is written as $\frac{x}{y}$ and represents the quotient of x being divided by y. More practically, it means dividing the whole into y equal parts, then taking x of those parts.

Examples of rational numbers include $\frac{1}{2}$ and $\frac{5}{4}$. The **numerator** is the number on the top of the fraction, while the **denominator** is the number on the bottom. Because every integer can be written as a fraction with a denominator of 1, (e.g., $\frac{3}{1} = 3$), every integer is also a rational number.

When adding integers and negative rational numbers, there are some basic rules to determine if the solution is negative or positive:

- Adding two positive numbers results in a positive value: $3.3 + 4.8 = 8.1$.
- Adding two negative numbers results in a negative number: $(-8) + (-6) = -14$.

Adding one positive and one negative number requires taking the absolute values and finding the difference between them. Then, the sign of the number that has the higher absolute value for the final solution is used.

For example, $(-9) + 11$, has a difference of absolute values of 2. The final solution is 2 because 11 has the higher absolute value. Another example is $9 + (-11)$, which has a difference of absolute values of 2. The final solution is -2 because 11 has the higher absolute value.

When subtracting integers and negative rational numbers, one has to change the problem to adding the opposite and then apply the rules of addition.

- Subtracting two positive numbers is the same as adding one positive and one negative number.

    For example, $4.9 - 7.1$ is the same as $4.9 + (-7.1)$. The solution is -2.2 since the absolute value of -7.1 is greater. Another example is $8.5 - 6.4$ which is the same as $8.5 + (-6.4)$. The solution is 2.1 since the absolute value of 8.5 is greater.

- Subtracting a positive number from a negative number results in negative value.

For example, $(-12) - 7$ is the same as $(-12) + (-7)$ with a solution of -19.

- Subtracting a negative number from a positive number results in a positive value.

  For example, $12 - (-7)$ is the same as $12 + 7$ with a solution of 19.

- For multiplication and division of integers and rational numbers, if both numbers are positive or both numbers are negative, the result is a positive value.

  For example, $(-1.7)(-4)$ has a solution of 6.8 since both numbers are negative values.

- For multiplication and division of integers and rational numbers, if one number is positive and another number is negative, the result is a negative value.

  For example, $(-15)/5$ has a solution of -3 since there is one negative number.

As mentioned, a rational number is any number that can be written as a fraction or ratio. Within the set of rational numbers, several subsets exist which are referenced throughout the mathematics topics. Counting numbers are the first numbers learned as a child. Counting numbers consist of 1,2,3,4, and so on. Whole numbers include all counting numbers and zero (0,1,2,3,4,...). Integers include counting numbers, their opposites, and zero (...,-3,-2,-1,0,1,2,3,...). Rational numbers include integers, fractions, and decimals that terminate (1.7, 0.04213) or repeat $(0.13\overline{6})$.

A **number line** typically consists of integers, and is used to visually represent the value of a rational number. Each rational number has a distinct position on the line determined by comparing its value with the displayed values on the line. For example, if plotting -1.5 on the number line below, it is necessary to recognize that the value of -1.5 is 0.5 less than -1 and 0.5 greater than -2. Therefore, -1.5 is plotted halfway between -1 and -2.

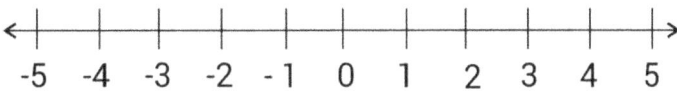

The **decimal system** consists of only ten different digits, 0 to 9, and is used to represent an infinite number of values. The **place value system** makes this infinite number of values possible. The position in which a digit is written corresponds to a given value. Starting from the decimal point (which is implied, if not physically present), each subsequent place value to the left represents a value greater than the one before it. Conversely, starting from the decimal point, each subsequent place value to the right represents a value less than the one before it.

The names for the place values to the left of the decimal point are as follows:

Billions	Hundred-Millions	Ten-Millions	Millions	Hundred-Thousands	Ten-Thousands	Thousands	Hundreds	Tens	Ones

*Note that this table can be extended infinitely further to the left.

The names for the place values to the right of the decimal point are as follows:

| Decimal Point (.) | Tenths | Hundredths | Thousandths | Ten-Thousandths | ... |

*Note that this table can be extended indefinitely further to the right.

When given a multi-digit number, the value of each digit depends on its place value. Consider the number 682,174.953. Referring to the chart above, it can be determined that the digit 8 is in the ten-thousands place. It is in the fifth place to the left of the decimal point. Its value is 8 ten-thousands or 80,000. The digit 5 is two places to the right of the decimal point. Therefore, the digit 5 is in the hundredths place. Its value is 5 hundredths or $\frac{5}{100}$ (equivalent to 0.05).

In accordance with the **base-10 system**, the value of a digit increases by a factor of ten each place it moves to the left. For example, consider the number 7. Moving the digit one place to the left (70) increases its value by a factor of 10:

$$(7 \times 10 = 70)$$

Moving the digit two places to the left (700) increases its value by a factor of 10 twice:

$$(7 \times 10 \times 10 = 700)$$

Moving the digit three places to the left (7,000) increases its value by a factor of 10 three times (10^3), and so on.

Conversely, the value of a digit decreases by a factor of ten each place it moves to the right. Note that multiplying by 10^{-1} is equivalent to dividing by 10. For example, consider the number 40. Moving the digit one place to the right (4) decreases its value by a factor of 10:

$$40 \div 10 = 4$$

Moving the digit two places to the right (0.4), decreases its value by a factor of 10 twice:

$$40 \div 10 \div 10 = 0.4$$

or

$$40 \times \frac{1}{10} \times \frac{1}{10} = 0.4$$

Moving the digit three places to the right (0.04) decreases its value by a factor of 10 three times:

$$40 \div 10 \div 10 \div 10 = 0.04$$

or

$$40 \times \frac{1}{10} \times \frac{1}{10} \times \frac{1}{10} = 0.04$$

Quantitative Reasoning and Mathematics Achievement

Basic Concepts of Addition, Subtraction, Multiplication, and Division

The four most basic and fundamental operations are addition, subtraction, multiplication, and division. The operations take a group of numbers and achieve an exact result, according to the operation. When dealing with positive integers greater than 1, addition and multiplication increase the result, while subtraction and division reduce the result.

Addition

Addition is the combination of two numbers; their quantities are added together cumulatively. The sign for an addition operation is the + symbol. For example, $9 + 6 = 15$. The 9 and 6 combine to achieve a cumulative value called a *sum*.

Addition follows the Commutative Property, which means that the order of numbers in an addition equation can be switched without altering the result. The formula for the Commutative Property is $a + b = b + a$. Let's look at a few examples to see how the Commutative Property works:

$$3 + 4 = 4 + 3 = 7$$

$$12 + 8 = 8 + 12 = 20$$

Addition also follows the Associative Property, which means that the groups of numbers don't matter in an addition problem. The formula for the Associative Property is $(a + b) + c = a + (b + c)$.

Here are some examples of the Associative Property at work:

$$(6 + 14) + 10 = 6 + (14 + 10) = 30$$

$$8 + (2 + 25) = (8 + 2) + 25 = 35$$

Subtraction

Subtraction is taking away one number from another, so their quantities are reduced. The sign designating a subtraction operation is the − symbol, and the result is called the *difference*. For example, $9 - 6 = 3$. The second number detracts from the first number in the equation to reach the difference.

Unlike addition, subtraction doesn't follow the Commutative or Associative Properties. The order and grouping in subtraction impact the result.

$$22 - 7 \neq 7 - 22$$

$$(10 - 5) - 2 \neq 10 - (5 - 2)$$

When working through subtraction problems involving larger numbers, it's necessary to regroup the numbers. Let's work through a practice problem using regrouping:

$$\begin{array}{r} 325 \\ - 77 \\ \hline \end{array}$$

Here, we see that the values in the ones and tens columns for 77 are greater than the values in the same columns in 325. Thus, we need to borrow from the tens and hundreds columns to complete the operation.

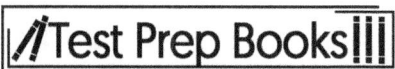

When borrowing from a column, we subtract one digit from the lender and add ten to the borrower's column:

$$3\overset{1}{\cancel{2}}5$$
$$-\ 77$$
$$\overline{8}$$

$$\overset{2}{\cancel{3}}\overset{11}{\cancel{2}}5$$
$$-\ 77$$
$$\overline{48}$$

$$\overset{2}{\cancel{3}}\overset{11}{\cancel{2}}5$$
$$-\ 77$$
$$\overline{248}$$

After ensuring greater numbers at the top of each column, we subtract as normal and arrive at the answer of 248.

Multiplication

Multiplication involves taking multiple copies of one number. The sign designating a multiplication operation is the × symbol. The result is called the product. For example, $9 \times 6 = 54$. Multiplication means adding together one number in the equation as many times as the number on the other side of the multiplication symbol:

$$9 \times 6 = 9 + 9 + 9 + 9 + 9 + 9 = 54$$

$$9 \times 6 = 6 + 6 + 6 + 6 + 6 + 6 + 6 + 6 + 6 = 54$$

Like addition, multiplication holds the Commutative and Associative Properties:

$$2 \times 4 = 4 \times 2$$

$$2 \times 5 = 5 \times 2$$

$$(2 \times 4)10 = 2(4 \times 10)$$

$$3(7 \times 4) = (3 \times 7)4$$

Multiplication also follows the Distributive Property, which allows the multiplication to be distributed through parentheses. The formula for distribution is $a \times (b + c) = ab + ac$. This will become clearer after some examples:

$$5(3 + 6) = (5 \times 3) + (5 \times 6) = 45$$

$$4(10 - 5) = (4 \times 10) - (4 \times 5) = 20$$

Multiplication becomes slightly more complicated when multiplying numbers with decimals. The easiest way to answer these problems is to ignore the decimals and multiply as if they were whole numbers. After multiplying the factors, add a decimal point to the product, and the decimal place should be equal to the total number of decimal places in the problem.

Here are two examples to familiarize you with the trick:

1.
$$\begin{array}{r} 0.7 \\ \times 3 \\ \hline 2.1 \end{array}$$

2.
$$\begin{array}{r} 2.6 \\ \times 4.2 \\ \hline 10.92 \end{array}$$

Let's tackle the first example. First, count the decimal places (one). Second, multiply the factors as if they were whole numbers to arrive at a product: 21. Finally, move the decimal place one position to the left, as the factors have only one decimal place. The second problem works the same exact away, except that there are two decimal places in the factors, so the product's decimal is moved two places over.

Division

Division is the opposite of multiplication as addition and subtraction are opposites. The signs designating a division operate are the ÷ or / symbols. In division, the second number divides the first. Like subtraction, it matters which number comes before the division sign. For example, $9 \div 6 \neq 6 \div 9$.

The number before the division sign is called the dividend, or, if expressed as a fraction, then it's the numerator. For example, in $a \div b$, a is the dividend. In $\frac{a}{b}$, a is the numerator.

The number after the division sign is called the **divisor**, or, if expressed as a fraction, then it's the denominator. For example, in $a \div b$, b is the divisor. In $\frac{a}{b}$, b is the denominator.

Division doesn't follow any of the Commutative, Associative, or Distributive Properties.

$$15 \div 3 \neq 3 \div 15$$
$$(30 \div 3) \div 5 \neq 30 \div (3 \div 5)$$
$$100 \div (20 + 10) \neq (100 \div 20) + (100 \div 10)$$

Division with decimals is similar to multiplication with decimals. When dividing a decimal by a whole number, ignore the decimal and divide as if it were a whole number. Once you solve for the answer (also called the **quotient**), then place the decimal at the decimal place equal to that in the dividend.

$$15.75 \div 3 = 5.25$$

When the divisor is a decimal, change it to a whole number by multiplying both the divisor and dividend by the factor of 10 that makes the divisor into a whole number. Then complete the division operation as described above.

$$17.5 \div 2.5 = 175 \div 25 = 7$$

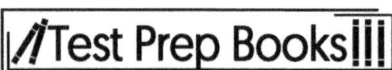

Use of Operations to Solve Problems

There are a variety of real-world situations in which one or more of the operators is used to solve a problem. The tables below display the most common scenarios.

Addition & Subtraction

	Unknown Result	**Unknown Change**	**Unknown Start**
Adding to	5 students were in class. 4 more students arrived. How many students are in class?	8 students were in class. More students arrived late. There are now 18 students in class. How many students arrived late? Solved by inverse operations	Some students were in class early. 11 more students arrived. There are now 17 students in class. How many students were in class early? Solved by inverse operations
Taking from	15 students were in class. 5 students left class. How many students are in class now?	12 students were in class. Some students left class. There are now 8 students in class. How many students left class? Solved by inverse operations	Some students were in class. 3 students left class. Then there were 13 students in class. How many students were in class before? Solved by inverse operations

	Unknown Total	**Unknown Addends (Both)**	**Unknown Addends (One)**
Putting together/ taking apart	The homework assignment is 10 addition problems and 8 subtraction problems. How many problems are in the homework assignment?	Bobby has $9. How much can Bobby spend on candy and how much can Bobby spend on toys?	Bobby has 12 pairs of pants. 5 pairs of pants are shorts, and the rest are long. How many pairs of long pants does he have? Solved by inverse operations

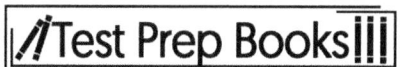

	Unknown Difference	**Unknown Larger Value**	**Unknown Smaller Value**
Comparing	Bobby has 5 toys. Tommy has 8 toys. How many more toys does Tommy have than Bobby? Solved by inverse operations Bobby has $6. Tommy has $10. How many fewer dollars does Bobby have than Tommy?	Tommy has 2 more toys than Bobby. Bobby has 4 toys. How many toys does Tommy have? Bobby has 3 fewer dollars than Tommy. Bobby has $8. How many dollars does Tommy have? Solved by inverse operations	Tommy has 6 more toys than Bobby. Tommy has 10 toys. How many toys does Bobby have? Bobby has $5 less than Tommy. Tommy has $9. How many dollars does Bobby have? Solved by inverse operations

Multiplication and Division

	Unknown Product	**Unknown Group Size**	**Unknown Number of Groups**
Equal groups	There are 5 students, and each student has 4 pieces of candy. How many pieces of candy are there in all?	14 pieces of candy are shared equally by 7 students. How many pieces of candy does each student have? Solved by inverse operations	If 18 pieces of candy are to be given out, 3 to each student, how many students will get candy? Solved by inverse operations

	Unknown Product	**Unknown Factor**	**Unknown Factor**
Arrays	There are 5 rows of students with 3 students in each row. How many students are there?	If 16 students are arranged into 4 equal rows, how many students will be in each row? Solved by inverse operations	If 24 students are arranged into an array with 6 columns, how many rows are there? Solved by inverse operations

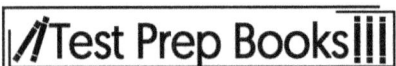

	Larger Unknown	Smaller Unknown	Multiplier Unknown
Comparing	A small popcorn costs $1.50. A large popcorn costs 3 times as much as a small popcorn. How much does a large popcorn cost?	A large soda costs $6 and that is 2 times as much as a small soda costs. How much does a small soda cost? Solved by inverse operations	A large pretzel costs $3 and a small pretzel costs $2. How many times as much does the large pretzel cost as the small pretzel? Solved by inverse operations

Order of Operations

When reviewing calculations consisting of more than one operation, the order in which the operations are performed affects the resulting answer. Consider $5 \times 2 + 7$. Performing multiplication then addition results in an answer of 17: ($5 \times 2 = 10; 10 + 7 = 17$). However, if the problem is written $5 \times (2 + 7)$, the order of operations dictates that the operation inside the parentheses must be performed first. The resulting answer is 45: ($2 + 7 = 9$, then $5 \times 9 = 45$).

The order in which operations should be performed is remembered using the acronym PEMDAS. PEMDAS stands for parentheses, exponents, multiplication/division, addition/subtraction. Multiplication and division are performed in the same step, working from left to right with whichever comes first. Addition and subtraction are performed in the same step, working from left to right with whichever comes first.

Consider the following example: $8 \div 4 + 8(7 - 7)$. Performing the operation inside the parentheses produces $8 \div 4 + 8(0)$ or $8 \div 4 + 8 \times 0$. There are no exponents, so multiplication and division are performed next from left to right resulting in: $2 + 8 \times 0$, then $2 + 0$. Finally, addition and subtraction are performed to obtain an answer of 2. Now consider the following example: $6 \times 3 + 3^2 - 6$. Parentheses are not applicable. Exponents are evaluated first, which brings us to $6 \times 3 + 9 - 6$. Then multiplication/division forms $18 + 9 - 6$. At last, addition/subtraction leads to the final answer of 21.

Properties of Operations

Properties of operations exist that make calculations easier and solve problems for missing values. The following table summarizes commonly used properties of real numbers.

Property	Addition	Multiplication
Commutative	$a + b = b + a$	$a \times b = b \times a$
Associative	$(a + b) + c = a + (b + c)$	$(a \times b) \times c = a \times (b \times c)$
Identity	$a + 0 = a; 0 + a = a$	$a \times 1 = a; 1 \times a = a$
Inverse	$a + (-a) = 0$	$a \times \frac{1}{a} = 1; a \neq 0$
Distributive	$a(b + c) = ab + ac$	

Quantitative Reasoning and Mathematics Achievement

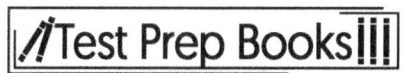

The commutative property of addition states that the order in which numbers are added does not change the sum. Similarly, the commutative property of multiplication states that the order in which numbers are multiplied does not change the product. The associative property of addition and multiplication state that the grouping of numbers being added or multiplied does not change the sum or product, respectively. The commutative and associative properties are useful for performing calculations. For example, $(47 + 25) + 3$ is equivalent to $(47 + 3) + 25$, which is easier to calculate.

The identity property of addition states that adding zero to any number does not change its value. The identity property of multiplication states that multiplying a number by 1 does not change its value. The inverse property of addition states that the sum of a number and its opposite equals zero. Opposites are numbers that are the same with different signs (ex. 5 and -5; $-\frac{1}{2}$ and $\frac{1}{2}$). The inverse property of multiplication states that the product of a number (other than 0) and its reciprocal equals 1. Reciprocal numbers have numerators and denominators that are inverted (ex. $\frac{2}{5}$ and $\frac{5}{2}$). Inverse properties are useful for canceling quantities to find missing values (see algebra content). For example, $a + 7 = 12$ is solved by adding the inverse of 7 (which is -7) to both sides in order to isolate a.

The distributive property states that multiplying a sum (or difference) by a number produces the same result as multiplying each value in the sum (or difference) by the number and adding (or subtracting) the products. Consider the following scenario: You are buying three tickets for a baseball game. Each ticket costs $18. You are also charged a fee of $2 per ticket for purchasing the tickets online. The cost is calculated: $3 \times 18 + 3 \times 2$. Using the distributive property, the cost can also be calculated: $3(18 + 2)$.

Estimation and Rounding

Estimation is finding a value that is close to a solution but is not the exact answer. For example, if there are values in the thousands to be multiplied, then each value can be estimated to the nearest thousand and the calculation performed. This value provides an approximate solution that can be determined very quickly.

Sometimes when performing operations such as multiplying numbers, the result can be estimated by *rounding*. For example, to estimate the value of 11.2×2.01, each number can be rounded to the nearest integer. This will yield a result of 22. Rounding numbers helps with estimation because it changes the given number to a simpler, although less accurate, number than the exact given number. Rounding allows for easier calculations, which estimate the results of using the exact given number. The accuracy of the estimate and ease of use depends on the place value to which the number is rounded.

Rounding is the process of either bumping a number up or leaving it the same, based on a specified place value. First, the place value is specified. Then, the digit to its right is looked at. For example, if rounding to the nearest hundreds place, the digit in the tens place is used. If it is a 0, 1, 2, 3, or 4, the digit being rounded is left alone. If it is a 5, 6, 7, 8 or 9, the digit being rounded to is increased by one. All other digits before the decimal point are then changed to zeros, and the digits in decimal places are dropped. If a decimal place is being rounded to, all subsequent digits are just dropped. For example, if 845,231.45 is rounded to the nearest thousands place, the answer is 845,000. The 5 would remain the same due to the 2 in the hundreds place. If 4.567 is rounded to the nearest tenths place, the answer is 4.6. The 5 increased to 6 due to the 6 in the hundredths place, and the rest of the decimal is dropped. To round 746,311 to the nearest ten-thousand, the digit in the ten-thousands place should be located first. In this case, this digit is 4 (7<u>4</u>6,311). The digit being examined is a 6, which means that the number will be rounded up by increasing the digit to the left by one. Therefore, the digit 4 is changed to a 5. For the given example, rounding 746,311 to the nearest ten-thousand will produce 750,000. To round 746,311 to the nearest hundred, the digit to the right of the 3 in the hundreds place is examined to determine whether to round up or keep

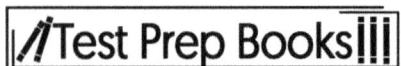

the same number. In this case, that digit is a 1, so the number will be kept the same and any digits to its right will be replaced with zeros. The resulting rounded number is 746,300.

Rounding place values to the right of the decimal follows the same procedure, but digits being replaced by zeros can simply be dropped. To round 3.752891 to the nearest thousandth, the desired place value is located (3.752891) and the digit to the right is examined. In this case, the digit 8 indicates that the number will be rounded up, and the 2 in the thousandths place will increase to a 3. Rounding up and replacing the digits to the right of the thousandths place produces 3.753000 which is equivalent to 3.753. Therefore, the zeros are not necessary, and the rounded number should be written as 3.753.

When rounding up, if the digit to be increased is a 9, the digit to its left is increased by 1 and the digit in the desired place value is changed to a zero. For example, the number 1,598 rounded to the nearest ten is 1,600. Another example shows the number 43.72961 rounded to the nearest thousandth is 43.730 or 43.73.

Mental Math

Mental math should always be considered as problems are worked through, as the ability to work through problems in one's head helps save time. If a problem is simple enough, such as $15 + 3 = 18$, it should be completed mentally. The ability to do this will increase once addition and subtraction in higher place values are grasped. Mental math is also important in multiplication and division. The times tables multiplying all numbers from 1 to 12 should be memorized. This will allow for division within those numbers to be memorized as well. For example, we should know easily that $121 \div 11 = 11$ because it should be memorized that $11 \times 11 = 121$.

Here is the multiplication table to be memorized:

x	1	2	3	4	5	6	7	8	9	10	11	12	13	14	15
1	1	2	3	4	5	6	7	8	9	10	11	12	13	14	15
2	2	4	6	8	10	12	14	16	18	20	22	24	26	28	30
3	3	6	9	12	15	18	21	24	27	30	33	36	39	42	45
4	4	8	12	16	20	24	28	32	36	40	44	48	52	56	60
5	5	10	15	20	25	30	35	40	45	50	55	60	65	70	75
6	6	12	18	24	30	36	42	48	54	60	66	72	78	84	90
7	7	14	21	28	35	42	49	56	63	70	77	84	91	98	105
8	8	16	24	32	40	48	56	64	72	80	88	96	104	112	120
9	9	18	27	36	45	54	63	72	81	90	99	108	117	126	135
10	10	20	30	40	50	60	70	80	90	100	110	120	130	140	150
11	11	22	33	44	55	66	77	88	99	110	121	132	143	154	165
12	12	24	36	48	60	72	84	96	108	120	132	144	156	168	180
13	13	26	39	52	65	78	91	104	117	130	143	156	169	182	195
14	14	28	42	56	70	84	98	112	126	140	154	168	182	196	210
15	15	30	45	60	75	90	105	120	135	150	165	180	195	210	225

Quantitative Reasoning and Mathematics Achievement

The shaded values along the diagonal of the table consist of **perfect squares**. A perfect square is the product of two of the same numbers.

Fractions

A **fraction** is an expression that represents a part of a whole but can also be used to present ratios or division problems. An example of a fraction is $\frac{x}{y}$. In this example, x is called the **numerator,** while y is the **denominator**. The numerator represents the number of parts, and the denominator is the total number of parts. They are separated by a line or slash, known as a fraction bar. In simple fractions, the numerator and denominator can be nearly any integer. However, the denominator of a fraction can never be zero because dividing by zero is a function that is undefined.

Imagine that an apple pie has been baked for a holiday party, and the full pie has eight slices. After the party, there are five slices left. How could the amount of the pie that remains be expressed as a fraction? The numerator is 5 since there are 5 pieces left, and the denominator is 8 since there were eight total slices in the whole pie. Thus, expressed as a fraction, the leftover pie totals $\frac{5}{8}$ of the original amount.

Fractions come in three different varieties: proper fractions, improper fractions, and mixed numbers. **Proper fractions** have a numerator less than the denominator, such as $\frac{3}{8}$, but **improper fractions** have a numerator greater than the denominator, such as $\frac{7}{2}$. **Mixed numbers** combine a whole number with a proper fraction, such as $3\frac{1}{2}$. Any mixed number can be written as an improper fraction by multiplying the integer by the denominator, adding the product to the value of the numerator, and dividing the sum by the original denominator. For example:

$$3\frac{1}{2} = \frac{3 \times 2 + 1}{2} = \frac{7}{2}$$

Whole numbers can also be converted into fractions by placing the whole number as the numerator and making the denominator 1. For example,

$$3 = \frac{3}{1}$$

One of the most fundamental concepts of fractions is their ability to be manipulated by multiplication or division. This is possible since $\frac{n}{n} = 1$ for any non-zero integer. As a result, multiplying or dividing by $\frac{n}{n}$ will not alter the original fraction since any number multiplied or divided by 1 doesn't change the value of that number. Fractions of the same value are known as equivalent fractions.

For example, $\frac{2}{4}, \frac{4}{8}, \frac{50}{100}$, and $\frac{75}{150}$ are equivalent, as they all equal $\frac{1}{2}$.

Although many equivalent fractions exist, they are easier to compare and interpret when reduced or simplified. The numerator and denominator of a simple fraction will have no factors in common other than 1. When reducing or simplifying fractions, divide the numerator and denominator by the greatest common factor. A simple strategy is to divide the numerator and denominator by low numbers, like 2, 3, or 5, until arriving at a simple fraction, but the same thing could be achieved by determining the greatest common factor for both the numerator and denominator and dividing each by it. Using the first method is preferable when both the numerator and denominator are even,

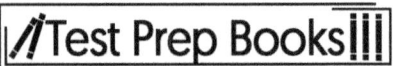

end in 5, or are obviously a multiple of another number. However, if no numbers seem to work, it will be necessary to factor the numerator and denominator to find the GCF. For example:

1) Simplify the fraction $\frac{6}{8}$:

Dividing the numerator and denominator by 2 results in $\frac{3}{4}$, which is a simple fraction.

2) Simplify the fraction $\frac{12}{36}$:

Dividing the numerator and denominator by 2 leaves $\frac{6}{18}$. This isn't a simple fraction, as both the numerator and denominator have factors in common. Dividing each by 3 results in $\frac{2}{6}$, but this can be further simplified by dividing by 2 to get $\frac{1}{3}$. This is the simplest fraction, as the numerator is 1. In cases like this, multiple division operations can be avoided by determining the greatest common factor between the numerator and denominator.

3) Simplify the fraction $\frac{18}{54}$ by dividing by the greatest common factor:

First, determine the factors for the numerator and denominator. The factors of 18 are 1, 2, 3, 6, 9, and 18. The factors of 54 are 1, 2, 3, 6, 9, 18, 27, and 54. Thus, the greatest common factor is 18. Dividing $\frac{18}{54}$ by 18 leaves $\frac{1}{3}$, which is the simplest fraction. This method takes slightly more work, but it definitively arrives at the simplest fraction.

Of the four basic operations that can be performed on fractions, the one that involves the least amount of work is multiplication. To multiply two fractions, simply multiply the numerators together, multiply the denominators together, and place the products of each as a fraction. Whole numbers and mixed numbers can also be expressed as a fraction, as described above, to multiply with a fraction. Here are a few examples:

1) $\frac{2}{5} \times \frac{3}{4} = \frac{6}{20} = \frac{3}{10}$

2) $\frac{4}{9} \times \frac{7}{11} = \frac{28}{99}$

Dividing fractions is similar to multiplication with one key difference. To divide fractions, flip the numerator and denominator of the second fraction, and then proceed as if it were a multiplication problem:

1) $\frac{7}{8} \div \frac{4}{5} = \frac{7}{8} \times \frac{5}{4} = \frac{35}{32}$

2) $\frac{5}{9} \div \frac{1}{3} = \frac{5}{9} \times \frac{3}{1} = \frac{15}{9} = \frac{5}{3}$

Addition and subtraction require more steps than multiplication and division, as these operations require the fractions to have the same denominator, also called a common denominator. It is always possible to find a common denominator by multiplying the denominators. However, when the denominators are large numbers, this method is unwieldy, especially if the answer must be provided in its simplest form. Thus, it's beneficial to find the least common denominator of the fractions—the least common denominator is incidentally also the least common multiple.

Once equivalent fractions have been found with common denominators, simply add or subtract the numerators to arrive at the answer:

1) $\frac{1}{2} + \frac{3}{4} = \frac{2}{4} + \frac{3}{4} = \frac{5}{4}$

2) $\frac{3}{12} + \frac{11}{20} = \frac{15}{60} + \frac{33}{60} = \frac{48}{60} = \frac{4}{5}$

3) $\frac{7}{9} - \frac{4}{15} = \frac{35}{45} - \frac{12}{45} = \frac{23}{45}$

4) $\frac{5}{6} - \frac{7}{18} = \frac{15}{18} - \frac{7}{18} = \frac{8}{18} = \frac{4}{9}$

Decimals

The **decimal system** is a way of writing out numbers that uses ten different numerals: 0, 1, 2, 3, 4, 5, 6, 7, 8, and 9. This is also called a "base ten" or "base 10" system. Other bases are also used. For example, computers work with a base of 2. This means they only use the numerals 0 and 1.

The **decimal place** denotes how far to the right of the decimal point a numeral is. The first digit to the right of the decimal point is in the *tenths* place. The next is the **hundredths**. The third is the **thousandths**.

So, 3.142 has a 1 in the tenths place, a 4 in the hundredths place, and a 2 in the thousandths place.

The **decimal point** is a period used to separate the **ones** place from the **tenths** place when writing out a number as a decimal.

A **decimal number** is a number written out with a decimal point instead of as a fraction, for example, 1.25 instead of $\frac{5}{4}$. Depending on the situation, it can sometimes be easier to work with fractions and sometimes easier to work with decimal numbers.

A decimal number is **terminating** if it stops at some point. It is called **repeating** if it never stops but repeats over and over. It is important to note that every rational number can be written as a terminating decimal or as a repeating decimal.

Addition with Decimals
To add decimal numbers, each number needs to be lined up by the decimal point in vertical columns. For each number being added, the zeros to the right of the last number need to be filled in so that each of the numbers has the same number of places to the right of the decimal. Then, the columns can be added together. Here is an example of $2.45 + 1.3 + 8.891$ written in column form:

$$\begin{array}{r} 2.450 \\ 1.300 \\ +8.891 \\ \hline \end{array}$$

Zeros have been added in the columns so that each number has the same number of places to the right of the decimal.

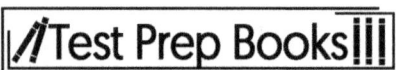

Added together, the correct answer is 12.641:

$$\begin{array}{r} 2.450 \\ 1.300 \\ +8.891 \\ \hline 12.641 \end{array}$$

Subtraction with Decimals

When subtracting decimal numbers, the decimals are lined up in vertical columns just as they are when adding decimals. Here is $7.89 - 4.235$ written in column form:

$$\begin{array}{r} 7.890 \\ -4.235 \\ \hline 3.655 \end{array}$$

A zero has been added in the column so that each number has the same number of places to the right of the decimal.

Multiplication with Decimals

The simplest way to multiply decimals is to calculate the product as if the decimals are not there, then count the number of decimal places in the original problem. Use that total to place the decimal the same number of places over in your answer, counting from right to left. For example, 0.5×1.25 can be rewritten and multiplied as:

$$5 \times 125 = 625$$

The final answer will have the same number of decimal places as the total number of decimal places in the problem. The first number has one decimal place, and the second number has two decimal places. Therefore, the final answer will contain three decimal places:

$$0.5 \times 1.25 = 0.625$$

Division with Decimals

Dividing a decimal by a whole number entails using long division first by ignoring the decimal point. Then, the decimal point is moved to the number of places given in the problem.

For example,

$$6.8 \div 4$$

This can be rewritten as:

$$68 \div 4$$

This is equal to 17. There is one non-zero integer to the right of the decimal point, so the final solution would have one decimal place to the right of the solution. In this case, the solution is 1.7.

Dividing a decimal by another decimal requires changing the divisor to a whole number by moving its decimal point. The decimal place of the dividend should be moved by the same number of places as the divisor. Then, the problem is the same as dividing a decimal by a whole number.

For example, $5.72 \div 1.1$ has a divisor with one decimal place. The expression can be rewritten as $57.2 \div 11$ by moving each decimal to the right to eliminate the decimal. The long division can be completed as $572 \div 11$ with a result of 52. Since there is one non-zero integer to the right of the decimal point in the problem, the final solution is 5.2.

In another example, $8 \div 0.16$ has a divisor with two decimal places. The expression can be rewritten as $800 \div 16$ by moving each decimal point two places to the right to eliminate the decimal in the divisor. The long division can be completed with a result of 50.

Percents

Think of **percents** as fractions with a denominator of 100. In fact, percent means "per hundred." Problems often require converting numbers from percents, fractions, and decimals.

The basic percent equation is the following:

$$\frac{is}{of} = \frac{\%}{100}$$

The placement of numbers in the equation depends on what the question asks.

Example 1: Find 40% of 80.

Basically, the problem is asking, "What is 40% of 80?" The 40 is the percent, and 80 is the number to find the percent "of." The equation is:

$$\frac{x}{80} = \frac{40}{100}$$

Solving the equation by cross-multiplication, the problem becomes $100x = 80(40)$. Solving for x produces the answer: $x = 32$.

Example 2: What percent of 100 is 20?

20 fills in the "is" portion, while 100 fills in the "of." The question asks for the percent, so that will be x, the unknown. The following equation is set up:

$$\frac{20}{100} = \frac{x}{100}$$

Cross-multiplying yields the equation $100x = 20(100)$. Solving for x gives the answer: 20%.

Example 3: 30% of what number is 30?

The following equation uses the clues and numbers in the problem:

$$\frac{30}{x} = \frac{30}{100}$$

Cross-multiplying results in the equation $30(100) = 30x$. Solving for x gives the answer: $x = 100$.

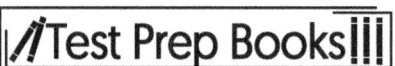

Quantitative Reasoning and Mathematics Achievement

Percentage Increase/Decrease

For questions asking for the increase in percentage, we need to calculate the difference, divide by the original amount, and multiply by 100. Written as an equation, the formula is

$$\frac{new\ quantity - old\ quantity}{old\ quantity} \times 100$$

This formula also works if you are asked for the percentage decrease. Here's an example of a percentage increase problem:

> Xavier was hospitalized with pneumonia. He was originally given 35mg of antibiotics. Later, after his condition continued to worsen, Xavier's dosage was increased to 60mg. What was the percentage increase of the antibiotics? Round the percent to the nearest tenth.

Here, the question tells us that the dosage increased from 35mg to 60mg, so we can plug those numbers into the formula to find the percentage increase.

$$\frac{60 - 35}{35} \times 100 = \frac{25}{35} \times 100 = .7142 \times 100 = 71.4\%$$

Converting Fractions, Decimals, and Percents

Decimals and Percents

Since a percent is based on "per hundred," decimals and percents can be converted by multiplying or dividing by 100. Practically speaking, this always amounts to moving the decimal point two places to the right or left, depending on the conversion. To convert a percent to a decimal, move the decimal point two places to the left and remove the % sign. To convert a decimal to a percent, move the decimal point two places to the right and add a % sign. Here are some examples:

$$65\% = 0.65$$

$$0.33 = 33\%$$

$$0.215 = 21.5\%$$

$$99.99\% = 0.9999$$

$$500\% = 5.00$$

$$7.55 = 755\%$$

Here's an example of a problem in which conversion to a decimal makes it easier to work out:

> At a general practice law firm, 30% of the lawyers work solely on tort cases. If 9 lawyers work solely on tort cases, how many lawyers work at the firm?

We need to solve for the total number of lawyers working at the firm, which we will represent with x. We know that 9 lawyers work solely on torts cases, and they make up 30% of the total lawyers at the firm. Thus, 30% multiplied by the total, x, will equal 9. Written as an equation, this is:

$$30\% \times x = 9$$

It's easier to deal with the equation if we convert the percent to a decimal, leaving us with $0.3x = 9$. Thus, $x = \frac{9}{0.3} = 30$ lawyers working at the firm.

Fractions and Percents

A percent can be converted to a fraction by making the number in the percent the numerator and putting 100 as the denominator:

$$43\% = \frac{43}{100}$$

$$97\% = \frac{97}{100}$$

To convert a fraction to a percent, follow the same logic. If the fraction happens to have 100 in the denominator, you're in luck. Just take the numerator and add a percent symbol:

$$\frac{28}{100} = 28\%$$

Otherwise, divide the numerator by the denominator to get a decimal:

$$\frac{9}{12} = 0.75$$

Then convert the decimal to a percent:

$$0.75 = 75\%$$

Another option is to make the denominator equal to 100. Be sure to multiply the numerator and the denominator by the same number. For example:

$$\frac{3}{20} \times \frac{5}{5} = \frac{15}{100}$$

$$\frac{15}{100} = 15\%$$

Changing Fractions to Decimals

To change a fraction into a decimal, divide the denominator into the numerator until there are no remainders. There may be repeating decimals, so rounding is often acceptable. A straight line above the repeating portion denotes that the decimal repeats.

Example: Express $\frac{4}{5}$ as a decimal.

Set up the division problem.

$$5\overline{)4}$$

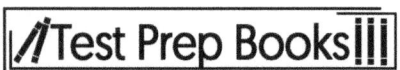

Quantitative Reasoning and Mathematics Achievement

5 does not go into 4, so place the decimal and add a zero.

$$5\overline{)4.0}$$

5 goes into 40 eight times. There is no remainder.

$$\begin{array}{r} 0.8 \\ 5\overline{)4.0} \\ -4.0 \\ \hline 0 \end{array}$$

The solution is 0.8.

Example: Express $33\frac{1}{3}$ as a decimal.

Since the whole portion of the number is known, set it aside to calculate the decimal from the fraction portion.

Set up the division problem.

$$3\overline{)1}$$

3 does not go into 1, so place the decimal and add zeros. 3 goes into 10 three times.

$$\begin{array}{r} 0.333 \\ 3\overline{)1.000} \end{array}$$

This will repeat with a remainder of 1, so placing a line over the 3 denotes the repetition.

$$\begin{array}{r} 0.333 \\ 3\overline{)1.000} \\ -\ 9 \\ \hline 10 \\ -\ 9 \\ \hline 10 \end{array}$$

The solution is $0.\overline{3}$.

Therefore, expressing $33\frac{1}{3}$ as a decimal is $33.\overline{3}$.

Changing Decimals to Fractions

To change decimals to fractions, place the decimal portion of the number, the numerator, over the respective place value, the denominator, then reduce, if possible.

Example: Express 0.25 as a fraction.

48

Quantitative Reasoning and Mathematics Achievement

This is read as twenty-five hundredths, so put 25 over 100. Then reduce to find the solution.

$$\frac{25}{100} = \frac{1}{4}$$

Example: Express 0.455 as a fraction

This is read as four hundred fifty-five thousandths, so put 455 over 1,000. Then reduce to find the solution.

$$\frac{455}{1,000} = \frac{91}{200}$$

Comparing or Ordering Numbers

When comparing or ordering numbers, the numbers should be written in the same format (decimal or fraction), if possible. For example, $\sqrt{49}$, 7.3, and $\frac{15}{2}$ are easier to order if each one is converted to a decimal: 7, 7.3, and 7.5. A number line is used to order and compare the numbers. Any number that is to the right of another number is greater than that number. Conversely, a number positioned to the left of a given number is less than that number.

Before discussing ordering all numbers, let's start with decimals.

To compare decimals and order them by their value, utilize a method similar to that of ordering large numbers.

The main difference is where the comparison will start. Assuming that any numbers to left of the decimal point are equal, the next numbers to be compared are those immediately to the right of the decimal point. If those are equal, then move on to compare the values in the next decimal place to the right.

For example:

Which number is greater, 12.35 or 12.38?

Check that the values to the left of the decimal point are equal:

$$12 = 12$$

Next, compare the values of the decimal place to the right of the decimal:

$$12.3 = 12.3$$

Those are also equal in value.

Finally, compare the value of the numbers in the next decimal place to the right on both numbers:

$$12.3\mathbf{5} \text{ and } 12.3\mathbf{8}$$

Here, the 5 is less than the 8, so the final way to express this inequality is:

$$12.35 < 12.38$$

Comparing decimals is regularly exemplified with money because the "cents" portion of money ends in the hundredths place. When paying for gasoline or meals in restaurants, and even in bank accounts, if enough errors are made when calculating numbers to the hundredths place, they can add up to dollars and larger amounts of money over time.

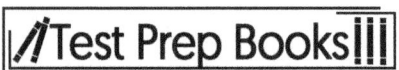

Quantitative Reasoning and Mathematics Achievement

Now that decimal ordering has been explained, let's expand and consider all real numbers. Whether the question asks to order the numbers from greatest to least or least to greatest, the crux of the question is the same—convert the numbers into a common format. Generally, it's easiest to write the numbers as whole numbers and decimals so they can be placed on a number line. Follow these examples to understand this strategy.

1) Order the following rational numbers from greatest to least:

$$\sqrt{36}, 0.65, 78\%, \frac{3}{4}, 7, 90\%, \frac{5}{2}$$

Of the seven numbers, the whole number (7) and decimal (0.65) are already in an accessible form, so concentrate on the other five.

First, the square root of 36 equals 6. If the test asks for the root of a non-perfect root, determine which two whole numbers the root lies between. Next, convert the percents to decimals. A percent means "per hundred," so this conversion requires moving the decimal point two places to the left, leaving 0.78 and 0.9. Lastly, evaluate the fractions:

$$\frac{3}{4} = \frac{75}{100} = 0.75; \frac{5}{2} = 2\frac{1}{2} = 2.5$$

Now, the only step left is to list the numbers in the requested order:

$$7, \sqrt{36}, \frac{5}{2}, 90\%, 78\%, \frac{3}{4}, 0.65$$

2) Order the following rational numbers from least to greatest:

$$2.5, \sqrt{9}, -10.5, 0.853, 175\%, \sqrt{4}, \frac{4}{5}$$

$$\sqrt{9} = 3$$

$$175\% = 1.75$$

$$\sqrt{4} = 2$$

$$\frac{4}{5} = 0.8$$

From least to greatest, the answer is:

$$-10.5, \frac{4}{5}, 0.853, 175\%, \sqrt{4}, 2.5, \sqrt{9}$$

Ratio Reasoning

Using Ratio Reasoning to Convert Rates

Ratios and rates can be used together to convert rates into different units. For example, if someone is driving 50 kilometers per hour, that rate can be converted into miles per hour by using a ratio known as the **conversion factor**.

Since the given value contains kilometers and the final answer needs to be in miles, the ratio relating miles to kilometers needs to be used. There are 0.62 miles in 1 kilometer. This, written as a ratio and in fraction form, is:

$$\frac{0.62 \text{ miles}}{1 \text{ km}}$$

To convert 50km/hour into miles per hour, the following conversion needs to be set up:

$$\frac{50 \text{ km}}{\text{hour}} \times \frac{0.62 \text{ miles}}{1 \text{ km}} = 31 \text{ miles per hour}$$

Using Ratios to Describe a Relationship Between Two Quantities

Ratios are used to show the relationship between two quantities. The ratio of oranges to apples in the grocery store may be 3 to 2, or 3:2. That means that for every 3 oranges, there are 2 apples. This comparison can be expanded to represent the actual number of oranges and apples, such as 36 oranges to 24 apples (36:24). Another example may be the number of boys to girls in a math class. If the ratio of boys to girls is given as 2 to 5 (2:5), that means there are 2 boys to every 5 girls in the class. Ratios can also be compared if the units in each ratio are the same. The ratio of boys to girls in the math class can be compared to the ratio of boys to girls in a science class by stating which ratio is higher and which is lower.

Example:

In a veterinary hospital, the veterinarian-to-pet ratio is $1:9$. The ratio is always constant. If there are 45 pets in the hospital, how many veterinarians are currently in the veterinary hospital?

We can set up a proportion to solve for the number of veterinarians: $\frac{1}{9} = \frac{x}{45}$

After cross-multiplying, we're left with $9x = 45$, which works out to 5 veterinarians.

Alternatively, as there are always 9 times as many pets as veterinarians, we can divide the number of pets (45) by 9. This also arrives at the correct answer of 5 veterinarians.

Solving Problems Involving Scale Factors

The ratio between two similar geometric figures is called the **scale factor**. This is the amount that the length or size is changed from the first object to the second. For example, a problem may depict two similar triangles, A and B, with A being the smaller triangle. If one side of triangle A has a length of 8 inches and the corresponding side of triangle B has a length of 16 inches, take the length of the second triangle and divide it by the length of the first triangle to find the scale factor of going from triangle A to triangle B. As a fraction this is 2/1, but it can also be written as 2:1. When divided, the result is a scale factor of 2, which is proven by the doubling of 8 to 16.

This scale factor can also be used to find the value of a missing side, side x, in triangle A. Since the scale factor from the smaller triangle (A) to the larger one (B) is 2, the larger corresponding side in triangle B (let's say it is 25) can be divided by 2 to find the missing side in A ($x = 12.5$). The scale factor can also be represented in the equation $2A = B$ because two times the lengths of A gives the corresponding lengths of B. Notice that the scale factor of going from a small object to a bigger object is more than 1. When going from a big object to smaller object, the scale factor will be less than 1. For example, if the length of one side of triangle A is 16 and the length of the corresponding side of triangle B is 8, the scale factor is found by dividing 8 by 16, or 8/16, or 8:16. This results in 1/2 or .5, which is proven by the halving of 16 to 8. The scale factor of .5 is less than 1.

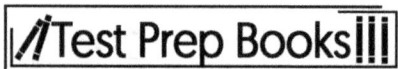

Exponents

An **exponent** is an operation used as shorthand for a number multiplied or divided by itself for a defined number of times.

$$3^7 = 3 \times 3 \times 3 \times 3 \times 3 \times 3 \times 3$$

In this example, the 3 is called the **base**, and the 7 is called the **exponent**. The exponent is typically expressed as a superscript number near the upper-right side of the base but can also be identified as the number following a caret symbol (^). This operation is verbally expressed as "3 to the 7th power" or "3 raised to the power of 7." Common exponents are 2 and 3. A base raised to the power of 2 is referred to as having been "squared," while a base raised to the power of 3 is referred to as having been "cubed."

Several special rules apply to exponents. First, the **Zero Power Rule** finds that any number raised to the zero power equals 1. For example, 100^0, 2^0, $(-3)^0$ and 0^0 all equal 1 because the bases are raised to the zero power.

Second, exponents can be negative. With negative exponents, the equation is expressed as a fraction, as in the following example:

$$3^{-7} = \frac{1}{3^7} = \frac{1}{3 \times 3 \times 3 \times 3 \times 3 \times 3 \times 3}$$

Whereas y^3 can also be rewritten as $\frac{y^3}{1}$, y^{-3} can be rewritten as $\frac{1}{y^3}$. A negative exponent means the exponential expression must be moved to the opposite spot in a fraction to make the exponent positive. If the negative appears in the numerator, it moves to the denominator. If the negative appears in the denominator, it is moved to the numerator. In general, $a^{-n} = \frac{1}{a^n}$, and a^{-n} and a^n are reciprocals.

Take, for example, the following expression:

$$\frac{a^{-4}b^2}{c^{-5}}$$

Since a is raised to the negative fourth power, it can be moved to the denominator. Since c is raised to the negative fifth power, it can be moved to the numerator. The b variable is raised to the positive second power, so it does not move.

The simplified expression is as follows:

$$\frac{b^2 c^5}{a^4}$$

Third, the **Power Rule** concerns exponents being raised by another exponent. When this occurs, the exponents are multiplied by each other:

$$(x^2)^3 = x^6 = (x^3)^2$$

Fourth, when multiplying two exponents with the same base, the **Product Rule** requires that the base remains the same, and the exponents are added. For example, $a^x \times a^y = a^{x+y}$. Since addition and multiplication are commutative, the two terms being multiplied can be in any order.

$$x^3 x^5 = x^{3+5} = x^8 = x^{5+3} = x^5 x^3$$

Quantitative Reasoning and Mathematics Achievement

Fifth, when dividing two exponents with the same base, the **Quotient Rule** requires that the base remains the same, but the exponents are subtracted. So, $a^x \div a^y = a^{x-y}$. Since subtraction and division are not commutative, the two terms must remain in order.

$$x^5 x^{-3} = x^{5-3} = x^2 = x^5 \div x^3 = \frac{x^5}{x^3}$$

Additionally, 1 raised to any power is still equal to 1, and any number raised to the power of 1 is equal to itself. In other words, $a^1 = a$ and $1^x = 1$. Therefore $14^1 = 14$ and $1^{14} = 1$.

Fractional exponents can be explained by looking first at the inverse of exponents, which are **roots.** Given the expression x^2, the square root can be taken, $\sqrt{x^2}$, canceling out the 2 and leaving x by itself, if x is positive. Cancelation occurs because $\sqrt{x}$ can be written with exponents, instead of roots, as $x^{\frac{1}{2}}$. The numerator of 1 is the exponent, and the denominator of 2 is called the **root** (which is why it's referred to as **square root**). Taking the square root of x^2 is the same as raising it to the $\frac{1}{2}$ power. Written out in mathematical form, it takes the following progression:

$$\sqrt{x^2} = (x^2)^{\frac{1}{2}} = x$$

Because $2 \times \frac{1}{2} = 1$, 1 is the actual exponent of x. Another example can be seen with $x^{\frac{4}{7}}$. The variable x, raised to four-sevenths, is equal to the seventh root of x to the fourth power: $\sqrt[7]{x^4}$. In general,

$$x^{\frac{1}{n}} = \sqrt[n]{x}$$

and

$$x^{\frac{m}{n}} = \sqrt[n]{x^m}$$

In mathematical expressions containing exponents and other operations, the order of operations must be followed. **PEMDAS** states that exponents are calculated after any parentheses and grouping symbols but before any multiplication, division, addition, and subtraction.

Scientific Notation

Scientific notation is used to represent numbers that are either very small or very large. For example, the distance to the Sun is approximately 150,000,000,000 meters. Instead of writing this number with so many zeros, it can be written in scientific notation as 1.5×10^{11} meters. The same is true for very small numbers, but the exponent becomes negative. If the mass of a human cell is 0.000000000001 kilograms, that measurement can be easily represented by 1.0×10^{-12} kilograms. In both situations, scientific notation makes the measurement easier to read and understand. Each number is translated to an expression with ones and tenths places multiplied by an expression corresponding to the zeros.

When two measurements are given and both involve scientific notation, it is important to know how these interact with each other:

- In addition and subtraction, the exponent on the ten must be the same before any operations are performed on the numbers. For example, $(1.3 \times 10^4) + (3.0 \times 10^3)$ cannot be added until one of the exponents on the ten is changed. The 3.0×10^3 can be changed to 0.3×10^4, then the 1.3 and 0.3 can be added. The answer comes out to be 1.6×10^4.

- For multiplication, the first numbers can be multiplied and then the exponents on the tens can be added. Once an answer is formed, it may have to be converted into scientific notation again depending on the change that occurred. The following is an example of multiplication with scientific notation:

$$(4.5 \times 10^3) \times (3.0 \times 10^{-5}) = 13.5 \times 10^{-2}$$

Since this answer is not in scientific notation, the decimal is moved over to the left one unit, and 1 is added to the ten's exponent. This results in the final answer:

$$1.35 \times 10^{-1}$$

- For division, the first numbers are divided, and the exponents on the tens are subtracted. Again, the answer may need to be converted into scientific notation form, depending on the type of changes that occurred during the problem.

- **Order of magnitude** relates to scientific notation and is the total count of powers of 10 in a number. For example, there are 6 orders of magnitude in 1,000,000. If a number is raised by an order of magnitude, it is multiplied by 10. Order of magnitude can be helpful in estimating results using very large or small numbers. An answer should make sense in terms of its order of magnitude. For example, if area is calculated using two dimensions with 6 orders of magnitude, because area involves multiplication, the answer should have around 12 orders of magnitude. Also, answers can be estimated by rounding to the largest place value in each number. For example: $5,493,302 \times 2,523,100$ can be estimated by $5 \times 3 = 15$ with 12 orders of magnitude.

Simplifying and Approximating Radicals

The **square root symbol** is expressed as $\sqrt{}$ and is commonly known as the **radical**. Taking the root of a number is the inverse operation of multiplying that number by itself some amount of times. For example, squaring the number 7 is equal to 7×7, or 49. Finding the square root is the opposite of finding an exponent, as the operation seeks a number that when multiplied by itself equals the number in the square root symbol.

For example,

$$\sqrt{36} = 6$$

6 multiplied by 6 equals 36. Note, the square root of 36 is also -6 since $-6 \times -6 = 36$.

This can be indicated using a plus/minus symbol like this: ± 6. However, square roots are often just expressed as a positive number for simplicity with it being understood that the true value can be either positive or negative.

Perfect squares are numbers with whole number square roots. The list of perfect squares begins with 0, 1, 4, 9, 16, 25, 36, 49, 64, 81, and 100.

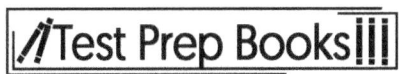

Quantitative Reasoning and Mathematics Achievement

Determining the square root of imperfect squares requires a calculator to reach an exact figure. It's possible, however, to approximate the answer by finding the two perfect squares that the number fits between. For example, the square root of 40 is between 6 and 7 since the squares of those numbers are 36 and 49, respectively.

Square roots are the most common root operation. If the radical doesn't have a number to the upper left of the symbol, $\sqrt{}$, then it's a square root. Sometimes a radical includes a number in the upper left, like $\sqrt[3]{27}$, as in the other common root type—the cube root. Complicated roots like the cube root often require a calculator.

Sequences and Series

Patterns within a sequence can come in 2 distinct forms: the items (shapes, numbers, etc.) either repeat in a constant order, or the items change from one step to another in some consistent way.

The most common patterns in which each item changes from one step to the next are arithmetic and geometric sequences. An arithmetic sequence is one in which the items increase or decrease by a constant difference. In other words, the same thing is added or subtracted to each item or step to produce the next. To determine if a sequence is arithmetic, determine what must be added or subtracted to step one to produce step two. Then, check if the same thing is added/subtracted to step two to produce step three. The same thing must be added/subtracted to step three to produce step four, and so on.

Consider the pattern 13, 10, 7, 4 ... To get from step one (13) to step two (10) by adding or subtracting requires subtracting by 3. The next step is determining whether subtracting 3 from step two (10) will produce step three (7), and subtracting 3 from step three (7) will produce step four (4). In this case, the pattern holds true. Therefore, this is an arithmetic sequence in which each step is produced by subtracting 3 from the previous step. To extend the sequence, 3 is subtracted from the last step to produce the next. The next three numbers in the sequence are 1, -2, -5.

A geometric sequence is one in which each step is produced by multiplying or dividing the previous step by the same number. To determine if a sequence is geometric, decide what step one must be multiplied or divided by to produce step two. Then determine whether multiplying or dividing step two by the same number produces step three, and so on. Consider the pattern 2, 8, 32, 128 ... To get from step one (2) to step two (8) requires multiplication by 4. The next step determines whether multiplying step two (8) by 4 produces step three (32), and multiplying step three (32) by 4 produces step four (128). In this case, the pattern holds true. Therefore, this is a geometric sequence in which each step is produced by multiplying the previous step by 4. To extend the sequence, the last step is multiplied by 4 and repeated. The next three numbers in the sequence are 512; 2,048; 8,192.

Although arithmetic and geometric sequences typically use numbers, these sequences can also be represented by shapes. For example, an arithmetic sequence could consist of shapes with three sides, four sides, and five sides (add one side to the previous step to produce the next). A geometric sequence could consist of eight blocks, four blocks, and two blocks (each step is produced by dividing the number of blocks in the previous step by 2).

Formulas
An arithmetic or geometric sequence can be written as a formula and used to determine unknown steps without writing out the entire sequence. An arithmetic sequence progresses by a **common difference**. To determine the common difference, any step is subtracted by the step that precedes it. In the sequence 4, 9, 14, 19 ... the common difference, or d, is 5. By expressing each step as a_1, a_2, a_3, etc., a formula can be written to represent the sequence. a_1 is the first step. To produce step two, step 1 (a_1) is added to the common difference (d): $a_2 = a_1 + d$. To produce step three, the common difference (d) is added twice to a_1: $a_3 = a_1 + 2d$. To produce step four, the common difference (d) is added three times to a_1: $a_4 = a_1 + 3d$. Following this pattern allows a general rule for arithmetic sequences to be written. For any term of the sequence (a_n), the first step (a_1) is added to the product of

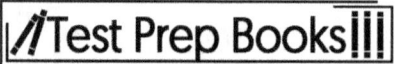

the common difference (d) and one less than the step of the term ($n - 1$): $a_1 + (n - 1)d$. Suppose the 8th term (a_8) is to be found in the previous sequence. By knowing the first step (a_1) is 4 and the common difference (d) is 5, the formula can be used:

$$a_n = a_1 + (n - 1)d \rightarrow a_8 = 4 + (7)5 \rightarrow a_8 = 39$$

In a geometric sequence, each step is produced by multiplying or dividing the previous step by the same number. The **common ratio**, or r, can be determined by dividing any step by the previous step. In the sequence 1, 3, 9, 27 ... the common ratio (r) is 3 $\left(\frac{3}{1} = 3 \text{ or } \frac{9}{3} = 3 \text{ or } \frac{27}{9} = 3\right)$. Each successive step can be expressed as a product of the first step a_1 and the common ratio (r) to some power. For example,

$$a_2 = a_1 \times r$$

$$a_3 = a_1 \times r \times r \text{ or } a_3 = a_1 \times r^2$$

$$a_4 = a_1 \times r \times r \times r \text{ or } a_4 = a_1 \times r^3$$

Following this pattern, a general rule for geometric sequences can be written. For any term of the sequence (a_n), the first step (a_1) is multiplied by the common ratio (r) raised to the power one less than the step of the term ($n - 1$): $a_n = a_1 \times r^{(n-1)}$. Suppose for the previous sequence, the 7th term (a_7) is to be found. Knowing the first step (a_1) is one, and the common ratio (r) is 3, the formula can be used:

$$a_n = a_1 \times r^{(n-1)} \rightarrow a_7 = (1) \times 3^6 \rightarrow a_7 = 729$$

Counting Techniques

There are many counting techniques that can help solve problems involving counting possibilities. For example, the **Addition Principle** states that if there are m choices from Group 1 and n choices from Group 2, then $n + m$ is the total number of choices possible from Groups 1 and 2. For this to be true, the groups can't have any choices in common. The **Multiplication Principle** states that if Process 1 can be completed n ways and Process 2 can be completed m ways, the total number of ways to complete both Process 1 and Process 2 is $n \times m$. For this rule to be used, both processes must be independent of each other. Counting techniques also involve permutations. A **permutation** is an arrangement of elements in a set for which order must be considered. For example, if three letters from the alphabet are chosen, ABC and BAC are two different permutations. The multiplication rule can be used to determine the total number of possibilities. If each letter can't be selected twice, the total number of possibilities is:

$$26 \times 25 \times 24 = 15{,}600$$

A formula can also be used to calculate this total. In general, the notation $P(n, r)$ represents the number of ways to arrange r objects from a set of n and, the formula is:

$$P(n, r) = \frac{n!}{(n - r)!}$$

In the previous example,

$$P(26, 3) = \frac{26!}{23!} = 15{,}600$$

Contrasting permutations, a **combination** is an arrangement of elements in which order doesn't matter. In this case, ABC and BAC are the same combination. In the previous scenario, there are six permutations that represent each single combination. Therefore, the total number of possible combinations is:

$$15{,}600 \div 6 = 2{,}600$$

In general, $C(n,r)$ represents the total number of combinations of n items selected r at a time where order doesn't matter. Another way to represent the combinations of r items selected out of a set of n items is $\binom{n}{r}$. The formula for select combinations of items is:

$$\binom{n}{r} = C(n,r) = \frac{n!}{(n-r)!\,r!}$$

Therefore, the following relationship exists between permutations and combinations:

$$C(n,r) = \frac{P(n,r)}{r!} = \frac{P(n,r)}{P(r,r)}$$

Corresponding Terms of Two Numerical Patterns

When given two numerical patterns, the corresponding terms should be examined to determine if a relationship exists between them. Corresponding terms between patterns are the pairs of numbers that appear in the same step of the two sequences. Consider the following patterns 1, 2, 3, 4 ... and 3, 6, 9, 12 ... The corresponding terms are: 1 and 3; 2 and 6; 3 and 9; and 4 and 12. To identify the relationship, each pair of corresponding terms is examined and the possibilities of performing an operation ($+$, $-$, $\times$, $\div$) to the term from the first sequence to produce the corresponding term in the second sequence are determined. In this case:

$$1 + 2 = 3 \text{ or } 1 \times 3 = 3$$

$$2 + 4 = 6 \text{ or } 2 \times 3 = 6$$

$$3 + 6 = 9 \text{ or } 3 \times 3 = 9$$

$$4 + 8 = 12 \text{ or } 4 \times 3 = 12$$

The consistent pattern is that the number from the first sequence multiplied by 3 equals its corresponding term in the second sequence. By assigning each sequence a label (input and output) or variable (x and y), the relationship can be written as an equation. If the first sequence represents the inputs, or x, and the second sequence represents the outputs, or y, the relationship can be expressed as: $y = 3x$.

Consider the following sets of numbers:

a	2	4	6	8
b	6	8	10	12

To write a rule for the relationship between the values for a and the values for b, the corresponding terms (2 and 6; 4 and 8; 6 and 10; 8 and 12) are examined. The possibilities for producing b from a are:

$$2 + 4 = 6 \text{ or } 2 \times 3 = 6$$

$$4 + 4 = 8 \text{ or } 4 \times 2 = 8$$

$$6 + 4 = 10$$

$$8 + 4 = 12 \text{ or } 8 \times 1.5 = 12$$

The consistent pattern is that adding 4 to the value of a produces the value of b. The relationship can be written as the equation $a + 4 = b$.

Frequencies

Frequencies refer to how often an event occurs or the number of times a particular quantity appears in a given series. To find the number of times a specific value appears, frequency tables are used to record the occurrences, which can then be summed. To construct a frequency table, one simply inputs the values into a tabular format with a column denoting each value, typically in ascending order, with a second column to tally up the number of occurrences for each value, and a third column to give a numerical frequency based on the number of tallies.

A **frequency distribution communicates** the number of outcomes of a given value or number in a data set. When displayed as a bar graph or histogram, a frequency distribution can visually indicate the spread and distribution of the data. A histogram resembling a bell curve approximates a normal distribution. A frequency distribution can also be displayed as a **stem-and-leaf plot**, which arranges data in numerical order and displays values similar to a tally chart with the stem being a range within the set and the leaf indicating the exact value (i.e., stems are whole numbers and leaves are tenths).

	Movie Ratings
4	7
5	2 6 9
6	1 4 6 8 8
7	0 3 5 9
8	1 3 5 6 8 8 9
9	0 0 1 3 4 6 6 9
Key	6	1 represents 61

Stem	Leaf
2	0 2 3 6 8 8 9
3	2 6 7 7
4	7 9
5	4 6 9

This plot provides more detail about individual data points and allows for easy identification of the median, as well as any repeated values in the set.

Data that isn't described using numbers is known as **categorical data.** For example, age is numerical data but hair color is categorical data. Categorical data can also be summarized using two-way frequency tables. A **two-way frequency table** counts the relationship between two sets of categorical data. There are rows and columns for each category, and each cell represents frequency information that shows the actual data count between each combination.

For example, below is a two-way frequency table showing the gender and breed of cats in an animal shelter:

	Domestic Shorthair	Persian	Domestic Longhair	Total
Male	12	2	7	21
Female	8	4	5	17
Total	20	6	12	38

Entries in the middle of the table are known as the **joint frequencies**. For example, the number of females that are Persians is 4, which is a joint frequency. The totals are the **marginal frequencies**. For example, the total number of males is 21, which is a marginal frequency. If the frequencies are changed into percentages based on totals, the table is known as a **two-way relative frequency table**. Percentages can be calculated using the table total, the row totals, or the column totals. Two-way frequency tables can help in making conclusions about the data.

Vectors

A **vector** can be thought of as an abstract list of numbers or as giving a location in a space. For example, the coordinates (x, y) for points in the Cartesian plane are vectors. Each entry in a vector can be referred to by its location in the list: first, second, third, and so on. The total length of the list is the **dimension** of the vector. A vector is often denoted as such by putting an arrow on top of it, e.g., $\vec{v} = (v_1, v_2, v_3)$.

Adding Vectors Graphically and Algebraically

There are two basic operations for vectors. First, two vectors can be added together. Let:

$$\vec{v} = (v_1, v_2, v_3)$$

$$\vec{w} = (w_1, w_2, w_3)$$

The sum of the two vectors is defined to be:

$$\vec{v} + \vec{w} = (v_1 + w_1, v_2 + w_2, v_3 + w_3)$$

Subtraction of vectors can be defined similarly.

Vector addition can be visualized in the following manner. First, each vector can be visualized as an arrow. Then, the base of one arrow is placed at the tip of the other arrow. The tip of this first arrow now hits some point in space, and there will be an arrow from the origin to this point. This new arrow corresponds to the new vector. In subtraction, the direction of the arrow being subtracted is reversed.

For example, if adding together the vectors $(-2, 3)$ and $(4, 1)$, the new vector will be $(-2 + 4, 3 + 1)$, or $(2, 4)$. Graphically, this may be pictured in the following manner:

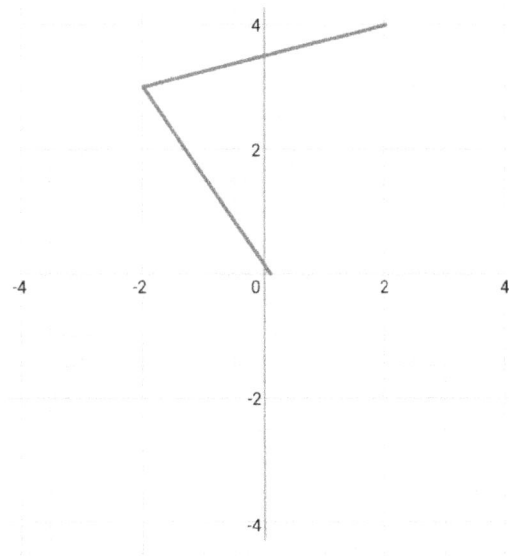

Performing Scalar Multiplications

The second basic operation for vectors is called **scalar multiplication**. Scalar multiplication is multiplying any vector by any real number, which is denoted here as a scalar. Let $\vec{v} = (v_1, v_2, v_3)$, and let a be an arbitrary real number. Then the scalar multiple $a\vec{v} = (av_1, av_2, av_3)$. Graphically, this corresponds to changing the length of the arrow corresponding to the vector by a factor, or scale, of a. That is why the real number is called a **scalar** in this instance.

As an example, let $\vec{v} = (2, -1, 1)$. Then $3\vec{v} = (3 \times 2, 3 \times -1, 3 \times 1) = (6, -3, 3)$.

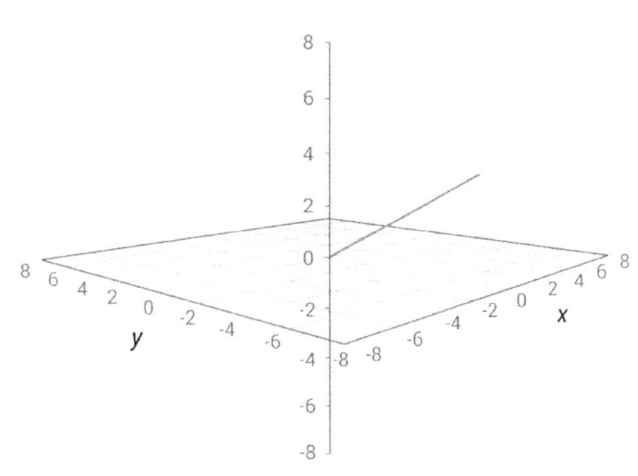

Note that scalar multiplication is **distributive** over vector addition, meaning that $a(\vec{v} + \vec{w}) = a\vec{v} + a\vec{w}$.

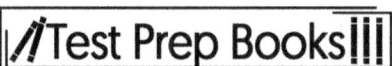

Determinants

A **matrix** is a rectangular arrangement of numbers in rows and columns. The **determinant** of a matrix is a special value that can be calculated for any square matrix.

Using the *square* 2×2 *matrix* $\begin{bmatrix} a & b \\ c & d \end{bmatrix}$, the determinant is $ad - bc$.

For example, the determinant of the matrix $\begin{bmatrix} -5 & 1 \\ 3 & 4 \end{bmatrix}$ is:

$$-5(4) - 1(3) = -20 - 3 = -23$$

Using a 3×3 *matrix* $\begin{bmatrix} a & b & c \\ d & e & f \\ g & h & i \end{bmatrix}$, the determinant is:

$$a(ei - fh) - b(di - fg) + c(dh - eg)$$

For example, the determinant of the matrix $\begin{bmatrix} 2 & 0 & 1 \\ -1 & 3 & 2 \\ 2 & -2 & -1 \end{bmatrix}$ is

$$2(3(-1) - 2(-2)) - 0(-1(-1) - 2(2)) + 1(-1(-2) - 3(2))$$

$$2(-3 + 4) - 0(1 - 4) + 1(2 - 6)$$

$$2(1) - 0(-3) + 1(-4)$$

$$2 - 0 - 4 = -2$$

The pattern continues for larger square matrices.

Word Problems

Arithmetic

Word problems present the opportunity to relate mathematical concepts learned in the classroom into real-world situations. These types of problems are situations in which some parts of the problem are known and at least one part is unknown.

There are three types of instances in which something can be unknown: the starting point, the modification, or the final result can all be missing from the provided information.

- For an addition problem, the modification is the quantity of a new amount added to the starting point.
- For a subtraction problem, the modification is the quantity taken away from the starting point.

Keywords in the word problems can signal what type of operation needs to be used to solve the problem. Words such as *total, increased, combined*, and *more* indicate that addition is needed. Words such as *difference, decreased*, and *minus* indicate that subtraction is needed.

Regarding addition, here's a sample equation:

$$3 + 7 = 10$$

The number 3 is the starting point. 7 is the modification, and 10 is the result from adding a new amount to the starting point. Different word problems can arise from this same equation, depending on which value is the unknown. For example, here are three problems:

- If a boy had three pencils and was given seven more, how many would he have in total?
- If a boy had three pencils and a girl gave him more so that he had ten in total, how many was he given?
- A boy was given seven pencils so that he had ten in total. How many did he start with?

All three problems involve the same equation, and determining which part of the equation is missing is the key to solving each word problem. The missing answers would be 10, 7, and 3, respectively.

In terms of subtraction, the same three scenarios can occur. Here's a sample equation:

$$6 - 4 = 2$$

The number 6 is the starting point, 4 is the modification, and 2 is the new amount that is the result from taking 4 away from the starting point. Again, different types of word problems can arise from this equation. For example, here are three possible problems:

- If a girl had six quarters and four were taken away, how many would be left over?
- If a girl had six quarters, purchased a pencil, and had two quarters left over, how many did she pay with?
- If a girl paid for a pencil with four quarters and had two quarters left over, how many did she have to start with?

Determining whether the starting point, the modification, or the final result is missing is the goal in solving the problem. The missing answers would be 2, 4, and 6, respectively.

The three addition problems and the three subtraction word problems can be solved by using a picture, a number line, or an algebraic equation. If an equation is used, a question mark can be utilized to represent the unknown quantity. For example, $6 - 2 =?$ can be written to show that the missing value is the result. Using equation form visually indicates what portion of the addition or subtraction problem is the missing value.

Similar instances can be seen in word problems involving multiplication and division. Key words within a multiplication problem involve *times, product, doubled,* and *tripled*. Key words within a division problem involve *split, quotient, divided, shared, groups*, and *half*. Like addition and subtraction, multiplication and division problems also have three different types of missing values.

Multiplication consists of a specific number of groups having the same size, the quantity of items within each group, and the total quantity within all groups. Therefore, each one of these amounts can be the missing value.

Here's a sample equation:

$$5 \times 3 = 15$$

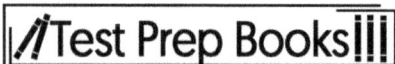

5 and 3 are interchangeable, so either amount can be the number of groups or the quantity of items within each group. 15 is the total number of items. Again, different types of word problems can arise from this equation. For example, here are three problems:

- If a classroom is serving 5 different types of apples for lunch and has three apples of each type, how many total apples are there to give to the students?
- If a classroom has 15 apples with 5 different types, how many of each type are there?
- If a classroom has 15 apples with 3 of each type, how many types are there to choose from?

Each question involves using the same equation to solve, and it is imperative to decide which part of the equation is the missing value. The answers to the problems are 15, 3, and 5, respectively.

Similar to multiplication, division problems involve a total amount, a number of groups having the same size, and a number of items within each group. The difference between multiplication and division is that the starting point is the total amount, which then gets divided into equal quantities.

Here's a sample equation:

$$48 \div 6 = 8$$

48 is the total number of items, which is being divided into 6 different groups. In order to do so, 8 items go into each group. Also, 6 and 8 are interchangeable, so the 48 items could be divided into 8 groups of 6 items each. Therefore, different types of word problems can arise from this equation depending on which value is unknown. For example, here are three types of problems:

- A boy needs 48 pieces of chalk. If there are 8 pieces in each box, how many boxes should he buy?
- A boy has 48 pieces of chalk. If he has 6 boxes that each contain an equal amount of chalk, how many pieces of chalk are in each box?
- A boy has partitioned all of his chalk into 8 piles, with 6 pieces in each pile. How many pieces does he have in total?

Each one of these questions involves the same equation, and the third question can easily utilize the multiplication equation $8 \times 6 = ?$ instead of division. The answers are 6, 8, and 48, respectively.

Word problems can appear daunting, but don't let the verbiage psyche you out. No matter the scenario or specifics, the key to answering them is to translate the words into a math problem. Always keep in mind what the question is asking and what operations could lead to that answer.

Word problems involving elapsed time, money, length, volume, and mass require:

- determining which operations (addition, subtraction, multiplication, and division) should be performed, and
- using and/or converting the proper unit for the scenario.

Quantitative Reasoning and Mathematics Achievement

The following table lists key words that can be used to indicate the proper operation.

Addition	Sum, total, in all, combined, increase of, more than, added to
Subtraction	Difference, change, remaining, less than, decreased by
Multiplication	Product, times, twice, triple, each
Division	Quotient, goes into, per, evenly, divided by half, divided by third, split

If a question asks to provide a mathematical expression and says "equals," then an = sign must be included in the answer. Similarly, "less than or equal to" is expressed by the inequality symbol ≤, and "greater than or equal to" is expressed as ≥. Furthermore, "less than" is represented by <, and "greater than" is expressed by >.

Example:

A store is having a spring sale, where everything is 70% off. You have $45.00 to spend. A jacket is regularly priced at $80.00. Do you have enough to buy the jacket and a pair of gloves regularly priced at $20.00?

There are two ways to approach this.

Method 1:

Set up the equations to find the sale prices (the original price minus the amount discounted):

$$\$80.00 - (\$80.00(0.70)) = sale\ cost\ of\ the\ jacket$$

$$\$20.00 - (\$20.00(0.70)) = sale\ cost\ of\ the\ gloves$$

Solve for the sale cost:

$$\$24.00 = sale\ cost\ of\ the\ jacket$$

$$\$6.00 = sale\ cost\ of\ the\ gloves$$

Determine if you have enough money for both:

$$\$24.00 + \$6.00 = total\ sale\ cost$$

$30.00 is less than $45.00, so you can afford to purchase both.

Method 2:

Determine the percent of the original price that you will pay:

$$100\% - 70\% = 30\%$$

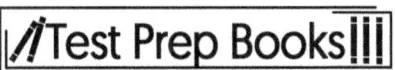

Set up the equations to find the sale prices:

$$\$80.00(0.30) = cost\ of\ the\ jacket$$

$$\$20.00(0.30) = cost\ of\ the\ gloves$$

Solve:

$$\$24.00 = cost\ of\ the\ jacket$$

$$\$6.00 = cost\ of\ the\ gloves$$

Determine if you have enough money for both:

$$\$24.00 + \$6.00 = total\ sale\ cost$$

$30.00 is less than $45.00, so you can afford to purchase both.

Unit Rate

Rates are used to compare two quantities with different units. **Unit rates** are the simplest form of rate. Some word problems will ask you to calculate the unit rate of something, and some will require you to use the unit rate in the calculation to find the answer. Unit rate is the amount or quantity of something per one of a certain measurement. For example, a problem might tell you that a car drove a certain number of miles in a certain number of hours and then ask how many miles per hour (the unit rate) the car was traveling. These questions involve solving proportions. With unit rates, the denominator in the comparison of two units is one.

For example, if someone can type at a rate of 1,000 words in 5 minutes, then their unit rate for typing is:

$$\frac{1,000}{5} = \frac{200}{1}$$

or

200 words per minute

Any rate can be converted into a unit rate by dividing to make the denominator one. 1,000 words in 5 minutes has been converted into the unit rate of 200 words per minute.

Example 1:

> Alexandra made $96 during the first 3 hours of her shift as a temporary worker at a law office. She will continue to earn money at this rate until she finishes in 5 more hours. How much does Alexandra make per hour? How much will Alexandra have made at the end of the day?

This problem can be solved in two ways. The first is to set up a proportion, as the rate of pay is constant. The second is to determine her hourly rate, multiply the 5 hours by that rate, and then add the $96. We'll solve it using both methods.

To set up a proportion, put the money already earned over the hours already worked on one side of an equation. The other side has x over 8 hours (the total hours worked in the day). It looks like this: $\frac{96}{3} = \frac{x}{8}$. Now, cross-multiply to get $768 = 3x$. To get x, we divide by 3, which leaves us with $x = 256$. Thus, Alexandra will make $256 at the end of the day. To calculate her hourly rate, we need to divide the total by 8, which gives us $32 per hour (the unit rate).

Alternatively, we could figure out the hourly rate by dividing $96 by 3 hours to get $32 per hour. Now we can figure out her total pay by multiplying $32 per hour by 8 hours, which comes out to $256.

Example 2:

> Jonathan is reading a novel. So far, he has read 215 of the 335 total pages. It takes Jonathan 25 minutes to read 10 pages, and the rate is constant. How long does it take Jonathan to read one page? How much longer will it take him to finish the novel? Express the answer in time.

To calculate how long it takes Jonathan to read one page, we need to divide the 25 minutes by 10 pages to determine the page per minute rate. Thus, it takes 2.5 minutes to read one page.

Jonathan must read 120 more pages to complete the novel. (This is calculated by subtracting the pages already read from the total.) Now, we need to multiply his rate per page by the number of pages. Thus, $120 \times 2.5 = 300$. Expressed in time, 300 minutes is equal to 5 hours.

Determining the Reasonableness of Results

When solving math word problems, the solution obtained should make sense within the given scenario. The step of checking the solution will reduce the possibility of a calculation error or a solution that may be mathematically correct but not applicable in the real world. Consider the following scenarios:

A problem states that Lisa got 24 out of 32 questions correct on a test and asks to find the percentage of correct answers. To solve the problem, a student divided 32 by 24 to get 1.33, and then multiplied by 100 to get 133%. By examining the solution within the context of the problem, the student should recognize that getting all 32 questions correct will produce a perfect score of 100%. Therefore, a score of 133% with 8 incorrect answers does not make sense, and the calculations should be checked.

A problem states that the maximum weight on a bridge cannot exceed 22,000 pounds. The problem asks to find the maximum number of cars that can be on the bridge at one time if each car weighs 4,000 pounds. To solve this problem, a student divided 22,000 by 4,000 to get an answer of 5.5. By examining the solution within the context of the problem, the student should recognize that although the calculations are mathematically correct, the solution does not make sense. Half of a car on a bridge is not possible, so the student should determine that a maximum of 5 cars can be on the bridge at the same time.

Estimating Absolute and Relative Error in the Numerical Answer to a Problem

Once a result is determined to be logical within the context of a given problem, the result should be evaluated by its nearness to the expected answer. This is performed by approximating given values to perform mental math. Numbers should be rounded to the nearest value possible to check the initial results.

Consider the following example:

> A customer is buying a new sound system for their home. The customer purchases a stereo for $435, 2 speakers for $67 each, and the necessary cables for $12. The customer chooses an option that allows him to spread the costs over equal payments for 4 months. How much will the monthly payments be?

After making calculations for the problem, a student determines that the monthly payment will be $145.25. To check the accuracy of the results, the student rounds each cost to the nearest ten:

$$(440 + 70 + 70 + 10)$$

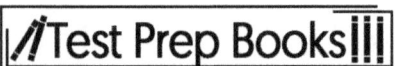

Then, the student determines that the total is approximately $590. Dividing by 4 months gives an approximate monthly payment of $147.50. Therefore, the student can conclude that the solution of $145.25 is very close to what should be expected.

When rounding, the place-value that is used in rounding can make a difference. Suppose the student had rounded to the nearest hundred for the estimation. The result:

$$400 + 100 + 100 + 0 = 600$$

$$600 \div 4 = 150$$

This will show that the answer is reasonable but not as close to the actual value as rounding to the nearest ten.

When considering the accuracy of estimates, the error in the estimated solution can be shown as absolute and relative. **Absolute error** tells the actual difference between the estimated value and the true, calculated value. The **relative error** tells how large the error is in relation to the true value. There may be two problems where the absolute error of the values (the estimated one and the calculated one) is 10. For one problem, this may mean the relative error in the estimate is very small because the estimated value is 15,000, and the true value is 14,990. Ten in relation to the true value of 15,000 is small: 0.06%. For the other problem, the estimated value is 50, and the true value is 40. In this case, the absolute error of 10 means a high relative error because the true value is smaller. The relative error is:

$$\frac{10}{40} = 0.25 \text{ or } 25\%$$

Algebra

Algebraic Expressions and Equations

An algebraic expression is a statement about an unknown quantity expressed in mathematical symbols. A variable is used to represent the unknown quantity, usually denoted by a letter. An equation is a statement in which two expressions (at least one containing a variable) are equal to each other. An algebraic expression can be thought of as a mathematical phrase and an equation can be thought of as a mathematical sentence.

Algebraic expressions and equations both contain numbers, variables, and mathematical operations. The following are examples of algebraic expressions: $5x + 3$, $7xy - 8(x^2 + y)$, and $\sqrt{a^2 + b^2}$. An expression can be simplified or evaluated for given values of variables. The following are examples of equations: $2x + 3 = 7$, $a^2 + b^2 = c^2$, and $2x + 5 = 3x - 2$. An equation contains two sides separated by an equal sign. Equations can be solved to determine the value(s) of the variable for which the statement is true.

Parts of Expressions

Algebraic expressions consist of variables, numbers, and operations. A term of an expression is any combination of numbers and/or variables, and terms are separated by addition and subtraction. For example, the expression $5x^2 - 3xy + 4 - 2$ consists of 4 terms: $5x^2$, $-3xy$, $4y$, and -2. Note that each term includes its given sign ($+$ or $-$). The variable part of a term is a letter that represents an unknown quantity. The coefficient of a term is the number by which the variable is multiplied. For the term $4y$, the variable is y, and the coefficient is 4. Terms are identified by the power (or exponent) of its variable.

A number without a variable is referred to as a constant. If the variable is to the first power (x^1 or simply x), it is referred to as a linear term. A term with a variable to the second power (x^2) is quadratic, and a term to the third power (x^3) is cubic. Consider the expression $x^3 + 3x - 1$. The constant is -1. The linear term is $3x$. There is no quadratic term. The cubic term is x^3.

An algebraic expression can also be classified by how many terms exist in the expression. Any like terms should be combined before classifying. A monomial is an expression consisting of only one term. Examples of monomials are: 17, $2x$, and $-5ab^2$. A binomial is an expression consisting of two terms separated by addition or subtraction. Examples include $2x - 4$ and $-3y^2 + 2y$. A trinomial consists of 3 terms. For example, $5x^2 - 2x + 1$ is a trinomial.

Simple Expressions for Given Values

An algebraic expression is a statement written in mathematical symbols, typically including one or more unknown values represented by variables. For example, the expression $2x + 3$ states that an unknown number (x) is multiplied by 2 and added to 3. If given a value for the unknown number, or variable, the value of the expression is determined. For example, if the value of the variable x is 4, the value of the expression 4 is multiplied by 2, and 3 is added. This results in a value of 11 for the expression.

When given an algebraic expression and values for the variable(s), the expression is evaluated to determine its numerical value. To evaluate the expression, the given values for the variables are substituted (or replaced), and the expression is simplified using the order of operations. Parentheses should be used when substituting. Consider the following: Evaluate $a - 2b + ab$ for $a = 3$ and $b = -1$. To evaluate, any variable a is replaced with 3 and any variable b with -1, producing $(3) - 2(-1) + 3(-1)$. Next, the order of operations is used to calculate the value of the expression, which is 2.

Adding and Subtracting Algebraic Expressions

An algebraic expression is simplified by combining like terms. For the algebraic expression $3x^2 - 4x + 5 - 5x^2 + x - 3$, the terms are $3x^2$, $-4x$, 5, $-5x^2$, x, and -3. Like terms have the same variables raised to the same powers (exponents). The like terms for this example are $3x^2$ and $-5x^2$, $-4x$ and x, and 5 and -3. To combine like terms, the coefficients (numerical factor of the term including sign) are added, and the variables and their powers are kept the same. Note that if a coefficient is not written, it is an implied coefficient of 1 ($x = 1x$). In this example, the equation will simplify to $-2x^2 - 3x + 2$.

When adding or subtracting algebraic expressions, each expression is written in parentheses. The negative sign is distributed when necessary, and like terms are combined. Consider the following: add $2a + 5b - 2$ to $a - 2b + 8c - 4$. The sum is set as follows: $(a - 2b + 8c - 4) + (2a + 5b - 2)$. In front of each set of parentheses is an implied positive one, which, when distributed, does not change any of the terms. Therefore, the parentheses are dropped and like terms are combined:

$$a - 2b + 8c - 4 + 2a + 5b - 2 = 3a + 3b + 8c - 6$$

Consider the following problem: Subtract $2a + 5b - 2$ from $a - 2b + 8c - 4$. The difference is set as follows:

$$(a - 2b + 8c - 4) - (2a + 5b - 2)$$

The implied one in front of the first set of parentheses will not change those four terms. However, distributing the implied -1 in front of the second set of parentheses will change the sign of each of those three terms:

$$a - 2b + 8c - 4 - 2a - 5b + 2$$

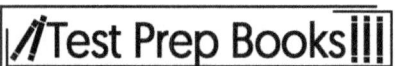

Combining like terms yields the simplified expression $-a - 7b + 8c - 2$.

Distributive Property

The distributive property states that multiplying a sum (or difference) by a number produces the same result as multiplying each value in the sum (or difference) by the number and adding (or subtracting) the products. Using mathematical symbols, the distributive property states $a(b + c) = ab + ac$. The expression $4(3 + 2)$ is simplified using the order of operations. Simplifying inside the parentheses first produces 4×5, which equals 20. The expression $4(3 + 2)$ can also be simplified using the distributive property:

$$4(3 + 2) = 4 \times 3 + 4 \times 2 = 12 + 8 = 20$$

Consider the following example: $4(3x - 2)$. The expression cannot be simplified inside the parentheses because $3x$ and -2 are not like terms and therefore cannot be combined. However, the expression can be simplified by using the distributive property and multiplying each term inside of the parentheses by the term outside of the parentheses: $12x - 8$. The resulting equivalent expression contains no like terms, so it cannot be further simplified. The algebraic expressions can be tested for equivalency by choosing values for the variables and evaluating both expressions. For example, $4(3x - 2)$ and $12x - 8$ are tested by substituting 3 for the variable x and calculating to determine whether equivalent values result.

Consider the expression $(3x + 2y + 1) - (5x - 3) + 2(3y + 4)$. The distributive property is used to simplify the expression. Note that there is an implied one in front of the first set of parentheses and an implied -1 in front of the second set of parentheses. Distributing the 1, -1, and 2 produces:

$$1(3x) + 1(2y) + 1(1) - 1(5x) - 1(-3) + 2(3y) + 2(4) = 3x + 2y + 1 - 5x + 3 + 6y + 8$$

This expression contains like terms that are combined to produce the simplified expression $-2x + 8y + 12$.

Verbal Statements and Algebraic Expressions

An algebraic expression is a statement about unknown quantities expressed in mathematical symbols. The statement *five times a number added to forty* is expressed as $5x + 40$. An equation is a statement in which two expressions (with at least one containing a variable) are equal to one another. The statement *five times a number added to forty is equal to ten* is expressed as $5x + 40 = 10$.

Real world scenarios can also be expressed mathematically. Suppose a job pays its employees $300 per week and $40 for each sale made. The weekly pay is represented by the expression $40x + 300$ where x is the number of sales made during the week.

Consider the following scenario: Bob had $20 and Tom had $4. After selling 4 ice cream cones to Bob, Tom has as much money as Bob. The cost of an ice cream cone is an unknown quantity and can be represented by a variable (x). The amount of money Bob has after his purchase is four times the cost of an ice cream cone subtracted from his original $20 → $20 - 4x$. The amount of money Tom has after his sale is four times the cost of an ice cream cone added to his original $4 → $4x + 4$. After the sale, the amount of money that Bob and Tom have is equal → $20 - 4x = 4x + 4$.

When expressing a verbal or written statement mathematically, it is vital to understand words or phrases that can be represented with symbols. The following are examples:

Symbol	Phrase
+	Added to; increased by; sum of; more than
−	Decreased by; difference between; less than; take away
×	Multiplied by; 3(4,5...) times as large; product of
÷	Divided by; quotient of; half (third, etc.) of
=	Is; the same as; results in; as much as; equal to
x, t, n, etc.	A number; unknown quantity; value of; variable

Rewriting Expressions

Expressions can be rewritten based on their factors. For example, the expression $6x + 4$ can be rewritten as $2(3x + 2)$ because 2 is a factor of both $6x$ and 4. More complex expressions can also be rewritten based on their factors.

The expression $x^4 - 16$ can be rewritten as $(x^2 - 4)(x^2 + 4)$. This is a different type of factoring, where a difference of squares is factored into a sum and difference of the same two terms. With some expressions, the factoring process is simple and only leads to a different way to represent the expression. With others, factoring and rewriting the expression leads to more information about the given problem.

In the following quadratic equation, factoring the binomial leads to finding the zeros of the function:

$$x^2 - 5x + 6 = y$$

This equation factors into $(x - 3)(x - 2) = y$, where 2 and 3 are found to be the zeros of the function when y is set equal to zero. The zeros of any function are the x-values where the graph of the function on the coordinate plane crosses the x-axis.

Factoring an equation is a simple way to rewrite the equation and find the zeros, but factoring is not possible for every quadratic. Completing the square is one way to find zeros when factoring is not an option. The following equation cannot be factored:

$$x^2 + 10x - 9 = 0$$

The first step in this method is to move the constant to the right side of the equation, making it:

$$x^2 + 10x = 9$$

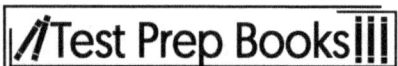

Then, the coefficient of x is divided by 2 and squared. This number is then added to both sides of the equation, to make the equation still true. For this example, $\left(\frac{10}{2}\right)^2 = 25$ is added to both sides of the equation to obtain:

$$x^2 + 10x + 25 = 9 + 25$$

This expression simplifies to $x^2 + 10x + 25 = 34$, which can then be factored into:

$$(x + 5)^2 = 34$$

Solving for x then involves taking the square root of both sides and subtracting 5. This leads to two zeros of the function:

$$x = \pm\sqrt{34} - 5$$

Depending on the type of answer the question seeks, a calculator may be used to find exact numbers.

Given a quadratic equation in standard form, $ax^2 + bx + c = 0$, the sign of a tells whether the function has a minimum value or a maximum value. If $a > 0$, the graph opens up and has a minimum value. If $a < 0$, the graph opens down and has a maximum value. Depending on the way the quadratic equation is written, multiplication may need to occur before a max/min value is determined.

Exponential expressions can also be rewritten, just as quadratic equations. Properties of exponents must be understood. Multiplying two exponential expressions with the same base involves adding the exponents:

$$a^m a^n = a^{m+n}$$

Dividing two exponential expressions with the same base involves subtracting the exponents:

$$\frac{a^m}{a^n} = a^{m-n}$$

Raising an exponential expression to another exponent includes multiplying the exponents:

$$(a^m)^n = a^{mn}$$

The zero power always gives a value of 1: $a^0 = 1$. Raising either a product or a fraction to a power involves distributing that power:

$$(ab)^m = a^m b^m \text{ and } \left(\frac{a}{b}\right)^m = \frac{a^m}{b^m}$$

Finally, raising a number to a negative exponent is equivalent to the reciprocal including the positive exponent:

$$a^{-m} = \frac{1}{a^m}$$

Solving Equations and Inequalities

Linear equations and linear inequalities are both comparisons of two algebraic expressions. However, unlike equations in which the expressions are equal, linear inequalities compare expressions that may be unequal. Linear equations typically have one value for the variable that makes the statement true. Linear inequalities generally have an infinite number of values that make the statement true.

When solving a linear equation, the desired result requires determining a numerical value for the unknown variable. If given a linear equation involving addition, subtraction, multiplication, or division, working backwards isolates the variable. Addition and subtraction are inverse operations, as are multiplication and division. Therefore, they can be used to cancel each other out.

The first steps to solving linear equations are distributing, if necessary, and combining any like terms on the same side of the equation. Sides of an equation are separated by an equal sign. Next, the equation is manipulated to show the variable on one side. Whatever is done to one side of the equation must be done to the other side of the equation to remain equal. Inverse operations are then used to isolate the variable and undo the order of operations backwards. Addition and subtraction are undone, then multiplication and division are undone.

For example, solve:

$$4(t - 2) + 2t - 4 = 2(9 - 2t)$$

Distributing:

$$4t - 8 + 2t - 4 = 18 - 4t$$

Combining like terms:

$$6t - 12 = 18 - 4t$$

Adding $4t$ to each side to move the variable:

$$10t - 12 = 18$$

Adding 12 to each side to isolate the variable:

$$10t = 30$$

Dividing each side by 10 to isolate the variable:

$$t = 3$$

The answer can be checked by substituting the value for the variable into the original equation, ensuring that both sides calculate to be equal.

Linear inequalities express the relationship between unequal values. More specifically, they describe in what way the values are unequal. A value can be greater than (>), less than (<), greater than or equal to (≥), or less than or equal to (≤) another value. $5x + 40 > 65$ is read as *five times a number added to forty is greater than sixty-five.*

When solving a linear inequality, the solution is the set of all numbers that make the statement true. The inequality $x + 2 \geq 6$ has a solution set of 4 and every number greater than 4 (4.01; 5; 12; 107; etc.). Adding 2 to 4 or any number greater than 4 results in a value that is greater than or equal to 6. Therefore, $x \geq 4$ is the solution set.

To algebraically solve a linear inequality, follow the same steps as those for solving a linear equation. The inequality symbol stays the same for all operations *except* when multiplying or dividing by a negative number. If multiplying or dividing by a negative number while solving an inequality, the relationship reverses (the sign flips). In other words,

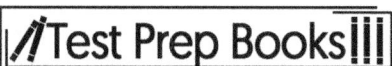

> switches to < and vice versa. Multiplying or dividing by a positive number does not change the relationship, so the sign stays the same. An example is shown below.

Solve $-2x - 8 \leq 22$ for the value of x.

Add 8 to both sides to isolate the variable: $-2x \leq 30$

Divide both sides by -2 to solve for x: $x \geq -15$

Solutions of a linear equation or a linear inequality are the values of the variable that make a statement true. In the case of a linear equation, the solution set (list of all possible solutions) typically consists of a single numerical value. To find the solution, the equation is solved by isolating the variable. For example, solving the equation $3x - 7 = -13$ produces the solution $x = -2$. The only value for x which produces a true statement is -2. This can be checked by substituting -2 into the original equation to check that both sides are equal. In this case, $3(-2) - 7 = -13 \rightarrow -13 = -13$; therefore, -2 is the solution.

Although linear equations generally have one solution, this is not always the case. If there is no value for the variable that makes the statement true, there is no solution to the equation. Consider the equation $x + 3 = x - 1$. There is no value for x in which adding 3 to the value produces the same result as subtracting one from the value. Conversely, if any value for the variable makes a true statement, the equation has an infinite number of solutions. Consider the equation $3x + 6 = 3(x + 2)$. Any number substituted for x will result in a true statement (both sides of the equation are equal).

By manipulating equations like the two above, the variable of the equation will cancel out completely. If the remaining constants express a true statement (ex. $6 = 6$), then all real numbers are solutions to the equation. If the constants left express a false statement (ex. $3 = -1$), then no solution exists for the equation.

Solving a linear inequality requires all values that make the statement true to be determined. For example, solving $3x - 7 \geq -13$ produces the solution $x \geq -2$. This means that -2 and any number greater than -2 produces a true statement. Solution sets for linear inequalities will often be displayed using a number line. If a value is included in the set ($\geq$ or $\leq$), a shaded dot is placed on that value and an arrow extends in the direction of the solutions. For a variable $>$ or $\geq$ a number, the arrow will point right on a number line, the direction where the numbers increase. If a variable is $<$ or $\leq$ a number, the arrow will point left on a number line, which is the direction where the numbers decrease. If the value is not included in the set ($>$ or $<$), an open (unshaded) circle is placed on that value and an arrow extends in the appropriate direction.

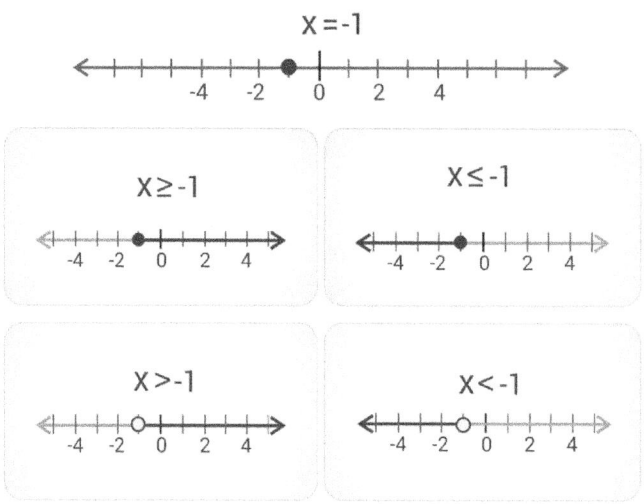

Quantitative Reasoning and Mathematics Achievement

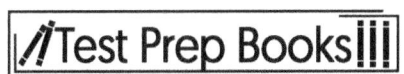

Similar to linear equations, a linear inequality may have a solution set consisting of all real numbers, or can contain no solution. When solved algebraically, a linear inequality in which the variable cancels out and results in a true statement (ex. $7 \geq 2$) has a solution set of all real numbers. A linear inequality in which the variable cancels out and results in a false statement (ex. $7 \leq 2$) has no solution.

Equations that require solving for a variable (*algebraic equations*) come in many forms. Here are some more examples:

No coefficient attached to the variable:

$$x + 8 = 20$$

$$x + 8 - 8 = 20 - 8$$

$$x = 12$$

A fractional coefficient:

$$\frac{1}{2}z + 24 = 36$$

$$\frac{1}{2}z + 24 - 24 = 36 - 24$$

$$\frac{1}{2}z = 12$$

Now we multiply the fraction by its inverse:

$$\frac{2}{1} \times \frac{1}{2}z = 12 \times \frac{2}{1}$$

$$z = 24$$

Multiple instances of x:

$$14x + x - 4 = 3x + 2$$

All instances of x can be combined.

$$15x - 4 = 3x + 2$$

$$15x - 4 + 4 = 3x + 2 + 4$$

$$15x = 3x + 6$$

$$15x - 3x = 3x + 6 - 3x$$

$$12x = 6$$

$$\frac{12x}{12} = \frac{6}{12}$$

$$x = \frac{1}{2}$$

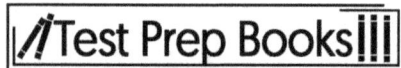

When solving radical and rational equations, extraneous solutions must be accounted for when finding the answers. For example, the equation $\frac{x}{x-5} = \frac{3x}{x+3}$ has two values that create a 0 denominator: $x \neq 5, -3$. When solving for x, these values must be considered because they cannot be solutions. In the given equation, solving for x can be done using cross-multiplication, yielding the equation:

$$x(x+3) = 3x(x-5)$$

Distributing results in the quadratic equation $x^2 + 3x = 3x^2 - 15x$; therefore, all terms must be moved to one side of the equal sign. This results in $2x^2 - 18x = 0$, which in factored form is:

$$2x(x-9) = 0$$

Setting each factor equal to zero, the apparent solutions are $x = 0$ and $x = 9$. These two solutions are neither 5 nor -3, so they are viable solutions. Neither 0 nor 9 create a 0 denominator in the original equation.

A similar process exists when solving radical equations. One must check to make sure the solutions are defined in the original equations. Solving an equation containing a square root involves isolating the root and then squaring both sides of the equal sign. Solving a cube root equation involves isolating the radical and then cubing both sides. In either case, the variable can then be solved for because there are no longer radicals in the equation.

Systems of Equations

A *system of equations* is a group of equations that have the same variables or unknowns. These equations can be linear, but they are not always so. Finding a solution to a system of equations means finding the values of the variables that satisfy each equation. For a linear system of two equations and two variables, there could be a single solution, no solution, or infinitely many solutions.

A single solution occurs when there is one value for x and y that satisfies the system. This would be shown on the graph where the lines cross at exactly one point. When there is no solution, the lines are parallel and do not ever cross. With infinitely many solutions, the equations may look different, but they are the same line. One equation will be a multiple of the other, and on the graph, they lie on top of each other.

The process of elimination can be used to solve a system of equations. For example, the following equations make up a system:

$$x + 3y = 10$$

$$2x - 5y = 9$$

Immediately adding these equations does not eliminate a variable, but it is possible to change the first equation by multiplying the whole equation by -2.

This changes the first equation to:

$$-2x - 6y = -20$$

The equations can be then added to obtain $-11y = -11$. Solving for y yields $y = 1$. To find the rest of the solution, 1 can be substituted in for y in either original equation to find the value of $x = 7$. The solution to the system is (7, 1) because it makes both equations true, and it is the point in which the lines intersect. If the system is *dependent*—having infinitely many solutions—then both variables will cancel out when the elimination method is used, resulting in an equation that is true for many values of x and y. Since the system is dependent, both equations can be simplified to the same equation or line.

A system can also be solved using *substitution*. This involves solving one equation for a variable and then plugging that solved equation into the other equation in the system. For example, $x - y = -2$ and $3x + 2y = 9$ can be solved using substitution. The first equation can be solved for x, where:

$$x = -2 + y$$

Then it can be plugged into the other equation:

$$3(-2 + y) + 2y = 9$$

Solving for y yields $-6 + 3y + 2y = 9$, where $y = 3$. If $y = 3$, then $x = 1$. This solution can be checked by plugging in these values for the variables in each equation to see if it makes a true statement.

Additionally, a solution to a system of equations can be found graphically. The solution to a linear system is the point or points where the lines cross. The values of x and y represent the coordinates (x, y) where the lines intersect. Using the same system of equations as above, they can be solved for y to put them in slope-intercept form, $y = mx + b$. These equations become $y = x + 2$ and:

$$y = -\frac{3}{2}x + 4.5$$

The slope is the coefficient of x, and the y-intercept is the constant value. This system with the solution is shown below:

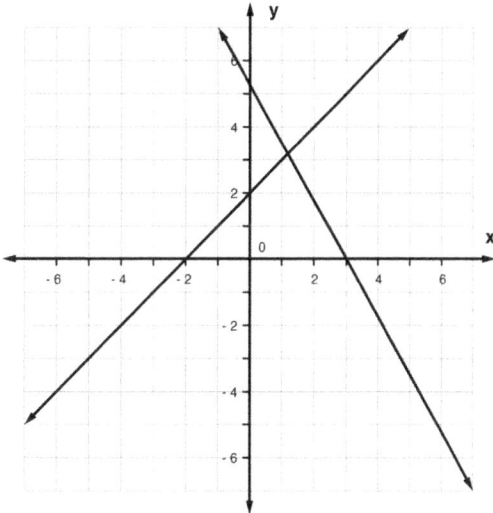

A system of equations may also be made up of a linear and a quadratic equation. These systems may have one solution, two solutions, or no solutions. The graph of these systems involves one straight line and one parabola. Algebraically, these systems can be solved by solving the linear equation for one variable and plugging that answer in to the quadratic equation. If possible, the equation can then be solved to find part of the answer. The graphing method is commonly used for these types of systems. On a graph, these two lines can be found to intersect at one point, at two points across the parabola, or at no points.

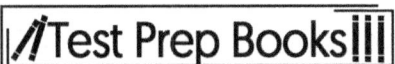

Finding solutions to systems of equations is essentially finding what values of the variables make both equations true. It is finding the input value that yields the same output value in both equations. For functions $g(x)$ and $f(x)$, the equation $g(x) = f(x)$ means the output values are being set equal to each other. Solving for the value of x means finding the x-coordinate that gives the same output in both functions. For example, $f(x) = x + 2$ and $g(x) = -3x + 10$ is a system of equations. Setting $f(x) = g(x)$ yields the equation:
$$x + 2 = -3x + 10$$

Solving for x, gives the x-coordinate $x = 2$ where the two lines cross. This value can also be found by using a table or a graph. On a table, both equations can be given the same inputs, and the outputs can be recorded to find the point(s) where the lines cross. Any method of solving finds the same solution, but some methods are more appropriate for some systems of equations than others.

Systems of Linear Inequalities

Systems of *linear inequalities* are like systems of equations, but the solutions are different. Since inequalities have infinitely many solutions, their systems also have infinitely many solutions. Finding the solutions of inequalities involves graphs. A system of two equations and two inequalities is linear; thus, the lines can be graphed using slope-intercept form. If the inequality has an equal sign, the line is solid. If the inequality only has a greater than or less than symbol, the line on the graph is dotted. Dashed lines indicate that points lying on the line are not included in the solution. After the lines are graphed, a region is shaded on one side of the line. This side is found by determining if a point—known as a *test point*—lying on one side of the line produces a true inequality. If it does, that side of the graph is shaded. If the point produces a false inequality, the line is shaded on the opposite side from the point. The graph of a system of inequalities involves shading the intersection of the two shaded regions.

Linear Relationships

Linear relationships describe the way two quantities change with respect to each other. The relationship is defined as linear because a line is produced if all the sets of corresponding values are graphed on a coordinate grid. When expressing the linear relationship as an equation, the equation is often written in the form $y = mx + b$ (slope-intercept form) where m and b are numerical values and x and y are variables (for example, $y = 5x + 10$). Given a linear equation and the value of either variable (x or y), the value of the other variable can be determined.

Suppose a teacher is grading a test containing 20 questions with 5 points given for each correct answer, adding a curve of 10 points to each test. This linear relationship can be expressed as the equation $y = 5x + 10$ where x represents the number of correct answers, and y represents the test score. To determine the score of a test with a given number of correct answers, the number of correct answers is substituted into the equation for x and evaluated. For example, for 10 correct answers, 10 is substituted for x:

$$y = 5(10) + 10 \rightarrow y = 60$$

Therefore, 10 correct answers will result in a score of 60. The number of correct answers needed to obtain a certain score can also be determined. To determine the number of correct answers needed to score a 90, 90 is substituted for y in the equation (y represents the test score) and solved:

$$90 = 5x + 10 \rightarrow 80 = 5x \rightarrow 16 = x$$

Therefore, 16 correct answers are needed to score a 90.

Linear relationships may be represented by a table of 2 corresponding values. Certain tables may determine the relationship between the values and predict other corresponding sets.

Consider the table below, which displays the money in a checking account that charges a monthly fee:

Month	0	1	2	3	4
Balance	$210	$195	$180	$165	$150

An examination of the values reveals that the account loses $15 every month (the month increases by one and the balance decreases by 15). This information can be used to predict future values. To determine what the value will be in month 6, the pattern can be continued, and it can be concluded that the balance will be $120. To determine which month the balance will be $0, $210 is divided by $15 (since the balance decreases $15 every month), resulting in month 14.

Similar to a table, a graph can display corresponding values of a linear relationship.

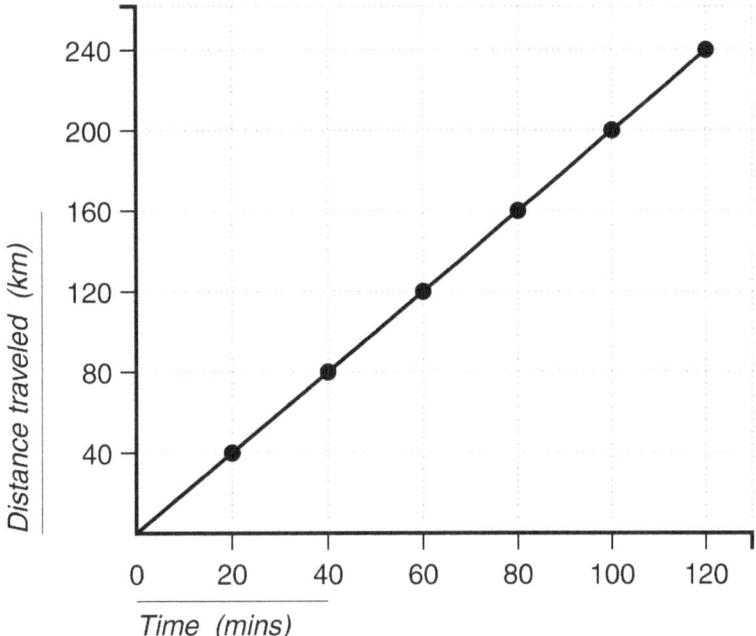

The graph above represents the relationship between distance traveled and time. To find the distance traveled in 80 minutes, the mark for 80 minutes is located at the bottom of the graph. By following this mark directly up on the graph, the corresponding point for 80 minutes is directly across from the 160-kilometer mark. This information indicates that the distance traveled in 80 minutes is 160 kilometers. To predict information not displayed on the graph, the way in which the variables change with respect to one another is determined. In this case, distance increases by 40 kilometers as time increases by 20 minutes. This information can be used to continue the data in the graph or convert the values to a table.

Functions

A *function* is defined as a relationship between inputs and outputs where there is only one output value for a given input. As an example, the following function is in function notation:

$$f(x) = 3x - 4$$

The $f(x)$ represents the output value for an input of x. If $x = 2$, the equation becomes:

$$f(2) = 3(2) - 4 = 6 - 4 = 2$$

The input of 2 yields an output of 2, forming the ordered pair $(2, 2)$. The following set of ordered pairs corresponds to the given function: $(2, 2), (0, -4), (-2, -10)$.

Domain and Range

The set of all possible inputs of a function is its *domain*, and all possible outputs is called the *range*. By definition, each member of the domain is paired with only one member of the range.

Functions can also be defined recursively. In this form, they are not defined explicitly in terms of variables. Instead, they are defined using previously-evaluated function outputs, starting with either $f(0)$ or $f(1)$. An example of a recursively-defined function is:

$$f(1) = 2, f(n) = 2f(n-1) + 2n, n > 1$$

The domain of this function is the set of all integers.

The domain and range of a function can be found visually by its plot on the coordinate plane. In the function $f(x) = x^2 - 3$, for example, the domain is all real numbers because the parabola stretches as far left and as far right as it can go, with no restrictions. This means that any input value from the real number system will yield an answer in the real number system. For the range, the inequality $y \geq -3$ would be used to describe the possible output values because the parabola has a minimum at $y = -3$. This means there will not be any real output values less than -3 because -3 is the lowest value it reaches on the y-axis.

These same answers for domain and range can be found by observing a table. The table below shows that from input values $x = -2$ to $x = 2$, the output results in a minimum of -3. On each side of $x = 0$, the numbers increase, showing that the range is all real numbers greater than or equal to -3.

x (domain/input)	y (range/output)
-2	1
-1	-2
0	-3
-1	-2
2	1

Common Functions

Three common functions used to model different relationships between quantities are linear, quadratic, and exponential functions. Linear functions are the simplest of the three, and the independent variable x has an exponent of 1. Written in the most common form, $y = mx + b$, the coefficient of x indicates how fast the function grows at a constant rate, and the b-value denotes the starting point. A quadratic function has an exponent of 2 on the independent variable x. Standard form for this type of function is $y = ax^2 + bx + c$, and the graph is a parabola. These type functions grow at a changing rate. An exponential function has an independent variable in the exponent $y = ab^x$. The graph of these types of functions is described as *growth* or *decay*, based on whether the base, b, is greater than or less than 1. These functions are different from quadratic functions because the base stays constant. A common base is base *e*.

The following three functions model a linear, quadratic, and exponential function respectively: $y = 2x$, $y = x^2$, and $y = 2^x$. Their graphs are shown below. The first graph, modeling the linear function, shows that the growth is constant over each interval. With a horizontal change of 1, the vertical change is 2. It models constant positive growth. The second graph shows the quadratic function, which is a curve that is symmetric across the y-axis. The growth is not constant, but the change is mirrored over the axis. The last graph models the exponential function, where the horizontal change of 1 yields a vertical change that increases more and more with each iteration of horizontal change. The exponential graph gets very close to the x-axis, but never touches it, meaning there is an asymptote there. The y-value can never be zero because the base of 2 can never be raised to an input value that yields an output of zero.

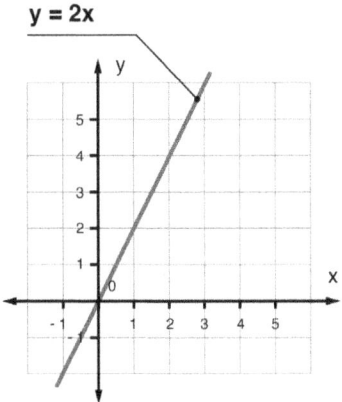
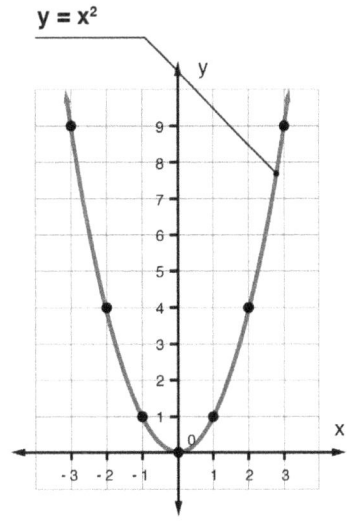
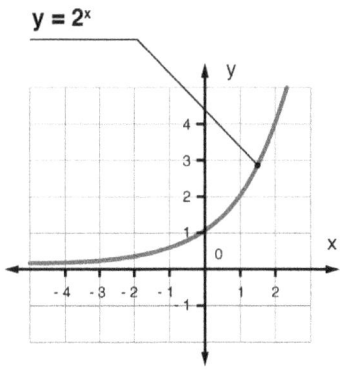

The three tables below show specific values for three types of functions. The third column in each table shows the change in the y-values for each interval. The first table shows a constant change of 2 for each equal interval, which matches the slope in the equation $y = 2x$. The second table shows an increasing change, but it also has a pattern. The increase is changing by 2 more each time, so the change is quadratic. The third table shows the change as factors of the base, 2. It shows a continuing pattern of factors of the base.

$y = 2x$		
x	y	Δy
1	2	
2	4	2
3	6	2
4	8	2
5	10	2

$y = x^2$		
x	y	Δy
1	1	
2	4	3
3	9	5
4	16	7
5	25	9

$y = 2^x$		
x	y	Δy
1	2	
2	4	2
3	8	4
4	16	8
5	32	16

Given a table of values, the type of function can be determined by observing the change in y over equal intervals. For example, the tables below model two functions. The changes in interval for the x-values is 1 for both tables. For the first table, the y-values increase by 5 for each interval. Since the change is constant, the situation can be described as a linear function. The equation would be $y = 5x + 3$.

For the second table, the change for y is 20, 100, and 500, respectively. The increases are multiples of 5, meaning the situation can be modeled by an exponential function. The equation below models this situation:

$$y = 5^x + 3$$

$y = 5x + 3$	
x	y
1	8
2	13
3	18
4	23

$y = 5^x + 3$	
x	y
1	8
2	28
3	128
4	628

Quadratic equations can be used to model real-world area problems. For example, a farmer may have a rectangular field that he needs to sow with seed. The field has length $x + 8$ and width $2x$. The formula for area should be used: $A = lw$. Therefore,

$$A = (x + 8) * 2x = 2x^2 + 16x$$

The possible values for the length and width can be shown in a table, with input x and output A. If the equation was graphed, the possible area values can be seen on the y-axis for the given x-values.

Exponential growth and decay can be found in real-world situations. For example, if a piece of notebook paper is folded 25 times, the thickness of the paper can be found. To model this situation, a table can be used. The initial point is one-fold, which yields a thickness of 2 papers. For the second fold, the thickness is 4. Since the thickness doubles each time, the table below shows the thickness for the next few folds. Notice the thickness changes by the same factor each time. Since this change for a constant interval of folds is a factor of 2, the function is exponential. The equation for this is $y = 2^x$. For twenty-five folds, the thickness would be 33,554,432 papers.

x (folds)	y (paper thickness)
0	1
1	2
2	4
3	8
4	16
5	32

One exponential formula that is commonly used is the *interest formula*: $A = Pe^{rt}$. In this formula, interest is compounded continuously. A is the value of the investment after the time, t, in years. P is the initial amount of the investment, r is the interest rate, and e is the constant equal to approximately 2.718. Given an initial amount of $200 and a time of 3 years, if interest is compounded continuously at a rate of 6%, the total investment value can be found by plugging each value into the formula. The invested value at the end is $239.44. In more complex problems, the final investment may be given, and the rate may be the unknown. In this case, the formula becomes $239.44 = 200e^{r3}$. Solving for r requires isolating the exponential expression on one side by dividing by 200, yielding the equation $1.20 = e^{r3}$. Taking the natural log of both sides results in $\ln(1.2) = r3$. Using a calculator to evaluate the logarithmic expression, $r = 0.06 = 6\%$.

When working with logarithms and exponential expressions, it is important to remember the relationship between the two. In general, the logarithmic form is $y = \log_b x$ for an exponential form $b^y = x$. Logarithms and exponential functions are inverses of each other.

Building a Function

Functions can be built out of the context of a situation. For example, the relationship between the money paid for a gym membership and the months that someone has been a member can be described through a function. If the one-time membership fee is $40 and the monthly fee is $30, then the function can be written:
$$f(x) = 30x + 40$$

The x-value represents the number of months the person has been part of the gym, while the output is the total money paid for the membership. The table below shows this relationship. It is a representation of the function because the initial cost is $40 and the cost increases each month by $30.

x (months)	y (money paid to gym)
0	40
1	70
2	100
3	130

Functions can also be built from existing functions. For example, a given function $f(x)$ can be transformed by adding a constant, multiplying by a constant, or changing the input value by a constant. The new function $g(x) = f(x) + k$ represents a vertical shift of the original function. In $f(x) = 3x - 2$, a vertical shift 4 units up would be:
$$g(x) = 3x - 2 + 4 = 3x + 2$$

Multiplying the function times a constant k represents a vertical stretch, based on whether the constant is greater than or less than 1. The function $g(x) = kf(x) = 4(3x - 2) = 12x - 8$ represents a stretch. Changing the input x by a constant forms the function $g(x) = f(x + k) = 3(x + 4) - 2 = 3x + 12 - 2 = 3x + 10$, and this represents a horizontal shift to the left 4 units. If $(x - 4)$ was plugged into the function, it would represent a horizontal shift to the right.

A composition function can also be formed by plugging one function into another. In function notation, this is written:
$$(f \circ g)(x) = f(g(x))$$

For two functions $f(x) = x^2$ and $g(x) = x - 3$, the composition function becomes:
$$f(g(x)) = (x - 3)^2 = x^2 - 6x + 9$$

The composition of functions can also be used to verify whether two functions are inverses of each other.

Given the two functions $f(x) = 2x + 5$ and $g(x) = \frac{x-5}{2}$, the composition function can be found $(f \circ g)(x)$. Solving this equation yields:
$$f(g(x)) = 2\left(\frac{x-5}{2}\right) + 5 = x - 5 + 5 = x$$

It also is true that $g(f(x)) = x$. Since the composition of these two functions gives a simplified answer of x, this verifies that $f(x)$ and $g(x)$ are inverse functions. The domain of $f(g(x))$ is the set of all x-values in the domain of $g(x)$ such that $g(x)$ is in the domain of $f(x)$. Basically, both $f(g(x))$ and $g(x)$ have to be defined.

To build an inverse of a function, $f(x)$ needs to be replaced with y, and the x and y values need to be switched. Then, the equation can be solved for y. For example, given the equation $y = e^{2x}$, the inverse can be found by rewriting the equation $x = e^{2y}$. The natural logarithm of both sides is taken down, and the exponent is brought down to form the equation $\ln(x) = \ln(e) 2y$. $\ln(e)=1$, which yields the equation $\ln(x) = 2y$. Dividing both sides by 2 yields the inverse equation:

$$\frac{\ln(x)}{2} = y = f^{-1}(x)$$

The domain of an inverse function is the range of the original function, and the range of an inverse function is the domain of the original function. Therefore, an ordered pair (x, y) on either a graph or a table corresponding to $f(x)$ means that the ordered pair (y, x) exists on the graph of $f^{-1}(x)$. Basically, if $f(x) = y$, then $f^{-1}(y) = x$. For a function to have an inverse, it must be one-to-one. That means it must pass the *Horizontal Line Test*, and if any horizontal line passes through the graph of the function twice, a function is not one-to-one. The domain of a function that is not one-to-one can be restricted to an interval in which the function is one-to-one, to be able to define an inverse function.

Functions can also be formed from combinations of existing functions. Given $f(x)$ and $g(x)$, $f + g, f - g, fg$, and $\frac{f}{g}$ can be built. The domains of $f + g, f - g$, and fg are the intersection of the domains of f and g. The domain of $\frac{f}{g}$ is the same set, excluding those values that make $g(x) = 0$. For example, if $f(x) = 2x + 3$ and $g(x) = x + 1$, then $\frac{f}{g} = \frac{2x+3}{x+1}$, and its domain is all real numbers except -1.

Rate of Change

Rate of change for any line calculates the steepness of the line over a given interval. Rate of change is also known as the slope or rise/run. The rates of change for nonlinear functions vary depending on the interval being used for the function. The rate of change over one interval may be zero, while the next interval may have a positive rate of change. The equation plotted on the graph below, $y = x^2$, is a quadratic function and non-linear.

The average rate of change from points $(0,0)$ to $(1,1)$ is 1 because the vertical change is 1 over the horizontal change of 1. For the next interval, $(1,1)$ to $(2,4)$, the average rate of change is 3 because the slope is $\frac{3}{1}$.

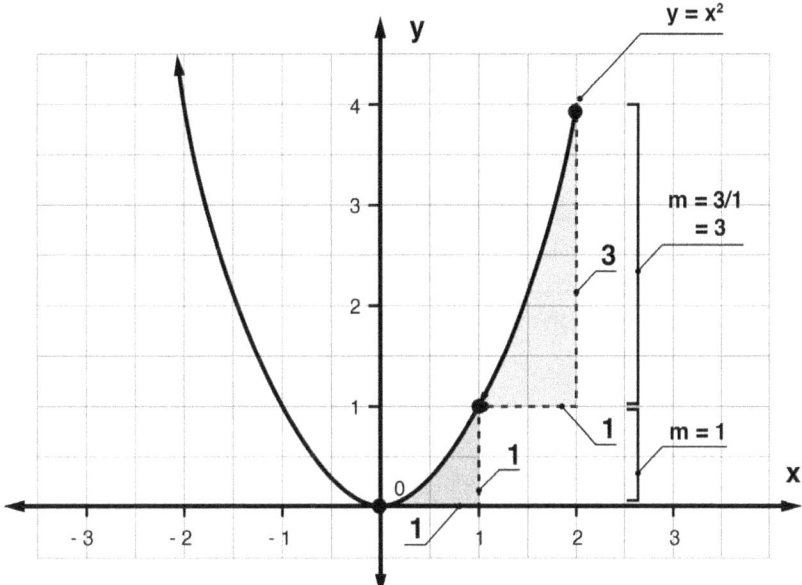

The rate of change for a linear function is constant and can be determined based on a few representations. One method is to place the equation in slope-intercept form: $y = mx + b$. Thus, m is the slope, and b is the y-intercept. In the graph below, the equation is $y = x + 1$, where the slope is 1 and the y-intercept is 1. For every vertical change of 1 unit, there is a horizontal change of 1 unit. The x-intercept is -1, which is the point where the line crosses the x-axis.

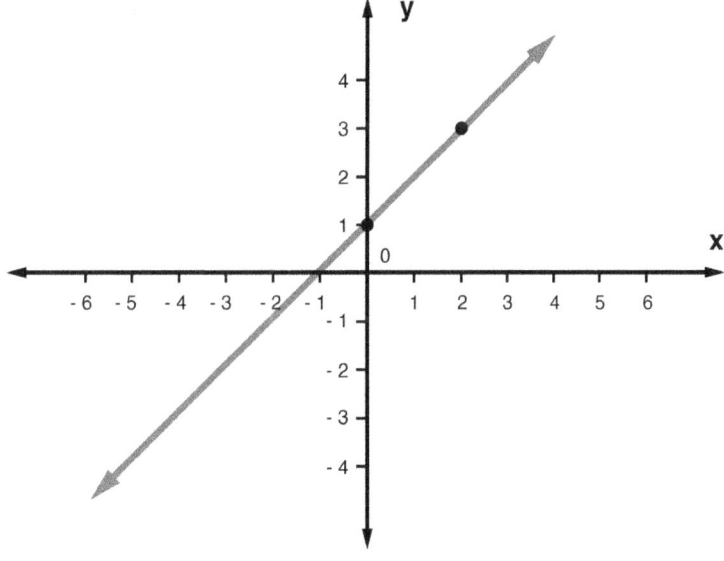

Solving Line Problems

Two lines are parallel if they have the same slope and a different intercept. Two lines are perpendicular if the product of their slope equals -1. Parallel lines never intersect unless they are the same line, and perpendicular lines intersect at a right angle. If two lines aren't parallel, they must intersect at one point. Determining equations of lines based on properties of parallel and perpendicular lines appears in word problems. To find an equation of a line, both the slope and a point the line goes through are necessary. Therefore, if an equation of a line is needed that's parallel to a given line and runs through a specified point, the slope of the given line and the point are plugged into the point-slope form of an equation of a line.

Second, if an equation of a line is needed that's perpendicular to a given line running through a specified point, the negative reciprocal of the slope of the given line and the point are plugged into the point-slope form. Also, if the point of intersection of two lines is known, that point will be used to solve the set of equations. Therefore, to solve a system of equations, the point of intersection must be found. If a set of two equations with two unknown variables has no solution, the lines are parallel.

Zeros of Polynomials

Finding the zeros of polynomial functions is the same process as finding the solutions of polynomial equations. These are the points at which the graph of the function crosses the x-axis. As stated previously, factors can be used to find the zeros of a polynomial function. The degree of the function shows the number of possible zeros. If the highest exponent on the independent variable is 4, then the degree is 4, and the number of possible zeros is 4. If there are complex solutions, the number of roots is less than the degree.

Given the function $y = x^2 + 7x + 6$, y can be set equal to zero, and the polynomial can be factored. The equation turns into $0 = (x + 1)(x + 6)$, where $x = -1$ and $x = -6$ are the zeros. Since this is a quadratic equation, the shape of the graph will be a parabola. Knowing that zeros represent the points where the parabola crosses the x-axis, the maximum or minimum point is the only other piece needed to sketch a rough graph of the function. By looking at the function in standard form, the coefficient of x is positive; therefore, the parabola opens *up*. Using the zeros and the minimum, the following rough sketch of the graph can be constructed:

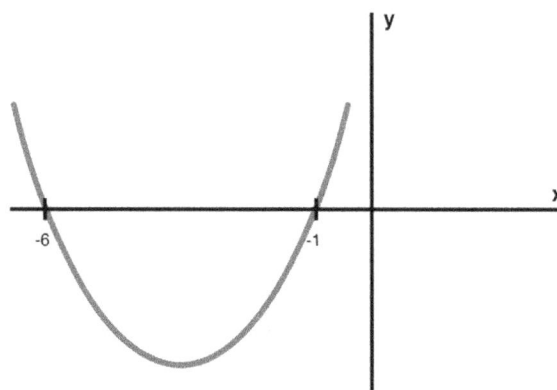

Finding the Zeros of a Function

The zeros of a function are the points where its graph crosses the x-axis. At these points, $y = 0$. One way to find the zeros is to analyze the graph. If given the graph, the x-coordinates can be found where the line crosses the x-axis.

Another way to find the zeros is to set $y = 0$ in the equation and solve for x. Depending on the type of equation, this could be done by using opposite operations, by factoring the equation, by completing the square, or by using the quadratic formula. If a graph does not cross the x-axis, then the function may have complex roots.

Translating Functions

A function can be translated in many ways. Typical translations involve shifting, reflecting, and scaling graphs. A shift is a translation that does not change the original shape of the function. A vertical shift adds or subtracts a constant from every y-coordinate and is represented as:

$$y = f(x) \pm c$$

A horizontal shift adds or subtracts a constant from every x-coordinate and is represented as:

$$y = f(x \pm c)$$

A reflection involves flipping a function over an axis. To reflect about the y-axis, every x-coordinate needs to be multiplied times -1. This reflection is represented as $y = f(-x)$. To reflect about the x-axis, every y-coordinate needs to be multiplied times -1. This reflection is represented as $y = -f(x)$.

Finally, a scale involves changing the shape of the graph through either a shrink or stretch. A scale either multiplies or divides each coordinate by a constant. A vertical scale involves multiplying or dividing every y-coordinate by a constant. This scaling is represented by $y = kf(x)$ and is a vertical stretch if $k > 1$ and vertical shrink if $0 < k < 1$. A horizontal scale involves multiplying or dividing every x-coordinate by a constant. This scaling is represented by $y = f(kx)$ and is a horizontal stretch if $0 < k < 1$ and horizontal shrink if $k > 1$.

Graphing Functions

Typically, a function can be graphed using a graphing calculator. However, some characteristics can be found that allow for enough information to be compounded to graph a very good sketch without technology. Such information includes significant points such as zeros, local extrema, and points where a function is not continuous and not differentiable. Zeros are points in which a function crosses the y-axis. These points are found by plugging 0 into the independent variable x and solving for the dependent variable y. Local extrema are points in which a function is either a local maxima or minima. These points occur where the derivative of the function is either equal to zero or undefined, and those points are known as critical values.

The first derivative test can be used to decide whether a critical value is a maximum or minimum. If a function increases to a point, showing that the first derivative is positive over that interval, and if a function decreases after that same point, showing that the derivative is negative over that interval, then the point is a local maximum. The opposite occurs at a local minimum. Finally, points in which a function is not continuous or not differentiable are also important points. A function is continuous over its domain. A function is not differentiable at a point if there exists a vertical tangent at that point, if there is a corner or a cusp at that point, or if the function is not defined at that point.

Asymptotes

An *asymptote* is a line that approaches the graph of a given function, but never meets it. Vertical asymptotes correspond to denominators of zero for a rational function. They also exist in logarithmic functions and trigonometric functions, such as tangent and cotangent. In rational functions and trigonometric functions, the asymptotes exist at x-values that cause a denominator equal to zero. For example, vertical asymptotes exist at $x = \pm 2$ for the function:

$$f(x) = \frac{x+1}{(x-2)(x+2)}$$

Horizontal and slant (oblique) asymptotes correspond to the behavior of a curve as the x-values approach either positive or negative infinity. For example, the graph of $f(x) = e^x$ has a horizontal asymptote of $y = 0$ as x approaches negative infinity. In regards to rational functions, there is a rule to follow. Consider the following rational function:

$$f(x) = \frac{ax^n + \cdots}{bx^m + \cdots}$$

The numerator is an nth degree polynomial and the denominator is an mth degree polynomial. If $m < n$, the line $y = 0$ is a horizontal asymptote. If $n = m$, the line $y = \frac{a}{b}$ is a horizontal asymptote. If $m > n$, then there is a slant asymptote. In order to find the equation of the slant asymptote, the denominator is divided into the numerator using long division. The result, minus the remainder, gives the equation of the slant asymptote.

Here is a graph that shows an example of both a slant and a vertical asymptote:

Graphed Asymptotes

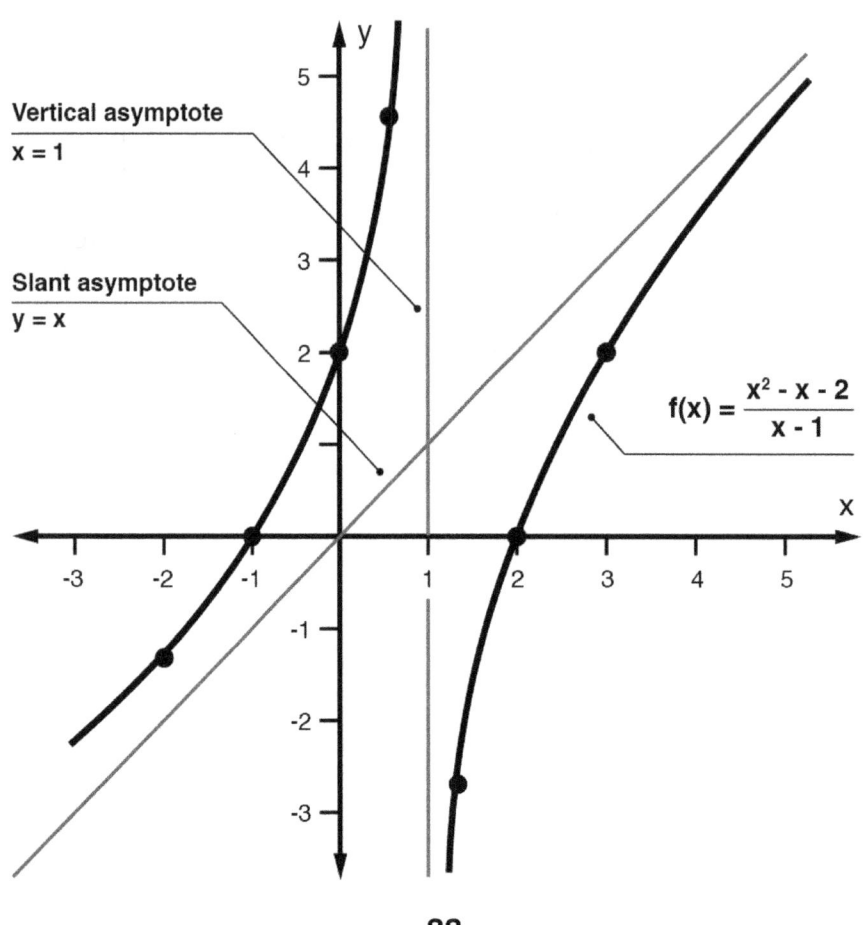

Geometry/Measurement

Geometry is the part of mathematics that deals with shapes and their properties. The basis of geometry involves being able to label and describe shapes and their properties. That knowledge will lead to working with formulas such as area, perimeter, and volume, which will help to solve problems involving shapes.

Flat or two-dimensional shapes include circles, triangles, hexagons, and rectangles, among others. Three-dimensional solid shapes, such as spheres and cubes, are also used in geometry. A shape can be classified based on whether it is open like the letter U or closed like the letter O. Further classifications involve counting the number of sides and vertices (corners) on the shapes. This will help you tell the difference between shapes.

Polygons can be drawn by sketching a fixed number of line segments that meet to create a closed shape. **Triangles** can be drawn by sketching a closed space using only three-line segments. **Quadrilaterals** are closed shapes with four-line segments. Note that a triangle has three vertices, and a quadrilateral has four vertices.

To draw circles, one curved line segment must be drawn that has only one endpoint. This creates a closed shape. Given such direction, every point on the line would be the same distance away from its center. The radius of a circle goes from an endpoint on the center of the circle to an endpoint on the circle. The diameter is the line segment created by placing an endpoint on the circle, drawing through the radius, and placing the other endpoint on the circle. A compass can be used to draw circles of a more precise size and shape.

Classifying Two-Dimensional Figures

A **polygon** is a closed geometric figure in a plane (flat surface) consisting of at least 3 sides formed by line segments. These are often defined as two-dimensional shapes. Common two-dimensional shapes include circles, triangles, squares, rectangles, pentagons, and hexagons. Note that a circle is a two-dimensional shape without sides.

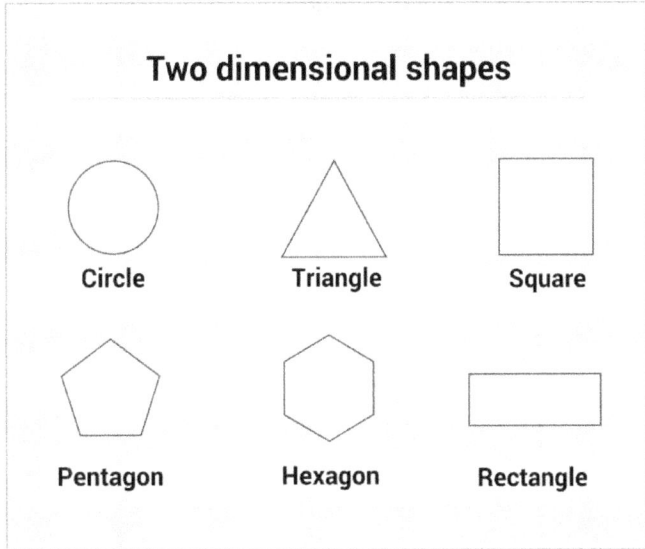

Polygons can be either convex or concave. A polygon that has interior angles all measuring less than 180° is convex. A concave polygon has one or more interior angles measuring greater than 180°. Examples are shown below.

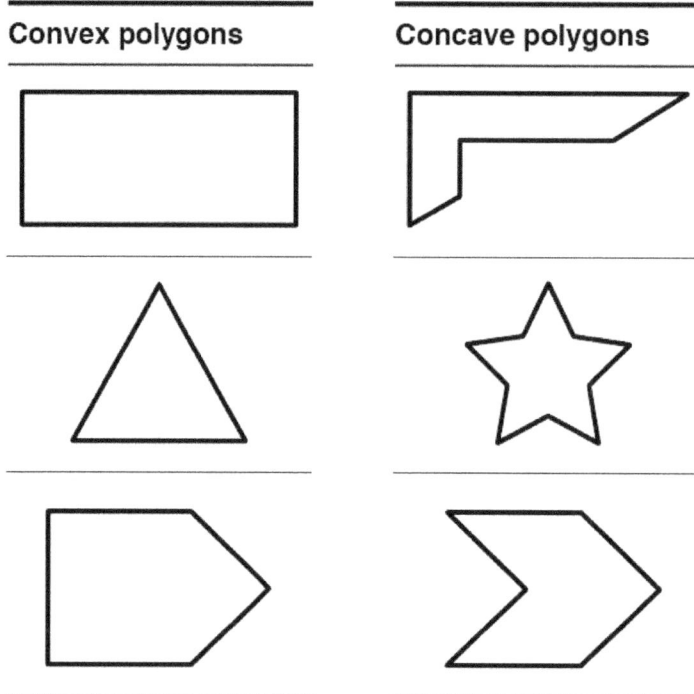

Polygons can be classified by the number of sides (also equal to the number of angles) they have. The following are the names of polygons with a given number of sides or angles:

# of Sides	Name of Polygon
3	Triangle
4	Quadrilateral
5	Pentagon
6	Hexagon
7	Septagon (or heptagon)
8	Octagon
9	Nonagon
10	Decagon

Equiangular polygons are polygons in which the measure of every interior angle is the same. The sides of equilateral polygons are always the same length. If a polygon is both equiangular and equilateral, the polygon is defined as a regular polygon.

Triangles can be further classified by their sides and angles. The sum of the angles within any triangle is always 180 degrees. A triangle with its largest angle measuring 90° is a right triangle. A triangle with the largest angle less than 90° is an acute triangle. A triangle with the largest angle greater than 90° is an obtuse triangle. Below is an example of a right triangle.

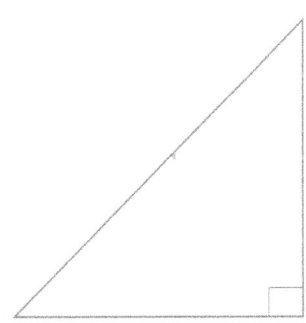

A triangle consisting of two equal sides and two equal angles is an **isosceles triangle**. A triangle with three equal sides and three equal angles is an **equilateral triangle**. A triangle with no equal sides or angles is a **scalene triangle**.

Isosceles triangle:

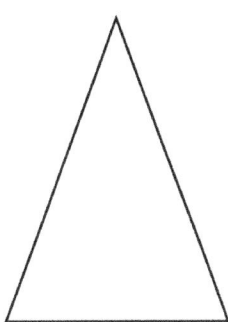

Equilateral triangle:

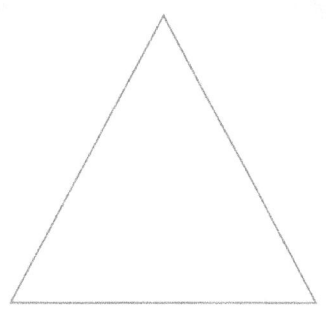

Scalene triangle:

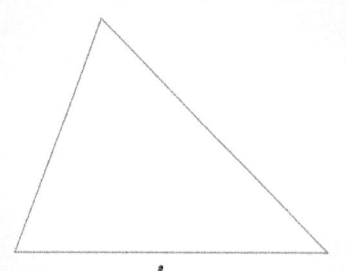

In an equilateral triangle, the measure of each angle is always 60 degrees. A *scalene triangle* can never be an equilateral or an isosceles triangle because it contains no equal sides and no equal angles. However, a *right triangle*, which is a triangle containing a 90-degree angle, can be a scalene triangle.

Quadrilaterals can be further classified according to their sides and angles. A quadrilateral with exactly one pair of parallel sides is called a **trapezoid**. A quadrilateral that shows both pairs of opposite sides parallel is a **parallelogram**. Parallelograms include rhombuses, rectangles, and squares. A **rhombus** has four equal sides. A **rectangle** has four equal angles (90° each). A **square** has four 90° angles and four equal sides. Therefore, a square is both a rhombus and a rectangle.

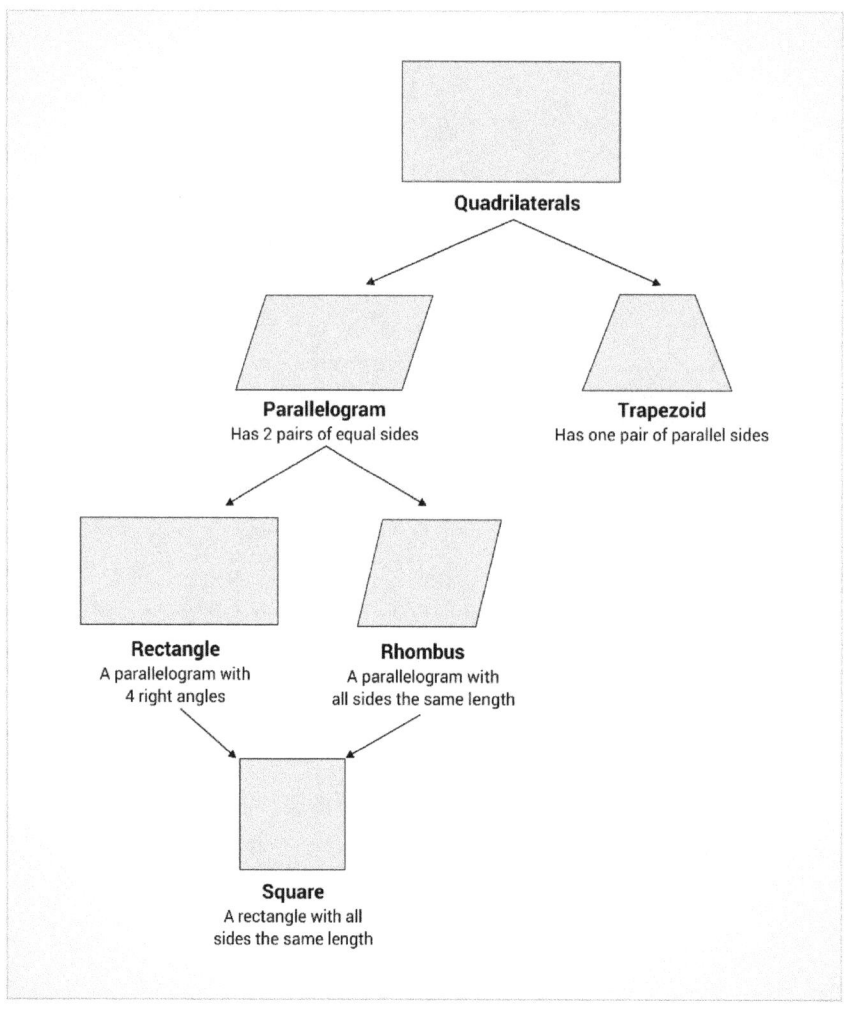

Quantitative Reasoning and Mathematics Achievement

Properties of Three-Dimensional Shapes

A **solid** is a three-dimensional figure that encloses a part of space. Common three-dimensional shapes include spheres, prisms, cubes, pyramids, cylinders, and cones.

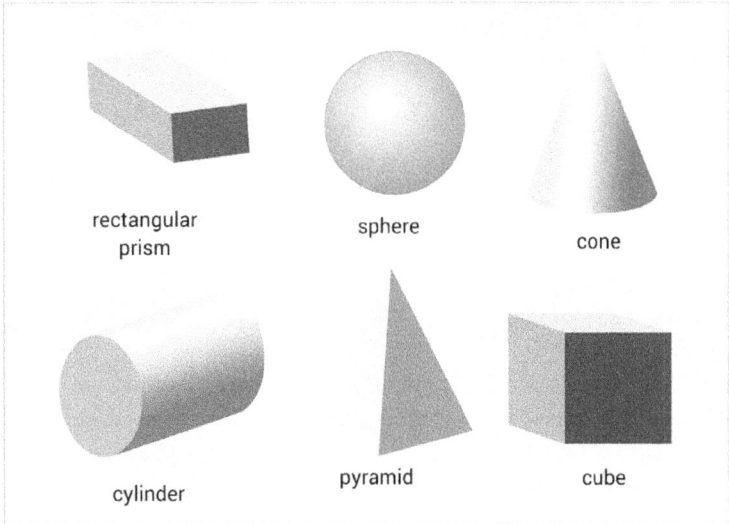

Solids consisting of all flat surfaces that are polygons are called **polyhedrons**. The two-dimensional surfaces that make up a polyhedron are called faces. Types of polyhedrons include prisms and pyramids. A **prism** consists of two parallel faces that are congruent (or the same shape and same size) and **lateral faces** going around (which are parallelograms).

A prism is further classified by the shape of its base, as shown below:

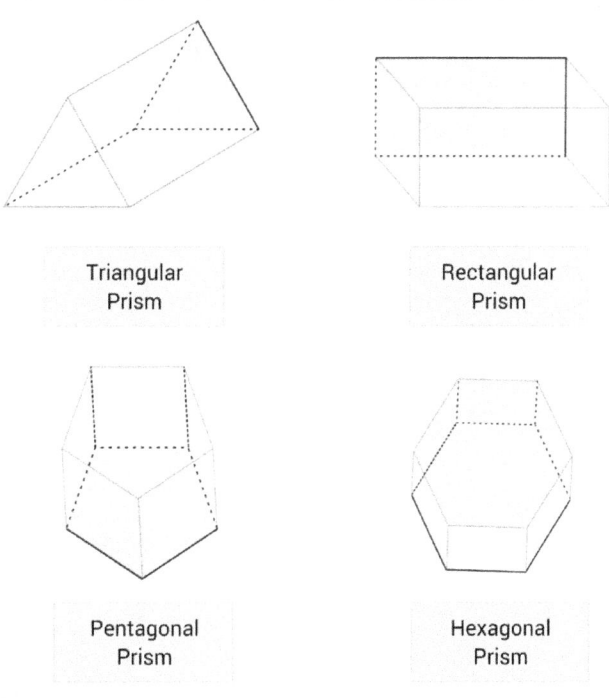

A pyramid consists of lateral faces (triangles) that meet at a common point called the vertex and one other face that is a polygon, called the base. A pyramid can be further classified by the shape of its base, as shown below.

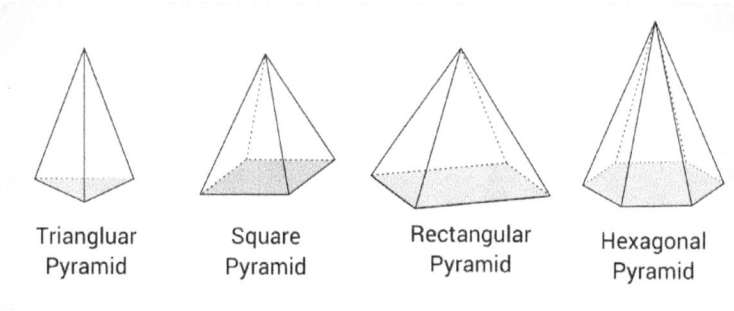

Triangluar Pyramid | Square Pyramid | Rectangular Pyramid | Hexagonal Pyramid

A tetrahedron is another name for a triangular pyramid. All the faces of a tetrahedron are triangles.

Solids that are not polyhedrons include spheres, cylinders, and cones. A sphere is the set of all points a given distance from a given center point. A sphere is commonly thought of as a three-dimensional circle. A cylinder consists of two parallel, congruent (same size) circles and a lateral curved surface. A cone consists of a circle as its base and a lateral curved surface that narrows to a point called the vertex.

Similar polygons are the same shape but different sizes. More specifically, their corresponding angle measures are congruent (or equal) and the length of their sides is proportional. For example, all sides of one polygon may be double the length of the sides of another. Likewise, similar solids are the same shape but different sizes. Any corresponding faces or bases of similar solids are the same polygons that are proportional by a consistent value.

Three-Dimensional Figures with Nets

A **net** is a construction of two-dimensional figures that can be folded to form a given three-dimensional figure. More than one net may exist to fold and produce the same solid, or three-dimensional figure. The bases and faces of the solid figure are analyzed to determine the polygons (two-dimensional figures) needed to form the net.

Consider the following triangular prism:

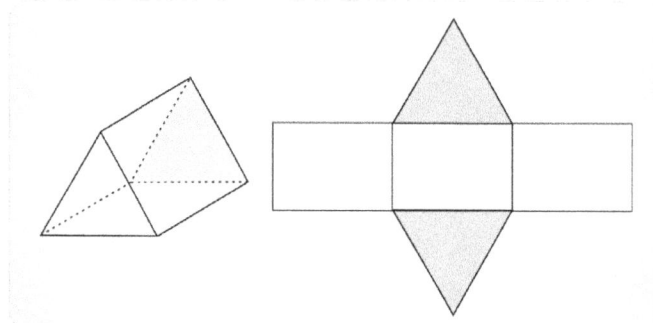

The surface of the prism consists of two triangular bases and three rectangular faces. The net beside it can be used to construct the triangular prism by first folding the triangles up to be parallel to each other, and then folding the two outside rectangles up and to the center with the outer edges touching.

Consider the following cylinder:

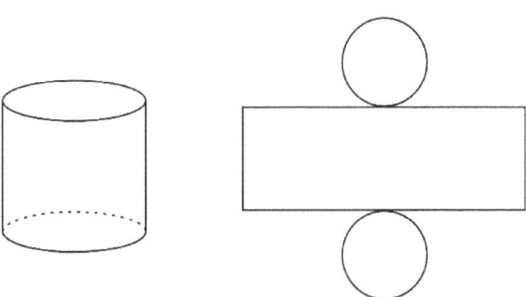

The surface consists of two circular bases and a curved lateral surface that can be opened and flattened into a rectangle. The net beside the cylinder can be used to construct the cylinder by first folding the circles up to be parallel to each other and then curving the sides of the rectangle up to touch each other. The top and bottom of the folded rectangle should be touching the outside of both circles.

Consider the following square pyramid below on the left. The surface consists of one square base and four triangular faces. The net below on the right can be used to construct the square pyramid by folding each triangle towards the center of the square. The top points of the triangle meet at the vertex.

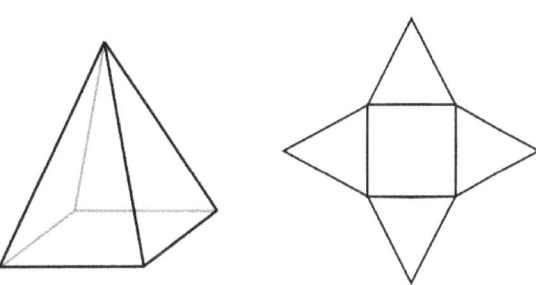

Symmetry

Symmetry is another concept in geometry. If a two-dimensional shape can be folded along a straight line and the halves line up exactly, the figure is **symmetric**. The line is known as a **line of symmetry**. Circles, squares, and rectangles are examples of symmetric shapes.

Perimeter and Area of Geometric Shapes

Perimeter is the measurement of a distance around something or the sum of all sides of a polygon. Think of perimeter as the length of the boundary, like a fence. In contrast, **area** is the space occupied by a defined enclosure, like a field enclosed by a fence.

When thinking about perimeter, think about walking around the outside of something. When thinking about area, think about the amount of space or **surface area** something takes up.

Square

The perimeter of a square is measured by adding together all of the sides. Since a square has four equal sides, its perimeter can be calculated by multiplying the length of one side by 4. Thus, the formula is $4 \times s$, where s equals one side.

For example, the following square has side lengths of 5 meters:

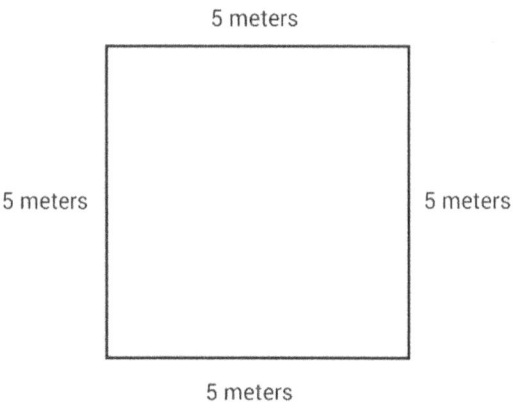

The perimeter is 20 meters because 4 times 5 is 20.

The area of a square is the length of a side squared. For example, if a side of a square is 7 centimeters, then the area is 49 square centimeters. The formula for this example is:

$$A = s^2 = 7^2 = 49 \text{ square centimeters}$$

Rectangle

Like a square, a rectangle's perimeter is measured by adding together all of the sides. But as the sides are unequal, the formula is different. A rectangle has equal values for its lengths (long sides) and equal values for its widths (short sides), so the perimeter formula for a rectangle is:

$$P = l + l + w + w = 2l + 2w$$

l equals length

w equals width

For example, if the length of a rectangle is 10 inches and the width 8 inches, then the perimeter is 36 inches:

$$P = 2l + 2w = 2(10) + 2(8)$$

$$20 + 16 = 36 \text{ inches}$$

The area is found by multiplying the length by the width, so the formula is $A = l \times w$.

An example is if the rectangle has a length of 6 inches and a width of 7 inches, then the area is 42 square inches:

$$A = lw = 6(7) = 42 \text{ square inches}$$

Quantitative Reasoning and Mathematics Achievement

Triangle

A triangle's perimeter is measured by adding together the three sides, so the formula is:

$$P = a + b + c$$

a, b, and c are the values of the three sides. The area is the product of one-half the base and height, so the formula is:

$$A = \frac{1}{2} \times b \times h$$

It can be simplified to:

$$A = \frac{bh}{2}$$

The base is the bottom of the triangle, and the height is the distance from the base to the peak. If a problem asks to calculate the area of a triangle, it will provide the base and height.

For example, if the base of the triangle is 2 feet and the height 4 feet, then the area is 4 square feet. The following equation shows the formula used to calculate the area of the triangle:

$$A = \frac{1}{2}bh = \frac{1}{2}(2)(4) = 4 \text{ square feet}$$

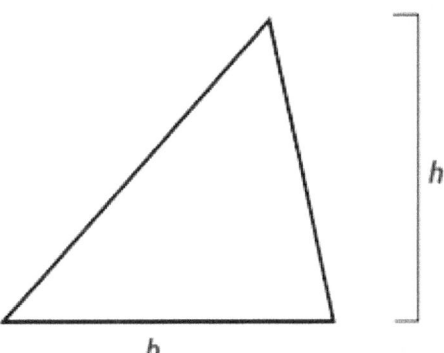

Circle

A circle's perimeter—also known as its **circumference**—is measured by multiplying the diameter by π.

Diameter is the straight line measured from a point on one side of the circle to a point directly across on the opposite side of the circle. π is referred to as pi and is equal to 3.14 (with rounding). So, the formula is $\pi \times d$. This is sometimes expressed by the formula $C = 2 \times \pi \times r$

r is the radius of the circle. These formulas are equivalent, as the radius equals half of the diameter.

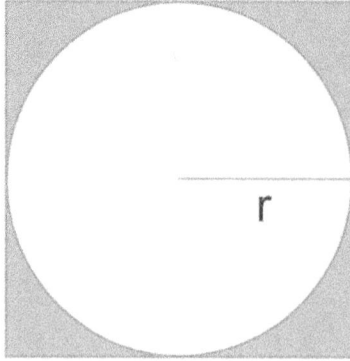

The area of a circle is calculated through the formula:

$$A = \pi \times r^2$$

The test will indicate whether to leave the answer with π attached or to calculate to the nearest decimal place, which means multiplying by 3.14 for π.

Parallelogram

The perimeter of a parallelogram is measured by adding the lengths and widths together. Thus, the formula is the same as for a rectangle:

$$P = l + l + w + w = 2l + 2w$$

However, the area formula differs from the rectangle. For a parallelogram, the area is calculated by multiplying the length by the height:

$$A = h \times l$$

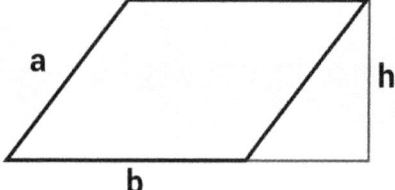

Area = bh

Perimeter = 2(a + b)

Quantitative Reasoning and Mathematics Achievement

Trapezoid
The perimeter of a trapezoid is calculated by adding the two unequal bases and two equal sides, so the formula is:

$$P = a + b_1 + c + b_2$$

The formula for the area of a trapezoid is:

$$A = \frac{b_1 + b_2}{2} \times h$$

h equals height, and b_1 and b_2 equal the bases.

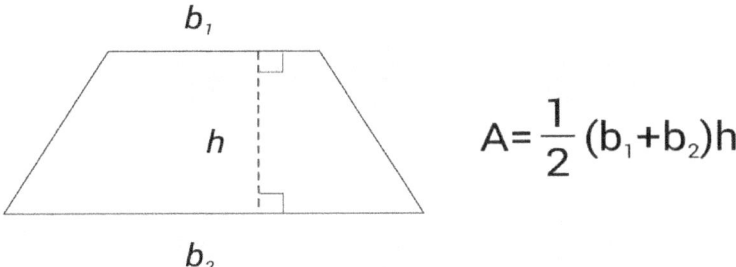

Irregular Shapes
The perimeter of an irregular polygon is found by adding the lengths of all of the sides. In cases where all of the sides are given, this will be very straightforward, as it will simply involve finding the sum of the provided lengths. Other times, a side length may be missing and must be determined before the perimeter can be calculated. Consider the example below:

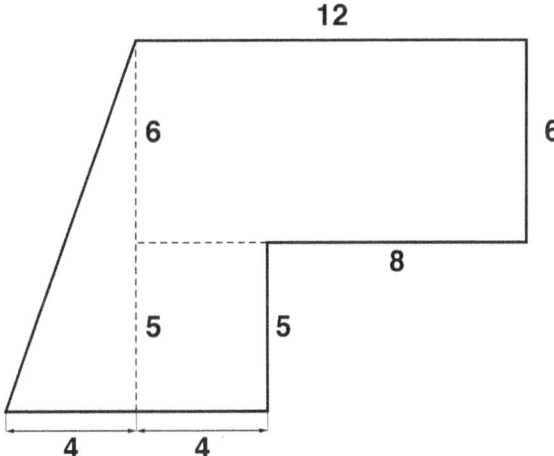

All of the side lengths are provided except for the angled side on the left. Test takers should notice that this is the hypotenuse of a right triangle. The other two sides of the triangle are provided (the base is 4 and the height is $6 + 5 = 11$). The Pythagorean Theorem can be used to find the length of the hypotenuse, remembering that $a^2 + b^2 = c^2$. Substituting the side values provided yields:

$$(4)^2 + (11)^2 = c^2$$

Therefore,

$$c = \sqrt{16 + 121} = 11.7$$

Finally, the perimeter can be found by adding this new side length with the other provided lengths to get the total length around the figure:

$$4 + 4 + 5 + 8 + 6 + 12 + 11.7 = 50.7$$

Although units are not provided in this figure, remember that reporting units with a measurement is important.

The area of an irregular polygon is found by decomposing, or breaking apart, the figure into smaller shapes. When the area of the smaller shapes is determined, these areas are added together to produce the total area of the original figure. Consider the same example provided before:

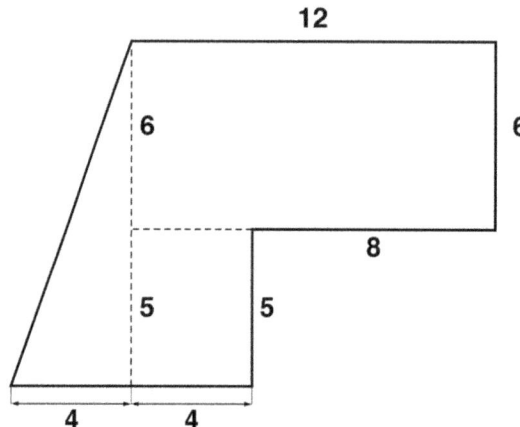

The irregular polygon is decomposed into two rectangles and a triangle. The area of the large rectangle is 72 square units.

$$A = l \times w \rightarrow A = 12 \times 6$$

The area of the small rectangle is 20 square units ($A = 4 \times 5$). The area of the triangle is 22 square units.

$$A = \frac{1}{2} \times b \times h \rightarrow A = \frac{1}{2} \times 4 \times 11$$

The sum of the areas of these figures produces the total area of the original polygon:

$$A = 72 + 20 + 22 \rightarrow A = 114 \text{ square units}$$

Surface Area

The area of a two-dimensional figure refers to the number of square units needed to cover the interior region of the figure. This concept is similar to wallpaper covering the flat surface of a wall. For example, if a rectangle has an area of 8 square inches (written 8 in^2), it will take 8 squares, each with sides one inch in length, to cover the interior region of the rectangle.

Note that area is measured in square units such as: square feet or ft²; square yards or yd²; square miles or mi².

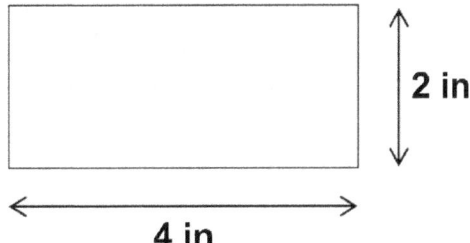

The **surface area** of a three-dimensional figure refers to the number of square units needed to cover the entire surface of the figure. This concept is similar to using wrapping paper to completely cover the outside of a box. For example, if a triangular pyramid has a surface area of 17 square inches (written 17 in²), it will take 17 squares, each with sides one inch in length, to cover the entire surface of the pyramid. Surface area is also measured in square units.

Many three-dimensional figures (solid figures) can be represented by nets consisting of rectangles and triangles. The surface area of such solids can be determined by adding the areas of each of its faces and bases. Finding the surface area using this method requires calculating the areas of rectangles and triangles. To find the area (A) of a rectangle, the length (l) is multiplied by the width (w):

$$A = l \times w$$

The area of a rectangle with a length of 8 cm and a width of 4 cm is calculated:

$$A = (8 \text{ cm}) \times (4 \text{ cm}) \rightarrow A = 32 \text{ cm}^2$$

To calculate the area (A) of a triangle, the product of $\frac{1}{2}$, the base (b), and the height (h) is found:

$$A = \frac{1}{2} \times b \times h$$

Note that the height of a triangle is measured from the base to the vertex opposite of it forming a right angle with the base. The area of a triangle with a base of 11 cm and a height of 6 cm is calculated:

$$A = \frac{1}{2} \times (11 \text{ cm}) \times (6 \text{ cm}) \rightarrow A = 33 \text{ cm}^2$$

Consider the following triangular prism, which is represented by a net consisting of two triangles and three rectangles.

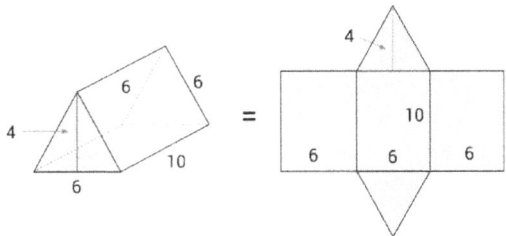

The surface area of the prism can be determined by adding the areas of each of its faces and bases. The surface area $(SA) = area\ of\ triangle + area\ of\ triangle + area\ of\ rectangle + area\ of\ rectangle + area\ of\ rectangle$.

$$SA = (\frac{1}{2} \times b \times h) + (\frac{1}{2} \times b \times h) + (l \times w) + (l \times w) + (l \times w)$$

$$SA = (\frac{1}{2} \times 6 \times 4) + (\frac{1}{2} \times 6 \times 4) + (6 \times 10) + (6 \times 10) + (6 \times 10)$$

$$SA = (12) + (12) + (60) + (60) + (60)$$

$$SA = 204 \text{ square units}$$

Volume

Volume is the measurement of how much space an object occupies, like how much space is in the cube. Volume is useful in determining the space within a certain three-dimensional object. Volume can be calculated for a cube, rectangular prism, cylinder, pyramid, cone, and sphere.

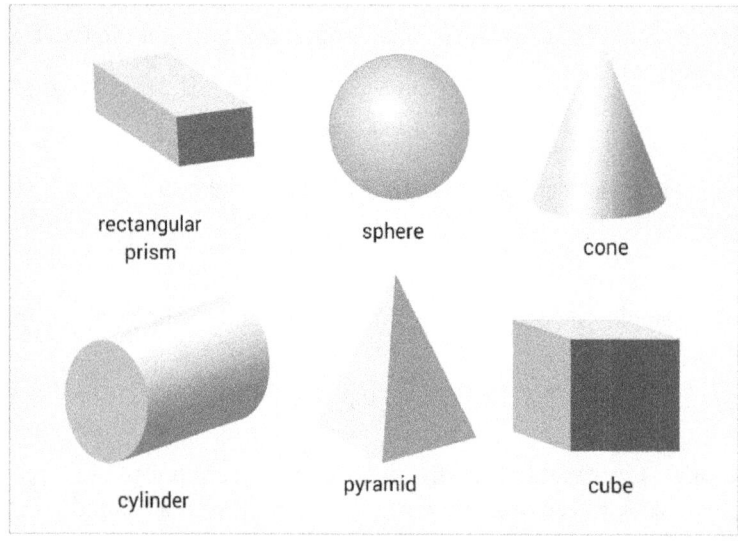

By knowing specific dimensions of the objects, the volume of the object is computed with these figures. The units for the volumes of solids can include cubic centimeters, cubic meters, cubic inches, and cubic feet.

Cube

The **cube** is the simplest figure for which volume can be determined because all dimensions in a cube are equal. In the following example, the length, width, and height of the cube are all represented by the variable a because these measurements are equal lengths.

The volume of any rectangular, three-dimensional object is found by multiplying its length by its width by its height. In the case of a cube, the length, width, and height are all equal lengths, represented by the variable a. Therefore, the equation used to calculate the volume is $(a \times a \times a)$ or a^3. In a real-world example of this situation, if the length of a side of the cube is 3 centimeters, the volume is calculated by utilizing the formula:

$$(3 \times 3 \times 3) = 27 \text{ cm}^3$$

Rectangular Prism

The dimensions of a **rectangular prism** are not necessarily equal as those of a cube. Therefore, the formula for a rectangular prism recognizes that the dimensions vary and use different variables to represent these lengths. The length, width, and height of a rectangular prism can be represented with the variables a, b, and c.

The equation used to calculate volume is length times width times height. Using these variables, this means $a \times b \times c$.

In a real-world application of this situation, if $a = 2$ cm, $b = 3$ cm, and $c = 4$ cm, the volume is calculated by utilizing the formula:

$$3 \times 4 \times 5 = 60 \text{ cm}^3$$

Cylinder

Discovering a cylinder's volume requires the measurement of the cylinder's base, length of the radius, and height. The height of the cylinder can be represented with variable h, and the radius can be represented with variable r.

The formula to find the volume of a cylinder is $\pi r^2 h$. Notice that πr^2 is the formula for the area of a circle. This is because the base of the cylinder is a circle. To calculate the volume of a cylinder, the slices of circles needed to build the entire height of the cylinder are added together. For example, if the radius is 5 feet and the height of the cylinder is 10 feet, the cylinder's volume is calculated by using the following equation:

$$\pi 5^2 \times 10$$

Substituting 3.14 for π, the volume is 785.4 ft³.

Pyramid

To calculate the volume of a pyramid, the area of the base of the pyramid is multiplied by the pyramid's height and by $\frac{1}{3}$. The area of the base of the pyramid is found by multiplying the base length by the base width.

Therefore, the formula to calculate a pyramid's volume is:

$$(L \times W \times H) \div 3$$

Cone

The formula to calculate the volume of a circular cone is similar to the formula for the volume of a pyramid. The primary difference in determining the area of a cone is that a circle serves as the base of a cone. Therefore, the area of a circle is used for the cone's base.

The variable r represents the radius, and the variable h represents the height of the cone. The formula used to calculate the volume of a cone is:

$$\frac{1}{3}\pi r^2 h$$

Essentially, the area of the base of the cone is multiplied by the cone's height. In a real-life example where the radius of a cone is 2 meters and the height of a cone is 5 meters, the volume of the cone is calculated by utilizing the formula:

$$\frac{1}{3}\pi 2^2 \times 5 = 21 \text{ m}^3$$

Sphere

The volume of a sphere uses π due to its circular shape.

The length of the radius, r, is the only variable needed to determine the sphere's volume. The formula to calculate the volume of a sphere is:

$$\frac{4}{3}\pi r^3$$

Therefore, if the radius of a sphere is 8 centimeters, the volume of the sphere is calculated by utilizing the formula:

$$\frac{4}{3}\pi(8)^3 = 2{,}144 \text{ cm}^3$$

Internal Angles of Polygons with More Than Four Sides

Mathematical problems involving polygons with more than four sides usually involve side length and angle measurements. The sum of all internal angles in a polygon equals $180(n-2)$ degrees, where n is the number of sides. Therefore, the total of all internal angles in a pentagon is 540 degrees because there are five sides so $180(5-2)$ = 540 degrees. Unfortunately, area formulas don't exist for polygons with more than four sides. However, their shapes can be split up into triangles, and the formula for area of a triangle can be applied and totaled to obtain the area for the entire figure.

Points, Lines, and Angles

Points

A point is a place, not a thing, and therefore has no dimensions or size. A set of points that lies on the same line is called collinear. A set of points that lies on the same plane is called coplanar.

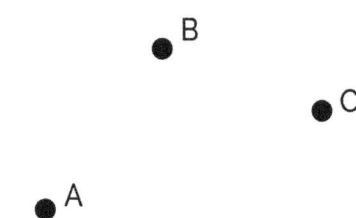

The image above displays point A, point B, and point C.

Lines

A line is as series of points that extends in both directions without ending. It consists of an infinite number of points and is drawn with arrows on both ends to indicate that it extends infinitely. Lines can be named by two points on the line or with a single, cursive, lower case letter. The lines below are named: line AB or line BA or $\overleftrightarrow{AB}$ or $\overleftrightarrow{BA}$; and line m.

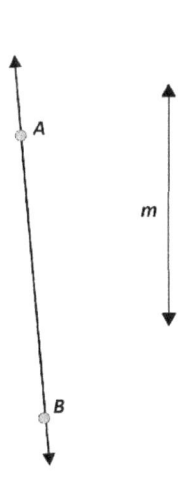

Lines are known as being **coplanar** if they are located in the same plane. Coplanar lines exist within the same two-dimensional surface. Two lines are **parallel** if they are coplanar, extend in the same direction, and never cross. They are known as being **equidistant** because they are always the same distance from each other. If lines do cross, they are **intersecting lines**. Two lines are considered perpendicular if they intersect to form right angles. Right angles are 90°. Typically, a small box is drawn at the intersection point to indicate the right angle.

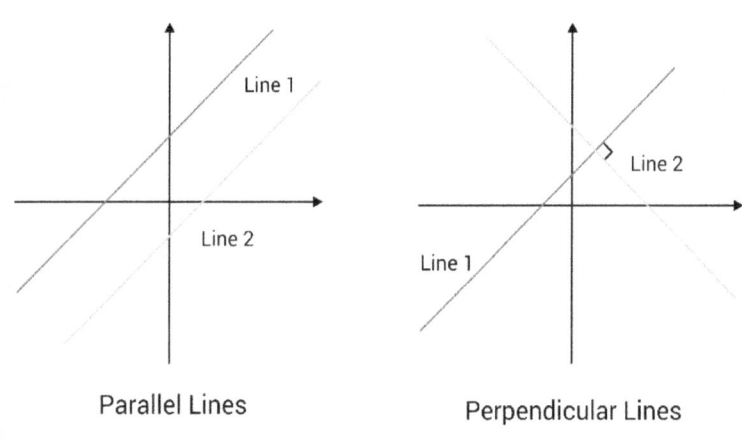

Line 1 is parallel to line 2 in the left image and is written as line 1 || line 2. Line 1 is perpendicular to line 2 in the right image and is written as line 1 ⊥ line 2.

A ray has a specific starting point and extends in one direction without ending. The endpoint of a ray is its starting point. Rays are named using the endpoint first and any other point on the ray. The following ray can be named ray AB and written $\overrightarrow{AB}$.

A line segment has specific starting and ending points. A line segment consists of two endpoints and all the points in between. Line segments are named by the two endpoints. The example below is named segment KL or segment LK, written $\overline{KL}$ or $\overline{LK}$.

Solving Parallel and Perpendicular Line Problems

Two lines are parallel if they have the same slope and a different intercept. Two lines are perpendicular if the product of their slope equals -1. Parallel lines never intersect unless they are the same line, and perpendicular lines intersect at a right angle. If two lines aren't parallel, they must intersect at one point. Determining equations of lines based on properties of parallel and perpendicular lines appears in word problems. To find an equation of a line, both the slope and a point the line goes through are necessary. Therefore, if an equation of a line is needed that's parallel to a given line and runs through a specified point, the slope of the given line and the point are plugged into the point-slope form of an equation of a line.

If an equation of a line is needed that's perpendicular to a given line running through a specified point, the negative reciprocal of the slope of the given line and the point are plugged into the point-slope form. If the point of intersection of two lines is known, that point will be used to solve the set of equations. Therefore, to solve a system of equations, the point of intersection must be found. If a set of two equations with two unknown variables has no solution, the lines are parallel.

Angles

An angle consists of two rays that have a common endpoint. This common endpoint is called the vertex of the angle. The two rays can be called sides of the angle. The angle below has a vertex at point B and the sides consist of ray BA and ray BC. An angle can be named in three ways:

1. Using the vertex and a point from each side, with the vertex letter in the middle.
2. Using only the vertex. This can only be used if it is the only angle with that vertex.
3. Using a number that is written inside the angle.

The angle below can be written ∠ABC (read angle ABC), ∠CBA, ∠B, or ∠1.

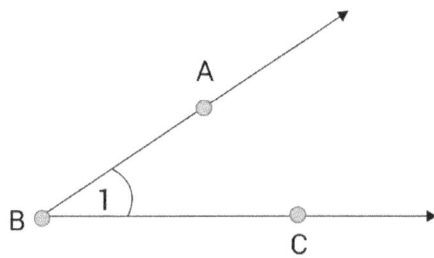

An angle divides a plane, or flat surface, into three parts: the angle itself, the interior (inside) of the angle, and the exterior (outside) of the angle. The figure below shows point M on the interior of the angle and point N on the exterior of the angle.

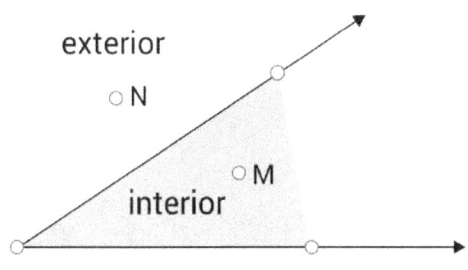

Angles can be measured in units called degrees, with the symbol °. The degree measure of an angle is between 0° and 180° and can be obtained by using a protractor.

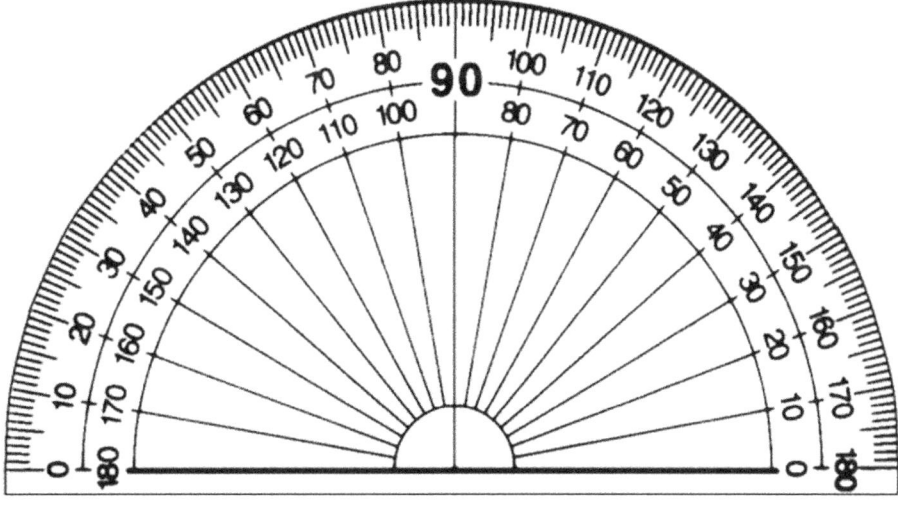

A straight angle (or simply a line) measures exactly 180°. A right angle's sides meet at the vertex to create a square corner. A right-angle measures exactly 90° and is typically indicated by a box drawn in the interior of the angle. An acute angle has an interior that is narrower than a right angle. The measure of an acute angle is any value less than 90° and greater than 0°. For example, 89.9°, 47°, 12°, and 1°. An obtuse angle has an interior that is wider than a right angle. The measure of an obtuse angle is any value greater than 90° but less than 180°. For example, 90.1°, 110°, 150°, and 179.9°.

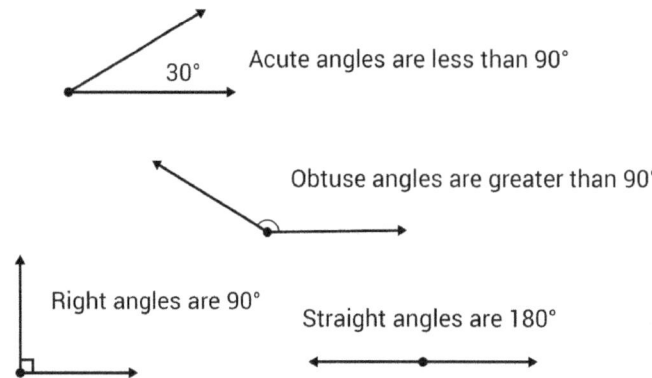

Here is an example of a 180-degree angle split up into an acute and obtuse angle:

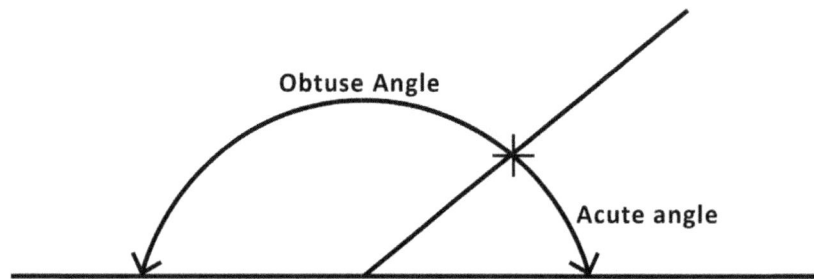

Adjacent angles can be formed by forming two angles out of one shared ray. They are two side-by-side angles that also share an endpoint. To determine angle measures for adjacent angles, at least one of the angles must be known. Other information that is necessary to determine such measures include that there are 90° in a right angle, and there are 180° in a straight line. Therefore, if two adjacent angles form a right angle, they will add up to 90°, and if two adjacent angles form a straight line, they add up to 180°.

If the measurement of one of the adjacent angles is known, the other can be found by subtracting the known angle from the total number of degrees.

For example, given the following situation, if angle a measures 55°, find the measure of unknown angle b:

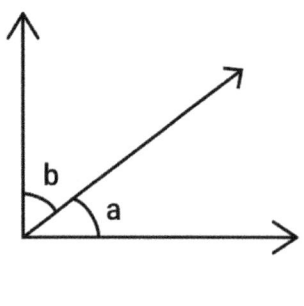

To solve this, subtract the known angle measure from 90°.

$$90° - 55° = 35°$$

The measure of $b = 35°$.

Given the following situation, if angle 1 measures 45°, find the measure of the unknown angle 2:

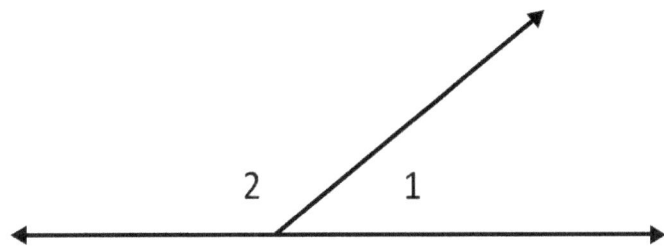

To solve this, subtract the known angle measure from 180°.

$$180° - 45° = 135°$$

The measure of angle $2 = 135°$

In the case that more than two angles are given, use the same method of subtracting the known angles from the total measure.

For example, given the following situation, if angle $y = 40°$, and angle $z = 25°$, find unknown angle x.

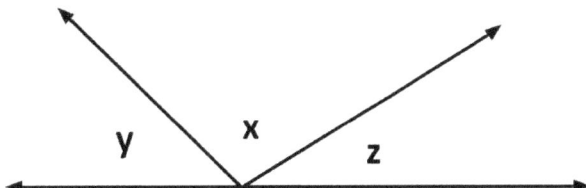

Subtract the known angles from 180°.

$$180° - 65° = 115°$$

The measure of angle $x = 115°$.

Supplementary angles add up to 180 degrees. **Vertical angles** are two nonadjacent angles formed by two intersecting lines. **Corresponding angles** are two angles in the same position whenever a straight line (known as a **transversal**) crosses two others. If the two lines are parallel, the corresponding angles are equal. **Alternate interior**

angles are also a pair of angles formed when two lines are crossed by a transversal. They are opposite angles that exist inside of the two lines.

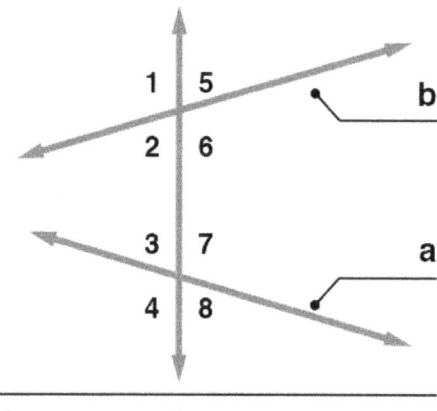

Corresponding Angles

In the corresponding angles diagram above, angles 2 and 7 are alternate interior angles, as well as angles 6 and 3. **Alternate exterior angles** are opposite angles formed by a transversal but, in contrast to interior angles, exterior angles exist outside the two original lines. Therefore, angles 1 and 8 are alternate exterior angles and so are angles 5 and 4. Finally, **consecutive interior angles** are pairs of angles formed by a transversal. These angles are located on the same side of the transversal and inside the two original lines. Therefore, angles 2 and 3 are a pair of consecutive interior angles, and so are angles 6 and 7. These definitions are instrumental in solving many problems that involve determining relationships between angles.

Application of Trigonometry to Triangles

The Area Formula

A triangle that isn't a right triangle is known as an *oblique triangle*. It should be noted that even if the triangle consists of three acute angles, it is still referred to as an oblique triangle. *Oblique*, in this case, does not refer to an angle measurement. Consider the following oblique triangle:

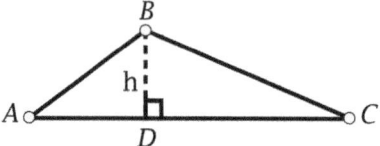

For this triangle, $Area = \frac{1}{2} \cdot base \cdot height = \frac{1}{2} \cdot AC \cdot BD$. The auxiliary line drawn from the vertex B perpendicular to the opposite side AC represents the height of the triangle. This line splits the larger triangle into two smaller right triangles, which allows for the use of the trigonometric functions (specifically that $\sin A = \frac{h}{AB}$). Therefore,

$$Area = \frac{1}{2} AC \cdot AB \cdot \sin A$$

Typically, the sides are labelled as the lowercase letter of the vertex that's opposite. Therefore, the formula can be written as $Area = \frac{1}{2} bc \sin A$. This area formula can be used to find areas of triangles when given side lengths and angle measurements, or it can be used to find side lengths or angle measurements based on a specific area and other characteristics of the triangle.

Laws of Sines and Cosines

The *law of sines* and *law of cosines* are two more relationships that exist within oblique triangles. Consider a triangle with sides *a*, *b*, and *c*, and angles *A*, *B*, and *C* opposite the corresponding sides.

The law of cosines states that:

$$c^2 = a^2 + b^2 - 2ab \cos C$$

The law of sines states that:

$$\frac{\sin A}{a} = \frac{\sin B}{b} = \frac{\sin C}{c}$$

In addition to the area formula, these two relationships can help find unknown angle and side measurements in oblique triangles.

Trigonometric Ratios and the Pythagorean Theorem in Right Triangles

Within similar triangles, corresponding sides are proportional, and angles are congruent. In addition, within similar triangles, the ratio of the side lengths is the same. This property is true even if side lengths are different. Within right triangles, trigonometric ratios can be defined for the acute angles within the triangle. The functions are defined through ratios in a right triangle. Sine of acute angle, A, is opposite over hypotenuse, cosine is adjacent over hypotenuse, and tangent is opposite over adjacent. Note that expanding or shrinking the triangle won't change the ratios. However, changing the angle measurements will alter the calculations.

Angles that add up to 90 degrees are *complementary*. Within a right triangle, two complementary angles exist because the third angle is always 90 degrees. In this scenario, the *sine* of one of the complementary angles is equal to the *cosine* of the other angle. The opposite is also true. This relationship exists because sine and cosine will be calculated as the ratios of the same side lengths.

The *Pythagorean theorem* is an important relationship between the three sides of a right triangle. It states that the square of the side opposite the right triangle, known as the *hypotenuse* (denoted as c^2), is equal to the sum of the squares of the other two sides ($a^2 + b^2$). Thus, $a^2 + b^2 = c^2$.

Both the trigonometric functions and the Pythagorean theorem can be used in problems that involve finding either a missing side or a missing angle of a right triangle. To do so, one must look to see what sides and angles are given and select the correct relationship that will help find the missing value. These relationships can also be used to solve application problems involving right triangles. Often, it's helpful to draw a figure to represent the problem to see what's missing.

Transformations in a Plane

A **transformation** occurs when a shape is altered in the plane where it exists. There are three major types of transformation: translations, reflections, and rotations. A **translation** consists of shifting a shape in one direction. A **reflection** results when a shape is transformed over a line to its mirror image. Finally, a **rotation** occurs when a shape moves in a circular motion around a specified point. The object can be turned clockwise or counterclockwise and, if rotated 360 degrees, returns to its original location.

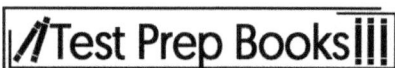

Distance and Angle Measure

The three major types of transformations preserve distance and angle measurement. The shapes stay the same, but are moved to another place in the plane. Therefore, the distance between any two points on the shape doesn't change. Also, any original angle measure between two line segments doesn't change. However, there are transformations that don't preserve distance and angle measurements, including those that don't preserve the original shape. For example, transformations that involve stretching and shrinking shapes don't preserve distance and angle measures. In these cases, the input variables are multiplied by either a number greater than 1 (*stretch*) or less than 1 (*shrink*).

Rotations and Reflections

A *point of symmetry* is used to determine translations that map a shape onto itself. When a line is drawn through a point of symmetry, it crosses the shape on one side of the point while crossing the shape on the other side at the exact same distance. A shape can be rotated 180 degrees around a point of symmetry to get back to its original shape. Simple examples are the center of a circle and a square. A *line of symmetry* is a line that a shape is folded over to have its sides align, and it goes through the point of symmetry. A combination of reflecting an original shape around a line of symmetry and rotating it can map the original image onto itself. A shape has *rotational symmetry* if it can be rotated to get back to its original shape, and it has *reflection symmetry* if it can be reflected onto itself over some line. Shapes such as rectangles, parallelograms, trapezoids, and regular polygons can be mapped onto themselves through such rotations and reflections.

Isometric Transformations

Rotations, reflections, and translations are isometric transformations, because throughout each transformation the distance of line segments is maintained, the angle measure is maintained, parallel lines in the original shape remain parallel, and points on lines remain on those lines.

A rotation turns a shape around a specific point (*O*) known as the *center of rotation*. An *angle of rotation* is formed by drawing a ray from the center of rotation to a point (*P*) on the original shape and to the point's image (*P'*) on the reflected shape. Thus, it's true that $OP=OP'$.

A reflection over a line (*l*), known as the *line of reflection*, takes an original point P and maps it to its image P' on the opposite side of *l*. The line of reflection is the perpendicular bisector of every line formed by an original point and its image.

A translation maps each point P in the original shape to a new point P'. The line segment formed between each point and its image consists of the same length, and the line segment formed by two original points is parallel to the line segment formed from their two images.

Dilation

A shape is dilated, or a *dilation* occurs, when each side of the original image is multiplied by a given scale factor. If the scale factor is less than 1 and greater than 0, the dilation contracts the shape, and the resulting shape is smaller. If the scale factor equals 1, the resulting shape is the same size, and the dilation is a rigid motion. Finally, if the scale factor is greater than 1, the resulting shape is larger and the dilation expands the shape. The *center of dilation* is the point where the distance from it to any point on the new shape equals the scale factor times the distance from the center to the corresponding point in the pre-image. Dilations aren't isometric transformations because distance isn't preserved. Dilations are also non-rigid transformations. However, angle measure, parallel lines, and points on a line all remain unchanged. The following figure is an example of translation, rotation, dilation, and reflection:

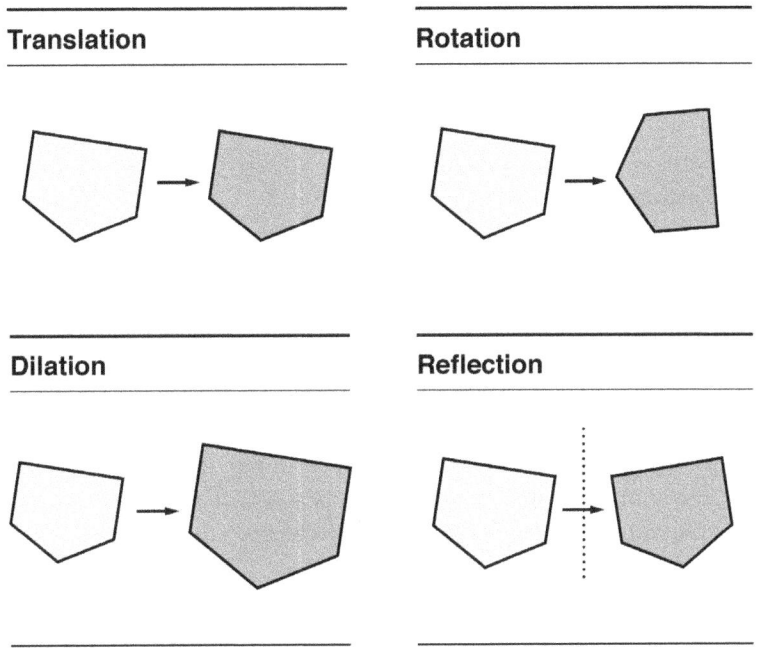

Rigid Motion

A *rigid motion* is a transformation that preserves distance and length. Every line segment in the resulting image is congruent to the corresponding line segment in the pre-image. Congruence between two figures means a series of transformations (or a rigid motion) can be defined that maps one of the figures onto the other. Basically, two figures are congruent if they have the same shape and size.

Congruency and Similarity

Two figures are congruent if they have the same shape and same size. The two figures could have been rotated, reflected, or translated. Both angle and side length are preserved in congruent figures. For example, in triangles, each pair of the three sides and three angles must be congruent. Similarly, in two four-sided figures, each pair of the four sides and four angles must be congruent. Two figures are similar if they have been rotated, reflected, translated, and resized. Angle measure is preserved in similar figures. Therefore, the difference between congruence and similarity is that dilation can be used in similarity, so side lengths between each shape can differ. However, angle measure must be preserved within this definition. If two polygons differ in size so that the lengths of corresponding line segments differ by the same factor, but corresponding angles have the same measurement, they are similar.

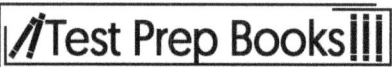

Quantitative Reasoning and Mathematics Achievement

Triangle Congruence and Similarity

There are five theorems to show that triangles are congruent when it's unknown whether each pair of angles and sides are congruent. Each theorem is a shortcut that involves different combinations of sides and angles that must be true for the two triangles to be congruent.

Side-side-side (SSS) states that if all sides are equal, the triangles are congruent.

Side-angle-side (SAS) states that if two pairs of sides are equal and the included angles are congruent, then the triangles are congruent.

Similarly, *angle-side-angle (ASA)* states that if two pairs of angles are congruent and the included side lengths are equal, the triangles are congruent.

Angle-angle-side (AAS) states that two triangles are congruent if they have two pairs of congruent angles and a pair of corresponding equal side lengths that aren't included.

Finally, *hypotenuse-leg (HL)* states that if two right triangles have equal hypotenuses and an equal pair of shorter sides, then the triangles are congruent.

An important item to note is that angle-angle-angle *(AAA)* is not enough information to have congruence. It's important to understand why these rules work by using rigid motions to show congruence between the triangles with the given properties. For example, three reflections are needed to show why *SAS* follows from the definition of congruence.

Similarity for Two Triangles

If two angles of one triangle are congruent with two angles of a second triangle, the triangles are similar. This is because, within any triangle, the sum of the angle measurements is 180 degrees. Therefore, if two are congruent, the third angle must also be congruent because their measurements are equal. Three congruent pairs of angles mean that the triangles are similar.

Proving Congruence and Similarity

The criteria needed to prove triangles are congruent involves both angle and side congruence. Both pairs of related angles and sides need to be of the same measurement to use congruence in a proof. The criteria to prove similarity in triangles involves proportionality of side lengths. Angles must be congruent in similar triangles; however, corresponding side lengths only need to be a constant multiple of each other. Once similarity is established, it can be used in proofs as well. Relationships in geometric figures other than triangles can be proven using triangle congruence and similarity. If a similar or congruent triangle can be found within another type of geometric figure, their criteria can be used to prove a relationship about a given formula. For instance, a rectangle can be broken up into two congruent triangles.

Locating Ordered Pairs in All Four Quadrants of a Rectangular Coordinate System

The **coordinate plane**, sometimes referred to as the Cartesian plane, is a two-dimensional surface consisting of a horizontal and a vertical number line. The horizontal number line is referred to as the x-axis, and the vertical number line is referred to as the y-axis. The x-axis and y-axis intersect (or cross) at a point called the origin. At the origin, the value of the x-axis is zero, and the value of the y-axis is zero. The coordinate plane identifies the exact location of a point that is plotted on the two-dimensional surface. Like a map, the location of all points on the plane are in relation to the origin. Along the x-axis (horizontal line), numbers to the right of the origin are positive and increasing in value (1,2,3, ...) and to the left of the origin numbers are negative and decreasing in value (-1,-2,-3, ...).

Along the y-axis (vertical line), numbers above the origin are positive and increasing in value and numbers below the origin are negative and decreasing in value.

The x- and y-axis divide the coordinate plane into four sections. These sections are referred to as quadrant one, quadrant two, quadrant three, and quadrant four, and are often written with Roman numerals I, II, III, and IV.

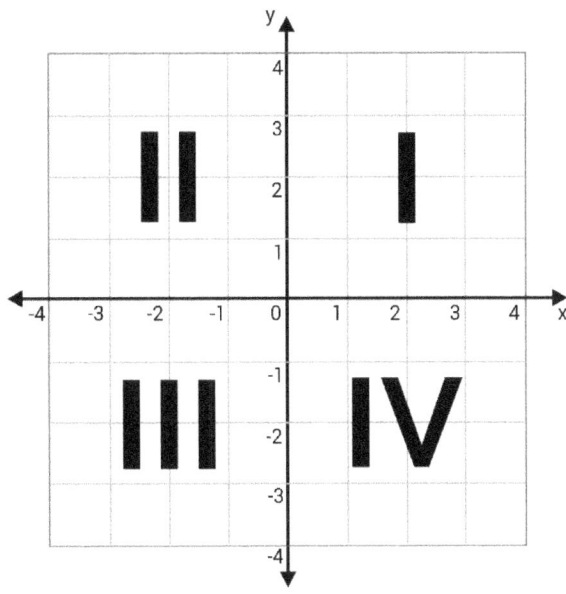

The upper right section is Quadrant I and consists of points with positive x-values and positive y-values. The upper left section is Quadrant II and consists of points with negative x-values and positive y-values. The bottom left section is Quadrant III and consists of points with negative x-values and negative y-values. The bottom right section is Quadrant IV and consists of points with positive x-values and negative y-values.

Any point within the plane can be defined by a set of **coordinates** (x, y). The coordinates consist of two numbers, x and y, which represent a position on each number line. The coordinates can also be referred to as an **ordered pair,** and $(0, 0)$ is the ordered pair known as the **vertex**, or the origin, the point in which the axes intersect. Positive x-coordinates go to the right of the vertex, and positive y-coordinates go up. Negative x-coordinates go left, and negative y-coordinates go down.

Here is an example of the coordinate plane with a point plotted:

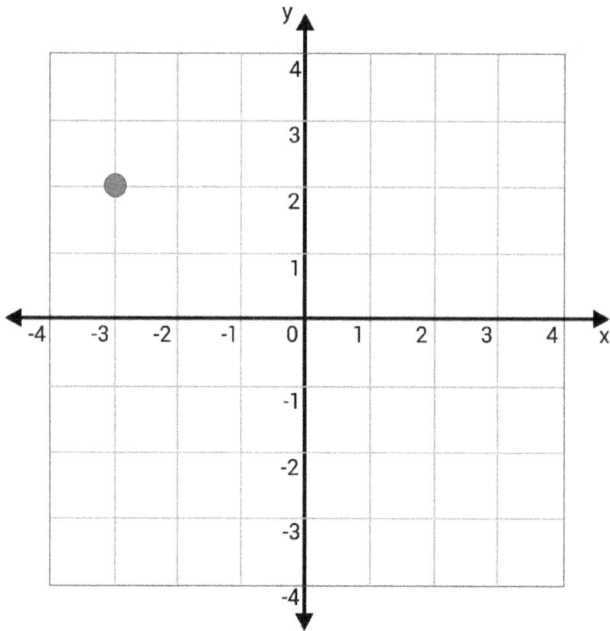

In order to plot a point on the coordinate plane, each coordinate must be considered individually. The value of x represents how many units away from the vertex the point lies on the x-axis. The value of y represents the number of units away from the vertex that the point lies on the y-axis.

The points on the coordinate plane are labeled based on their position in relation to the origin. If a point is found 4 units to the right and 2 units up from the origin, the location is described as $(4, 2)$. These numbers are the x- and y-coordinates, always written in the order (x, y). This point is also described as lying in the first quadrant. Every point in the first quadrant has a location that is positive in the x and y directions. The point plotted in the coordinate plane above is (-3, 2).

The following figure shows the coordinate plane with examples of points that lie in each quadrant:

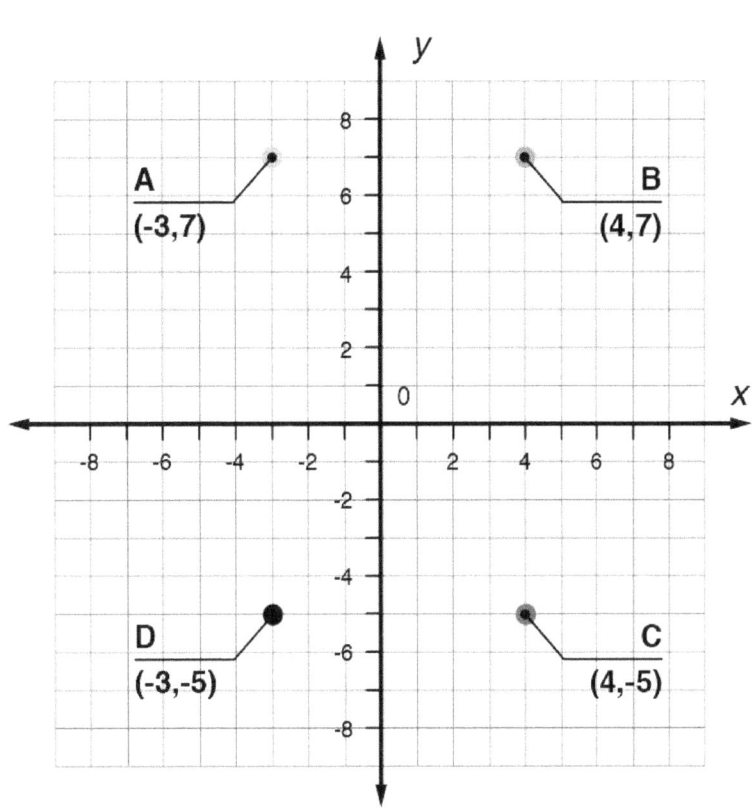

Point B lies in the first quadrant, described with positive x- and y-values, above the x-axis and to the right of the y-axis. Point A lies in the second quadrant, where the x-value is negative and the y-value is positive. This quadrant is above the x-axis and to the left of the y-axis. Point D lies in the third quadrant, where both the x- and y-values are negative. Points in this quadrant are below the x-axis and to the left of the y-axis. Point C is in the fourth quadrant, where the x-value is positive and the y-value is negative.

Graphing on the Coordinate Plane Using Mathematical Problems, Tables, and Patterns

Data can be recorded using a coordinate plane. Graphs are utilized frequently in real-world applications and can be seen in everyday life. A relationship can exist between the x- and y-coordinates that are plotted on a graph, and those values can represent a set of data that can be listed in a table. Going back and forth between the table and the graph is an important concept, and defining the relationship between the variables is the key that links the data to a real-life application.

For example, temperature increases during a summer day. The x-coordinate can be used to represent hours in the day, and the y-coordinate can be used to represent the temperature in degrees. The graph would show the temperature at each hour of the day. Time is almost always plotted on the x-axis, and utilizing different units on each axis, if necessary, is important. Labeling the axes with units is also important.

Within the first quadrant of the coordinate plane, both the x and y values are positive. Most real-world problems can be plotted in this quadrant because most real-world quantities, such as time and distance, are positive.

Consider the following table of values:

X	Y
1	2
2	4
3	6
4	8

Each row gives a coordinate pair. For example, the first row gives the coordinates $(1, 2)$. Each x-value tells you how far to move from the origin, the point $(0, 0)$, to the right, and each y-value tells you how far to move up from the origin. Here is the graph of the points listed above in the table in addition to the origin:

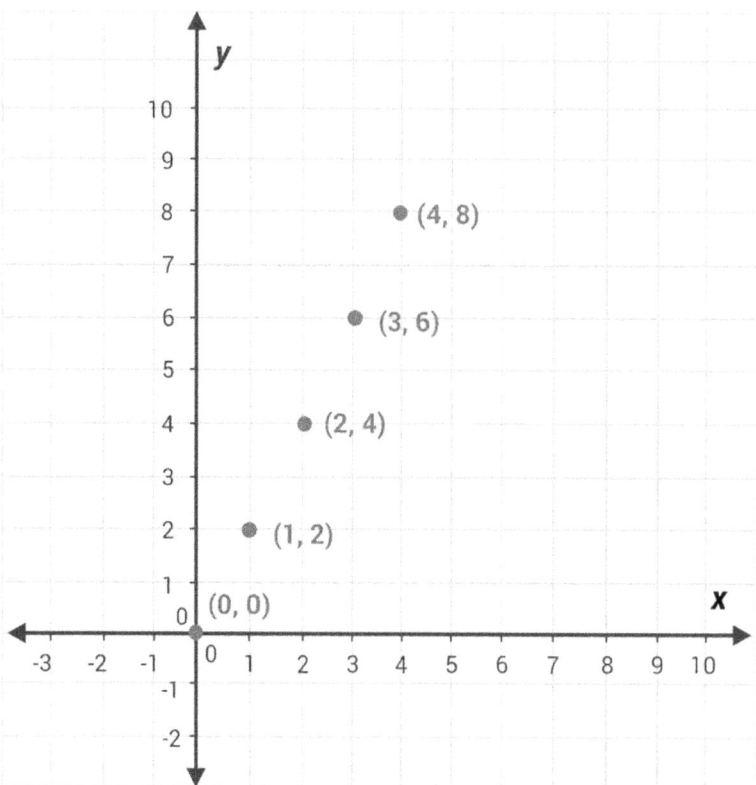

Notice that each y-value is found by doubling the x-value that forms the other portion of its coordinate pair.

The coordinate plane can also be used in problems involving two-dimensional geometric shapes. Polygons can be drawn in the coordinate plane given the coordinates of their vertices. These coordinates can be used to determine the perimeter and area of the figure. Suppose triangle RQP has vertices located at the points: R(-2, 0), Q(2, 2), and P(2, 0). By plotting the points for the three vertices, the triangle can be constructed as follows:

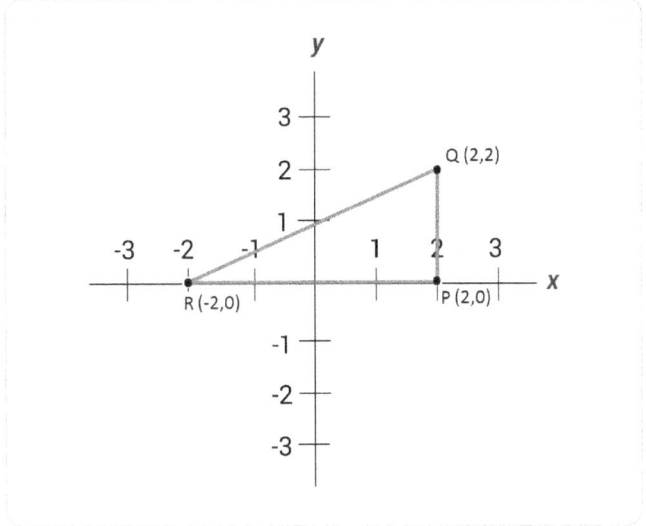

Because points R and P have the same y-coordinates (they are directly across from each other), the distance between them is determined by subtracting their x-coordinates (or simply counting units from one point to the other): 2 − (-2) = 4. Therefore, the length of side RP is 4 units. Because points Q and P have the same x-coordinate (they are directly above and below each other), the distance between them is determined by subtracting their y-coordinates (or counting units between them): 2 − 0 = 2. Therefore, the length of side PQ is 2 units. Knowing the length of side RP, which is the base of the triangle, and the length of side PQ, which is the height of the triangle, the area of the figure can be determined by using the formula $A = \frac{1}{2}bh$.

To determine the perimeter of the triangle, the lengths of all three sides are needed. Points R and Q are neither directly across nor directly above and below each other. Therefore, the distance formula must be used to find the length of side RQ. The distance formula is as follows:

$$d = \sqrt{(x_2 - x_1)^2 + (y_2 - y_1)^2}$$

$$d = \sqrt{(2 - (-2))^2 + (2 - 0)^2}$$

$$d = \sqrt{(4)^2 + (2)^2}$$

$$d = \sqrt{16 + 4} \rightarrow d = \sqrt{20}$$

The perimeter is determined by adding the lengths of the three sides of the triangle.

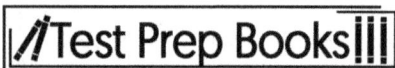

Quantitative Reasoning and Mathematics Achievement

Measuring Lengths of Objects

The length of an object can be measured using standard tools such as rulers, yard sticks, meter sticks, and measuring tapes. The following image depicts a yardstick:

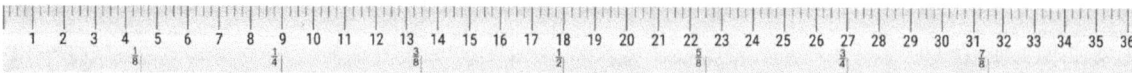

Choosing the right tool to perform the measurement requires determining whether United States customary units or metric units are desired, and having a grasp of the approximate length of each unit and the approximate length of each tool. The measurement can still be performed by trial and error without the knowledge of the approximate size of the tool.

For example, to determine the length of a room in feet, a United States customary unit, various tools can be used for this task. These include a ruler (typically 12 inches/1 foot long), a yardstick (3 feet/1 yard long), or a tape measure displaying feet (typically either 25 feet or 50 feet). Because the length of a room is much larger than the length of a ruler or a yardstick, a tape measure should be used to perform the measurement.

When the correct measuring tool is selected, the measurement is performed by first placing the tool directly above or below the object (if making a horizontal measurement) or directly next to the object (if making a vertical measurement). The next step is aligning the tool so that one end of the object is at the mark for zero units, then recording the unit of the mark at the other end of the object. To give the length of a paperclip in metric units, a ruler displaying centimeters is aligned with one end of the paper clip to the mark for zero centimeters.

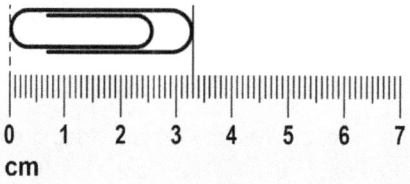

Directly down from the other end of the paperclip is the mark that measures its length. In this case, that mark is three small dashes past the 3-centimeter mark. Each small dash is 1 millimeter (or .1 centimeters). Therefore, the length of the paper clip is 3.3 centimeters.

To compare the lengths of objects, each length must be expressed in the same unit. If possible, the objects should be measured with the same tool or with tools utilizing the same units. For example, a ruler and a yardstick can both measure length in inches. If the lengths of the objects are expressed in different units, these different units must be converted to the same unit before comparing them. If two lengths are expressed in the same unit, the lengths may be compared by subtracting the smaller value from the larger value. For example, suppose the lengths of two gardens are to be compared. Garden A has a length of 4 feet, and garden B has a length of 2 yards. 2 yards is converted to 6 feet so that the measurements have similar units. Then, the smaller length (4 ft) is subtracted from the larger length (6 ft): 6 ft − 4 ft = 2 ft. Therefore, garden B is 2 feet larger than garden A.

Relative Sizes of United States Customary Units and Metric Units

The United States customary system and the metric system each consist of distinct units to measure lengths and volume of liquids. The U.S. customary units for length, from smallest to largest, are: inch (in), foot (ft), yard (yd), and mile (mi). The metric units for length, from smallest to largest, are: millimeter (mm), centimeter (cm), decimeter (dm), meter (m), and kilometer (km). The relative size of each unit of length is shown below.

U.S. Customary	Metric	Conversion
12 in = 1 ft	10 mm = 1 cm	1 in = 2.54 cm
36 in = 3 ft = 1 yd	10 cm = 1 dm (decimeter)	1 m ≈ 3.28 ft ≈ 1.09 yd
5,280 ft = 1,760 yd = 1 mi	100 cm = 10 dm = 1 m	1 mi ≈ 1.6 km
	1,000 m = 1 km	

The U.S. customary units for volume of liquids, from smallest to largest, are: fluid ounces (fl oz), cup (c), pint (pt), quart (qt), and gallon (gal). The metric units for volume of liquids, from smallest to largest, are: milliliter (mL), centiliter (cL), deciliter (dL), liter (L), and kiloliter (kL). The relative size of each unit of liquid volume is shown below.

U.S. Customary	Metric	Conversion
8 fl oz = 1 c	10 mL = 1 cL	1 pt ≈ 0.473 L
2 c = 1 pt	10 cL = 1 dL	1 L ≈ 1.057 qt
4 c = 2 pt = 1 qt	1,000 mL = 100 cL = 10 dL = 1 L	1 gal ≈ 3.785 L
4 qt = 1 gal	1,000 L = 1 kL	

The U.S. customary system measures weight (how strongly Earth is pulling on an object) in the following units, from least to greatest: ounce (oz), pound (lb), and ton. The metric system measures mass (the quantity of matter within an object) in the following units, from least to greatest: milligram (mg), centigram (cg), gram (g), kilogram (kg), and metric ton (MT). The relative sizes of each unit of weight and mass are shown below.

U.S. Measures of Weight	Metric Measures of Mass
16 oz = 1 lb	10 mg = 1 cg
2,000 lb = 1 ton	100 cg = 1 g
	1,000 g = 1 kg
	1,000 kg = 1 MT

Note that weight and mass DO NOT measure the same thing.

Time is measured in the following units, from shortest to longest: second (sec), minute (min), hour (h), day (d), week (wk), month (mo), year (yr), decade, century, millennium. The relative size of each unit of time is shown below:

- 60 sec = 1 min
- 60 min = 1 h
- 24 hr = 1 d
- 7 d = 1 wk
- 52 wk = 1 yr
- 12 mo = 1 yr
- 10 yr = 1 decade
- 100 yrs = 1 century
- 1,000 yrs = 1 millennium

Conversion of Units

Converting measurements in different units between the two systems can be difficult because they follow different rules. The best method is to look up an English to Metric system conversion factor and then use a series of equivalent fractions to set up an equation to convert the units of one of the measurements into those of the other. The table below lists some common conversion values that are useful for problems involving measurements with units in both systems:

English System	Metric System
1 inch	2.54 cm
1 foot	0.3048 m
1 yard	0.914 m
1 mile	1.609 km
1 ounce	28.35 g
1 pound	0.454 kg
1 fluid ounce	29.574 mL
1 quart	0.946 L
1 gallon	3.785 L

Consider the example where a scientist wants to convert 6.8 inches to centimeters. One method for converting units is to write and solve a proportion. The arrangement of values in a proportion is extremely important. The table above is used to find that there are 2.54 centimeters in every inch, so the following equation should be set up and solved:

$$\frac{6.8 \text{ in}}{1} \times \frac{2.54 \text{ cm}}{1 \text{ in}} = 17.272 \text{ cm}$$

Notice how the inches in the numerator of the initial figure and the denominator of the conversion factor cancel out. (This equation could have been written simply as $6.8 \text{ in} \times 2.54 \text{ cm} = 17.272 \text{ cm}$ but it was shown in detail to illustrate the steps). The goal in any conversion equation is to set up the fractions so that the units you are trying to convert from cancel out and the units you desire remain.

For a more complicated example, consider converting 2.15 kilograms into ounces. The first step is to convert kilograms into grams and then grams into ounces. Note that the measurement you begin with does not have to be put in a fraction.

So, in this case, 2.15 kg is by itself although it's technically the numerator of a fraction:

$$2.15 \text{ kg} \times \frac{1{,}000 \text{ g}}{\text{kg}} = 2{,}150 \text{ g}$$

Then, use the conversion factor from the table to convert grams to ounces:

$$2{,}150 \text{ g} \times \frac{1 \text{ oz}}{28.35 \text{ g}} = 75.8 \text{ oz}$$

When working with different systems of measurement, conversion from one unit to another may be necessary. The conversion rate must be known to convert units. One method for converting units is to write and solve a proportion. The arrangement of values in a proportion is extremely important. Suppose that a problem requires converting 20 fluid ounces to cups. To do so, a proportion can be written using the conversion rate of $8 \text{ fl oz} = 1 \text{ c}$ with x representing the missing value.

The proportion can be written in any of the following ways:

$$\frac{1}{8} = \frac{x}{20} \left(\frac{c \text{ for conversion}}{fl \text{ oz for conversion}} = \frac{\text{unknown } c}{fl \text{ oz given}} \right); \quad \frac{8}{1} = \frac{20}{x} \left(\frac{fl \text{ oz for conversion}}{c \text{ for conversion}} = \frac{fl \text{ oz given}}{\text{unknown } c} \right);$$

$$\frac{1}{x} = \frac{8}{20} \left(\frac{c \text{ for conversion}}{\text{unknown } c} = \frac{fl \text{ oz for conversion}}{fl \text{ oz given}} \right)$$

$$\frac{x}{1} = \frac{20}{8} \left(\frac{\text{unknown } c}{c \text{ for conversion}} = \frac{fl \text{ oz given}}{fl \text{ oz for conversion}} \right)$$

To solve a proportion, the ratios are cross-multiplied and the resulting equation is solved. When cross-multiplying, all four proportions above will produce the same equation:

$$(8)(x) = (20)(1) \rightarrow 8x = 20$$

Divide by 8 to isolate the variable x, the result is $x = 2.5$. The variable x represents the unknown number of cups. Therefore, the conclusion is that 20 fluid ounces converts (is equal) to 2.5 cups.

Sometimes converting units requires writing and solving more than one proportion. Suppose an exam question asks to determine how many hours are in 2 weeks. Without knowing the conversion rate between hours and weeks, this can be determined knowing the conversion rates between weeks and days, and between days and hours. First, weeks are converted to days, then days are converted to hours. To convert from weeks to days, the following proportion can be written:

$$\frac{7}{1} = \frac{x}{2} \left(\frac{\text{days conversion}}{\text{weeks conversion}} = \frac{\text{days unknown}}{\text{weeks given}} \right)$$

Cross-multiplying produces:

$$(7)(2) = (x)(1) \rightarrow 14 = x$$

Quantitative Reasoning and Mathematics Achievement

Therefore, 2 weeks is equal to 14 days. Next, a proportion is written to convert 14 days to hours:

$$\frac{24}{1} = \frac{x}{14} \left(\frac{conversion\ hours}{conversion\ days} = \frac{unknown\ hours}{given\ days} \right)$$

Cross-multiplying produces:

$$(24)(14) = (x)(1) \rightarrow 336 = x$$

Therefore, the answer is that there are 336 hours in 2 weeks.

Data Analysis/Probability

Measures of Center and Range

The center of a set of data (statistical values) can be represented by its mean, median, or mode. These are sometimes referred to as measures of central tendency. The mean is the average of the data set. The mean can be calculated by adding the data values and dividing by the sample size (the number of data points). Suppose a student has test scores of 93, 84, 88, 72, 91, and 77.

To find the mean, or average, the scores are added and the sum is divided by 6 because there are 6 test scores:

$$\frac{93 + 84 + 88 + 72 + 91 + 77}{6} = \frac{505}{6} = 84.17$$

Given the mean of a data set and the sum of the data points, the sample size can be determined by dividing the sum by the mean. Suppose you are told that Kate averaged 12 points per game and scored a total of 156 points for the season. The number of games that she played (the sample size or the number of data points) can be determined by dividing the total points (sum of data points) by her average (mean of data points): $\frac{156}{12} = 13$. Therefore, Kate played in 13 games this season.

If given the mean of a data set and the sample size, the sum of the data points can be determined by multiplying the mean and sample size. Suppose you are told that Tom worked 6 days last week for an average of 5.5 hours per day. The total number of hours worked for the week (sum of data points) can be determined by multiplying his daily average (mean of data points) by the number of days worked (sample size): $5.5 \times 6 = 33$. Therefore, Tom worked a total of 33 hours last week.

The median of a data set is the value of the data point in the middle when the sample is arranged in numerical order. To find the median of a data set, the values are written in order from least to greatest. The lowest and highest values are simultaneously eliminated, repeating until the value in the middle remains. Suppose the salaries of math teachers are: $35,000; $38,500; $41,000; $42,000; $42,000; $44,500; $49,000. The values are listed from least to greatest to find the median. The lowest and highest values are eliminated until only the middle value remains. Repeating this step three times reveals a median salary of $42,000. If the sample set has an even number of data points, two values will remain after all others are eliminated. In this case, the mean of the two middle values is the median. Consider the following data set: 7, 9, 10, 13, 14, 14. Eliminating the lowest and highest values twice leaves two values, 10 and 13, in the middle. The mean of these values $\left(\frac{10+13}{2}\right)$ is the median. Therefore, the set has a median of 11.5.

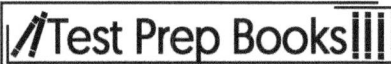

The mode of a data set is the value that appears most often. A data set may have a single mode, multiple modes, or no mode. If different values repeat equally as often, multiple modes exist. If no value repeats, no mode exists. Consider the following data sets:

A: 7, 9, 10, 13, 14, 14
B: 37, 44, 33, 37, 49, 44, 51, 34, 37, 33, 44
C: 173, 154, 151, 168, 155

Set A has a mode of 14. Set B has modes of 33, 37, and 44. Set C has no mode.

The range of a data set is the difference between the highest and the lowest values in the set. The range can be considered the span of the data set. To determine the range, the smallest value in the set is subtracted from the largest value. The ranges for the data sets A, B, and C above are calculated as follows: $A: 14 - 7 = 7$; $B: 51 - 33 = 18$; $C: 173 - 151 = 22$.

Best Description of a Set of Data

Measures of central tendency, namely mean, median, and mode, describe characteristics of a set of data. Specifically, they are intended to represent a *typical* value in the set by identifying a central position of the set. Depending on the characteristics of a specific set of data, different measures of central tendency are more indicative of a typical value in the set.

When a data set is grouped closely together with a relatively small range and the data is spread out somewhat evenly, the mean is an effective indicator of a typical value in the set. Consider the following data set representing the height of sixth grade boys in inches: 61 inches, 54 inches, 58 inches, 63 inches, 58 inches. The mean of the set is 58.8 inches. The data set is grouped closely (the range is only 9 inches) and the values are spread relatively evenly (three values below the mean and two values above the mean). Therefore, the mean value of 58.8 inches is an effective measure of central tendency in this case.

When a data set contains a small number of values either extremely large or extremely small when compared to the other values, the mean is not an effective measure of central tendency. Consider the following data set representing annual incomes of homeowners on a given street: $71,000; $74,000; $75,000; $77,000; $340,000. The mean of this set is $127,400. This figure does not indicate a typical value in the set, which contains four out of five values between $71,000 and $77,000. The median is a much more effective measure of central tendency for data sets such as these. Finding the middle value diminishes the influence of outliers, or numbers that may appear out of place, like the $340,000 annual income. The median for this set is $75,000 which is much more typical of a value in the set.

The mode of a data set is a useful measure of central tendency for categorical data when each piece of data is an option from a category. Consider a survey of 31 commuters asking how they get to work with results summarized below.

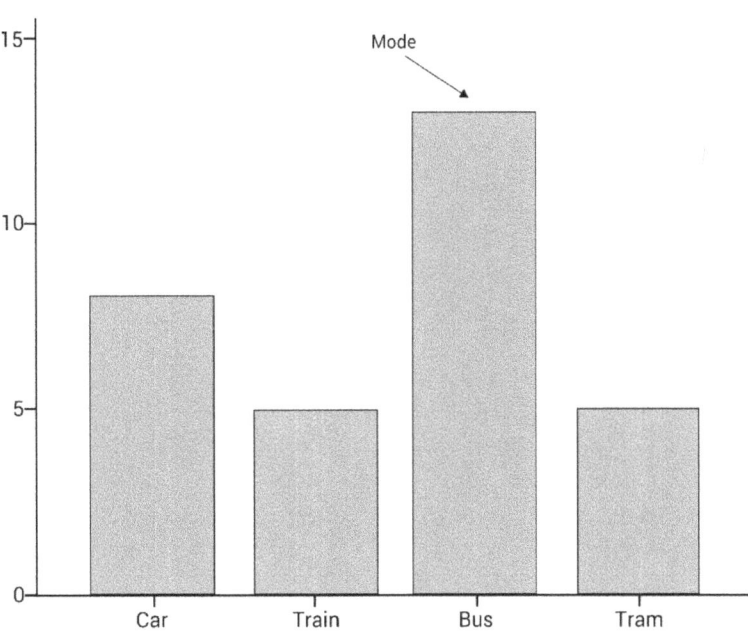

The mode for this set represents the value, or option, of the data that repeats most often. This indicates that the bus is the most popular method of transportation for the commuters.

Effects of Changes in Data

Changing all values of a data set in a consistent way produces predictable changes in the measures of the center and range of the set. A linear transformation changes the original value into the new value by either adding a given number to each value, multiplying each value by a given number, or both. Adding (or subtracting) a given value to each data point will increase (or decrease) the mean, median, and any modes by the same value. However, the range will remain the same due to the way that range is calculated. Multiplying (or dividing) a given value by each data point will increase (or decrease) the mean, median, and any modes, and the range by the same factor.

Consider the following data set, call it set P, representing the price of different cases of soda at a grocery store: $4.25, $4.40, $4.75, $4.95, $4.95, $5.15. The mean of set P is $4.74. The median is $4.85. The mode of the set is $4.95. The range is $0.90. Suppose the state passes a new tax of $0.25 on every case of soda sold. The new data set, set T, is calculated by adding $0.25 to each data point from set P. Therefore, set T consists of the following values: $4.50, $4.65, $5.00, $5.20, $5.20, $5.40. The mean of set T is $4.99. The median is $5.10. The mode of the set is $5.20. The range is $.90. The mean, median and mode of set T is equal to $0.25 added to the mean, median, and mode of set P. The range stays the same.

Now suppose, due to inflation, the store raises the cost of every item by 10%. Raising costs by 10% is calculated by multiplying each value by 1.1. The new data set, set I, is calculated by multiplying each data point from set T by 1.1. Therefore, set I consists of the following values: $4.95, $5.12, $5.50, $5.72, $5.72, $5.94. The mean of set I is $5.49. The median is $5.61. The mode of the set is $5.72. The range is $0.99. The mean, median, mode, and range of set I is equal to 1.1 multiplied by the mean, median, mode, and range of set T because each increased by a factor of 10%.

Describing a Set of Data

A set of data can be described in terms of its center, spread, shape and any unusual features. The center of a data set can be measured by its mean, median, or mode. Measures of central tendency are covered in the *Measures of Center and Range* section. The spread of a data set refers to how far the data points are from the center (mean or median). The spread can be measured by the range or by the quartiles and interquartile range. A data set with all its data points clustered around the center will have a small spread. A data set covering a wide range of values will have a large spread.

When a data set is displayed as a histogram or frequency distribution plot, the shape indicates whether a sample is normally distributed, symmetrical, or has measures of skewness or kurtosis. When graphed, a data set with a normal distribution will resemble a bell curve.

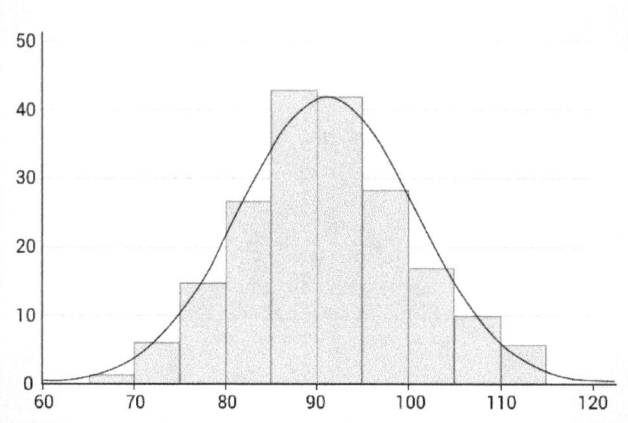

If the data set is symmetrical, each half of the graph when divided at the center is a mirror image of the other. If the graph has fewer data points to the right, the data is skewed right. If it has fewer data points to the left, the data is skewed left.

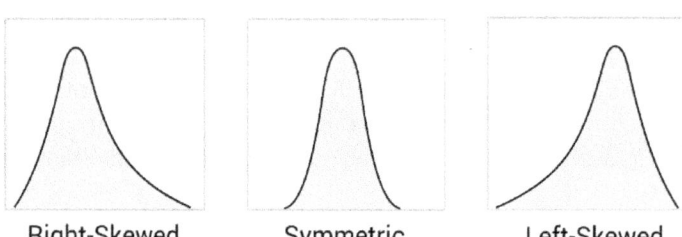

Kurtosis is a measure of whether the data is heavy-tailed with a high number of outliers, or light-tailed with a low number of outliers.

A description of a data set should include any unusual features such as gaps or outliers. A gap is a span within the range of the data set containing no data points. An outlier is a data point with a value either extremely large or extremely small when compared to the other values in the set.

Interpreting Displays of Data

A set of data can be visually displayed in various forms allowing for quick identification of characteristics of the set. Histograms, such as the one shown below, display the number of data points (vertical axis) that fall into given intervals (horizontal axis) across the range of the set. Suppose the histogram below displays IQ scores of students. Histograms can describe the center, spread, shape, and any unusual characteristics of a data set.

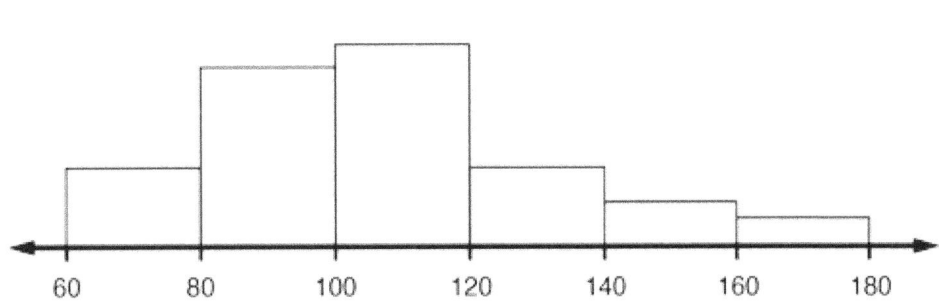

A box plot, also called a box-and-whisker plot, divides the data points into four groups and displays the five-number summary for the set as well as any outliers. The five-number summary consists of:

- The lower extreme: the lowest value that is not an outlier
- The higher extreme: the highest value that is not an outlier
- The median of the set: also referred to as the second quartile or Q_2
- The first quartile or Q_1: the median of values below Q_2
- The third quartile or Q_3: the median of values above Q_2

Calculating each of these values is covered in the next section, *Graphical Representation of Data*.

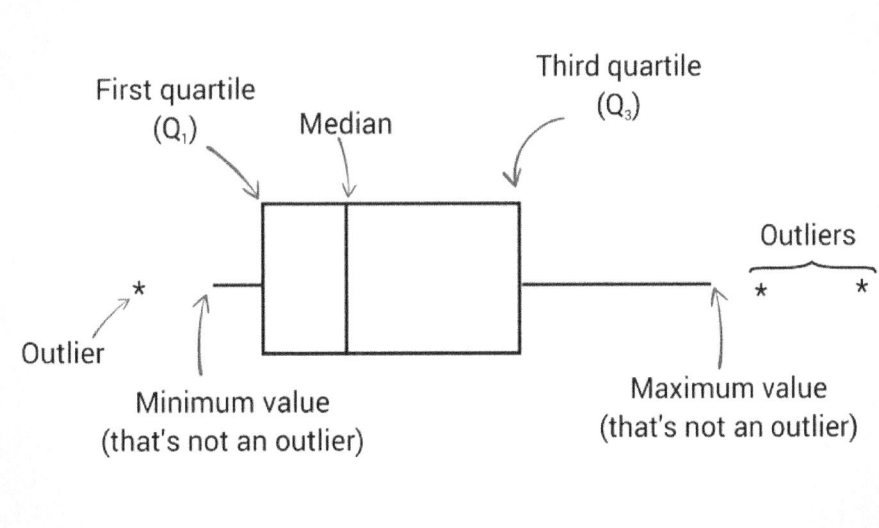

Suppose the box plot displays IQ scores for 12th grade students at a given school. The five number summary of the data consists of: lower extreme (67); upper extreme (127); Q_2 or median (100); Q_1 (91); Q_3 (108); and outliers (135 and 140). Although all data points are not known from the plot, the points are divided into four quartiles each, including 25% of the data points. Therefore, 25% of students scored between 67 and 91, 25% scored between 91 and 100, 25% scored between 100 and 108, and 25% scored between 108 and 127. These percentages include the normal values for the set and exclude the outliers. This information is useful when comparing a given score with the rest of the scores in the set.

A scatter plot is a mathematical diagram that visually displays the relationship or connection between two variables. The independent variable is placed on the x-axis, or horizontal axis, and the dependent variable is placed on the y-axis, or vertical axis. When visually examining the points on the graph, if the points model a linear relationship, or if a line of best-fit can be drawn through the points with the points relatively close on either side, then a correlation exists. If the line of best-fit has a positive slope (rises from left to right), then the variables have a positive correlation. If the line of best-fit has a negative slope (falls from left to right), then the variables have a negative correlation. If a line of best-fit cannot be drawn, then no correlation exists. A positive or negative correlation can be categorized as strong or weak, depending on how closely the points are graphed around the line of best-fit.

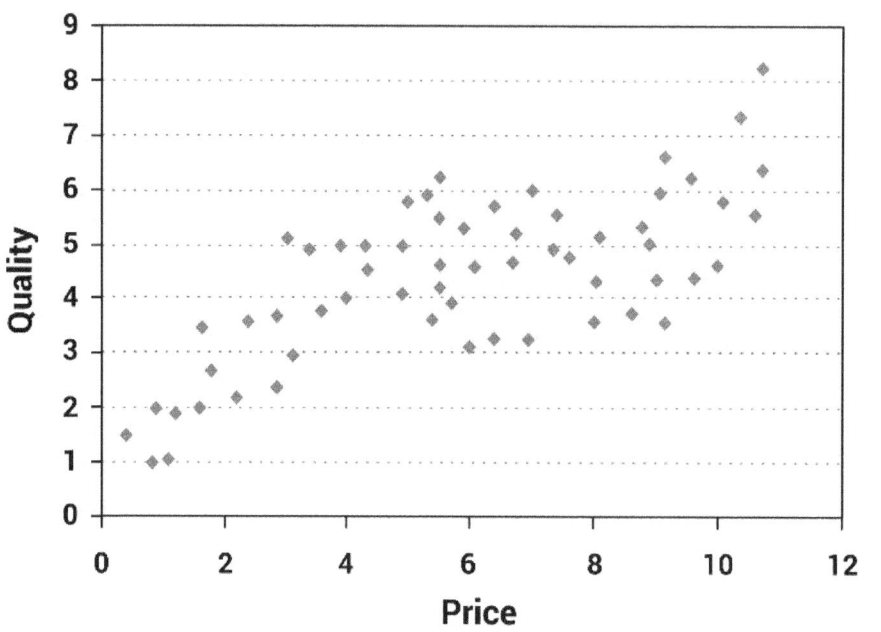

Graphical Representation of Data

Various graphs can be used to visually represent a given set of data. Each type of graph requires a different method of arranging data points and different calculations of the data. Examples of histograms, box plots, and scatter plots are discussed in the previous section *Interpreting Displays of Data*. To construct a histogram, the range of the data points is divided into equal intervals. The frequency for each interval is then determined, which reveals how many points fall into each interval. A graph is constructed with the vertical axis representing the frequency and the horizontal axis representing the intervals. The lower value of each interval should be labeled along the horizontal axis. Finally, for each interval, a bar is drawn from the lower value of each interval to the lower value of the next interval with a height equal to the frequency of the interval. Because of the intervals, histograms do not have any gaps between bars along the horizontal axis.

Quantitative Reasoning and Mathematics Achievement

To construct a box (or box-and-whisker) plot, the five-number summary for the data set is calculated as follows: the second quartile (Q_2) is the median of the set. The first quartile (Q_1) is the median of the values below Q_2. The third quartile (Q_3) is the median of the values above Q_2. The upper extreme is the highest value in the data set if it is not an outlier (greater than 1.5 times the interquartile range $Q_3 - Q_1$). The lower extreme is the least value in the data set if it is not an outlier (more than 1.5 times lower than the interquartile range).

To construct the box-and-whisker plot, each value is plotted on a number line, along with any outliers. The box consists of Q_1 and Q_3 as its top and bottom and Q_2 as the dividing line inside the box. The whiskers extend from the lower extreme to Q_1 and from Q_3 to the upper extreme.

Box Plot

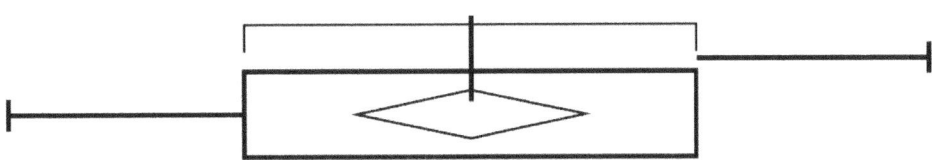

A scatter plot displays the relationship between two variables. Values for the independent variable, typically denoted by x, are paired with values for the dependent variable, typically denoted by y. Each set of corresponding values are written as an ordered pair (x, y). To construct the graph, a coordinate grid is labeled with the x-axis representing the independent variable and the y-axis representing the dependent variable. Each ordered pair is graphed.

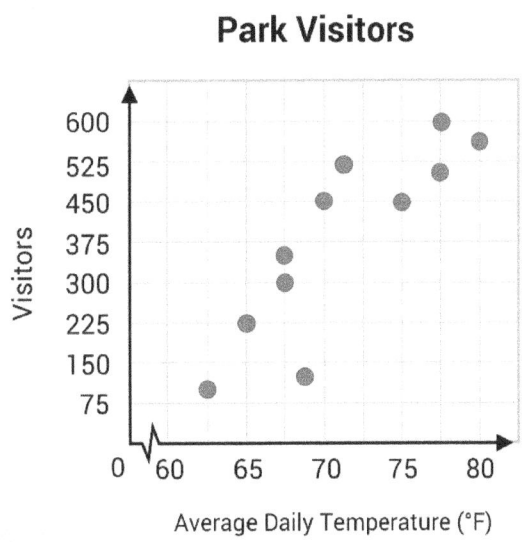

Like a scatter plot, a line graph compares variables that change continuously, typically over time. Paired data values (ordered pairs) are plotted on a coordinate grid with the x- and y-axis representing the variables. A line is drawn from each point to the next, going from left to right.

Quantitative Reasoning and Mathematics Achievement

The line graph below displays cell phone use for given years (two variables) for men, women, and both sexes (three data sets).

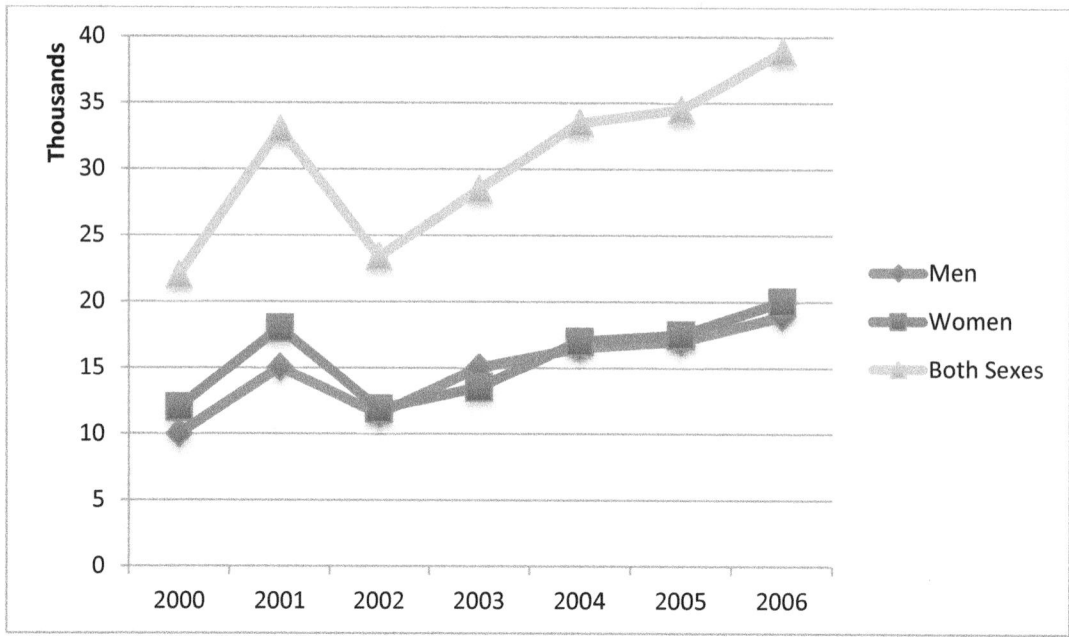

A line plot, also called dot plot, displays the frequency of data (numerical values) on a number line. To construct a line plot, a number line is used that includes all unique data values. It is marked with x's or dots above the value the number of times that the value occurs in the data set.

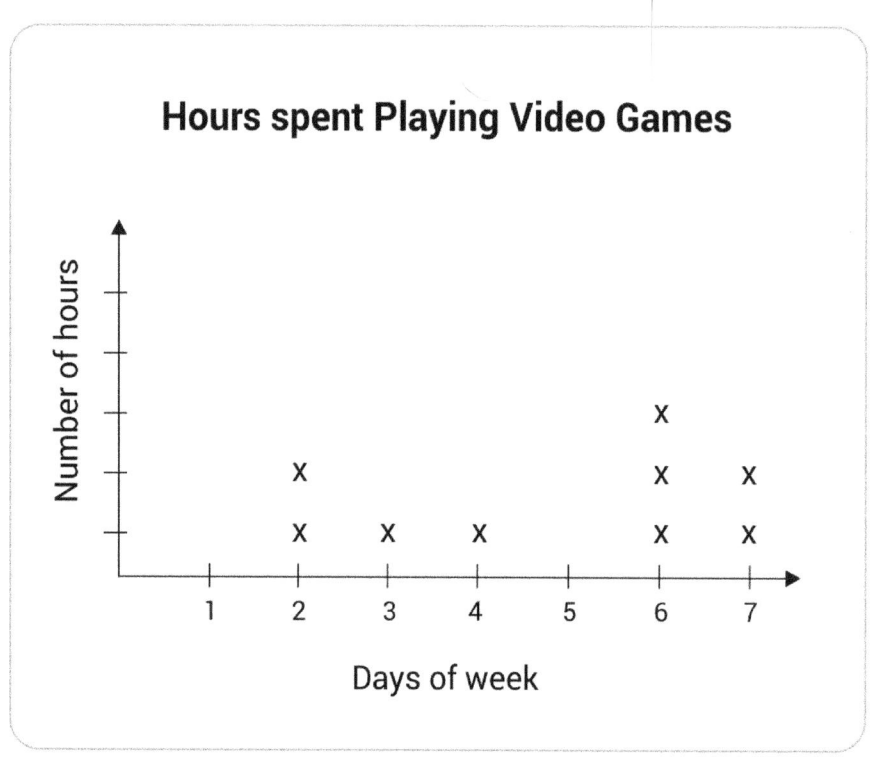

Quantitative Reasoning and Mathematics Achievement

A bar graph looks similar to a histogram but displays categorical data. The horizontal axis represents each category and the vertical axis represents the frequency for the category. A bar is drawn for each category (often different colors) with a height extending to the frequency for that category within the data set. A double bar graph displays two sets of data that contain data points consisting of the same categories.

The double bar graph below indicates that two girls and four boys like Pad Thai the most out of all the foods, two boys and five girls like pizza, and so on.

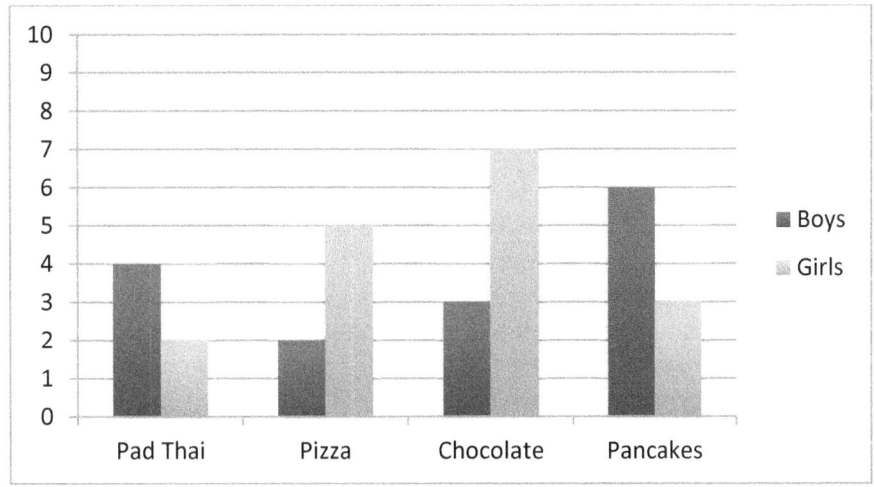

A circle graph, also called a pie chart, displays categorical data with each category representing a percentage of the whole data set. To construct a circle graph, the percent of the data set for each category must be determined. To do so, the frequency of the category is divided by the total number of data points and converted to a percent. For example, if 80 people were asked their favorite pizza topping and 20 responded cheese, then cheese constitutes 25% of the data ($\frac{20}{80} = .25 = 25\%$).

Each category in a data set is represented by a **slice** of the circle proportionate to its percentage of the whole.

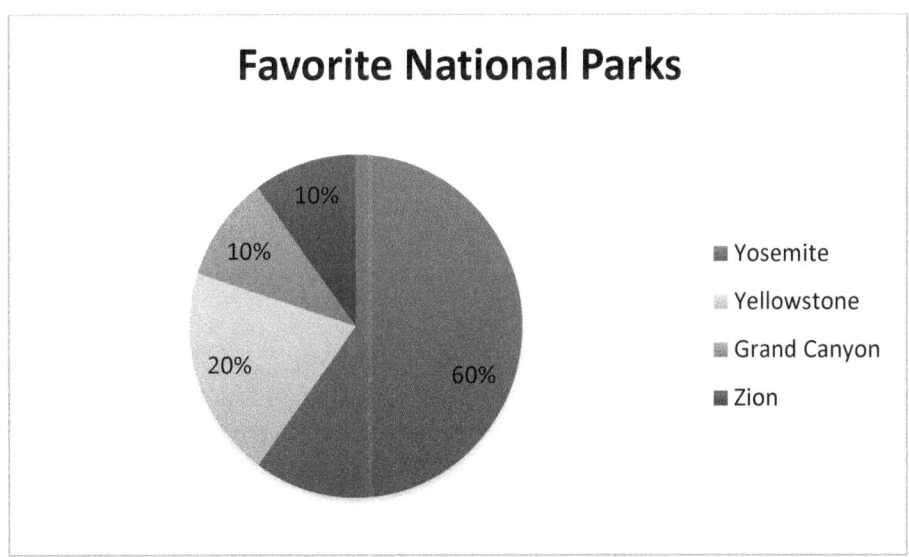

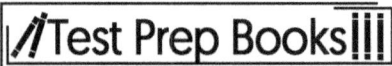

Choice of Graphs to Display Data

Choosing the appropriate graph to display a data set depends on what type of data is included in the set and what information must be displayed. Histograms and box plots can be used for data sets consisting of individual values across a wide range. Examples include test scores and incomes. Histograms and box plots will indicate the center, spread, range, and outliers of a data set. A histogram will show the shape of the data set, while a box plot will divide the set into quartiles (25% increments), allowing for comparison between a given value and the entire set.

Scatter plots and line graphs can be used to display data consisting of two variables. Examples include height and weight, or distance and time. A correlation between the variables is determined by examining the points on the graph. Line graphs are used if each value for one variable pairs with a distinct value for the other variable. Line graphs show relationships between variables.

Line plots, bar graphs, and circle graphs are all used to display categorical data, such as surveys. Line plots and bar graphs both indicate the frequency of each category within the data set. A line plot is used when the categories consist of numerical values. For example, the number of hours of TV watched by individuals is displayed on a line plot. A bar graph is used when the categories consist of words. For example, the favorite ice cream of individuals is displayed with a bar graph. A circle graph can be used to display either type of categorical data. However, unlike line plots and bar graphs, a circle graph does not indicate the frequency of each category. Instead, the circle graph represents each category as its percentage of the whole data set.

Probabilities Relative to Likelihood of Occurrence

Probability is a measure of how likely an event is to occur. Probability is written as a fraction between zero and one. If an event has a probability of zero, the event will never occur. If an event has a probability of one, the event will definitely occur. If the probability of an event is closer to zero, the event is unlikely to occur. If the probability of an event is closer to one, the event is more likely to occur. For example, a probability of $\frac{1}{2}$ means that the event is equally as likely to occur as it is not to occur. An example of this is tossing a coin. The probability of an event can be calculated by dividing the number of favorable outcomes by the number of total outcomes. For example, suppose you have 2 raffle tickets out of 20 total tickets sold. The probability that you win the raffle is calculated:

$$\frac{number\ of\ favorable\ outcomes}{total\ number\ of\ outcomes} = \frac{2}{20} = \frac{1}{10} \text{ (always reduce fractions)}$$

Therefore, the probability of winning the raffle is $\frac{1}{10}$ or 0.1.

Chance is the measure of how likely an event is to occur, written as a percent. If an event will never occur, the event has a 0% chance. If an event will certainly occur, the event has a 100% chance. If an event will sometimes occur, the event has a chance somewhere between 0% and 100%. To calculate chance, probability is calculated, and the fraction is converted to a percent.

The probability of multiple events occurring can be determined by multiplying the probability of each event. For example, suppose you flip a coin with heads and tails, and roll a six-sided die numbered one through six. To find the probability that you will flip heads AND roll a two, the probability of each event is determined, and those fractions are multiplied. The probability of flipping heads is $\frac{1}{2}$ ($\frac{1\ side\ with\ heads}{2\ sides\ total}$), and the probability of rolling a two is $\frac{1}{6}$ ($\frac{1\ side\ with\ a\ 2}{6\ total\ sides}$). The probability of flipping heads AND rolling a 2 is:

$$\frac{1}{2} \times \frac{1}{6} = \frac{1}{12}$$

The above scenario with flipping a coin and rolling a die is an example of independent events. Independent events are circumstances in which the outcome of one event does not affect the outcome of the other event. Conversely, dependent events are ones in which the outcome of one event affects the outcome of the second event. Consider the following scenario: a bag contains 5 black marbles and 5 white marbles. What is the probability of picking 2 black marbles without replacing the marble after the first pick?

The probability of picking a black marble on the first pick is $\frac{5}{10}$ $\left(\frac{5\ black\ marbles}{10\ total\ marbles}\right)$. Assuming that a black marble was picked, there are now 4 black marbles and 5 white marbles for the second pick. Therefore, the probability of picking a black marble on the second pick is $\frac{4}{9}$ $\left(\frac{4\ black\ marbles}{9\ total\ marbles}\right)$. To find the probability of picking two black marbles, the probability of each is multiplied:

$$\frac{5}{10} \times \frac{4}{9} = \frac{20}{90} = \frac{2}{9}$$

Practice Quiz

Word Problems

1. Kaleigh is completing a school workbook at a rate of 3 pages every 50 minutes. If she continues to complete the workbook at the same rate, how long is the workbook if she completes the entire thing in 30 hours?
    a. 500 pages
    b. 2 pages
    c. 108 pages
    d. 88 pages

2. The total cost of 50 identical textbooks is x dollars. What is the total cost of 80 of these same textbooks in terms of x?
    a. $\frac{30}{x}$
    b. $3x$
    c. $\frac{8}{5}x$
    d. $\frac{5}{8}x$

Quantitative Comparisons

3.

Quantity A	Quantity B
The number of odd integers between -8 and 8	The number of even integers between -8 and 8

   a. Quantity A is greater.
   b. Quantity B is greater.
   c. The two quantities are equal.
   d. The relationship cannot be determined from the information givens

Mathematics Achievement

4. $(6 + 9) \times 14 \div 10 + (3^2 - 9 + 1) =$ _____
    a. 16
    b. 21
    c. 17.4
    d. 22

5. Calculate the following quantity: 40% of $2\frac{7}{10}$.
    a. $\frac{27}{25}$
    b. $\frac{27}{100}$
    c. $\frac{7}{25}$
    d. $\frac{25}{27}$

See answers on the next page.

Answer Explanations

Word Problems

1. C: 30 hours is equal to $30 \cdot 60 = 1800$ minutes. We can set up a proportion to solve this. Let x be equal to the number of pages in the workbook. Therefore,

$$\frac{3}{50} = \frac{x}{1800}$$

Cross-multiply to obtain $5400 = 50x$. Then, divide by 50 to obtain $x = 108$.

2. B: The price of each textbook is equal to $\frac{x}{50}$. Therefore, the total cost of 80 textbooks would be $80\left(\frac{x}{50}\right) = \frac{8}{5}x$.

Quantitative Comparisons

3. A: The odd integers between -8 and 8 are -7, -5, -3, -1, 1, 3, 5, and 7. There are 8 of them. The even integers between -8 and 8 are -6, -4, -2, 0, 2, 4, and 6. There are 7 of them. Quantity A is greater.

Mathematics Achievement

4. D: We must follow order of operations. The quantities in the parentheses are calculated first. Inside the second set of parentheses, the exponent is calculated first. Therefore, we have $15 \times 14 \div 10 + (9 - 9 + 1)$. Then, inside the parentheses, the addition and subtraction are performed from left to right, leaving us with $15 \times 14 \div 10 + 1$. Next, the multiplication is performed, resulting in $210 \div 10 + 1$. Then, the division is performed: $21 + 1$, leaving us with a final answer of 22.

5. A: First, we convert the mixed number to an improper fraction, resulting in $2\frac{7}{10} = \frac{2 \cdot 10 + 7}{10} = \frac{27}{10}$. Then we convert 40% to a fraction: $40\% = 0.4 = \frac{4}{10}$. Calculating 40% of $2\frac{7}{10}$ is the same as multiplying $\frac{4}{10} \cdot \frac{27}{10} = \frac{108}{100} = \frac{27}{25}$.

Reading Comprehension

The Reading Comprehension section of the ISEE Upper Level exam consists of six passages, each followed by 6 questions. The questions will test the student's abilities in the areas of main idea, supporting ideas, inference, vocabulary, organization/logic, and tone/style/figurative language.

Main Idea

Topic Versus the Main Idea

Typically, in a piece of narrative writing there are only a couple of ideas that the author is trying to convey to the reader. It is very important to know the difference between the **topic** and the **main idea** of the text. Even though these two are similar because they both present the central point of a text, they have distinctive differences. A **topic** is the subject of the text; This can usually be described in a concise one- to two-word phrase. A topic might be "horses." On the other hand, the **main idea** is more detailed and provides the author's central point of the text. It can be expressed through a complete sentence and is often found in the beginning, the middle, or at the end of a paragraph. A main idea might be, "Racehorses run faster when they have a good relationship with the jockey." Here are some guidelines, tips, and tricks to follow that will help identify the main idea:

Identifying the Main Idea
The most important part of the text
Text title and pictures may reveal clues
Opening sentences and final sentences may reveal clues
Key vocabulary words that are repeatedly used may reveal clues

In most nonfiction books, the first sentence of the passage usually (but not always) states the main idea. Take a look at the passage below to review the **topic** versus the **main idea**:

Cheetahs

Cheetahs are one of the fastest mammals on the land, reaching up to 70 miles an hour over short distances. Even though cheetahs can run as fast as 70 miles an hour, they usually only have to run half that speed to catch up with their choice of prey. Cheetahs cannot maintain a fast pace over long periods of time because they will overheat their bodies. After a chase, cheetahs need to rest for approximately 30 minutes prior to eating or returning to any other activity.

In the example above, the *topic* of the passage is "Cheetahs" simply because that is the subject of the text. The *main idea* of the text is "Cheetahs are one of the fastest mammals on the land but can only maintain a fast pace for shorter distances." While it covers the topic, it is more detailed and refers to the text in its entirety. The text continues to provide additional details called **supporting details**.

Theme

The **theme** of a text is the central message of the story. The theme can be about a moral or lesson that the author wants to share with the audience. Although authors do not directly state the theme of a story, it is the "big picture" that they intend readers to walk away with. For example, the fairy tale *The Boy Who Cried Wolf* features the tale of a little boy who continued to lie about seeing a wolf. When the little boy actually saw a wolf, no one believed him because of all of the previous lies. The author of this fairy tale does not directly tell readers, "Don't lie because people will question the credibility of the story." The author simply portrays the story of the little boy and presents the moral through the tale.

The theme of a text centers around varying subjects such as courage, friendship, love, bravery, facing challenges, or adversity. It often leaves readers with more questions than answers. Authors tend to insinuate certain themes in texts; however, readers are left to interpret the true meaning of the story.

Message

An author's **message** is the same as the overall meaning of a passage. It is the main idea, or the main concept that the author wishes to convey. An author's message may be stated outright, or it may be implied. Regardless, the test taker will need to use careful reading skills to identify an author's message or purpose.

Often, the message of a particular passage can be determined by thinking about why the author wrote the information. Many historical passages are written to inform and to teach readers established, factual information. However, many historical works are also written to convey biased ideas to readers. Gleaning bias from an author's message in a historical passage can be difficult, especially if the reader is presented with a variety of established facts as well. Readers tend to accept historical writing as factual. This is not always the case. Any discerning reader who has tackled historical information on topics such as United States political party agendas can attest that two or more works on the same topic may have completely different messages supporting or refuting the value of the identical policies. Therefore, it is important to critically assess an author's message separate from factual information. One author, for example, may point to the rise of unorthodox political candidates in an election year based on the failures of the political party in office while another may point to the rise of the same candidates in the same election year based on the current party's successes. The historical facts of what has occurred leading up to an election year are not in refute. Labeling those facts as a failure or a success is a bias within an author's overall message, as is excluding factual information in order to further a particular point. In a standardized testing situation, a reader must be able to critically assess what the author is trying to say separate from the historical facts that surround their message.

Using the example of Lincoln's Gettysburg Address, a test question may ask the following:

> What message is the speaker trying to convey through this address?

Then they will ask the test taker to select an answer that best expresses Lincoln's message to his audience. Based on the options given, a test taker should be able to select the answer expressing the idea that Lincoln's audience should recognize the efforts of those who died in the war as a sacrifice to preserving human equality and self-government.

Supporting Ideas

Locating Details

Supporting details of texts are defined as those elements of a text that help readers make sense of the main idea. They either qualitatively and/or quantitatively describe the main idea, strengthening the reader's understanding.

Supporting details answer questions like *who, what, where, when, why,* and *how*. Different types of supporting details include examples, facts and statistics, anecdotes, and sensory details.

Persuasive and informative texts often use supporting details. In persuasive texts, authors attempt to make readers agree with their points of view, and supporting details are often used as "selling points." If authors make a statement, they need to support the statement with evidence in order to adequately persuade readers. Informative texts use supporting details such as examples, facts, and details to inform readers. Take a look at the "Cheetahs" example again below to find examples of supporting details.

Cheetahs

Cheetahs are one of the fastest mammals on the land, reaching up to 70 miles an hour over short distances. Even though cheetahs can run as fast as 70 miles an hour, they usually only have to run half that speed to catch up with their choice of prey. Cheetahs cannot maintain a fast pace over long periods of time because they will overheat their bodies. After a chase, cheetahs need to rest for approximately 30 minutes prior to eating or returning to any other activity.

In the previous example, supporting details include:

- Cheetahs reach up to 70 miles per hour over short distances.
- They usually only have to run half that speed to catch up with their prey.
- Cheetahs will overheat their bodies if they exert a high speed over longer distances.
- They need to rest for 30 minutes after a chase.

Look at the diagram below (applying the cheetah example) to help determine the hierarchy of *topic, main idea,* and *supporting details.*

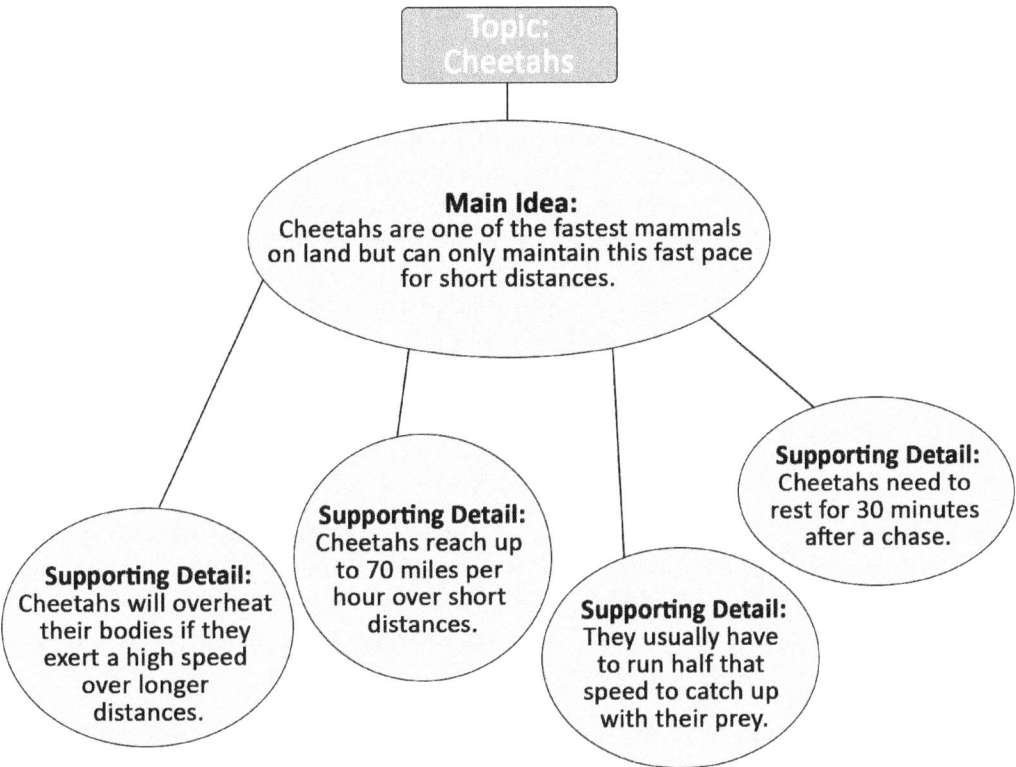

Inference

Making Inferences

Simply put, an **inference** is an educated guess drawn from evidence, logic, and reasoning. The key to making inferences is identifying clues within a passage, and then using common sense to arrive at a reasonable conclusion. Consider it "reading between the lines."

One way to make an inference is to look for main topics. When doing so, pay particular attention to any titles, headlines, or opening statements made by the author. Topic sentences or repetitive ideas can be clues in gleaning inferred ideas. For example, if a passage contains the phrase *While some consider DNA testing to be infallible, it is an inherently flawed technique,* the test taker can infer the rest of the passage will contain information that points to problems with DNA testing.

The test taker may be asked to make an inference based on prior knowledge but may also be asked to make predictions based on new ideas. For example, the test taker may have no prior knowledge of DNA other than its genetic property to replicate. However, if the reader is given passages on the flaws of DNA testing with enough factual evidence, the test taker may arrive at the inferred conclusion that the author does not support the infallibility of DNA testing in all identification cases.

When making inferences, it is important to remember that the critical thinking process involved must be fluid and open to change. While a reader may infer an idea from a main topic, general statement, or other clues, they must be open to receiving new information within a particular passage. New ideas presented by an author may require the test taker to alter an inference. Similarly, when asked questions that require making an inference, it's important to read the entire test passage and all of the answer options. Often, a test taker will need to refine a general inference based on new ideas that may be presented within the test itself.

Inferences also refer to the ability to make logical assumptions based on clues from the text. People make inferences about the world around them on a daily basis but may not be aware of what they are doing. For example, a young boy may infer that it is likely cold outside if he wakes up and his bedroom is chilly or the floor is cold. While being driven somewhere on the highway and a girl notices a person at the side of the road with a parked car, that girl will likely infer that the individual is having car problems and is awaiting some assistance. Both of these are example of how inferences are used every day and the same skill can be applied to different stories and texts.

In a way, making inferences is similar to detective work by collecting evidence. Sometimes clues can be found in the pictures or visual aids (like diagrams) that accompany a story or text. For example, a story may show a picture of a school in which all children are gathered in the parking lot. Upon closer examination, careful readers might spot a fire truck parked at the side of the road and may infer that the school had a fire drill or an actual fire.

Conclusions

Determining **conclusions** requires being an active reader, as a reader must make a prediction and analyze facts to identify a conclusion. There are a few ways to determine a logical conclusion, but careful reading is the most important. It's helpful to read a passage a few times, noting details that seem important to the text. A reader should also identify key words in a passage to determine the logical conclusion or determination that flows from the information presented.

Textual evidence helps readers draw a conclusion about a passage. **Textual evidence** refers to information—facts and examples that support the main point; it will likely come from outside sources and can be in the form of quoted or paraphrased material. In order to draw a conclusion from evidence, it's important to examine the credibility and validity of that evidence as well as how (and if) it relates to the main idea.

If an author presents a differing opinion or a **counterargument** in order to refute it, the reader should consider how and why the information is being presented. It is meant to strengthen the original argument and shouldn't be confused with the author's intended conclusion, but it should also be considered in the reader's final evaluation.

Sometimes, authors explicitly state the conclusion they want readers to understand. Alternatively, a conclusion may not be directly stated. In that case, readers must rely on the implications to form a logical conclusion:

> On the way to the bus stop, Michael realized his homework wasn't in his backpack. He ran back to the house to get it and made it back to the bus just in time.

In this example, though it's never explicitly stated, it can be inferred that Michael is a student on his way to school in the morning. When forming a conclusion from implied information, it's important to read the text carefully to find several pieces of evidence to support the conclusion.

Synthesis

Synthesis also requires a reader to make inferences while reading. Inference has been addressed earlier in this guide. Review the section and take note of the required skills in making inferences.

In order to achieve synthesis and full reading comprehension, a reader must take their prior knowledge, the knowledge or main ideas an author presents, and fill in the gaps to reach a logical conclusion. In a testing situation, a test taker may be asked to infer ideas from a given passage, asked to choose from a set of inferences that best express a summary of what the author hints at, or arrive at a logical conclusion based on their inferences. This is not an easy task, but it is approachable.

While inference requires a reader to make educated guesses based on stated information, it's important that the reader does not assume too much. It's important that the reader does not insert information into a passage that's not there. It's important to make an inference based solely on the presented information and to make predictions using a logical thought process.

After reviewing the earlier section on making inferences, keep the following in mind:

- Do not jump to conclusions early in the passage. Read the full text before trying to infer meaning.
- Rely on asking questions. What is the author stating? What is the author not saying? What information is missing? What conclusions can be made about that missing information, if any.
- Make an inference then apply it back to the text passage. Does the inference make sense? Is it likely an idea with which the author would agree?
- What inferences can be made from any data presented? Are these inferences sound and logical?

While this is not an exhaustive list of questions related to making inferences, it should help the reader with the skill of synthesis in achieving full reading comprehension.

Vocabulary

Deriving the Meaning of a Word or Phrase from its Context

It's common to find words that aren't familiar in writing. When you don't know a word, there are some "tricks" that can be used to find out its meaning. *Context clues* are words or phrases in a sentence or paragraph that provide hints about a word and what it means. For example, if an unknown word is attached to a noun with other surrounding words as clues, these can help you figure out the word's meaning. Consider the following example:

After the treatment, Grandma's natural rosy cheeks looked *wan* and ghostlike.

The word we don't know is *wan*. The first clue to its meaning is in the phrase *After the treatment,* which tells us that something medical possibly happened. A second clue is the word *rosy*, which describes Grandma's natural cheek color that changed after the treatment. Finally, the word *ghostlike* infers that Grandma's cheeks now look white. By using the context clues in the sentence, we can figure out that the meaning of the word *wan* means *pale*.

Contrasts
Look for context clues that **contrast** the unknown word. When reading a sentence with a word we don't know, look for an opposite word or idea. Here's an example:

Since Mary didn't cite her research sources, she lost significant points for *plagiarizing* the content of her report.

In this sentence, *plagiarizing* is the word we don't know. Notice that when Mary *didn't cite her research sources,* it resulted in her losing points for *plagiarizing the content of her report*. These contrasting ideas tell us that Mary did something wrong with the content. This makes sense because the definition of *plagiarizing* is "taking the work of someone else and passing it off as your own."

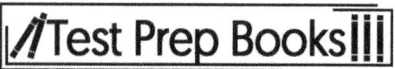

Reading Comprehension

Contrasts often use words like *but, however, although,* or phrases like *on the other hand*. For example:

    The *gargantuan* television won't fit in my car, but it will cover the entire wall in the den.

The word we don't know is *gargantuan*. Notice that the television is too big to fit in a car, <u>but it will cover the entire wall in the den</u>. This tells us that the television is extremely large. The word *gargantuan* means *enormous*.

Synonyms

Another way to find out a word you don't know is to think of synonyms for that word. **Synonyms** are words with the same meaning. To do this, replace synonyms one at a time. Then read the sentence after each synonym to see if the meaning is clear. By replacing a word we don't know with a word we do know, it's easier to uncover its meaning. For example:

    Gary's clothes were *saturated* after he fell into the swimming pool.

In this sentence, we don't know the word *saturated*. To brainstorm synonyms for *saturated*, think about what happens to Gary's clothes after falling into the swimming pool. They'd be *soaked* or *wet*. These both turn out to be good synonyms to try. The actual meaning of *saturated* is "thoroughly soaked."

Antonyms

Sometimes sentences contain words or phrases that oppose each other. Opposite words are known as **antonyms**. An example of an antonym is *hot* and *cold*. For example:

    Although Mark seemed *tranquil*, you could tell he was actually nervous as he paced up and down the hall.

The word we don't know is *tranquil*. The sentence says that Mark was in fact not *tranquil*. He was *actually nervous*. The opposite of the word *nervous* is *calm*. *Calm* is the meaning of the word *tranquil*.

Explanations or Descriptions

Explanations or descriptions of other things in the sentence can also provide clues to an unfamiliar word. Take the following example:

    Golden Retrievers, Great Danes, and Pugs are the top three *breeds* competing in the dog show.

We don't know the word *breeds*. Look at the sentence for a clue. The subjects (*Golden Retrievers, Great Danes,* and *Pugs*) describe different types of dogs. This description helps uncover the meaning of the word *breeds*. The word *breeds* means "a particular type of animal."

Inferences

Inferences are clues to an unknown word that tell us its meaning. These inferences can be found within the sentence where the word appears. Or, they can be found in a sentence before the word or after the word. Look at the following example:

    The *wretched* old lady was kicked out of the restaurant. She was so mean and nasty to the waiter!

Here, we don't know the word *wretched*. The first sentence says that the *old lady was kicked out of the restaurant*, but it doesn't say why. The sentence after tells us why: *She was so mean and nasty to the waiter!* This infers that the old lady was *kicked out* because she was *so mean and nasty* or, in other words, *wretched*.

When you prepare for a vocabulary test, try reading harder materials to learn new words. If you don't know a word on the test, look for prefixes and suffixes to find out what the word means and get rid of wrong answers. If two

Reading Comprehension

answers both seem right, see if there are any differences between them. Then select the word that best fits. Context clues in the sentence or paragraph can also help you find the meaning of a word you don't know. By learning new words, a person can expand their knowledge. They can also improve the quality of their writing.

Organization/Logic

Recognizing the Structure of Texts in Various Formats

Writing can be classified under four passage types: narrative, expository, descriptive (sometimes called technical), and persuasive. Though these types are not mutually exclusive, one form tends to dominate the rest. By recognizing the *type* of passage you're reading, you gain insight into *how* you should read. If you're reading a narrative, you can assume the author intends to entertain, which means you may skim the text without losing meaning. A technical document might require a close read because skimming the passage might cause the reader to miss salient details.

Narrative
Narrative writing, at its core, is the art of storytelling. A narrative can either be fiction or nonfiction, although in order to still be categorized as a narrative, certain elements need to be present. A narrative must have:

- **Plot**: what happens in the story, or what is going to happen
- **Series of events**: beginning, middle, and end, but not necessarily in that order
- **Characters**: people, animals, or inanimate objects
- **Figurative language**: metaphors, similes, personification, etc.
- **Setting**: when and where the story takes place

Expository
Expository writing is designed to instruct or inform. It sometimes involves directions and steps written in second person ("you" voice), lacking any persuasive or narrative elements. Sequence words such as *first*, *second*, and *third*, or *in the first place*, *secondly*, and *lastly* are often given to add fluency and cohesion. Common examples of expository writing include instructor's lessons, cookbook recipes, and repair manuals.

Because expository passages are meant to educate readers, they often do not use flamboyant language, unless the subject area requires it. Expository passages can also be informative texts written as memoirs or autobiographies.

Biography
A **biography** is a work written about a real person (historical or currently living). It involves factual accounts of the person's life, often in a re-telling of those events based on available, researched factual information. The re-telling and dialogue, especially if related within quotes, must be accurate and reflect reliable sources. A biography reflects the time and place in which the person lived, with the goal of creating an understanding of the person and their human experience. Examples of well-known biographies include *The Life of Samuel Johnson* by James Boswell and *Steve Jobs* by Walter Isaacson.

Autobiography
An **autobiography** is a factual account of a person's life written by that person. It may contain some or all of the same elements as a biography, but the author is the subject matter. An autobiography will be told in first person narrative. Examples of well-known autobiographies in literature include *Night* by Elie Wiesel and *Margaret Thatcher: The Autobiography* by Margaret Thatcher.

Memoir
A **memoir** is a historical account of a person's life and experiences written by one who has personal, intimate knowledge of the information. The line between memoir, autobiography, and biography is often muddled, but

generally speaking, a memoir covers a specific timeline of events as opposed to the other forms of nonfiction. A memoir is less all-encompassing. It is also less formal in tone and tends to focus on the emotional aspect of the presented timeline of events. Some examples of memoirs in literature include *Angela's Ashes* by Frank McCourt and *All Creatures Great and Small* by James Herriot.

Descriptive or Technical

Due to its empirical nature, **descriptive** or **technical writing** can be filled with steps, charts, graphs, data, and statistics. **Technical** passages are written to describe how to do or make something. Technical passages are often manuals or guides written in a very organized and logical manner. The texts usually have outlines with subtitles and very little jargon. The vocabulary used in technical passages is very straightforward so as not to confuse readers. Technical texts often explore cause and effect relationships and can also include authors' purposes.

Persuasive

Persuasive passages are written with the intent to convince readers to agree with the author's viewpoint on the subject. Authors generally stick to one main point and present smaller arguments that concur with the initial central claim. The author's intent or purpose is to persuade readers by presenting them with evidence or clues (such as facts, statistics, and observations) to make them stray away from their own thoughts on the matter and agree with the author's ideas. By using evidence and clues to support their ideas, authors may or may not be strategically placing strong thoughts and emotions in their readers' minds, causing them to lean in one direction more than the other.

Organization of the Text

The **structure of the text** is how authors organize information in their writing. The organization of text depends on the authors' intentions and writing purposes for the text itself. Text structures can vary from paragraph to paragraph or from piece to piece, depending on the author. There are various types of patterns in which authors can organize texts, some of which include problem and solution, cause and effect, chronological order, and compare and contrast. These four text structures are described below.

Problem and Solution

One way authors can organize their text is by following a **problem and solution** pattern. This type of structure may present the problem first without offering an immediately clear solution. The problem and solution pattern may also offer the solution first and then hint at the problem throughout the text. Some texts offer multiple solutions to the same problem, which then leaves the decision as to the "best" solution to the minds of readers.

Even though the problem and solution text may seem easy to recognize, it is often confused with another organizational text pattern, cause and effect. One way of determining the difference between the two patterns is by searching for key words that indicate a problem and solution organizational text pattern is being followed, such as *propose, answer, prevention, issue, fix,* and *problematic*. Also, in problem and solution patterned texts, solutions are offered to all problems, even negative problems, unlike the cause-and-effect pattern.

Cause and Effect

Cause and effect is one of the more common ways that authors organize texts. In a cause and effect patterned text, the author explains what caused something to happen. For example, "It rained, so we got all wet." In this sentence, the cause is "the rain," and the effect is "we got all wet." Authors tend to use key words such as *because, as a result, due to, effected, caused, since, in order,* and *so* when writing cause and effect patterned texts.

Persuasive and expository writing models frequently use a cause and effect organizational pattern as well. In **persuasive texts**, authors try to convince readers to sway their opinions to align with the authors' thoughts. Authors may use cause and effect patterns or relationships to present supporting evidence to try to persuade the readers' judgment on a particular subject.

In **expository texts**, authors write to inform and educate readers about certain subjects. By using cause and effect patterns in expository writing, authors show relationships between events—basically, how one event may affect the other in chronological order.

Chronological Order
When using a **chronological order** organizational pattern, authors simply state information in the order in which it occurs. Nonfiction texts often include specific dates listing events in chronological order (such as timelines), whereas fiction texts may list events in order but not provide detailed dates (such as describing a daily routine: wake up, eat breakfast, get dressed, and so on). Narratives usually follow the chronological order pattern of beginning, middle, and end, with the occasional flashback in between.

Compare and Contrast
The **compare and contrast** organizational text pattern explores the differences and similarities of two or more objects. If authors describe how two or more objects are similar, they are comparing the items. If they describe how two or more objects are different, they are contrasting them. In order for texts to follow a compare and contrast organizational pattern, authors must include both similarities and differences within the text and hold each to the same guidelines. The following Venn diagram compares and contrasts oranges and apples.

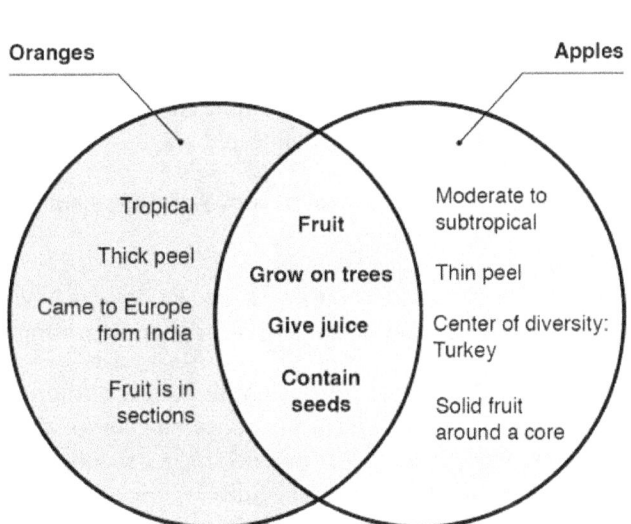

Compare and Contrast Example

In this diagram, readers should notice how the author uses the same guidelines when comparing and contrasting oranges and apples. The origin, peel type, climate, outcomes, and classifications are all used for both fruits. The author does not use different categories for each fruit to compare or contrast the two fruits.

Even though authors may agree or disagree with each side of an argument, they should remain impartial when presenting the facts in a compare and contrast text(s). Authors should present all information using neutral language and allow readers to form their individual conclusions about the subject matter. Authors tend to use key words such as *like, unlike, different, similar, both,* and *neither* when following a compare and contrast pattern.

Overall, organization of texts helps readers better understand an author's intent and purpose.

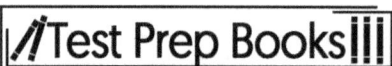

Summarizing

Summarizing is a strategy in which readers determine what is important throughout the text or passage, shorten those ideas, and rewrite or retell it in their own words. A summary should identify the main idea of the text or passage. Important details or supportive evidence should also be accurately reported in the summary. Irrelevant details in a summary may cloud the greater meaning of the text or passage. A clear summary provides clarity of the text or passage to the readers.

Tone/Style/Figurative Language

Tone

Tone refers to the writer's attitude toward the subject matter. For example, the tone conveys how the writer feels about the topic they are writing about. A lot of nonfiction writing has a neutral tone, which is an important tone for the writer to take. A neutral tone demonstrates that the writer is presenting a topic impartially and letting the information speak for itself. On the other hand, nonfiction writing can be just as effective and appropriate if the tone isn't neutral. For instance, consider this example:

> Seat belts save more lives than any other automobile safety feature. Many studies show that airbags save lives as well; however, not all cars have airbags. For instance, some older cars don't. Furthermore, air bags aren't entirely reliable. For example, studies show that in 15% of accidents, airbags don't deploy as designed; but, on the other hand, seat belt malfunctions are extremely rare. The number of highway fatalities has plummeted since laws requiring seat belt usage were enacted.

In this passage, the writer mostly chooses to retain a neutral tone when presenting information. If the writer would instead include their own personal experience of losing a friend or family member in a car accident, the tone would change dramatically. The tone would no longer be neutral and would show that the writer has a personal stake in the content, allowing them to interpret the information in a different way.

Writers also use particular words, phrases, and writing style to convey an overall meaning or tone. For example, a historical reading passage may begin like the following:

> The presidential election of 1960 ushered in a new era, a new Camelot, a new phase of forward thinking in U.S. politics that embraced brash action and unrest and responded with admirable leadership.

From this opening statement, a reader can draw some conclusions about the author's attitude towards President John F. Kennedy. Furthermore, the reader can make additional, educated guesses about the state of the Union during the 1960 presidential election. By close reading, the test taker can determine that the repeated use of the word *new* and words such as *admirable leadership* indicate the author's tone of admiration regarding President Kennedy's boldness. In addition, the author assesses that the era during President Kennedy's administration was problematic through the use of the words *brash action* and *unrest.* Therefore, if a test taker encountered a test question asking about the author's use of tone and their assessment of the Kennedy administration, the test taker should be able to identify an answer indicating admiration. Similarly, if asked about the state of the Union during the 1960s, a test taker should be able to correctly identify an answer indicating political unrest.

Reading Comprehension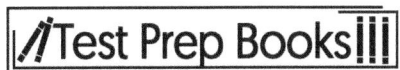

When analyzing tone, consider what the writer is trying to achieve in the text and how they *create* the tone using style. The following list of words may be helpful when identifying tone. This is not an inclusive list. Generally, parts of speech that indicate attitude will also indicate tone:

- Comical
- Angry
- Ambivalent
- Scary
- Lyrical
- Matter-of-fact
- Judgmental
- Sarcastic
- Malicious
- Objective
- Pessimistic
- Patronizing
- Gloomy
- Instructional
- Satirical
- Formal
- Casual

Style

Style can include any number of technical writing choices. A few examples of style choices include:

- Sentence Construction: When presenting facts, does the writer use shorter sentences to create a quicker sense of the supporting evidence, or do they use longer sentences to elaborate and explain the information?

- Technical Language: Does the writer use jargon to demonstrate their expertise in the subject, or do they use ordinary language to help the reader understand things in simple terms?

- Formal Language: Does the writer refrain from using contractions such as *won't* or *can't* to create a more formal tone, or do they use a colloquial, conversational style to connect to the reader?

- Formatting: Does the writer use a series of shorter paragraphs to help the reader follow a line of argument, or do they use longer paragraphs to examine an issue in great detail and demonstrate their knowledge of the topic?

Understanding the Effect of Word Choice

An author's choice of words—also referred to as **diction**—helps to convey meaning in a particular way. Through diction, an author can convey a particular tone—e.g., a humorous tone, a serious tone—in order to support the thesis in a meaningful way to the reader.

Connotation and Denotation

Connotation is when an author chooses words or phrases that invoke ideas or feelings other than their literal meaning. An example of the use of connotation is the word *cheap*, which suggests something is poor in value or negatively describes a person as reluctant to spend money. When something or someone is described this way, the reader is more inclined to have a particular image or feeling. Thus, connotation can be a very effective language tool in creating emotion and swaying opinion. However, connotations are sometimes hard to pin down because varying emotions can be associated with a word. Generally, though, connotative meanings tend to be fairly consistent within a specific cultural group.

Denotation refers to words or phrases that mean exactly what they say. It is helpful when a writer wants to present hard facts or vocabulary terms with which readers may be unfamiliar. Some examples of denotation are the words *inexpensive* and *frugal*. *Inexpensive* refers to the cost of something, not its value, and *frugal* indicates that a person is conscientiously watching their spending. These terms do not elicit the same emotions that *cheap* does.

Authors sometimes choose to use both, but what they choose and when they use it is what critical readers need to differentiate. One method isn't inherently better than the other; however, one may create a better effect depending upon an author's intent. If, for example, an author's purpose is to inform, to instruct, and to familiarize readers with a difficult subject, their use of connotation may be helpful. However, it may also undermine credibility and confuse readers. An author who wants to create a credible, scholarly effect in their text would most likely use denotation, which emphasizes literal, factual meaning and examples.

Technical Language
Test takers and critical readers alike should be very aware of technical language used within informational text. **Technical language** refers to terminology that is specific to a particular industry and is best understood by those specializing in that industry. This language is fairly easy to differentiate since it will most likely be unfamiliar to readers. It's critical to be able to define technical language either by the author's written definition, through the use of an included glossary—if offered—or through context clues that help readers clarify word meaning.

Determining the Author's Purpose

Authors want to capture the interest of the reader. An effective reader is attentive to an author's *position*. Authors write with intent, whether implicit or explicit. An author may hold a bias or use emotional language, which in turn creates a very clear *position*. Finding an author's *purpose* is usually easier than figuring out their position. An author's **purpose** of a text may be to persuade, inform, entertain, or be descriptive. Most narratives are written with the intent to entertain the reader, although some may also be informative or persuasive. When an author tries to persuade a reader, the reader must be cautious of the intent or argument. Therefore, the author keeps the persuasion lighthearted and friendly to maintain the entertainment value in narrative texts even though he or she is still trying to convince the reader of something.

An author's **purpose** will influence their writing style. As mentioned previously, the purpose can inform, entertain, or persuade a reader. If an author writes an informative text, their purpose is to educate the reader about a certain topic. Informative texts are usually nonfiction, and the author rarely states their opinion. The **purpose** of an informative text is also indicated by the outline of the text itself. In some cases, an informative text may have headings, subtitles, and bold key words. The purpose for this type of text is to educate the reader.

Entertaining texts, whether fiction or nonfiction, are meant to captivate readers' attention. Entertaining texts are usually stories that describe real or fictional people, places, or things. These narratives often use expressive language, emotions, imagery, and figurative language to captivate the readers. If readers do not want to put the entertaining text down, the author has fulfilled their purpose for this type of text.

Descriptive texts use adjectives and adverbs to describe people, places, or things to provide a clear image to the reader throughout the story. If an author fails to provide detailed descriptions, readers may find texts boring or confusing. Descriptive texts are almost always informative but can also be persuasive or entertaining pending the author's purpose.

Figurative Language

Figurative language is a specific style of speaking or writing that uses tools for a variety of effects. It entertains readers, ignites imagination, and promotes creativity. Instead of writing in realistic terms or literal terms, figurative language plays with words and prompts readers to infer the underlying meaning. As with connotative language, figures of speech tend to be shared within a cultural group and may be difficult to pick up on for learners outside of that group. In some cases, a figure of speech may be based on the literal denotation of the words it contains, but in other cases, a figure of speech is far removed from its literal meaning. A case in point is *irony*, where what is said is the exact opposite of what is meant:

> The new tax plan is poorly planned, based on faulty economic data, and unable to address the financial struggles of middle-class families. Yet legislators remain committed to passing this brilliant proposal.

When the writer refers to the proposal as brilliant, the opposite is implied—the plan is "faulty" and "poorly planned." By using irony, the writer means that the proposal is anything but brilliant by using the word in a non-literal sense.

There are several other types of figurative language:

Type	Definition	Example
Personification	Giving animate qualities to an inanimate object	The tree stood tall and still, staring up at the sky.
Simile	The comparison of two unlike things using connecting words	Your eyes are as blue as the ocean.
Metaphor	The comparison of two unlike things without the use of connecting words	Kayla is a walking encyclopedia!
Hyperbole	An over-exaggeration	I could eat a million of these cookies!
Alliteration	The patterned repetition of an initial consonant sound	The bunnies are bouncing in baskets.
Onomatopoeia	Words that are formed by using the very sound associated with the word itself	"Drip, drip, drip" went the kitchen faucet.
Idioms	Common sayings that carry a lesson or meaning that must be inferred	We were sure to turn back the hands of time.

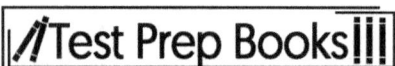

Writing Devices

Analogy
An **analogy** is a comparison between two things that are quite different from one another. Authors commonly use analogies to add meaning and make ideas relatable in texts. Metaphors and similes are specific types of analogies. Metaphors compare two things that are not similar and directly connect them. Similes also compare two unlike items but connect them using the words *like* or *as*. For example,

> In the library, Alice was asked to be as quiet as a mouse.

Clearly, Alice and a mouse are very different. However, when Alice is asked to be as quiet as a mouse, readers understand that mice are small and therefore have small and soft voices—appropriate voice noise level for the library.

Irony
Irony is a device that authors use when pitting two contrasting items or ideas against each other in order to create an effect. It's frequently used when an author wants to employ humor or convey a sarcastic tone. Additionally, it's often used in fictional works to build tension between characters or between a particular character and the reader. An author may use **verbal irony** (sarcasm), **situational irony** (where actions or events have the opposite effect than what's expected), and **dramatic irony** (where the reader knows something a character does not). Examples of irony include:

- Dramatic Irony: An author describing the presence of a hidden killer in a murder mystery, unbeknownst to the characters but known to the reader.

- Situational Irony: An author relating the tale of a fire captain who loses her home in a five-alarm conflagration.

- Verbal Irony: This is where an author or character says one thing but means another. For example, telling a police officer "Thanks a lot" after receiving a ticket.

Point of View
Point of view is the perspective in which authors tell stories. Authors can tell stories in either the first or third person. When authors write in the first person, they are a character within a story telling about their own experiences. The pronouns *I* and *we* are used when writing in the first person. If an author writes in the third person, the narrator (the person telling the story) is telling the story from an outside perspective and is completely detached from the story. The author is not a character in the story, but rather tells about the characters' actions and dialogues. Pronouns such as *he, she, it,* and *they* are used in texts written in the third person.

Transitional Words and Phrases
There are approximately 200 transitional words and phrases that are commonly used in the English language. Below are lists of common transition words and phrases used throughout transitions:

- Time
    - After
    - Before
    - During
    - In the middle

- Example about to be Given
    - For example
    - In fact
    - For instance
- Compare
    - Likewise
    - Also
- Contrast
    - However
    - Yet
    - But
- Addition
    - And
    - Also
    - Furthermore
    - Moreover
- Logical Relationships
    - If
    - Then
    - Therefore
    - As a result
    - Since
- Steps in a Process
    - First
    - Second
    - Last

Transitional words and phrases are important writing devices because they connect sentences and paragraphs. Transitional words and phrases present logical order to writing and provide more coherent meaning to readers.

Practice Quiz

Questions 1–5 are based on the following passage:

[1]Although many Missourians know that Harry S. Truman and Walt Disney hailed from their great state, probably far fewer know that it was also home to the remarkable George [3]Washington Carver. At the end of the Civil War, Moses Carver, the slave owner who owned George's parents, decided to keep George and his brother and raise them on his farm. As a [5]child, George was driven to learn and he loved painting. He even went on to study art while in college but was encouraged to pursue botany instead. He spent much of his life helping others [7]by showing them better ways to farm; his ideas improved agricultural productivity in many countries. One of his most notable contributions to the newly emerging class of Black farmers [9]was to teach them the negative effects of agricultural monoculture (i.e., growing the same crops in the same fields year after year, depleting the soil of much needed nutrients and [11]resulting in a lesser crop yield). Carver was an innovator, always thinking of new and better ways to do things, and is most famous for his over three hundred uses for the peanut. Toward [13]the end of his career, Carver returned to his first love of art. Through his artwork, he hoped to inspire people to see the beauty around them and to do great things themselves. When [15]Carver died, he left his money to help fund ongoing agricultural research. Today, people still visit and study at the George Washington Carver Foundation at Tuskegee Institute.

1. Which of the following describes the kind of writing used in the above passage?
    a. Narrative
    b. Persuasive
    c. Technical
    d. Expository

2. According to the passage, what was George Washington Carver's first love?
    a. Plants
    b. Art
    c. Animals
    d. Soil

3. According to the passage, what is the best definition for agricultural monoculture?
    a. The practice of producing or growing a single crop or plant species over a wide area and for a large number of consecutive years
    b. The practice of growing a diversity of crops and rotating them from year to year
    c. The practice of growing crops organically to avoid the use of pesticides
    d. The practice of charging an inflated price for cheap crops to obtain a greater profit margin

4. Which of the following is the best summary of this passage?
    a. George Washington Carver was born at a time when scientific discovery was at a virtual standstill.
    b. Because he was African American, there were not many opportunities for George Washington Carver.
    c. George Washington Carver was an intelligent man whose research and discoveries had an impact worldwide.
    d. George Washington Carver was far more successful as an artist than he was as a scientist.

Reading Comprehension

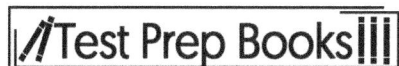

5. Which of the following is closest in meaning to the word *hailed* as it is used in line 1 of the passage:
   a. Flagged down
   b. Praised
   c. Originated
   d. Frozen rain

See answers on the next page.

Answer Explanations

1. D: Expository writing involves straightforward, factual information and analysis. It is unbiased and does not rely on the writer's personal feelings or opinions. Choice *A* is incorrect because narrative writing tells a story. Choice *B* is incorrect because persuasive writing is intended to change the reader's mind or position on a topic. Choice *C* is incorrect because technical writing attempts to outline a complex object or process.

2. B: The passage begins by describing Carver's childhood fascination with painting and later returns to this point when it states that at the end of his career "Carver returned to his first love of art." For this reason, all the other answer choices are incorrect.

3. A: This is the correct answer choice because the passage contains a definition of the term, *agricultural monoculture*, which is very similar to this answer.

4. C: There is ample evidence in the passage that refers to Carver's brilliance and the fact that his discoveries had a far-reaching impact both then and now. There is no evidence in the passage to support any of the other answer choices.

5. C: *Hailed* means originated, or "came from." The other choices, also synonyms for hailed, do not fit in the context of the sentence.

Essay

The Short Overview

The essay may seem challenging, but following these steps can help writers focus:

- Take one to two minutes to think about the topic.
- Generate some ideas through brainstorming (three to four minutes).
- Organize ideas into a brief outline, selecting just three to four main points to cover in the essay
- Develop essay in parts:
    o Introduction paragraph, with intro to topic and main points
    o Viewpoint on the subject at the end of the introduction
    o Body paragraphs, based on outline, each should make a main point, explain the viewpoint, and use examples to support the point
    o Brief conclusion highlighting the main points and closing
- Read over the essay (last five minutes).
- Look for any obvious errors, making sure that the writing makes sense.

Writing an essay can be overwhelming, and performance panic is a natural response. The outline serves as a basis for the writing and help writers keep focused. Getting stuck can also happen, and it's helpful to remember that brainstorming can be done at any time during the writing process. Following the steps of the writing process is the best defense against writer's block.

Timed essays can be particularly stressful, but assessors are trained to recognize the necessary planning and thinking for these timed efforts. Using the plan above and sticking to it helps with time management. Timing each part of the process helps writers stay on track. Sometimes writers try to cover too much in their essays. If time seems to be running out, this is an opportunity to determine whether all of the ideas in the outline are necessary. Three body paragraphs are sufficient, and more than that is probably too much to cover in a short essay.

More isn't always *better* in writing. A strong essay will be clear and concise. It will avoid unnecessary or repetitive details. It is better to have a concise, five-paragraph essay that makes a clear point, than a ten-paragraph essay that doesn't. The goal is to write one to two pages of quality writing. Paragraphs should also reflect balance; if the introduction goes to the bottom of the first page, the writing may be going off-track or may be repetitive. It's best to fall into the one to two-page range, but a complete, well-developed essay is the ultimate goal.

Parts of the Essay

The **introduction** has to do a few important things:

- Establish the **topic** of the essay in original wording (i.e., not just repeating the prompt)
- Clarify the significance/importance of the topic or purpose for writing. This should provide a brief overview rather than share too many details.
- Offer a **thesis statement** that identifies the writer's own viewpoint on the topic. Typically, the thesis statement is one or two brief sentences that offer a clear, concise explanation of the main point on the topic.

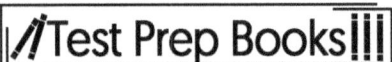

Body paragraphs reflect the ideas developed in the outline. Three or four points is probably sufficient for a short essay, and they should include the following:

- A **topic sentence** that identifies the sub-point (e.g., a reason why, a way how, a cause or effect)
- A detailed **explanation** of each sub-point, explaining why the writer thinks each point is valid
- **Illustrative examples**, such as personal examples or real-world examples, that support and validate the point (i.e., "prove" the point)
- A **concluding sentence** that connects the examples, reasoning, and analysis to the point being made

The **conclusion,** or final paragraph, should be brief and should reiterate the focus, clarifying why the discussion is significant or important. It is important to avoid adding specific details or new ideas to this paragraph. The purpose of the conclusion is to sum up what has been said to bring the discussion to a close.

Practice Makes Prepared Writers

Like any other useful skill, writing only improves with practice. While writing may come more easily to some than others, it is still a skill to be honed and improved. Regardless of a person's natural abilities, there is always room for growth in writing. Practicing the basic skills of writing can aid in preparations for the ISEE.

One way to build vocabulary and enhance exposure to the written word is through reading. This can be through reading books, but reading of any materials such as newspapers, magazines, and even social media count towards practice with the written word. This also helps to enhance critical reading and thinking skills, through analysis of the ideas and concepts read. Think of each new reading experience as a chance to sharpen these skills.

Planning

Brainstorming

One of the most important steps in writing an essay is prewriting. Before drafting an essay, it's helpful to think about the topic for a moment or two, in order to gain a more solid understanding of the task. Then, spending about five minutes jotting down the immediate ideas that could work for the essay is recommended. Brainstorming is a way to get some words on the page and offer a reference for ideas when drafting. Scratch paper is provided for writers to use any prewriting techniques such as webbing, free writing, or listing. The goal is to get ideas out of the mind and onto the page.

In the planning stage, it's important to consider all aspects of the topic, including different viewpoints on the subject. There are more than two ways to look at a topic, and a strong argument considers those opposing viewpoints. Considering opposing viewpoints can help writers present a fair, balanced, and informed essay that shows consideration for all readers. This approach can also strengthen an argument by recognizing and potentially refuting opposing viewpoint(s).

Drawing from personal experience may help to support ideas. For example, if the goal for writing is a personal narrative, then the story should come from the writer's own life. Many writers find it helpful to draw from personal experience, even in an essay that is not strictly narrative. Personal anecdotes or short stories can help to illustrate a point in other types of essays as well.

Once the ideas are on the page, it's time to turn them into a solid plan for the essay. The best ideas from the brainstorming results can then be developed into a more formal outline.

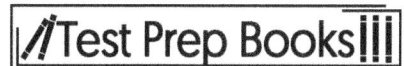

Outlining

An **outline** is a system used to organize writing. When reading texts, outlining is important because it helps readers organize important information in a logical pattern using Roman numerals. Usually, outlines start out with the main idea(s) and then branch out into subgroups or subsidiary thoughts or subjects. The outline should be methodical, with at least two main points followed each by at least two subpoints. Outlines provide a visual tool for readers to reflect on how events, characters, settings, or other key parts of the text or passage relate to one another. They can also lead readers to a stronger conclusion. The sample below demonstrates what a general outline looks like.

- I. Main Topic 1
    - a. Subtopic 1
    - b. Subtopic 2
        - 1. Detail 1
        - 2. Detail 1
- II. Main Topic 2
    - a. Subtopic 1
    - b. Subtopic 2
        - 1. Detail 1
        - 2. Detail 2

Free Writing

Like brainstorming, **free writing** is another prewriting activity to help the writer generate ideas. This method involves setting a timer for 2 or 3 minutes and writing down all ideas that come to mind about the topic using complete sentences. Once time is up, review the sentences to see what observations have been made and how these ideas might translate into a more coherent direction for the topic. Even if sentences lack sense as a whole, this is an excellent way to get ideas onto the page in the very beginning stages of writing. Using complete sentences can make this a bit more challenging than brainstorming, but overall, it is a worthwhile exercise, as it may force the writer to come up with more complete thoughts about the topic.

Writing

Now it comes time to actually write your essay. Follow the outline you developed in the brainstorming process and try to incorporate the sentences you wrote in the free writing exercise.

Basing the essay on the outline aids in both organization and coherence. The goal is to ensure that there is enough time to develop each sub-point in the essay, roughly spending an equal amount of time on each idea. Keeping an eye on the time will help. If there are fifteen minutes left to draft the essay, then it makes sense to spend about 5 minutes on each of the ideas. Staying on task is critical to success and timing out the parts of the essay can help writers avoid feeling overwhelmed.

During the essay portion of a test, leaving a few minutes at the end to revise and proofread offers an opportunity for writers to polish things up. Putting one's self in the reader's shoes and focusing on what the essay actually says

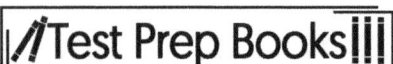

helps writers identify problems—it's a movement from the mindset of writer to the mindset of editor. The goal is to have a clean, clear copy of the essay. The following areas should be considered when proofreading:

- Sentence fragments
- Awkward sentence structure
- Run-on sentences
- Incorrect word choice
- Grammatical agreement errors
- Spelling errors
- Punctuation errors
- Capitalization errors

Developing a Well-Organized Paragraph

Forming Paragraphs

A good **paragraph** should have the following characteristics:

- Be logical with organized sentences
- Have a unified purpose within itself
- Use sentences as building blocks
- Be a distinct section of a piece of writing
- Present a single theme introduced by a topic sentence
- Maintain a consistent flow through subsequent, relevant, well-placed sentences
- Tell a story of its own or have its own purpose, yet connect with what is written before and after
- Enlighten, entertain, and/or inform

Though certainly not set in stone, the length should be a consideration for the reader's sake, not merely for the sake of the topic. When paragraphs are especially short, the reader might experience an irregular, uneven effect; when they're much longer than 250 words, the reader's attention span, and probably their retention, is challenged. While a paragraph can technically be a sentence long, a good rule of thumb is for paragraphs to be at least three sentences long and no more than ten sentence long. An optimal word length is 100 to 250 words.

Main Point of a Paragraph

What is the main point of a paragraph? It is *the* point all of the other important and lesser important points should lead up to, and it should be summed up in the topic sentence.

Sometimes there is a fine line between a paragraph's topic sentence and its main point. In fact, they actually might be one and the same. Often, though, they are two separate, but closely related, aspects of the same paragraph.

Depending upon the purpose of the essay, the topic sentence or the paragraph's main point might not be fully revealed until the paragraph's conclusion.

Sometimes, while developing paragraphs, one might deviate from the main point, which means they have to delete and rework their materials to stay on point.

Coherent Paragraphs

Coherence is simply defined as the quality of being logical and consistent. In order to have coherent paragraphs, the writing must be logical and consistent. The **topic sentence**, usually the first in a paragraph, holds the essential features that will be brought forth in the paragraph. The topic sentence can either grab or lose the reader's attention. The coherent paragraph progresses from the topic sentence in a logical order. It utilizes transitional words and phrases, parallel sentence structure, clear pronoun references, and reasonable repetition of key words and phrases. Synonyms should be considered for variety. Verb tense should remain consistent.

A paragraph's purpose should be accomplished before moving on to the next paragraph. To ensure that the purpose has been conveyed, while writing, the paragraph should be read over and edited as needed. Paragraphs should not go on too long: information can be broken up into a few paragraphs if necessary and logical. Also, if a paragraph doesn't seem to fully accomplish its purpose, it should be revised before the next paragraph is written. Before a paragraph can be considered complete, the main point should be identifiable and the related sentences should stay on point.

Distinguishing Between Formal and Informal Language

It is important to be able to distinguish between formal or informal language and to implement the most appropriate and effective one for a given situation. One would use formal language to write an informative or argumentative essay. Formal language is less personal and more informative and pragmatic than informal language. It is more "buttoned-up" and business-like, adhering to proper grammatical rules. Formal language avoids contractions, slang, colloquialisms, and first-person pronouns. **Slang** refers to non-standard expressions that are not used in elevated speech and writing. Slang creates linguistic in-groups and out-groups of people, those who can understand the slang terms and those who can't. Slang is often tied to a specific time period. For example, "groovy" and "far out" are connected to the 1970s, and "as if!" and "4-1-1-" are connected to the 1990s. **Colloquial language** is language that is used conversationally or familiarly—e.g., "What's up?"—in contrast to formal, professional, or academic language—"How are you this evening?" Formal language uses sentences that are usually more complex and often in passive voice. Punctuation can differ as well. For example, **exclamations point (!)** are used to show strong emotion or can be used as an interjection but should be used sparingly in formal writing situations.

Informal language is often used when communicating with family members, friends, peers, and those known more personally. It is more casual, spontaneous, and forgiving in its conformity to grammatical rules and conventions. Informal language is used for personal emails, some light fiction stories, and some correspondence between coworkers or other familial relationships. The tone is more relaxed, and slang, contractions, clichés, and the first and second person may be used in writing. The imperative voice may be used as well.

Point of View

The perspectives from which something may be written or conveyed are detailed below:

- First-person point of view: This is told from the writer's perspective. In fiction, this would mean that the main character is also the narrator. First-person point of view is easily recognized by the use of personal pronouns such as *I, me, we, us, our, my,* and *myself.*

- Second-person point of view: This point of view isn't commonly used in fiction or nonfiction writing because it directly addresses the reader using the pronouns *you, your,* and *yourself.* Second-person perspective is more appropriate in direct communication, such as business letters or emails.

- Third-person point of view: In a more formal essay, this would be an appropriate perspective because the focus should be on the subject matter, not the writer or the reader. Third-person point of view is recognized by the use of the pronouns *he, she, they,* and *it.*

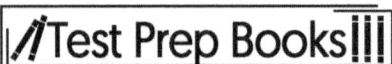

Tips for the Essay

- Don't panic! This section isn't scored. It's just a great way to show teachers how smart you are and how well you can tell a story and write. You can do it!

- Use your time well. 30 minutes is quick! Don't spend too much time doing any one thing. Try to brainstorm briefly and then get writing. Leave a few minutes to read it over and correct any spelling mistakes or confusing parts.

- Be yourself! You are smart and interesting, and teachers want to get to know you and your unique ideas. Don't feel pressured to use big vocabulary words if you aren't positive what they mean. You will be more understandable if you use the right word, not the fanciest word.

Practice Essay

You have 30 minutes to plan and write your essay. Do not worry too much about length; it's most important to focus on the content and quality of your writing.

Describe your favorite family tradition and explain why it is important to you.

Practice Test #1

Verbal Reasoning

Synonyms

1. DEDUCE
    a. Explain
    b. Gamble
    c. Reason
    d. Undo

2. ELUCIDATE
    a. Conscious
    b. Corroborate
    c. Enlighten
    d. Learn

3. VERIFY
    a. Criticize
    b. Resolve
    c. Substantiate
    d. Teach

4. INSPIRE
    a. Collaborate
    b. Exercise
    c. Motivate
    d. Patronize

5. PERCEIVE
    a. Comprehend
    b. Lead
    c. Prove
    d. Sustain

6. NOMAD
    a. Blissful
    b. Conscientious
    c. Propose
    d. Wanderer

7. PERPLEXED
    a. Annoyed
    b. Confused
    c. Injured
    d. Prepared

Practice Test #1

8. LYRICAL
   a. Expressive
   b. Playful
   c. Vague
   d. Whimsical

9. BREVITY
   a. Ancient
   b. Brief
   c. Calamity
   d. Dullness

10. IRATE
    a. Angry
    b. Confused
    c. Taciturn
    d. Tired

11. LUXURIOUS
    a. Bright
    b. Faded
    c. Lavish
    d. Overwhelming

12. IMMOBILE
    a. Fast
    b. Sedentary
    c. Slow
    d. Vivacious

13. OVERBEARING
    a. Amicable
    b. Clandestine
    c. Domineering
    d. Formidable

14. AVERT
    a. Endow
    b. Ensure
    c. Prevent
    d. Rejoice

15. REPLENISH
    a. Dwell
    b. Falsify
    c. Nominate
    d. Refresh

16. REGALE
    a. Entertain
    b. Grow
    c. Outnumber
    d. Remember

17. WEARY
    a. Clothing
    b. Hot
    c. Tired
    d. Whiny

18. VAST
    a. Expansive
    b. Ocean
    c. Rapid
    d. Small

19. DEMONSTRATE
    a. Build
    b. Complete
    c. Make
    d. Show

Sentence Completion

For the next questions, choose the best word(s) to fill in the blank(s) in each sentence.

20. The paramedic's _____ response during _____ moments made him an excellent fit for working in emergency services.
    a. composed/insignificant
    b. expeditious/critical
    c. foolhardy/catastrophic
    d. nonchalant/perilous

21. The candidate's political promises were met with _____ reactions from the public, as many questioned the sincerity and feasibility of her proposed policies.
    a. accepting
    b. amenable
    c. dubious
    d. exuberant

22. Despite the challenging circumstances, Jaci approached her new responsibilities with remarkable _____, eager to contribute and have a positive impact on the team.
    a. alacrity
    b. apathy
    c. indifference
    d. reluctance

23. Natalia's years of hard work and planning finally came to _____ when she successfully opened her own bakery in the heart of the city.
    a. closure
    b. deterioration
    c. fruition
    d. interruption

24. The animal rehabilitator felt _____ about her work, but found it to be _____ when she saw injured animals who might not make it.
    a. educated/spontaneous
    b. fierce/agitating
    c. passionately/distressing
    d. sympathetic/challenging

25. The neighborhood's _____ was evident in the luxurious mansions, upscale boutiques, and exclusive restaurants that lined the streets.
    a. affluence
    b. barrenness
    c. congeniality
    d. decrepitude

26. Although many consider a college degree to be _____ for getting a high-paying job, there are many tradesmen, such as plumbers, who make _____ money without formal education.
    a. essential/trivial
    b. futile/substantial
    c. mandatory/significant
    d. necessity/negligible

27. When the boy saw how sincere the girl's apology was, he decided to _____ her of her faults.
    a. acquire
    b. acquit
    c. stall
    d. quit

28. Genevieve was feeling _____ when she gave the homeless man a ten-dollar bill, but quickly switched to feeling _____ when he aggressively demanded even more.
    a. banal/dignified
    b. charitable/regretful
    c. miserly/rapacious
    d. philanthropy/avaricious

29. When she saw the crayon drawings on the wall, the mother had no choice but to _____ her sons.
    a. choose
    b. disown
    c. honor
    d. rebuke

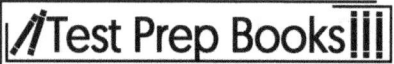

30. Normally, I enjoy hearing new music that has an edgy sound; however, the _____ of the tones and beats of the music tonight made me want to cover my ears.
    a. accord
    b. concordance
    c. dissonance
    d. harmony

31. The company had a(n) _____ rate of high turnover, yet they remained _____ about taking measures to prevent people from continuing to leave.
    a. alarming/unperturbed
    b. catastrophe/proactive
    c. distressed/nonchalant
    d. negligible/inattentive

32. The woman's dirty and disheveled outfit was a(n) _____ from her usual tidy wardrobe.
    a. aberration
    b. altercation
    c. distraction
    d. selection

33. There was one particular NFL football player who consistently delivered abrupt and _____ answers when the media approached him after the game.
    a. interesting
    b. obnoxious
    c. tedious
    d. terse

34. Jennifer struggled to find a _____ balance between her work life and personal life, especially due to the _____ demands of her children that were never-ending.
    a. feasible/incessant
    b. impartial/interminable
    c. inconsistent/predictable
    d. reasonable/sporadically

35. The teacher recognized the average writing style of the freshman because his essays used _____ language.
    a. apt
    b. astute
    c. disappointing
    d. mediocre

36. The two countries went through months of _____ peace negotiations before finally deciding on a ceasefire that would be _____ to both nations.
    a. enraging/disadvantageous
    b. fruitless/confounding
    c. hostile/beneficial
    d. triumphant/detrimental

37. Walking through the heavily wooded park by the river in October, I was amazed at the beautiful colors of the _____, the bright blue sky, and the crystal-clear water.
    a. fauna
    b. foliage
    c. orchard
    d. ravine

38. Jeremy showed great _____ as he took months to learn how to walk again following a severe car accident.
    a. apathy
    b. benevolence
    c. tenacity
    d. wariness

39. The skilled hacker was _____ in his efforts of breaching the government's database, but couldn't figure out how to get past the _____ defense system no matter how many times he tried.
    a. fervent/feeble
    b. hesitant/compromised
    c. persistent/impenetrable
    d. triumphant/incomprehensible

40. The judge was _____ on Jenny's extreme shoplifting case, only giving her seventy-two hours in jail due to the _____ effect that a longer stay would have on her young children.
    a. impartial/inconsequential
    b. lenient/detrimental
    c. merciless/profound
    d. stringent/traumatizing

Quantitative Reasoning

Word Problems

1. The variable y is directly proportional to x. If $y = 3$ when $x = 5$, then what is y when $x = 20$?
    a. 10
    b. 12
    c. 14
    d. 16

2. The hospital has a nurse-to-patient ratio of $1:25$. If there are a maximum of 325 patients admitted at a time, how many nurses are there?
    a. 12 nurses
    b. 13 nurses
    c. 25 nurses
    d. 325 nurses

3. Greg buys a $10 lunch with 5% sales tax. He leaves a $2 tip after paying his bill. How much money does he spend?
    a. $12.00
    b. $12.50
    c. $13.00
    d. $13.25

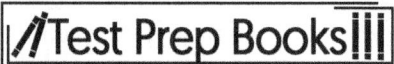

Practice Test #1

4. Taylor works two jobs. The first pays $20,000 per year. The second pays $10,000 per year. She donates 15% of her income to charity. How much does she donate each year?
   a. $4,500
   b. $5,000
   c. $5,500
   d. $6,000

5. Suppose an investor deposits $1,200 into a bank account that accrues 1 percent interest per month. Assuming x represents the number of months since the deposit and y represents the money in the account, which of the following exponential functions models the scenario?
   a. $y = (0.01)(1,200^x)$
   b. $y = (1.01)(1,200^x)$
   c. $y = (1,200)(0.01^x)$
   d. $y = (1,200)(1.01^x)$

6. Mom's car drove 72 miles in 90 minutes. There are 5,280 feet per mile. Which of the following equations would be used to calculate how fast she drove in feet per second?
   a. $\frac{72\ mi \times 90\ min}{5,280\ ft} \times 60\ s$
   b. $\frac{90\ min \times 5,280\ ft \times 72\ mi}{60\ s}$
   c. $\frac{72\ mi \times 5,280\ ft}{90\ min}$
   d. $\frac{72\ mi}{90\ min} \times \frac{1\ min}{60\ s} \times \frac{5,280\ ft}{1\ mi}$

7. A family purchased a vehicle in 2005 for $20,000. In 2010, they decided to sell the car for $8,000. By what percentage did the value of the family's car drop?
   a. 33%
   b. 40%
   c. 60%
   d. 68%

8. On May 1, 2010, a couple purchased a house for $100,000. On September 1, 2016, the couple sold the house for $93,000 so they could purchase a bigger one to start a family. How many months did they own the house?
   a. 54 months
   b. 76 months
   c. 85 months
   d. 93 months

9. A shipping box has a length of 8 inches, a width of 14 inches, and a height of 4 inches. If all three dimensions are doubled, what is the relationship between the volume of the new box and the volume of the original box?
   a. The volume of the new box is double the volume of the original box.
   b. The volume of the new box is four times as large as the volume of the original box.
   c. The volume of the new box is six times as large as the volume of the original box.
   d. The volume of the new box is eight times as large as the volume of the original box.

10. The phone bill is calculated each month using the equation $c = 50g + 75$. The cost of the phone bill per month is represented by c, and g represents the gigabytes of data used that month. What is the value and interpretation of the slope of this equation?
    a. 50 dollars per day
    b. 50 dollars per gigabyte
    c. 75 dollars per day
    d. 75 gigabytes per day

11. Which of the following equations best represents the problem below?

    The width of a rectangle is 2 centimeters less than the length. If the perimeter of the rectangle is 44 centimeters, then what are the dimensions of the rectangle?

    a. $(l + 2) + (l + 2) + l = 44$
    b. $l \times (l - 2) = 44$
    c. $2l + 2(l - 2) = 44$
    d. $(l + 2) + (l + 2) + l = 48$

12. A company invests $50,000 in a building where they can produce saws. If the cost of producing one saw is $40, then which function expresses the total amount of money the company spends on producing saws? The variable y is the money paid, and x is the number of saws produced.
    a. $y = 40x - 50{,}000$
    b. $y = 40x + 50{,}000$
    c. $y = 50{,}000x + 40$
    d. $y + 40 = x - 50{,}000$

13. A piggy bank contains 12 dollars' worth of nickels. A nickel weighs 5 grams, and the empty piggy bank weighs 1,050 grams. What is the total weight of the full piggy bank?
    a. 1,110 grams
    b. 1,200 grams
    c. 2,200 grams
    d. 2,250 grams

Questions 14 and 15 are based on the following stem-and-leaf plot:

The following stem-and-leaf plot shows plant growth in cm for a group of tomato plants:

Stem	Leaf
2	0 2 3 6 8 8 9
3	2 6 7 7
4	7 9
5	4 6 9

14. What is the range of measurements for the tomato plants' growth?
    a. 29 cm
    b. 37 cm
    c. 39 cm
    d. 59 cm

15. How many plants grew more than 35 cm?
    a. 4 plants
    b. 5 plants
    c. 8 plants
    d. 9 plants

16. Five students took a test. Jenny scored the highest with a 94. James scored the lowest with a 79. Hector scored lower than Jenny, but higher than Sam. Sam scored lower than Mary who scored an 84. Which of the following statements must be true?
    a. Hector scored lower than Mary.
    b. Jenny is the only student who scored above 90.
    c. The median test score was an 84.
    d. There were 3 people who scored higher than Sam.

17. Because of an increase in demand, the price of a designer purse has increased 25% from the original price of $128. What is the new price of the purse?
    a. $32
    b. $96
    c. $160
    d. $192

18. Which of the following is equivalent to the value of the digit 3 in the number 792.134?
    a. 3×10
    b. 3×100
    c. $\frac{3}{10}$
    d. $\frac{3}{100}$

19. Write the following number in standard form: $(1 \times 10^4) + (3 \times 10^3) + (7 \times 10^1) + (8 \times 10^0)$
    a. 137
    b. 3,780
    c. 8,731
    d. 13,078

20. If Danny takes 48 minutes to walk 3 miles, how long should it take him to walk 5 miles maintaining the same speed?
    a. 32 min
    b. 64 min
    c. 80 min
    d. 96 min

21. A construction company is building a new housing development with the property of each house measuring 30 feet wide. If the length of the street is zoned off at 345 feet, how many houses can be built on the street?
    a. 10 houses
    b. 11 houses
    c. 11.5 houses
    d. 12 houses

Quantitative Comparison

For questions 22–37, compare Quantity A to Quantity B, using additional information presented above the two quantities if provided:

22. h is an integer in the following mathematical series: 4, h, 19, 39, 79

Quantity A	Quantity B
The value of h	9

    a. Quantity A is greater.
    b. Quantity B is greater.
    c. The two quantities are equal.
    d. The relationship cannot be determined from the information given.

23.

g inches

[Rectangle: Area = 56 square inches, 4 inches]

Quantity A	Quantity B
The value of g	13

a. Quantity A is greater.
b. Quantity B is greater.
c. The two quantities are equal.
d. The relationship cannot be determined from the information given.

24. $4x - 12 = -2x$

Quantity A	Quantity B
The value of x	3

a. Quantity A is greater.
b. Quantity B is greater.
c. The two quantities are equal.
d. The relationship cannot be determined from the information given.

25.

Jimmy	Steve
7 red marbles	6 green marbles
8 blue marbles	4 blue marbles

Quantity A	Quantity B
All of Jimmy's marbles divided by all of Steve's marbles	Jimmy's blue marbles divided by Steve's green marbles

a. Quantity A is greater.
b. Quantity B is greater.
c. The two quantities are equal.
d. The relationship cannot be determined from the information given.

Practice Test #1

26.

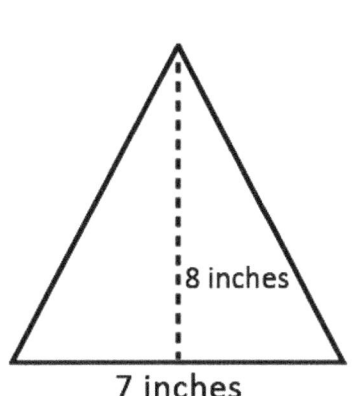

Quantity A	Quantity B
7 times the area of the triangle	2 times the area of the rectangle

a. Quantity A is greater.
b. Quantity B is greater.
c. The two quantities are equal.
d. The relationship cannot be determined from the information given.

27. Truck A drives 1,236 yards and truck B drives 3,680 feet.

Quantity A	Quantity B
The distance that truck A drove	The distance that truck B drove

a. Quantity A is greater.
b. Quantity B is greater.
c. The two quantities are equal.
d. The relationship cannot be determined from the information given.

28. $x > 6 > z$

Quantity A	Quantity B
$x + z$	$x - 6$

a. Quantity A is greater.
b. Quantity B is greater.
c. The two quantities are equal.
d. The relationship cannot be determined from the information given.

29. There are 16 rocks in a bag. 12 of them are smooth and 4 of them are rough.

Quantity A	Quantity B
The probability of choosing a rough rock	$\frac{2}{8}$

a. Quantity A is greater.
b. Quantity B is greater.
c. The two quantities are equal.
d. The relationship cannot be determined from the information given.

30. Bill is four years older than Jim.

Quantity A	Quantity B

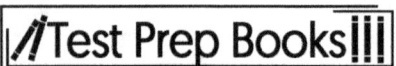

        Twice Jim's age   Bill's age

a. Quantity A is greater.
b. Quantity B is greater.
c. The two quantities are equal.
d. The relationship cannot be determined from the information given.

31. Angie has more cats than Janet.

        Quantity A   Quantity B
    Angie's number of cats   4 more than Janet's number of cats

a. Quantity A is greater.
b. Quantity B is greater.
c. The two quantities are equal.
d. The relationship cannot be determined from the information given.

32. Gage is twice as old as Cam.

        Quantity A   Quantity B
        Cam's age   Half of Gage's age

a. Quantity A is greater.
b. Quantity B is greater.
c. The two quantities are equal.
d. The relationship cannot be determined from the information given.

33.

        Quantity A   Quantity B
Largest prime number less than 35   Smallest prime number greater than 25

a. Quantity A is greater.
b. Quantity B is greater.
c. The two quantities are equal.
d. The relationship cannot be determined from the information given.

34.

        Quantity A   Quantity B
     28% of 345 $\frac{1}{5}$ of 300

a. Quantity A is greater.
b. Quantity B is greater.
c. The two quantities are equal.
d. The relationship cannot be determined from the information given.

35.

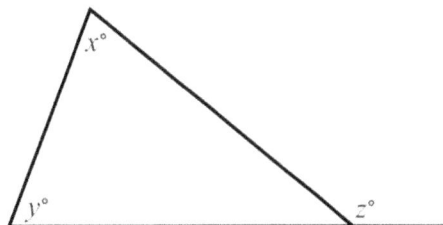

Quantity A	Quantity B
$x + y$	z

a. Quantity A is greater.
b. Quantity B is greater.
c. The two quantities are equal.
d. The relationship cannot be determined from the information given.

36.

Quantity A	Quantity B
Circumference of a circle with radius 4 cm	Perimeter of a rectangle with sides 5 cm and 7 cm

a. Quantity A is greater.
b. Quantity B is greater.
c. The two quantities are equal.
d. The relationship cannot be determined from the information given.

37. A square has side length l. A new square is formed by tripling the length of l.

Quantity A	Quantity B
The area of the new square	The area of the original square tripled

a. Quantity A is greater.
b. Quantity B is greater.
c. The two quantities are equal.
d. The relationship cannot be determined from the information given.

Reading Comprehension

Passage 1

¹In recent years, some modern approaches to public transportation have made significant additions to conventional modes, such as city buses, subways, and taxis. ³Private transportation has become convenient and affordable to anyone with access to the Internet.

⁵One of the most well-known modern transportation companies is Uber. Uber employs individuals to pick up and drop off riders with the touch of a button. When a rider needs ⁷to be picked up, they simply log into the Uber app and request a car. Once the app verifies the rider's location, a driver

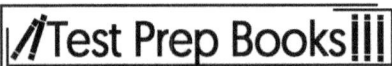

arrives for pick-up within minutes. Payment for the [9]ride is done through the app, so riders don't need to worry about carrying cash in order to catch a ride.

[11]Uber is a great resource; it is commonly used by adult commuters. Smaller cities have launched their own versions of Uber. For example, Deer Park, Texas, created DeerHaul. [13]DeerHaul operates under the same idea as Uber, only it caters to kids. Many working parents find it difficult to transport their children themselves during work hours, and [15]DeerHaul is a viable alternative. If a child needs to be picked up from school and dropped off at Little League baseball practice, but his or her parents can't leave work, a [17]ride with DeerHaul can be arranged. All DeerHaul drivers are previous or current teachers who have passed a battery of fingerprint background checks. Like Uber, [19]DeerHaul rides are arranged through an internet app, and all payments are handled electronically, so no cash is exchanged between the child and the driver.

1. What is the author's tone in the passage?
    a. Hopeful
    b. Humorous
    c. Concerned
    d. Positive

2. Which statement about DeerHaul is best supported by the passage?
    a. DeerHaul is a convenient way for parents to transport their kids.
    b. DeerHaul takes no special safety measures to ensure safe rides for kids.
    c. DeerHaul is a better transportation option than Uber.
    d. Anyone can apply to be a driver for DeerHaul.

3. According to the passage, how are payments handled for private transportation?
    a. Bus or subway tickets are purchased.
    b. Riders pay the driver at the end of each ride.
    c. Tipping drivers with cash is always appreciated.
    d. Rides are paid for electronically when the ride is requested.

4. In line 18, the word *battery* most nearly means
    a. cell.
    b. artillery.
    c. series.
    d. violence.

5. How could this passage be categorized?
    a. Persuasive
    b. Informative
    c. Narrative
    d. Creative

6. Which of the following best describes the subject matter of the passage?
    a. Two modes of private transportation are explained.
    b. The best method of private transportation is discussed.
    c. The analysis of one transportation company is refuted by the analysis of a second company.
    d. Conventional transportation methods are compared to more modern transportation.

Practice Test #1

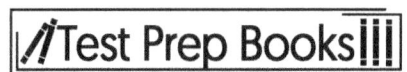

Passage 2

[1]Rudolph the Red-Nosed Reindeer hasn't always been an iconic staple in the tradition of Christmas. In 1939, Montgomery Ward department stores gave Robert L. May an [3]assignment that would change the tradition of Christmas around the world. May, a copywriter for Montgomery Ward, was asked to create a promotional Christmas [5]coloring book. The coloring book was to be a gift for children from the store Santa. Montgomery Ward hoped the gift would increase store traffic.

[7]The poem, "A Visit from St. Nicholas," published in 1823, originally depicted eight flying reindeer as members of Santa's team. In 1939, May added Rudolph. May's story depicts [9]Rudolph as a misfit among the other reindeer because of his red nose. Rudolph has the opportunity to prove his worth as he leads Santa's team through a blizzard on Christmas [11]Eve. For this, Rudolph becomes known as "the most famous reindeer of all". At the time, Montgomery Ward officials were unsure of Rudolph's red nose because this was [13]also known as a symptom of drunkenness. However, after May and coworker Denver Gillan created a sketch of the red-nosed reindeer, officials approved the story.

[15]Montgomery Ward's promotion was a great success during the Christmas season, with 2.4 million copies of "Rudolph the Red-Nosed Reindeer" gifted from Santas in their [17]stores. In 1947, "Rudolph the Red-Nosed Reindeer" was commercially printed as a children's literature book available for purchase in bookstores.

7. Which of the following best describes the subject matter in the passage?
   a. A Montgomery Ward advertising project made Rudolph a famous Christmas tradition.
   b. Denver Gillan first created the character of Rudolph for Montgomery Ward.
   c. Robert L. May's work helped him climb the ranks at Montgomery Ward.
   d. Without Montgomery Ward's Rudolph, Christmas would have been canceled in many countries.

8. Which of the following statements can be inferred based on the information in the passage?
   a. When first presented to the public, the character of Rudolph was associated with drunkenness.
   b. Rudolph the Red-Nosed Reindeer may have never existed if the sketch had not been created.
   c. Gillan is responsible for turning Way's story into a poem.
   d. The Rudolph Christmas promotional saved Montgomery Ward from having to close many stores.

9. According to the passage, *Rudolph the Red-Nosed Reindeer* was
   a. Commercially printed in 1949
   b. Originally a promotional coloring book
   c. Part of an earlier poem called "A Visit from St. Nicholas"
   d. Written by Denver Gillan

10. In line 9, the word *misfit* most nearly means
    a. member.
    b. conformist.
    c. insider.
    d. oddball.

11. Which of the following best describes the author's tone in this passage?

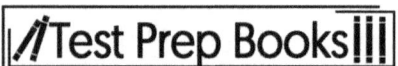

   a. Humorous
   b. Apologetic
   c. Informative
   d. Sad

12. What is the meaning of the word *iconic* in line 1?
   a. Cartoon
   b. Sarcastic
   c. Classic
   d. Essential

Passage 3

¹Water is the only substance on Earth that can occur in three states: liquid, gas, and solid. The liquid state of water is the type of water you drink, cook with, or find in ³streams and rivers. The gas form is called water vapor, or steam, and the solid, or frozen, form of water is known as ice.

⁵Water, also known as H_2O, is made up of hydrogen and oxygen atoms. These atoms join together to form water molecules.

⁷Water molecules move at various rates of speed and distances from each other depending on the state of water. When the temperature of water reaches its boiling ⁹point at 212°F, water molecules move more rapidly and spread farther apart, allowing some of them to escape into the air. This turns liquid water into water vapor, or steam.

¹¹On the other hand, when the temperature of liquid water becomes cooler, the water molecules begin to slow down and move closer together. Eventually, the water ¹³molecules stop moving and stick together to form a solid called ice. Conversely, when the temperature of ice becomes warmer, water molecules begin to spread apart, ¹⁵causing the ice to melt and return to a liquid state.

13. According to the passage, the water molecules of boiling water
   a. move rapidly and spread farther apart.
   b. move more slowly and spread farther apart.
   c. move closer together and slow down.
   d. move rapidly and get closer together.

14. If water vapor is formed when the temperature of water reaches 212°F, what happens to water vapor when it rises into the air and cools?
   a. As the water vapor cools, the molecules will return to a liquid state.
   b. The water molecules will move closer together to form a solid.
   c. The water molecules will disappear into the atmosphere.
   d. Once water becomes a gas, it always remains a gas.

15. Which of the following is the main idea of this passage?
   a. Water can exist in three different states.
   b. As water cools down, the molecules slow down and move closer together.
   c. The movement of water molecules depends on temperature.
   d. The three states of matter are liquid, gas, and solid.

16. In line 6, the word *molecules* most nearly means

a. masses.
   b. bundles.
   c. vast amounts.
   d. particles.

17. According to this passage, what state of water is steam?
    a. Liquid
    b. Gas
    c. Solid
    d. Molecule

18. In line 13, the term *conversely* most nearly means
    a. identically.
    b. comparably.
    c. similarly.
    d. the other way around.

Passage 4

[1]My friend Alyssa and I had spent most of the day getting ready. Our moms had treated us to manicures and pedicures, followed by a fancy lunch at Burgdorf's Tea Room and [3]then a trip to the hair salon for some curls and up-dos. Alyssa and I had smiled and giggled all day in disbelief that the big day had finally arrived.

[5]At seven o'clock sharp, Ricky and Bobby came to pick us up. There was an exchange of corsages and boutonnieres as our moms took an abundance of pictures to remember [7]the night. The four of us giggled and laughed as the limo driver whisked us off to the eighth-grade dance.

[9]We blared the radio and sang our favorite songs as the limo hustled into town. It was all fun and games until the car suddenly swerved and we tumbled over each other in the [11]back seat like rag dolls. The tires screeched like an alley cat just before everything went black.

[13]It's been three months since everything went dark that night, although it feels like a lifetime. The driver swerved to avoid a deer in the road. He might have seen it sooner if [15]he hadn't been texting while he was driving. We never made it to the eighth-grade dance. The only dancing lights I got to see that night were those of ambulances and [17]police cars. Ricky, Bobby, and Alyssa never even got to see those.

19. What is the main purpose of this passage?
    a. To persuade
    b. To inform
    c. To illustrate
    d. To entertain

20. The phrase *screeched like an alley cat* in line 11 is an example of a
    a. Metaphor
    b. Simile
    c. Alliteration
    d. Cliché

21. This story is told in which point of view?

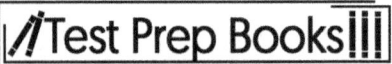

   a. First person
   b. Second person
   c. Third person
   d. Fourth person

22. According to the last sentence in the passage, readers can conclude that
   a. Ricky, Bobby, and Alyssa did not survive the accident.
   b. Ricky, Bobby, and Alyssa did not have to ride in an ambulance.
   c. Ricky, Bobby, and Alyssa had never planned to attend the dance.
   d. Ricky, Bobby, and Alyssa were blinded in the accident.

23. What is the overall message of this passage?
   a. Limo drivers are not required to take driving safety courses.
   b. Don't text and drive.
   c. Car accidents are common occurrences on special nights.
   d. Friends should not travel together in a limo.

24. Which statement can be inferred based on the information in the passage?
   a. The girls had been best friends since kindergarten.
   b. Ricky and Bobby came to pick up the girls in a limo.
   c. The girls' mothers were very supportive of their decision to go to the dance.
   d. The town has a great emergency response team.

Passage 5

[1]Princess Diana, born Diana Spencer on July 1, 1961 in Sandringham, England, left this world on August 31, 1997, at the age of thirty-six.

[3]Princess Diana was a graduate of Riddlesworth Hall School and West Heath School. After completing further schooling at Institut Alpin Videmanette in Switzerland, she [5]worked as a teacher's assistant so she could pursue her passion for working with children.

[7]Princess Diana was known for her big heart and support of various charities. Some of her most influential work included helping the homeless and children in need. She also [9]worked to provide support to people living with HIV and AIDS. Princess Diana also partnered with her sons, working diligently to raise awareness in Angola about the [11]dangers of landmines left behind after war.

Princess Diana is survived by son, Prince William Arthur Philip Louis; son, Prince Henry [13]Charles Albert David; and ex-husband, Prince Charles of Wales.

Funeral services will be held September 6 at Westminster Abbey. A family-only [15]graveside ceremony will be held at the Spencer family estate, Althorp.

In lieu of flowers, the family requests donations be made to the Diana, Princess of Wales [17]Memorial Fund in an effort to continue the valuable charity work Princess Diana cherished.

25. What type of article is this passage?
   a. News article
   b. Preface
   c. Obituary
   d. Short story

Practice Test #1

26. In line 16, the phrase *in lieu of* most nearly means
    a. because of.
    b. instead of.
    c. preferably.
    d. do not send.

27. With the information in this passage, readers can conclude Princess Diana was passionate about
    a. having children.
    b. doing charity work.
    c. getting an education.
    d. funding charities.

28. After Princess Diana completed school, she
    a. moved to Sandringham, England.
    b. had children.
    c. became a teacher's assistant.
    d. did charity work.

29. With the information in the passage, readers can infer donations to the Diana, Princess of Wales Memorial Fund will
    a. pay for her funeral at the family estate.
    b. buy clothes and school supplies for less fortunate children.
    c. be transferred to the family trust.
    d. send her sons to college.

30. How is this passage organized?
    a. Biographical information is followed by current events.
    b. An opinion is offered about an individual.
    c. Evidence is presented to refute an individual's popularity.
    d. A thesis statement is followed by supporting paragraphs.

Passage 6

[1]Mr. Walter lived here in Vinson, Oklahoma, for his entire life. He owned the little green house in town where he and his wife, Hilda, raised four boys. Mr. Walter worked at the [3]paper mill as a welder for forty-eight years.

When he retired, he became the school crossing guard. Every day, Mr. Walter stood on [5]that corner and helped kids safely cross the street. He knew the name of every kid who stopped at his corner, and he was always happy to see each one. In the wintertime, he [7]handed out hats and gloves to kids who'd left theirs at home. Mr. Walter was always smiling as he waved to every driver that passed his corner.

[9]After he got too old to be the crossing guard, Mr. Walter bought himself a bicycle. It was a three-wheeled bike, metallic red with a basket on the front. At eighty years old, [11]Mr. Walter put on his helmet and started cruising the streets.

Mr. Walter rode that red bike around town picking up cans and trash. He said it was his [13]ob to look out for his city. It wasn't uncommon to see his bike parked at the McDonald's on Main. He'd be standing out near the street waving at every car that [15]passed.

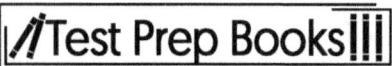

The whole town showed up at Mr. Walter's funeral. In eighty-four years, there wasn't a [17]day that had gone by where Mr. Walter hadn't touched one of our lives. Mr. Walter had been a hero to us.

31. Which of the following would most likely be found in the basket on Mr. Walter's bike?
    a. Lunch from McDonald's
    b. Hats and gloves
    c. Trash
    d. Toys for children

32. What can readers conclude from this passage?
    a. Mr. Walter retired from the paper mill and started riding his bike around town.
    b. Mr. Walter could never remember the names of the children he crossed at his corner.
    c. Mr. Walter picked up cans and trash when he worked at the paper mill.
    d. Mr. Walter touched the lives of everyone in the town of Vinson.

33. This passage can be categorized as a(n)
    a. informational text.
    b. short story.
    c. news article.
    d. persuasive letter.

34. According to the passage, it was common for Mr. Walter to
    a. give kids hats and gloves in the winter.
    b. forget to wear his safety helmet.
    c. encourage kids to pick up their trash.
    d. take his cans to the McDonald's.

35. What is the overall message of this passage?
    a. Heroes should save people from burning buildings.
    b. Sometimes it's the little things that make you a hero.
    c. Kids think all adults like Mr. Walter are heroes.
    d. All school crossing guards are special people.

36. Which of the following statements about Mr. Walter can be inferred based on the details in the passage?
    a. He was a caring person.
    b. He got bored easily.
    c. He did not like being at home.
    d. He did not have a car.

Practice Test #1

Mathematics Achievement

1. Which of the following represents the new coordinates of the ordered pair A if the triangle was reflected over the y-axis and then shifted down 3 units?

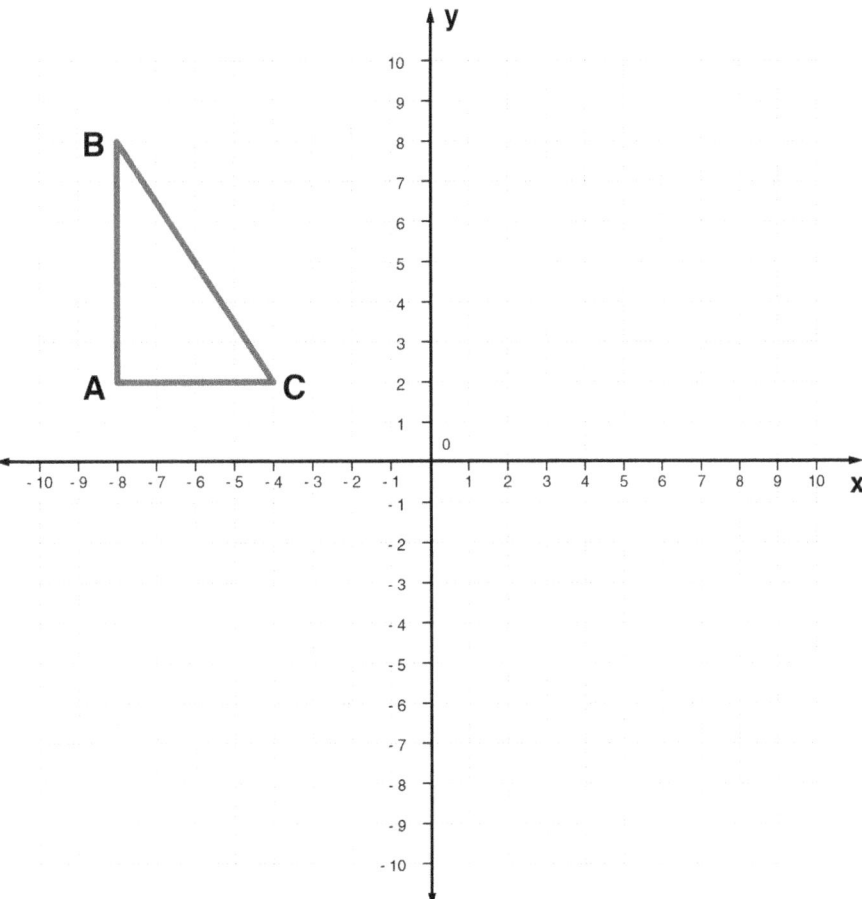

a. $(-8, -5)$
b. $(8, -1)$
c. $(8, 2)$
d. $(8, 5)$

2. A bag contains flashcards with the numbers 1 to 15 written individually. What is the probability that if one flashcard is selected, it is even?

a. $\frac{8}{15}$
b. $\frac{7}{16}$
c. $\frac{7}{15}$
d. $\frac{1}{2}$

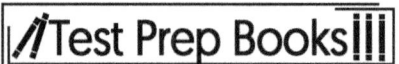

3. What is the simplified form of the expression $(7n + 3n^3 + 3) + (8n + 5n^3 + 2n^4)$?
   a. $2n^4 + 5n^3 + 15n - 2$
   b. $2n^4 + 8n^3 + 15n + 3$
   c. $9n^4 + 8n^3 + 15n$
   d. $9n^4 + 15n - 2$

4. Multiply and reduce $\frac{15}{23} \times \frac{54}{127}$.
   a. $\frac{810}{2929}$
   b. $\frac{810}{2,921}$
   c. $\frac{81}{292}$
   d. $\frac{69}{150}$

5. What is the solution for the following equation?
$$\frac{x^2 + x - 30}{x - 5} = 11$$
   a. There is no solution.
   b. $x = -6$
   c. $x = 5$
   d. $x = 16$

6. A circle on the Cartesian coordinate plane has a center of (-5,5). It is reflected across the y-axis and then shifted to the left six units. What is the new center?
   a. (-11,-5)
   b. (-1,5)
   c. (5,-1)
   d. (11,5)

7. Which of the ordered pairs below is a solution to the following system of inequalities?
$$\begin{cases} y > 2x - 3 \\ y < -4x + 8 \end{cases}$$
   a. $(-3, -2)$
   b. $(3, -1)$
   c. $(4, 5)$
   d. $(5, 2)$

8. Convert $\frac{2}{9}$ to a percentage.
   a. 0.22%
   b. 4.5%
   c. 22.22%
   d. 450%

9. A rectangle has a length that is 5 feet longer than 3 times its width. If the perimeter is 90 feet, what is the length in feet?
    a. 10 feet
    b. 20 feet
    c. 25 feet
    d. 35 feet

10. What is the measure of each angle in the following shape? Assume that each angle is equal.

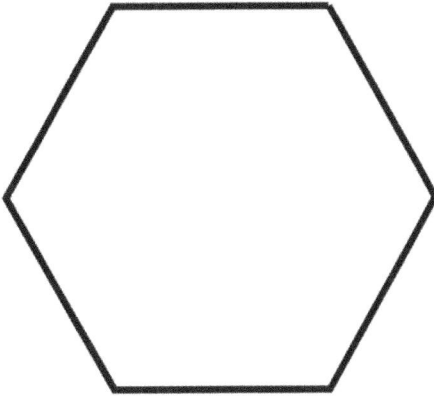

    a. 90°
    b. 100°
    c. 120°
    d. 180°

11. If a car can travel 300 miles in four hours, how far can it go in an hour and a half?
    a. 100 miles
    b. 112.5 miles
    c. 135.5 miles
    d. 150 miles

12. One apple costs $2. One papaya costs $3. If Samantha spends $35 and gets 15 pieces of fruit, how many papayas did she buy?
    a. 3 papayas
    b. 4 papayas
    c. 5 papayas
    d. 6 papayas

13. Shawna buys $2\frac{1}{2}$ gallons of paint. If she uses $\frac{1}{3}$ of it on the first day, how much does she have left?
    a. $1\frac{1}{2}$ gallons
    b. $1\frac{2}{3}$ gallons
    c. $1\frac{5}{6}$ gallons
    d. 2 gallons

14. If you flipped 4 coins, what is the probability that all 4 coins will land on heads?
    a. 0.0625
    b. 0.125
    c. 0.25
    d. 0.5

15. Solve this equation:
$$9x + x - 7 = 16 + 2x$$

   a. $x = -4$
   b. $x = \frac{9}{8}$
   c. $x = \frac{23}{8}$
   d. $x = 3$

16. What is the equation for the line passing through the origin and the point (2,1)?
    a. $y = x - 2$
    b. $y = \frac{1}{2}x$
    c. $y = 2x$
    d. $2y = x + 1$

17. A line segment connects the two ordered pairs (4,5) and (2,-8). What is the slope of a line that is perpendicular to this line?
    a. $-\frac{13}{2}$
    b. $-\frac{2}{3}$
    c. $-\frac{2}{13}$
    d. $\frac{2}{13}$

18. A line goes through the point $(-4, 0)$ and the point $(0, 2)$. What is the slope of the line?
    a. $\frac{1}{2}$
    b. $\frac{3}{2}$
    c. 2
    d. 4

19. Simplify the following fraction:

$$\frac{\left(\frac{5}{7}\right)}{\left(\frac{9}{11}\right)}$$

a. $\frac{7}{1,000}$

b. $\frac{5}{11}$

c. $\frac{13}{15}$

d. $\frac{55}{63}$

20. What is the slope of this line?

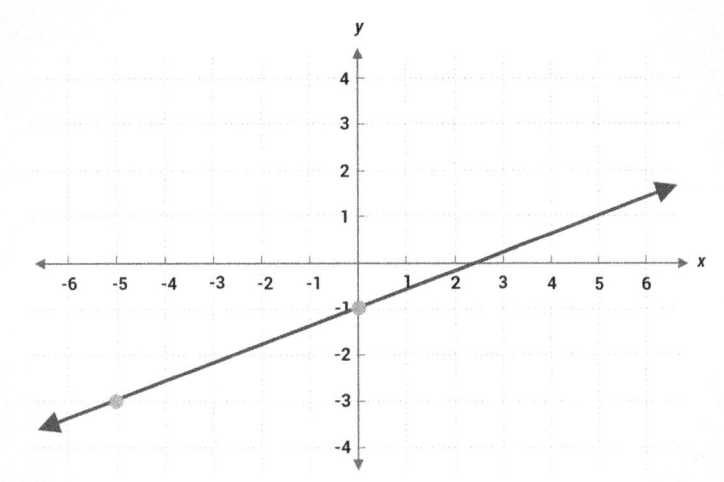

a. $\frac{2}{5}$

b. $\frac{1}{2}$

c. 2

d. $\frac{5}{2}$

21. What is the perimeter of the figure below? Note that the solid outer line is the perimeter.

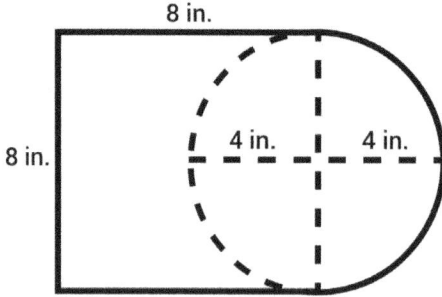

a. 36.565 in
b. 39.565 in
c. 39.78 in
d. 48.565 in

22. Five students take a test. The scores of the first four students are 80, 85, 75, and 60. If the median score is 80, which of the following could NOT be the score of the fifth student?
a. 60
b. 80
c. 85
d. 100

23. Find the missing angle x:

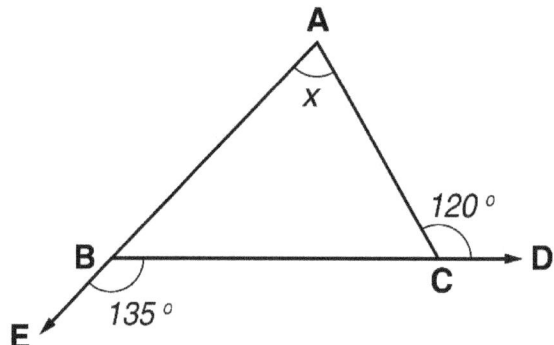

a. 45°
b. 60°
c. 75°
d. 105°

24. The volume of a rectangular prism $is\ V = length \times width \times height$. What is the volume of a rectangular prism with a height of 2 inches, a width of 4 inches, and a depth of 6 inches?
a. $12\ in^3$
b. $24\ in^3$
c. $48\ in^3$
d. $96\ in^3$

Practice Test #1

25. Ten students take a test. Five students get a 50. Four students get a 70. If the average score is 55, what was the last student's score?
    a. 20
    b. 40
    c. 50
    d. 60

26. A National Hockey League store in the state of Michigan advertises 50% off all items. Sales tax in Michigan is 6%. How much would a hat originally priced at $32.99 and a jersey originally priced at $64.99 cost during this sale? Round to the nearest penny.
    a. $48.99
    b. $51.93
    c. $97.98
    d. $103.86

27. A square has a side length of 4 inches. A triangle has a base of 2 inches and a height of 8 inches. What is the total area of the square and triangle?
    a. 24 square inches
    b. 28 square inches
    c. 32 square inches
    d. 36 square inches

28. Simplify $(2x - 3)(4x + 2)$.
    a. $-4x^2 - 8x - 1$
    b. $4x^2 - 4x - 6$
    c. $6x^2 + 8x - 5$
    d. $8x^2 - 8x - 6$

29. Which of the following expressions is equivalent to this expression?

$$\frac{2xy^2 + 4x - 8y}{16xy}$$

   a. $\frac{y}{8} + \frac{1}{4y} - \frac{1}{2x}$
   b. $8xy + 4y - 2x$
   c. $xy^2 + \frac{x}{4y} - \frac{1}{2x}$
   d. $\frac{y}{8} + 4y - 8y$

30. Simplify the following expression:

$$(3x + 5)(x - 8)$$

   a. $3x^2 - 19x - 40$
   b. $4x - 19x - 13$
   c. $3x^2 + 5x - 3$
   d. $4x - 5x + 9$

31. It costs Chad $12 to produce three necklaces. If he can sell each necklace for $20, how much profit would he make if he sold 60 necklaces?
   a. $240
   b. $360
   c. $960
   d. $1,200

32. In an office, there are 50 workers. A total of 60% of the workers are women. 50% of the women are wearing skirts. If no men wear skirts, how many workers are wearing skirts?
   a. 12 workers
   b. 15 workers
   c. 16 workers
   d. 20 workers

33. A bag contains 30 red crayons, 20 blue crayons, and 10 yellow crayons. What is the probability that if 1 crayon is randomly selected, it is not yellow?
   a. $\frac{1}{6}$
   b. $\frac{1}{5}$
   c. $\frac{4}{5}$
   d. $\frac{5}{6}$

34. What is 20% of the difference between the number of degrees in a rectangle and the number of degrees in an isosceles triangle?
   a. 3.6
   b. 36
   c. 72
   d. 80

35. Four people split a bill. The first person pays for $\frac{1}{5}$, the second person pays for $\frac{1}{4}$, and the third person pays for $\frac{1}{3}$. What fraction of the bill does the fourth person pay?
   a. $\frac{13}{60}$
   b. $\frac{1}{4}$
   d. $\frac{4}{15}$
   c. $\frac{47}{60}$

36. Consider a four-year private institution that you would like to attend for college. The tuition per year is $22,000. It is estimated that room and board will be $5,000 per year, and books will cost you $500 per year. Your family is expected to pay for 25% of your total expenses, and you will be paying for the rest. How much will you have to have in a savings account to cover your portion if you would like to have the total amount for all four years available before you even attend?
   a. $27,500
   b. $82,500
   c. $88,000
   d. $110,000

37. The table below shows tickets purchased during the week for entry to the local zoo. What is the mean number of adult tickets sold for the week?

Day of the Week	Age	Tickets Sold
Monday	Adult	22
Monday	Child	30
Tuesday	Adult	16
Tuesday	Child	15
Wednesday	Adult	24
Wednesday	Child	23
Thursday	Adult	19
Thursday	Child	26
Friday	Adult	29
Friday	Child	38

a. 21 tickets
b. 22 tickets
c. 24.2 tickets
d. 26.4 tickets

38. What is the value of x for the right triangle shown below?

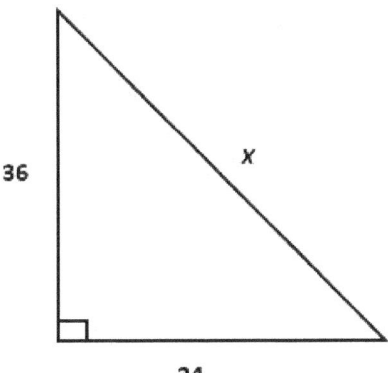

a. 26.8
b. 42.7
c. 43.3
d. 44.1

39. The following chart shows the number of baseball team runs per inning. Calculate the median of the data set.

Baseball Team Runs Per Inning	
Number of Runs	**Frequency**
0	4
1	3
2	1
3	1

a. 0.78
b. 0
c. 1
d. 2

40. What is the value of $x^2 - 2xy + 2y^2$ when $x = 2, y = 3$?
a. 8
b. 10
c. 12
d. 14

41. In the figure below, what is the area of the shaded region?

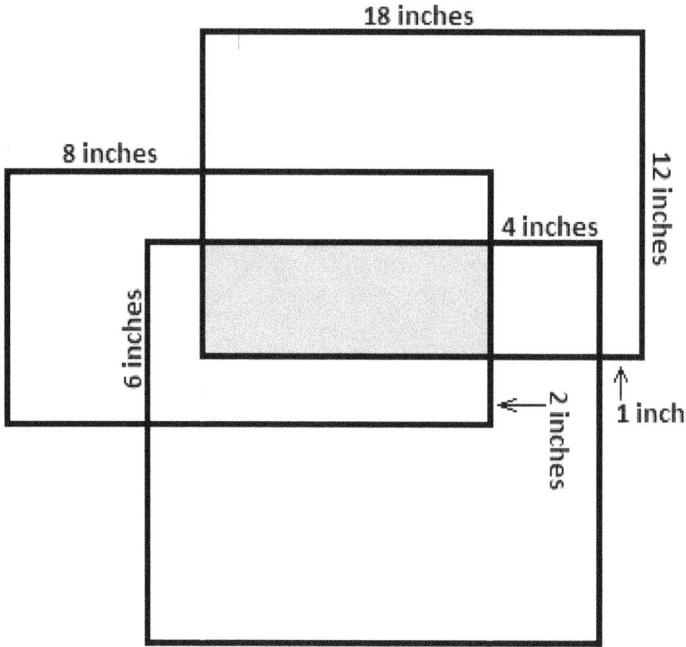

a. 44 square inches
b. 48 square inches
c. 52 square inches
d. 56 square inches

42. The following pie chart represents the results of a survey for a high school class. They tracked how many hours per day they spent performing each activity. There are 24 hours in a day. How many hours are spent on average watching TV and listening to music?

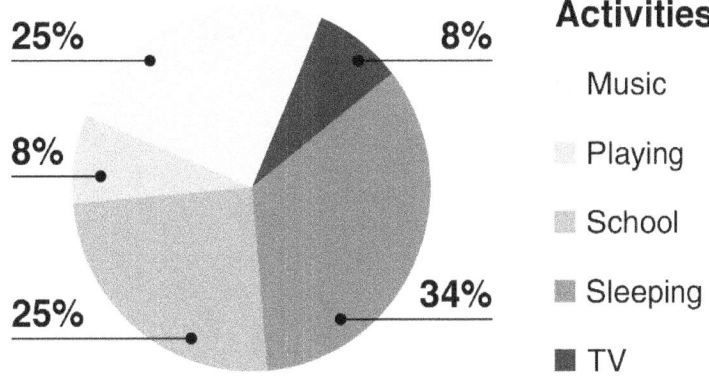

a. 1.92
b. 4.08
c. 6
d. 7.92

43. A student gets an 85% on a test with 20 questions. How many questions did the student solve correctly?
a. 15 questions
b. 16 questions
c. 17 questions
d. 18 questions

44. Consider the following set of similar triangles. What is the length of side y?

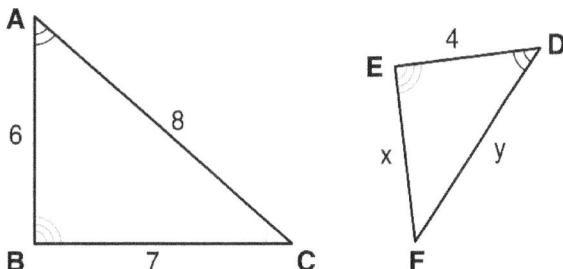

a. $\frac{8}{3}$
b. $\frac{14}{3}$
c. $\frac{16}{3}$
d. 24

45. The mean of a set of 14 numbers is 72. What is the sum of these numbers?
a. 504
b. 720
c. 1,008
d. 2016

46. A donut box contains 5 glazed, 6 chocolate, and 9 vanilla donuts. If 2 donuts are removed from the box, what is the probability that both donuts are vanilla?
   a. $\frac{1}{20}$
   b. $\frac{1}{19}$
   c. $\frac{2}{19}$
   d. $\frac{1}{4}$

47. If $(x - 14)^2 = x^2 + bx + 196$, what is the value of b?
   a. -28
   b. 14
   c. 28
   d. 196

Essay

You have 30 minutes to plan and write your essay. Do not worry too much about length; it's most important to focus on the content and quality of your writing.

What would you like to pursue as a career and why?

Answer Explanations #1

Synonyms

1. C: To *deduce* something is to figure it out using reasoning. While you can explain something you've *deduced*, *explain* is not a synonym for *deduce*.

2. C: To *elucidate* is to figuratively shine a light on a previously unknown or confusing subject. This Latin root, "lux" meaning "light," prominently figures into the solution. *Enlighten* means to educate or bring to light.

3. C: Looking at the Latin word "veritas," meaning "truth," will yield a clue as to the meaning of *verify*. To *verify* is the act of finding or assessing the truthfulness of something. This usually means amassing evidence to substantiate a claim. *Substantiate*, of course, means to provide evidence to prove a point.

4. C: If someone is *inspired*, they are *motivated* to do something. Someone who is an inspiration motivates others to follow their example.

5. A: All the connotations of *perceive* involve the concept of seeing. Whether figuratively or literally, *perceiving* implies the act of understanding what is presented. *Comprehending* is synonymous with *understanding*.

6. D: *Nomadic* tribes are those who, throughout history and even today, prefer to wander their lands instead of settling in any specific place. *Wanderer* best describes these people.

7. B: Perplexed means *baffled* or *puzzled*, which are synonymous with *confused*.

8. A: *Lyrical* is used to refer to something being poetic or song-like, characterized by showing enormous imagination and description. While the context of *lyrical* can be playful or even whimsical, the best choice is *expressive*, since whatever emotion *lyrical* may be used to convey in its context will be expressive in nature.

9. B: *Brevity* literally means *brief* or *concise*. Note the similar beginnings of *brevity* and *brief*—from the Latin "brevis," meaning *brief*.

10. A: *Irate* means being in a state of anger. Clearly this is a negative word that can be paired with another word in kind. The closest word to match this is obviously *angry*. Research would also reveal that *irate* comes from the Latin "ira," which means *anger*.

11. C: *Lavish* is a synonym for *luxurious*. Both words describe elaborate, elegant lifestyles and/or settings.

12. B: *Immobile* means "not able to move." The two best selections are *B* and *D*—but *slow* still implies some form of motion, whereas *sedentary* has the connotation of being seated and/or inactive for a significant portion of time and/or as a natural tendency.

13. C: *Overbearing* refers to *domineering* or being *oppressive*. This is emphasized in the "over" prefix, which emphasizes an excess in definitions.

14. C: *Avert* literally means to turn away or ward off an impending circumstance The "pre" prefix describes something that occurs before an event. *Prevent* means to stop something before it happens.

15. D: *Refresh* is synonymous with *replenish*. Both words mean to restore or refill. Additionally, these terms do share the "re" prefix as well.

16. A: *Regale* literally means to *amuse* someone with a story, making *entertain* the best choice.

Answer Explanations #1

17. C: *Weary* most closely means tired. Someone who is *weary* and *tired* may be *whiny*, but they do not necessarily mean the same thing.

18. A: Something that is *vast* is far-reaching and expansive. Choice *D*, *ocean*, may be described as *vast*, but the word alone doesn't mean *vast*.

19. D: To *demonstrate* something means to show it. The word *demonstration* comes from *demonstrate*, and a *demonstration* is a modeling or show-and-tell type of example that is usually visual.

Sentence Completion

20. B: Choice *B* is the correct answer because *expeditious* means quick and efficient, which is fitting for a paramedic's response during emergencies. *Critical* means extremely serious, which also fits the nature of a paramedic's work. Choice *A* is incorrect because although *composed* means calm, which fits the situation, *insignificant* which means unimportant, does not fit the seriousness of life-threatening scenarios. Choice *C* is incorrect because *foolhardy* means reckless, which does not fit a paramedic's demeanor on the job. Although *catastrophic* may fit some paramedic situations, they are not all at that level of severity. Choice *D* is incorrect because *nonchalant* means indifferent, which doesn't accurately capture a paramedic's focus on the job, even though *perilous*, which means dangerous, would otherwise fit.

21. C: The best answer for the blank is *dubious* because it accurately conveys the doubt felt by people who "questioned the sincerity and feasibility of her proposed policies." The other choices imply a positive response that does not fit the sentence. Choices *A* and *B* suggest a receptive response, while Choice *D* implies enthusiasm and excitement. Each of these options contradicts the more critical tone conveyed by *dubious* in this context.

22. A: In the given sentence, the word *alacrity* is the best choice for the blank because it conveys a sense of initiative and enthusiasm in approaching "challenging circumstances." The meaning of *alacrity* is promptness in response. This definition aligns well with Jaci's willingness to "contribute and make a positive impact on the team." The other options convey opposite meanings and would not accurately capture Jaci's positive and eager attitude.

23. C: The best answer for the blank is Choice *C* because it perfectly captures the idea of "Natalia's years of hard work and planning" leading to success. *Fruition* refers to the point at which something is achieved or realized, and in this context, it conveys the successful opening of Natalia's bakery after a period of dedicated effort. Choice *A* is tempting because it suggests an end result; however, *closure* generally refers to the resolution of an emotional situation rather than the realization of a plan or goal. *Deterioration* implies a decline in quality or condition, and *interruption* suggests a disruption or hindrance.

24. C: Choice *C* is the correct answer because *passionately* means with strong commitment to something, which accurately describes the animal rehabilitator's investment in her work. It is also in the adverb form necessary for this sentence. *Distressing* means emotionally painful, which also aligns with her reaction to animals who will not survive. Choice *A* is incorrect because *educated* or knowledgeable is more of a state of being than a feeling, and *spontaneous* or random is not an appropriate word to describe feelings about an injured animal. Choice *B* is incorrect because *fierce* should read *fiercely*; the adverb version of the word is needed. *Agitating* may be accurate but does not capture the emotional pain of not being able to help an injured animal. Choice *D* is incorrect because *sympathetic* means to connect with someone's pain, which would work if the sentence were referring to her sympathy for animals. However, it states that she feels that way about work, which does not exactly fit. *Challenging*, which means difficult, would otherwise be accurate.

25. A: Choice *A* is best because it accurately describes the wealth, prosperity, and abundance of the neighborhood. "Luxurious mansions, upscale boutiques, and exclusive restaurants" are indicative of a high socioeconomic status. *Affluence* means having a great deal of wealth, and in this context, it aligns well with the opulent characteristics of

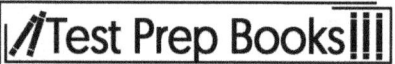

the neighborhood. Choice *D* does not fit because *decrepitude* implies a state of decline or deterioration. Choice *B*, barrenness, implies emptiness or abandonment. *Congeniality* refers to friendliness or compatibility, which is unrelated to the economic status of the neighborhood, so Choice *C* is incorrect.

26. C: Choice *C* is the correct answer because *mandatory* means required, which fits the assumption that a degree is necessary for a high paying job. *Significant* means considerable, which fits the context of the sentence saying that people who do not have degrees can make considerable money as well. Choice *A* is incorrect because although *essential* works well since it means necessary, *trivial* means of little value, which does not align with the sentence's argument about how much money non-degree-holders can make. Choice *B* is incorrect because *futile* means pointless, which does not align with the sentence's point that degrees are viewed as a necessity for high income. *Substantial* may work, but not with *futile* in this sentence. Choice *D* is incorrect because *necessity* is a noun, but the sentence calls for an adjective. *Negligible* means insignificant, which does not fit the sentence context.

27. B: *Acquit* means to free of blame or charge, or to forgive. *Stall* means to hinder, *acquire* means to gain, and *quit* means to stop. None of these choices fit with the context of the sentence. *Acquit* is the only choice that completes the sentence appropriately.

28. B: Choice *B* is the correct answer because *charitable* means generous, which fits Genevieve's initial action with the homeless person. *Regretful* also fits well since the person demanding more money is not appreciative of the gift; therefore, it is reasonable to infer that Genevieve regrets giving away her money to him. Choice *A* is incorrect because *banal* means boring which does not fit this sentence. *Dignified* means composed which does not fit the context of the sentence either. Choice *C* is incorrect because *miserly* means stingy, which does not describe Genevieve's charity. *Rapacious* means aggressively greedy, which does not describe Genevieve even after the man's demands. Choice *D* is incorrect because *philanthropy* should read as *philanthropic* for the structure of this sentence. *Avaricious* means greedy, which does not describe Genevieve, even after the man's demands.

29. D: *Rebuke* means to reprimand severely. Choices *A* and *C*, *choose* and *honor*, would not make sense in this sentence. Choice *B*, *disown*, would be an extreme reaction to drawings on a wall and can be eliminated.

30. C: Even if readers don't know what *dissonance* means, they can tell that three of the words are closely related. Readers should try to eliminate what they know in order to focus on the remaining words. The words *accord*, *concordance*, and *harmony* have a relationship with each other; therefore, the word that has a different meaning than those three words and maintains the meaning of the sentence is *dissonance*. If two notes are not in perfect accord with each other, they are demonstrating dissonance.

31. A: Choice *A* is the correct answer because *alarming*, which means worrying, fits the description of a company losing employees. *Unperturbed* also fits since it means unconcerned, which accurately describes the lack of action. Choice *B* is incorrect because *catastrophe* is the incorrect form of the word as it should read *catastrophic*. *Proactive* does not work either as the sentence is suggesting that the company does nothing about the high turnover. Choice *C* is incorrect because *distressed* is the wrong form of the word; it should read *distressing*. *Nonchalant* or unworried would otherwise fit. Choice *D* is incorrect because *negligible* means insignificant, which does not fit the high turnover rate. *Inattentive* does not fit well because that would suggest the company is ignoring an issue, but the word *negligible* would suggest there is no issue. This all contradicts the sentence's content.

32. A: Choice *A* is correct. *Aberration* means deviation or departure, which would fit in this sentence since dirty and disheveled contrast with tidy, making the woman's outfit a deviation or departure from her normal appearance. Choices *B* means fight, which does not make sense in the sentence. Choice *C* is incorrect. Although the outfit may cause a distraction, it's not a distraction from her wardrobe. Choice *D* is incorrect because a dirty and disheveled outfit would not be a selection from a tidy wardrobe.

Answer Explanations #1

33. D: The word *terse* means blunt or brief, which works best with the word *abrupt* in the sentence. There is no reason to assume that the football player's answers were interesting, obnoxious, or tedious (boring).

34. A: Choice *A* is the correct answer because *feasible* means achievable, which describes the attainable balance that Jennifer is looking for. *Incessant* means constant, which accurately describes the never-ending disturbances from her children. Choice *B* is incorrect because *impartial*, meaning unbiased, does not fit in this sentence even though *interminable*, meaning endless, would fit well. Choice *C* is incorrect because *inconsistent* goes against the idea of balance. *Predictable* means foreseeable, which would not explain why the children's demands are a problem. Choice *D* is incorrect because although *reasonable*, or moderate, fits the sentence, the word *sporadically*, meaning irregularly, would suggest that the distractions are not constant. It is also in the wrong form for the sentence, which requires a simple adjective and not an adverb.

35. D: Readers should choose the word that best fits the meaning the writer intended. Notice the word *average*. Since the student's language is what helped the teacher classify his writing as average, we need to find the correct adjective to go with the word *language*. *Apt* means relevant, and this doesn't fit with the meaning of the sentence, making Choice *A* incorrect. *Astute* means "intelligent," so Choice *B* is incorrect. Choice *C*, *disappointing*, is not specific enough to qualify his writing as average. In fact, if he used disappointing language, his writing style may be less than average. *Mediocre* means ordinary or average, therefore Choice *D* is correct.

36. C: Choice *C* is the correct answer because *hostile*, or unfriendly, accurately describes two countries who are exchanging violence. *Beneficial*, meaning positive, works in this sentence since peace negotiations would bring peace to both nations. Choice *A* is incorrect because although *enraging*, or angering, may fit the description of failed peace negotiations, *disadvantageous*, which means reducing chance for success, does not accurately capture the benefit that a ceasefire would bring for both nations. Choice *B* is incorrect because although *fruitless*, meaning without product, may be accurate, *confounding*, which means confusing, does not fit the description of a ceasefire. Choice *D* is incorrect because *triumphant* would mean that the peace negotiations were successful throughout, rather than taking a long time to come to fruition. The peace negotiations are also not *detrimental*.

37. B: The word *foliage* is defined as leaves on plants or trees. In this sentence, the type of word we're looking for can be drawn from the fact that a heavily wooded area in October would be characterized by the beautiful changing colors of the leaves. Therefore, Choice *B* is correct. The other answer choices do not accurately fit in the sentence. *Fauna* refers to the animals that are found in an area. Depending on which animals are found in the wooded area, this could be a possible answer, but the fact that it's October and heavily wooded, it makes more sense that the beautiful colors are the leaves of the trees in the fall. An orchard is a piece of land that has fruit trees growing on it, which is not likely to be found in a heavily wooded park. A ravine is a narrow and deep valley and is not the correct answer.

38. C: Choice *C* is the correct answer because it is the best word to describe Jeremy during his situation. *Tenacity* means to show determination and persistence. Since Jeremy went through a great hardship that took months of recovery, the word *tenacity* fits appropriately. Choice *A* is incorrect because *apathy* means to lack interest. Jeremy's dedication to his healing shows the opposite of that. Choice *B* is incorrect because *benevolence* means to show kindness to others. No other person is mentioned in this sentence. Choice *D* is incorrect because there is nothing to suggest that Jeremy feels *wariness*, which would mean uncertainty and caution.

39. C: Choice *C* is the correct answer because *persistent* means determined, which aligns with the hacker's attempts. *Impenetrable* means impossible to break into, which accurately describes the defense system that the hacker was up against. Choice *A* is incorrect because *fervent* means passionate, which may work, but *feeble*, which means weak, does not work since the hacker could not get past the strong defenses. Choice *B* is incorrect because *hesitant* means cautious, which does not capture the hacker's numerous attempts. *Compromised* does not work because the system would not be impossible to hack if it were already compromised. Choice *D* is incorrect because *triumphant* means

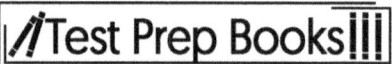

Answer Explanations #1

victorious, which the hacker is not because he failed. *Incomprehensible* means difficult to understand, which may fit the context but not with *triumphant*.

40. B: Choice B is the correct answer because *lenient* means forgiving, which fits the judge giving Jenny a light sentence. *Detrimental* means harmful, which accurately describes the negative impact that jailtime would have on Jenny's children. Choice A is incorrect because *impartial* means unbiased, which doesn't emphasize the light sentence Jenny received. *Inconsequential* means without consequence, which does not describe the impact on Jenny's children if she were sent to jail for a long time. Choice C is incorrect because *merciless* means showing no mercy, which contradicts the light sentence given. *Profound* means meaningful, which may work but tends to have a more positive connotation than a child having a negative experience. Choice D is incorrect because *stringent* means strict, the opposite of a light sentence. *Traumatizing* may otherwise work, but not with *stringent*.

Quantitative Reasoning

Word Problems

1. B: To be directly proportional means that $y = kx$. If x is changed from 5 to 20, the value of x is multiplied by 4. Applying the same rule to the y-value, also multiply the value of y by 4. Therefore:

$$y = 12$$

2. B: Using the given information of one nurse to 25 patients and 325 total patients, set up an equation to solve for the number of nurses (N):

$$\frac{N}{325} = \frac{1}{25}$$

Multiply both sides by 325 to get N by itself on one side.

$$\frac{N}{1} = \frac{325}{25} = 13 \text{ nurses}$$

3. B: The tip is not taxed, so he pays 5% tax only on the $10. To find 5% of $10, calculate $0.05 \times \$10 = \$0.50$. Add up $\$10 + \$0.50 + \$2$ to get $12.50.

4. A: Taylor's total income is $\$20,000 + \$10,000 = \$30,000$. 15% as a fraction is $\frac{15}{100} = \frac{3}{20}$. So:

$$\frac{3}{20} \times \$30,000 = \frac{\$90,000}{20} = \frac{\$9,000}{2}$$

$$\frac{\$9,000}{2} = \$4,500$$

5. D: Exponential functions can be written in the form: $y = a \times b^x$. The equation for an exponential function can be written given the y-intercept (a) and the growth rate (b). The y-intercept is the output (y) when the input (x) equals zero. It can be thought of as an "original value," or starting point. The value of b is the rate at which the original value increases ($b > 1$) or decreases ($b < 1$). In this scenario, the y-intercept, a, would be $1200, and the growth rate, b, would be 1.01 (100% of the original value combined with 1% interest, or $100\% + 1\% = 101\% = 1.01$).

6. D: This problem can be solved by using unit conversion. The initial units are miles per minute. The final units need to be feet per second. Converting miles to feet uses the equivalence statement 1 mi = 5,280 ft. Converting minutes

Answer Explanations #1

to seconds uses the equivalence statement 1 min = 60 s. Setting up the ratios to convert the units is shown in the following equation:

$$\frac{72 \text{ mi}}{90 \text{ min}} \times \frac{1 \text{ min}}{60 \text{ s}} \times \frac{5{,}280 \text{ ft}}{1 \text{ mi}} = 70.4 \frac{\text{ft}}{\text{s}}$$

The initial units cancel out, and the new units are left.

7. C: To find the drop in value, subtract the new value from the old value. To see what percentage of the initial value this is, divide the difference by the initial value, then multiply by 100.

$$\frac{20{,}000 - 8{,}000}{20{,}000} = 0.6$$

$$(0.60) \times 100 = 60\%$$

8. B: The question only asks how long they owned the house, so ignore the extra details about prices. There are 6 years between May 1, 2010 and May 1, 2016. There are another 4 months between May 1, 2016 and September 1, 2016. Therefore, they owned the house for a total of 6 years and 4 months. Each year has 12 months, so the total number of months is $(6 \times 12) + 4 = 72 + 4 = 76 \text{ months}$.

9. D: The formula for finding the volume of a rectangular prism is $V = l \times w \times h$, where l is the length, w is the width, and h is the height. The volume of the original box is calculated:

$$V = 8 \text{ in} \times 14 \text{ in} \times 4 \text{ in} = 448 \text{ in}^3$$

The volume of the new box is calculated:

$$V = 16 \text{ in} \times 28 \text{ in} \times 8 \text{ in} = 3{,}584 \text{ in}^3$$

The volume of the new box divided by the volume of the old box equals 8.

10. B: The slope from this equation is 50, and it is interpreted as the cost per gigabyte used. Since the g-value represents the number of gigabytes and the equation is set equal to the cost in dollars, the slope relates these two values. For every gigabyte used on the phone, the bill goes up 50 dollars.

11. C: The perimeter of a rectangle is $P = 2l + 2w$. We are told $P = 44$, so $2l + 2w = 44$. We are also told that the width is 2 cm less than the length: $w = l - 2$. Substituting this for w in the perimeter equation, we get $2l + 2(l - 2) = 44$. Although it's not necessary to answer the test question, we could solve the equation to find the length and width. The equation simplifies to $4l - 4 = 44$, or $l = 12$, and since $w = l - 2$, we find $w = 10$.

12. B: For manufacturing costs, there is a linear relationship between the cost to the company and the number produced, with a y-intercept given by the base cost of acquiring the means of production, and a slope given by the cost to produce one unit. In this case, that base cost is $50,000, while the cost per unit is $40. So:

$$y = 40x + 50{,}000$$

13. D: A dollar contains 20 nickels. Therefore, if there are 12 dollars' worth of nickels, there are:

$$12 \times 20 = 240 \text{ nickels}$$

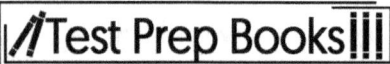

Answer Explanations #1

Each nickel weighs 5 grams. Therefore, the weight of the nickels is:

$$240 \times 5 = 1{,}200 \text{ grams}$$

To find the total weight of the filled piggy bank, add the weight of the nickels and the weight of the empty bank:

$$1{,}200 + 1{,}050 = 2{,}250 \text{ grams.}$$

14. C: The range of the entire stem-and-leaf plot is found by subtracting the lowest value from the highest value, as follows:

$$59 - 20 = 39 \text{ cm}$$

All other choices are miscalculations read from the chart.

15. C: To calculate the total greater than 35, the number of measurements above 35 must be totaled; 36, 37, 37, 47, 49, 54, 56, 59 = 8 measurements. Choice *A* is the number of measurements in the 3 category, Choice *B* is the number in the 4 and 5 categories, and Choice *D* is the number in the 3, 4, and 5 categories.

16. D: It can be determined from reading the information given that Jenny, Hector, and Mary scored higher than Sam, so Choice *D* is correct. There is no relation given between Hector and Mary's scores. This means that Hector could have scored higher or lower than Mary. So, Choice *A* is incorrect. With the information given, it is possible that Hector scored above 90, so Choice *B* is incorrect. Given that Mary could have scored higher or lower than Hector, it cannot be determined if her score is the median, so Choice *C* is incorrect.

17. C: The new price of the purse can be found by first multiplying the original price by 25%, or 0.25. This yields an increase of $32. Taking the original price of $128 and adding the increase in price of $32 yields a new price of $160.

18. D: Digits to the left of the decimal point represent the digit value times increasing multiples of 10 (first 1, then 10, 100, 1,000, and so on). Digits to the right of the decimal point represent the digit value divided by increasing multiples of 10 (first $\frac{1}{10}$, then $\frac{1}{100}$, $\frac{1}{1000}$, and so on). So, the second digit to the right of the decimal point equals the digit value divided by 100.

19. D: The power of 10 by which a digit is multiplied corresponds with the number of zeros following the digit when expressing its value in standard form. Therefore:

$$(1 \times 10^4) + (3 \times 10^3) + (7 \times 10^1) + (8 \times 10^0)$$

$$10{,}000 + 3{,}000 + 70 + 8$$

$$13{,}078$$

20. C: To solve the problem, we can write a proportion consisting of ratios comparing distance and time. One way to set up the proportion is: $\frac{3}{48} = \frac{5}{x}$. x represents the unknown value of time. To solve this proportion, we can cross-multiply:

$$(3)(x) = (5)(48) \text{ or } 3x = 240$$

To isolate the variable, we divide by 3 on both sides, getting $x = 80$.

Answer Explanations #1

21. B: To determine the number of houses that can fit on the street, we can divide the length of the street by the width of each house's property:

$$345 \div 30 = 11.5$$

However, the construction company is not going to build half a house, so they will need to build either 11 or 12 houses. Since the width of 12 houses (360 feet) would extend past the length of the street, only 11 houses can be built.

Quantitative Comparison

22. C: The equation that produces this series is $2x + 1$. This gives $2(4) + 1 = 9, 2(9) + 1 = 19$, and so on. This means that the value of h in the series is 9, so Quantity A and Quantity B are equal.

23. A: The value of g can be found using the formula for area of a rectangle ($A = l \times w$). So, $56 = g \times 4$, and $g = 14$. This means that Quantity A is greater than Quantity B.

24. B: The first step is to solve for x. For this equation, that is:

$$4x - 12 = -2x$$

$$6x - 12 = 0$$

$$6x = 12$$

$$x = 2$$

The value of x is 2 and Quantity B is 3, so Quantity B is greater.

25. A: The first step here is to solve each of the ratios. The first ratio is all of Jimmy's marbles divided by all of Steve's marbles. This gives:

$$\frac{15}{10} = \frac{3}{2}$$

The second ratio is all of Jimmy's blue marbles divided by all of Steve's green marbles. This gives:

$$\frac{8}{6} = \frac{4}{3}$$

Since $\frac{3}{2}$ is greater than $\frac{4}{3}$, Quantity A is greater.

26. B: First, find the area of both figures. The area of the triangle is:

$$\frac{1}{2}(7) \times 8 = 28 \text{ square inches}$$

The area of the rectangle is $13 \times 8 = 104$ square inches. So, 7 times the area of the triangle would be 196 square inches, and 2 times the area of the rectangle would be 208 square inches. This means that Quantity B is greater.

27. A: First, convert the distance that Truck A drove to feet. This is:

$$1{,}236 \times 3 = 3{,}708 \text{ feet}$$

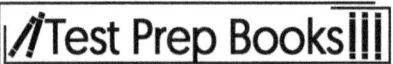

This means that Truck A drove further than Truck B. So, Quantity A is greater than Quantity B.

28. D: Either quantity could be greater for given values of x and z. For example, if $x = 7$ and $z = 1$, then Quantity A is 8 and Quantity B is 1. If $x = 10$ and $z = -8$, then Quantity A is 2, and Quantity B is 4.

29. C: The probability of choosing a rough rock is $\frac{4}{16}$. This is equal to $\frac{2}{8}$.

30. D: If Jim is 2 years old, then Bill is 6 years old. Twice Jim's age is 4, so Quantity B is greater. However, if Jim is 20 years old, then Bill is 24. Twice Jim's age is 40, so Quantity A is greater. Thus, the relationship cannot be determined from the given information.

31. D: If Angie has 5 cats, then Janet may have 4 cats. Four more than Janet is 8 cats, so Quantity B would be greater. But if Angie has 10 cats and Janet has 2 cats, then four more cats than Janet is 6, and Quantity A is greater. Thus, there is not enough information to determine which quantity is greater.

32. C: Call Gage's age g and Cam's age c. The sentence above, "Gage is twice as old as Cam," can be written as $2c = g$. Dividing both sides by 2, we find $c = (\frac{1}{2})g$, that is, Cam's age equals half of Gage's age.

33. A: A prime number is a number that only has factors of 1 and itself. Quantity A is the largest prime number less than 35. The number 34 is even, or divisible by 2, so it is not prime. 33 is divisible by 3 and 11, and 32 is even, so neither of those is prime. 31 has factors of only 1 and itself, so it is the largest prime number less than 35. Quantity B is the smallest prime number greater than 25. The next number is 26, which is even. 27 has factors of 3 and 9, while 28 is even. 29 has factors of only 1 and itself; therefore, it is the smallest prime number greater than 25. Comparing these two numbers, 31 and 29, Quantity A is greater. The correct answer is Choice A because Quantity A is greater.

34. A: To find a percentage of a number, convert the percentage to a decimal and multiply. Quantity A is $0.28 \times 345 = 96.6$. Quantity B is $(\frac{1}{5}) \times 300 = 300 \div 5 = 60$, so Quantity A is greater.

35. C: The angles inside a triangle are supplementary, which means they add up to 180 degrees. The third angle not named in the triangle and the exterior angle z are also supplementary because they add up to a straight line, or 180 degrees. If the unnamed angle is given the value w, then the equations can be written: $x + y + w = 180$ and $w + z = 180$. By the transitive property of equality, the equation can be written:

$$x + y + w = w + z$$

Subtracting w from both sides yields the equation $x + y = z$. Using this equation, Quantity A and Quantity B can be stated as equal. The correct answer is Choice C because Quantity B is equal to Quantity A.

36. A: The circumference of a circle can be found by using the formula $C = 2\pi r$. The radius of this circle is 4 cm, so its circumference is $C=2\pi(4)$, or 8π. The perimeter of a rectangle is $P=2l+2w$, or in this case, $P = 2(7) + 2(5) = 24$. 8π is about 25.13, which is greater than 24. Therefore, Quantity A is greater than Quantity B.

37. A: The new side length is $3l$. The area of a square is equal to the side squared, so the area of the original square was l^2, and the area of the new square is $(3l)^2 = 9l^2$. The area of the new square is 9 times as large as the original square. Therefore, Quantity A is greater.

Answer Explanations #1

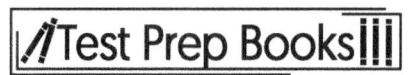

Reading Comprehension

1. D: The tone of the passage can best be described as positive. All of the information given about the two types of modern public transportation is favorable. Choice A is incorrect because a hopeful tone would imply that there's something coming in the future to look forward to. The passage only presents two transportation options that already exist, not types that might be expected or hoped for in the future. Choice B is incorrect because there is no humor in the passage. Choice C is incorrect because there is no indication that the author is worried about any aspect of these two modern choices for public transportation.

2. A: This item asks you to determine which statement can be supported based on information that is given in the passage. Choice A is the correct answer because the text explains how parents can use DeerHaul to help transport their children when they are unavailable. Choices B and D are incorrect because the third paragraph explains who can drive for DeerHaul and what safety precautions are taken by the company. Choice C is incorrect because the author offers no opinion on which company is the better option.

3. D: The task here is to use information from the text to determine which detail is correct. The passage explains how payments are made electronically through the app. Choice A is incorrect since buses and subways are considered public transportation. Choices B and C are incorrect because when payments are made and tipping are not discussed in the article.

4. C: In this context, *battery* is synonymous with *series*, so the correct answer is C. Although a battery can be a cell used to provide power to something, an artillery of guns, or an act of violence, none of these are the meaning that best fits this sentence. Thus, Choices A, B, and D are incorrect.

5. B: Choice B is correct because the author simply presents information to the reader. Choice A is incorrect because the author is not attempting to persuade the reader. Choices C and D are incorrect because the author does not tell a story or express their original ideas or emotions.

6. A: Choice A is correct because both the second and third paragraphs explain a means of private transportation. Choices B, C, and D are incorrect because the author does not offer an opinion on the best method of transportation or the best company to use.

7. A: Choice A is correct because the passage discusses how a department store's advertising project made Rudolph a famous Christmas tradition. Choice B is mentioned in the passage as a supporting detail. Choices C and D are not mentioned in the passage.

8. B: The passage explains that at that time, a red nose was considered a symptom of drunkenness, so the store's officials were unsure of the idea. After the sketch was created, the story was approved, most likely because the sketch showed a cute reindeer, not a character that appeared to be drunk. If the sketch had not been created, the officials may have never approved the story. Therefore, Choice B is the correct answer. The passage does not support the claims made in Choices A, C, or D.

9. B: Originally, May was asked to create a promotional coloring book, so Choice B is correct. The passage does not support the claims made in choices A, C, or D.

10. D: The task here is to identify the meaning of the word *misfit*. The word *misfit* means "oddball," so Choice D is correct. The words *member, conformist,* and *insider* are all antonyms, or opposites, for the word *misfit,* so Choices A, B, and C are incorrect.

11. C: The author's tone is informative, so Choice C is correct. The author is not humorous, apologetic, or sad in this passage, so Choices A, B, and D are incorrect.

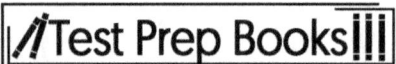

Answer Explanations #1

12. C: The word *iconic* means familiar, widely known, or classic, so Choice *C* is the correct answer. Although it is true that the story has not always been a cartoon, and the word *icon* can also mean image, the word *iconic* is not synonymous with the word *cartoon*, so Choice *A* is incorrect. One might confuse the word iconic with the word *ironic*, which would be a close match for Choice *B*, sarcastic, but this is not the correct answer because the now-classic story is not a sarcastic staple. Choice *D* is incorrect because *essential* is closer in meaning to the word *staple*; "essential staple" would be redundant. The choice that fits the context best is Choice *C*, classic.

13. A: Sentence 8 indicates that as the temperature of water increases, water molecules move rapidly and spread farther apart, so Choice *A* is correct.

14. A: Choice *A* is correct because as water vapor cools, the water molecules move closer together and move more slowly to form a liquid.

15. A: The passage discusses water having the ability to occupy three states of matter, so Choice *A* is the correct answer. Choices *B, C,* and *D* are supporting details in the passage, so they are incorrect.

16. D: Molecules are tiny units, or particles, of something, so Choice *D* is correct. Choices *A, B,* and *C* are antonyms for the word *molecule,* so they are incorrect.

17. B: Because steam, also known as *water vapor,* is water in the form of gas, Choice *B* is correct.

18. D: *Conversely* is a word used to mean "the other way around." The words in Choices *A, B,* and *C* have the opposite meaning and are incorrect.

19. C: The author tells this sad story to illustrate the impact texting while driving can have, not just on the driver, but also on the passengers, so Choice *C* is correct.

20. B: Choice *B* is correct because the phrase *screeched like an alley cat* is a simile. A simile is a comparison of two similar things (the sound of the tires and the screech of an alley cat) using the words *like* or *as*. Choice *A* is incorrect because a metaphor does not contain the words *like* or *as*. An alliteration is the repetition of a consonant sound at the beginning of several consecutive words, so choice *C* is incorrect. A cliché is an overused phrase. Therefore, Choice *D* is incorrect.

21. A: Choice *A* is correct because the story is told from a first-person point of view. In first-person narratives, the author is a character in the story and uses words such as *I, me,* and *we*. Second person, Choice *B*, which is uncommon, includes words such as *you, your,* and *yours*. In third person, Choice *C*, narratives, the narrator is not a character in the story and uses words such as *he, she,* and *they*. Choice *D*, fourth person, is a made-up choice.

22. A: The author says that Ricky, Bobby, and Alyssa never got to see the dancing lights of the ambulances and police cars. Thus, readers can conclude that they didn't survive the accident.

23. B: This story serves to highlight the potential consequences of texting and driving to dissuade readers from doing it. This means Choice *B* is the answer.

24. C: The first paragraph explains in detail how the girls' mothers wanted the day to be fun. Readers can conclude Choice *C* is the correct answer. The story includes no information to indicate that Choices *A* or *D* are correct. Choice *B* might be correct, but the text does not provide enough information for that conclusion.

25. C: Choice *C*, an obituary, is the correct answer. Obituaries are biographies written to honor someone who has passed away.

Answer Explanations #1

26. B: *In lieu of* means "instead of"; thus, the family is requesting that instead of sending flowers, people donate money to Princess Diana's memorial fund.

27. B: Paragraph 3 explains her dedication to charity work, so Choice *B* is the correct answer.

28. C: Lines 4–5 explain that after school, Princess Diana became a teacher's assistant, so Choice *C* is the correct answer.

29. B: The passage explains that Diana did a great deal of charity work for children in need. The passage also states that the family is asking mourners to donate to the Diana, Princess of Wales Memorial Fund instead of purchasing flowers for the funeral. Readers can safely assume at least some of the donation money will help needy children, so Choice *B* is correct.

30. A: Choice *A* is correct because basic information given about Princess Diana's life is followed by current events, such as details about the funeral and where to send donations.

31. C: Trash is the most likely item to be found in the basket. When Mr. Walter bought the bike, he started riding around town and cleaning up the cans and trash he would find. It's reasonable to assume that he would put the trash in the basket. Choice *A* is incorrect. Lunch from McDonald's is not a likely item to be found in the basket because from the details in the passage, it seems that Mr. Walter spent his time near the street waving to people in passing cars, not eating lunch. Choice *B* is incorrect because Mr. Walter used to hand out hats and gloves when he was a crossing guard. He didn't buy the bike until he got too old to be a crossing guard, so it's probably safe to assume that he was not carrying hats and gloves in the basket. Choice *D* is incorrect because there are no details in the passage that mention Mr. Walter handing out toys to children.

32. D: Throughout the passage, the author speaks of ways Mr. Walter touched the lives of everyone in the town of Vinson, so Choice *D* is correct.

33. B: This passage is considered a short story because it has a message, a sequence of events, and characters. Thus, Choice *B* is correct.

34. A: Choice *A* is correct because lines 6–7 tell readers that Mr. Walter gave out gloves and hats during the winter to children who needed them.

35. B: Choice *B* is correct because the author is trying to point out that heroes can be everyday people who consistently do little things in their communities to impact the lives of others.

36. A: Details in the story support the inference that Mr. Walter was a caring person. He cared about the kids in his town and showed this by helping them cross the street, remembering their names, and having hats and gloves for them when it was cold outside. He also cared about his town and showed this by cleaning up trash because "it was his job to look out for the city." These details make Choice *A* correct. Although the other choices could possibly be true, there is no evidence in the passage to back up the inferences made in Choices *B*, *C*, or *D*.

Mathematics Achievement

1. B: The coordinates of A in the graph are $(-8, 2)$. First, the triangle is reflected over the *y*-axis, placing point *A* at $(8, 2)$. Then, shifting it down 3 units moves it to $(8, -1)$.

2. C: The even numbers between 1 and 15 are 2, 4, 6, 8, 10, 12, and 14. Therefore, 7 out of the 15 numbers are even. This is equal to the probability.

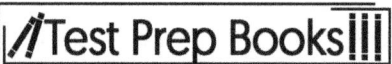

3. B: The expression is simplified by collecting like terms. Terms with the same variable and exponent are like terms, and their coefficients can be added.

4. B: $\frac{810}{2,921}$

Multiply across the top and across the bottom.

$$\frac{15 \times 54}{23 \times 127} = \frac{810}{2921}$$

This matches Choice B, but we must decide whether it can be reduced. Because the numbers are so large, it may be difficult to tell, so the easiest method may be to look at each of the other answer choices. In Choice A, the numerator is the same as in our original fraction, but the denominator isn't, so this can't have the same value. With Choice C, we can tell that the denominator, 292, is not a factor of 2,921 because $292 \times 10 = 2,920$, not 2,921, so that doesn't work. With Choice D, again, we can see that the denominator, 150, is not a factor of 2,921, because 150 is a multiple of 10 and 2,921 isn't. The other choices are eliminated, so the answer must be Choice B.

5. A: We can try to solve the equation by factoring the numerator into $(x + 6)(x - 5)$. Since $(x - 5)$ is on the top and bottom, that factor cancels out. This leaves the equation $x + 6 = 11$. Solving the equation gives the answer $x = 5$. When this value is plugged into the equation, it yields a zero in the denominator of the fraction. Since this is undefined, there is no solution.

6. B: Reflecting the circle across the y-axis changes the sign of the x-coordinate, so the new center would be (5,5). Then, shifting to the left would decrease the same coordinate by 6. The new center is (-1,5).

7. A: For an ordered pair to be a solution to a system of inequalities, it must make a true statement for both inequalities when substituting its values for x and y. Substituting $(-3,-2)$ into the inequalities produces $(-2) > 2(-3) - 3$ which becomes $-2 > -9$, and $(-2) < -4(-3) + 8$, which becomes $-2 < 20$. Both are true statements.

8. C: Converting a fraction to a percentage takes two steps. First, divide the numerator by the denominator to turn the fraction into a decimal:

$$\frac{2}{9} = 0.2222 \ldots$$

The "…" indicates a repeating decimal with an infinite number of 2s. Now, to convert to a percentage, move the decimal point two places to the right: 22.22%

9. D: Denote the width as w and the length as l. Then, $l = 3w + 5$. The perimeter is $2w + 2l = 90$. Substituting the first expression for l into the second equation yields:

$$2(3w + 5) + 2w = 90$$

$$6w + 10 + 2w = 90$$

$$8w = 80$$

$$w = 10$$

Putting this into the first equation, it yields:

$$l = 3(10) + 5 = 35$$

10. C: The shape has 6 sides of equal length. This is known as a hexagon. Because there are 6 sides and the total number of degrees in an n-sided polygon is $(n - 2) \cdot 180$, the total number of degrees in a hexagon is $4 \times 180° = 720°$. Each angle has $\frac{720}{6} = 120°$.

11. B: 300 miles in four hours is $\frac{300}{4} = 75$ miles per hour. In 1.5 hours, the car will go 1.5×75 miles, or 112.5 miles.

12. C: Let a be the number of apples purchased, and let p be the number of papayas purchased. There is a total of 15 pieces of fruit, so one equation is:

$$a + p = 15$$

The total cost is $35, which in terms of the total apples and papayas purchased can be written as:

$$2a + 3p = 35$$

If we multiply the first equation by 2 on both sides, it becomes:

$$2a + 2p = 30$$

We then subtract this equation from the second equation:

$$2a + 3p - (2a + 2p) = 35 - 30$$

$$p = 5$$

So, 5 papayas were purchased.

13. B: If Shawna has used $\frac{1}{3}$ of the paint, she has $\frac{2}{3}$ remaining. The mixed fraction can be converted because $2\frac{1}{2}$ gallons is the same as $\frac{5}{2}$ gallons. The calculation is:

$$\frac{2}{3} \times \frac{5}{2} = \frac{10}{6} = \frac{5}{3} = 1\frac{2}{3} \text{ gallons}$$

14. A: The probability that a single coin lands on heads is $\frac{1}{2}$. Therefore, the probability that all 4 coins land on heads is $\left(\frac{1}{2}\right)\left(\frac{1}{2}\right)\left(\frac{1}{2}\right)\left(\frac{1}{2}\right) = \left(\frac{1}{2}\right)^4 = \frac{1}{16} = 0.0625$.

Answer Explanations #1

15. C:

$$9x + x - 7 = 16 + 2x \quad \text{Combine } 9x \text{ and } x.$$

$$10x - 7 = 16 + 2x$$

$$10x - 7 + 7 = 16 + 2x + 7 \quad \text{Add 7 to both sides to remove } (-7).$$

$$10x = 23 + 2x$$

$$10x - 2x = 23 + 2x - 2x \quad \text{Subtract } 2x \text{ from both sides to move it to the other side of the equation.}$$

$$8x = 23$$

$$\frac{8x}{8} = \frac{23}{8} \quad \text{Divide by 8 to get } x \text{ by itself.}$$

$$x = \frac{23}{8}$$

16. B: The origin is (0,0). The slope is given by $\frac{(y^2 - y^1)}{(x^2 - x^1)} = \frac{1-0}{2-0} = \frac{1}{2}$.

The y-intercept will be 0 since it passes through the origin. Using slope-intercept form, the equation for this line is:

$$y = \frac{1}{2}x$$

17. C: The slope of the line given is $m = \frac{-8-5}{2-4} = \frac{-13}{-2} = \frac{13}{2}$. The slope of a line perpendicular is the negative reciprocal, which is $-\frac{2}{13}$.

18. A: The slope is given by the change in y divided by the change in x. The change in y is $2 - 0 = 2$, and the change in x is $0 - (-4) = 4$. The slope is $\frac{2}{4} = \frac{1}{2}$.

19. D: First, simplify the larger fraction by separating it into two. When dividing one fraction by another, remember to invert the second fraction and multiply the two as follows:

$$\frac{5}{7} \div \frac{9}{11} = \frac{5}{7} \times \frac{11}{9}$$

The resulting fraction $\frac{55}{63}$ cannot be simplified further, so this is the answer to the problem.

20. A: The slope is given by the change in y divided by the change in x. Specifically, it's:

$$slope = \frac{y_2 - y_1}{x_2 - x_1}$$

Work from left to right when identifying coordinates. The first point is $(-5, -3)$, and the second point is $(0, -1)$. Now we just need to plug those numbers into the equation:

$$slope = \frac{-1 - (-3)}{0 - (-5)}$$

Answer Explanations #1

It can be simplified to:

$$slope = \frac{-1+3}{0+5}$$

$$slope = \frac{2}{5}$$

21. A: The figure is composed of three sides of a square and a semicircle. The sides of the square are simply added:

$$8 \text{ in} + 8 \text{ in} + 8 \text{ in} = 24 \text{ in}$$

The circumference of a circle is found by the equation $C = 2\pi r$. The radius is 4 in, so the circumference of the circle is approximately 25.13 in. Only half of the circle makes up the outer border of the figure (part of the perimeter), and half of 25.13 is 12.565. Therefore, the total perimeter is:

$$24 \text{ in} + 12.565 \text{ in} = 36.565 \text{ in}$$

The other answer choices use the incorrect formula or fail to include all of the necessary sides.

22. A: Putting the scores in order from least to greatest, we have 60, 75, 80, and 85, as well as one unknown. The median is 80, so 80 must be the middle data point out of these five. Therefore, the unknown data point must be the fourth or fifth data point, meaning it must be greater than or equal to 80. The only answer that fails to meet this condition is 60.

23. C: The sum of angle ACD and ACB is 180°. Therefore, Angle ACB is 180 – 120 = 60°. Similarly, the sum of angle EBC and ABC is 180°. Therefore, angle ABC is 180 – 135 = 45°. The 3 angles ABC, BCA, and BAC add up to 180° as well. Therefore, x = 180 – 45 – 60 = 75°.

24. C: The volume of a rectangular prism $is\ V = length \times width \times height$. Substituting the values given in the problem, we find $V = 2 \times 4 \times 6 = 48$.

25. A: Let the unknown score be x. The average will be:

$$\frac{5 \times 50 + 4 \times 70 + x}{10} = \frac{530 + x}{10} = 55$$

Multiply both sides by 10 to get $530 + x = 550$, or $x = 20$.

26. B: We can first find the total cost of the hat and jersey, then multiply by 0.5 to apply the 50% off:

$$(32.99 + 64.99) \times 0.5 = 48.99$$

Finally, we calculate the sales tax of 6% (that is, 0.06) and add it to the total:

$$48.99 + (48.99 \times 0.06) = 51.93$$

27. A: The area of the square is the square of its side length, so $4^2 = 16$ square inches. The area of a triangle is half the base times the height. So,

$$\frac{1}{2} \times 2 \times 8 = 8 \text{ square inches}$$

The total area is $16 + 8 = 24$ square inches.

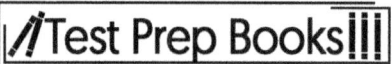

28. D: Multiply each of the terms in the first parentheses with each of the terms in the second parentheses.

$$(2x - 3)(4x + 2)$$
$$2x(4x) + 2x(2) - 3(4x) - 3(2)$$
$$8x^2 + 4x - 12x - 6$$
$$8x^2 - 8x - 6$$

29. A: First, separate each element of the numerator with the denominator as follows:

$$\frac{2xy^2}{16xy} + \frac{4x}{16xy} - \frac{8y}{16xy}$$

Simplify each expression accordingly, reaching Choice A:

$$\frac{y}{8} + \frac{1}{4y} - \frac{1}{2x}$$

30. A: When parentheses are around two expressions, they need to be multiplied. In this case, separate each expression into its parts (separated by addition and subtraction) and multiply by each of the parts in the other expression. Remember that when multiplying a positive integer by a negative integer, it will remain negative. Then, add the products together:

$$(3x)(x) + (3x)(-8) + (+5)(x) + (+5)(-8)$$
$$3x^2 - 24x + 5x - 40$$

Then add $-24x$ and $5x$ together to get the final simplified expression $3x^2 - 19x - 40$, Choice A.

31. C: In order to calculate the profit, we need to create an equation that models the total income minus the cost of the materials.

$$60 \times \$20 = \$1,200 \text{ total income}$$
$$60 \div 3 = 20 \text{ sets of materials}$$
$$20 \times \$12 = \$240 \text{ cost of materials}$$
$$\$1,200 - \$240 = \$960 \text{ profit}$$

32. B: If 60% of 50 workers are women, then there are 30 women working in the office. If half of them are wearing skirts, then that means 15 women wear skirts. Since nobody else wears skirts, this means there are 15 people wearing skirts.

33. D: There are 30 + 20 + 10 = 60 total crayons. 10 out of the 60 are yellow. Therefore, 50 out of the 60 are not yellow. The probability of selecting a crayon that is not yellow is $\frac{50}{60} = \frac{5}{6}$.

34. B: The total number of degrees in a rectangle is 360 since each corner represents a right angle, which is 90°. The total number of degrees in any type of triangle is 180. 360 – 180 = 180. Therefore, 20% of 180 is $0.2(180) = 36$.

Answer Explanations #1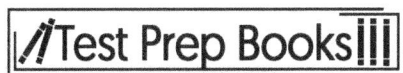

35. A: To find the fraction of the bill that the first three people pay, the fractions need to be added, which means finding the common denominator. The common denominator will be 60:

$$\frac{1}{5} + \frac{1}{4} + \frac{1}{3} = \frac{12}{60} + \frac{15}{60} + \frac{20}{60} = \frac{47}{60}$$

The remainder of the bill is:

$$1 - \frac{47}{60} = \frac{60}{60} - \frac{47}{60} = \frac{13}{60}$$

36. B: Total tuition for 4 years is:

$$\$22{,}000 \times 4 = \$88{,}000$$

Total room and board for 4 years is:

$$\$5{,}000 \times 4 = \$20{,}000$$

Total cost of books for four years is $\$500 \times 4 = \$2{,}000$. Therefore, it is estimated that you will spend $\$88{,}000 + \$20{,}000 + \$2{,}000 = \$110{,}000$ on college. Your family is going to pay 25% of this cost, which is:

$$0.25 \times \$110{,}000 = \$27{,}500$$

Therefore, you will be responsible for:

$$\$110{,}000 - \$27{,}500 = \$82{,}500$$

Therefore, to obtain your goal, you will need to have $82,500 in your account before college starts.

37. B: To find the mean, or average, of a set of values, add the values together and then divide by the total number of values. We will need to add up the number of adult tickets sold for the week and divide by the total number of days. The equation is as follows:

$$\frac{22 + 16 + 24 + 19 + 29}{5} = 22$$

38. C: The Pythagorean theorem states that, for right triangles, $c^2 = a^2 + b^2$, with c being the side opposite the 90° angle. Substituting 24 as a, 36 as b, and x as c, the equation becomes:

$$x^2 = 24^2 + 36^2 = 576 + 1{,}296 = 1{,}872$$

The last step is to take the square root of both sides to remove the exponent:

$$x = \sqrt{1{,}872} \approx 43.3$$

39. C: The data set is the following: {0, 0, 0, 0, 1, 1, 1, 2, 3}. There are odd number of values, so the median is the middle number, which is 1.

40. B: Start with the original equation: $x^2 - 2xy + 2y$, then replace each instance of x with a 2 and each instance of y with a 3 to get:

$$2^2 - 2 \times 2 \times 3 + 2 \times 3^2 = 4 - 12 + 18 = 10$$

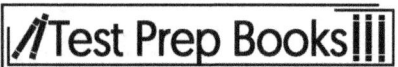

41. C: This can be determined by finding the length and width of the shaded region. The length can be found using the length of the top rectangle, which is 18 inches, and then subtracting the extra length of 4 inches and 1 inch. This means the length of the shaded region is 13 inches. Next, the width can be determined using the 6-inch measurement and subtracting the 2-inch measurement. This means that the width is 4 inches. Thus, the area is:

$$13 \times 4 = 52 \text{ sq. in.}$$

42. D: 25% of the day on average is spent listening to music. 8% of the day on average is spent watching TV. The total of both TV and music is 33%. 33% of 24 hours is $0.33 \times 24 = 7.92$ hours.

43. C: To find what 85% of 20 questions is, multiply 20 by 0.85:

$$20 \times 0.85 = 17 \text{ questions}$$

44. C: The triangles are similar, so we can set up the following proportion:

$$\frac{6}{4} = \frac{8}{y}$$

Cross-multiply to obtain $6y = 32$. Divide both sides by 6 to obtain $y = \frac{32}{6} = \frac{16}{3}$.

45. C: The mean of a set of numbers is equal to the sum of the numbers divided by the total number of values. Therefore, $72 = \frac{sum}{14}$. Therefore, the sum is $72 \times 14 = 1,008$.

46. B: There are 5 + 6 + 9 = 20 total donuts in the box. The probability of the first donut being vanilla is $\frac{5}{20}$. The first donut is not replaced. Therefore, the probability that the second donut is vanilla is $\frac{4}{19}$. Multiply these quantities together to find the probability that they are both vanilla: $\frac{5}{20} \times \frac{4}{19} = \frac{20}{380} = \frac{1}{19}$.

47. A: The quantity $(x - 14)^2$ is equivalent to $(x - 14)(x - 14) = x^2 - 14x - 14x + 196$, which is equal to $x^2 - 28x + 196$. Therefore, $b = -28$.

Practice Test #2

Verbal Reasoning

Synonyms

1. ORCHARD
    a. Farm
    b. Flower
    c. Fruit
    d. Grove

2. TEXTILE
    a. Document
    b. Fabric
    c. Knit
    d. Mural

3. OFFSPRING
    a. Bounce
    b. Child
    c. Parent
    d. Skip

4. PERMIT
    a. Allow
    b. Jail
    c. Law
    d. Parking

5. TAUT
    a. Instruct
    b. Rigid
    c. Unstable
    d. Sour

6. ROTATION
    a. Flip
    b. Orbit
    c. Spin
    d. Wheel

7. CONSISTENT
    a. Steady
    b. Sticky
    c. Stubborn
    d. Texture

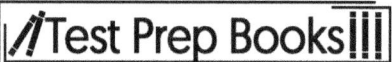

8. PRINCIPLE
    a. Foundation
    b. Leader
    c. Primary
    d. Royal

9. PERIMETER
    a. Area
    b. Inside
    c. Outline
    d. Side

10. SYMBOL
    a. Clang
    b. Drum
    c. Emblem
    d. Music

11. GERMINATE
    a. Grow
    b. Infect
    c. Plant
    d. Sick

12. LOQUACIOUS
    a. Loud
    b. Overbearing
    c. Quiet
    d. Talkative

13. FACETIOUS
    a. Annoying
    b. Lighthearted
    c. Serious
    d. Wry

14. PROFUSE
    a. Abundant
    b. Scarce
    c. Sincere
    d. Speedy

15. ASSIMILATE
    a. Abandon
    b. Conceal
    c. Integrate
    d. Restrict

Practice Test #2

16. INCREDULOUS
    a. Gullible
    b. Plausible
    c. Open-minded
    d. Unbelieving

17. SCHISM
    a. Filtration
    b. Laceration
    c. Separation
    d. Unification

18. DEXTERITY
    a. Incompetence
    b. Intelligence
    c. Skill
    d. Slowness

19. DILAPIDATED
    a. Decorated
    b. Deteriorated
    c. Expensive
    d. Inherited

Sentence Completion

For the next questions, choose the best word(s) to fill in the blank(s) in each sentence.

20. The animal shelter offered a free dog training program to _____ volunteers who were the top hard workers for the year, and funded it through the _____ donation from a wealthy benefactor.
    a. ambitious/munificent
    b. diligent/diminutive
    c. indolent/benevolent
    d. inspiring/paltry

21. After Harry lost his job, he had to learn how to be _____ and stop buying unnecessary items.
    a. conventional
    b. frugal
    c. mundane
    d. reclusive

22. The _____ school was in need of many repairs, but the costs were _____ due to its small budget.
    a. deteriorate/impractical
    b. dilapidated/prohibitive
    c. ruinous/tenable
    d. unreasonable/decaying

23. The professor made an effort to _____ answer student questions so that they felt at ease and _____ to share their thoughts during class.
    a. hastily/encouraged
    b. kindly/hesitant

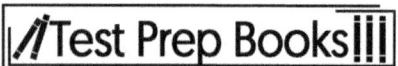

c. patiently/emboldened
d. vaguely/inquisitive

24. The archaeologist let out a(n) _____ cry after an intern broke a priceless artifact.
    a. anguished
    b. defiant
    c. ecstatic
    d. nonchalant

25. Marvin became _____ as he realized he couldn't get out of the cave and began to wish he had been more _____ in preparing his equipment.
    a. diligent/agitated
    b. frantic/methodical
    c. morose/fortified
    d. panicked/haphazard

26. Jeremy was on a mission to take a rare video of the _____ red panda, who lives in high-altitude forests that are _____ for most people due to treacherous terrain.
    a. coveted/laborious
    b. elusive/inaccessible
    c. prevalent/unattainable
    d. secretive/treacherous

27. The student's paper was so _____ that the teacher used it as a model example for years afterwards.
    a. austere
    b. exemplary
    c. intrepid
    d. pedantic

28. Marianne's favorite band was coming to town and she was _____ that she didn't have the funds to go, so she cried and _____ her mother for help paying for the tickets.
    a. apathetic/pleaded
    b. devastated/implored
    c. envious/belittled
    d. exasperation/beseeched

29. Penelope's wedding cake tasting left much to be desired as five out of the six cakes were _____.
    a. ambitious
    b. delectable
    c. dubious
    d. inadequate

30. Carlos, a medical school student, was _____ due to his final exam grade, which was lower than he _____ based on his success during his studies.
    a. detached/foreseen
    b. distraught/anticipated
    c. jubilant/dreaded
    d. lethargic/expectation

31. Cynthia's classmates happily provided her with _____ support as she fought against a(n) _____ chronic illness that left her bedbound throughout the school year.
    a. reluctant/manageable
    b. steadfast/debilitate
    c. unconditional/temperate
    d. unwavering/incapacitating

32. Thanksgiving is typically a time of practicing _____ for all that you are thankful for, but some people view it as simply a holiday to enjoy _____ food.
    a. clemency/palatable
    b. compassion/unappetizing
    c. gratitude/delectable
    d. pondering/abundant

33. Meghan became_____ at work despite her subpar performance, which ultimately led to her being fired.
    a. complacent
    b. diligent
    c. overzealous
    d. punctual

34. Tiffany struggled to build her first model train due to the _____ instructions that even an expert couldn't make sense of.
    a. adequate
    b. convoluted
    c. pragmatic
    d. precarious

35. Patients with the flu report feeling _____ to the point where they are unable to get out of bed.
    a. fervent
    b. lethargic
    c. melancholic
    d. nostalgic

36. After being CEO for twenty-five years, it was difficult for Adam to retire and _____ his power.
    a. assimilate
    b. condescend
    c. relinquish
    d. sustain

37. Because Cathy already had over twenty mugs at home, she looked at the pretty one on the shelf and painfully decided that it was _____.
    a. affluent
    b. insentient
    c. obsolete
    d. superfluous

38. During a heated argument, Janet blurted out a(n) _____ remark that caused her husband to feel enraged.
    a. ambiguous
    b. formidable
    c. incendiary

d. trivial

39. Carrie didn't want to make any mistakes as she was knitting a large blanket, so each stitch was done _____.
   a. abnormally
   b. hastily
   c. meticulously
   d. valiantly

40. The student would not calm down after the teacher had yelled at him; so, the principal decided to take a _____ approach to put him at ease.
   a. cautious
   b. conciliatory
   c. neutral
   d. skeptical

Quantitative Reasoning

Word Problems

1. Carly purchased 84 bulbs for her flower garden. Tulips came in trays containing six bulbs and daffodils came in trays containing 8 bulbs. Carly bought an equal number of tulip and daffodil trays. How many of each type of flower bulb were purchased?
   a. 3 trays
   b. 4 trays
   c. 6 trays
   d. 8 trays

2. Kassidy drove for 3 hours at a speed of 60 miles per hour. How far did Kassidy travel?
   a. 65 miles
   b. 90 miles
   c. 120 miles
   d. 180 miles

3. Karen gets paid a weekly salary and a commission for every sale that she makes. The table below shows the number of sales and her pay for different weeks.

Sales	2	7	4	8
Pay	$380	$580	$460	$620

Which of the following equations represents Karen's weekly pay?
   a. $y = 40x - 300$
   b. $y = 40x + 300$
   c. $y = 90x - 200$
   d. $y = 90x + 200$

4. What is the 42nd item in the pattern: ▲oo□▲oo□▲...?
   a. o
   b. ▲
   c. □
   d. oo

5. Which of the following statements is true about the two lines below?

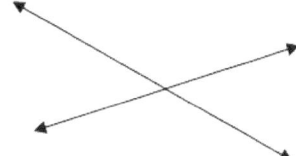

   a. The two lines are parallel but not perpendicular.
   b. The two lines are perpendicular but not parallel.
   c. The two lines are both parallel and perpendicular.
   d. The two lines are neither parallel nor perpendicular.

6. Which of the following figures is NOT a polygon?
   a. Pentagon
   b. Triangle
   c. Rhombus
   d. Cone

7. What are the coordinates of the point plotted on the grid?

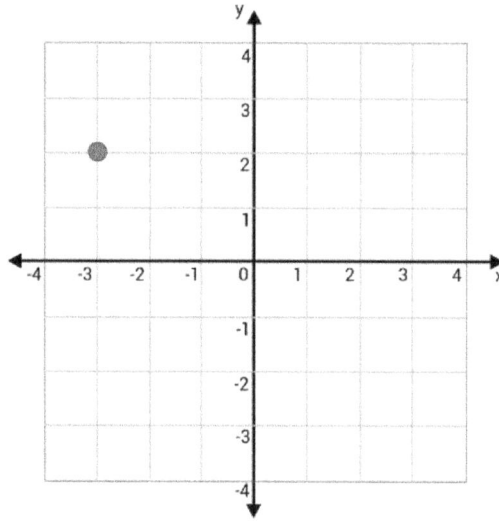

   a. (2, -3)
   b. (2, 3)
   c. (-3, -2)
   d. (-3, 2)

8. The perimeter of a 6-sided polygon is 56 cm. The lengths of 3 sides are 9 cm each. The lengths of 2 other sides are 8 cm each. What is the length of the final side?
   a. 10 cm
   b. 11 cm
   c. 12 cm
   d. 13 cm

9. Katie works at a clothing company and sold 192 shirts over the weekend. One-third of the shirts that were sold were patterned, and the rest were solid. Which mathematical expression would calculate the number of solid shirts Katie sold over the weekend?
   a. $192 \div \frac{1}{3}$
   b. $192 \times \frac{1}{3}$
   c. $192 \div (1 - \frac{1}{3})$
   d. $192 \times (1 - \frac{1}{3})$

10. Before a race of 4 horses, you make a random guess of which horse will get first place and which will get second place. What is the probability that both your guesses will be correct?

  a. $\frac{1}{16}$
  b. $\frac{1}{12}$
  c. $\frac{1}{4}$
  d. $\frac{1}{2}$

11. This chart indicates how many sales of CDs, vinyl records, and MP3 downloads occurred over the last year. Approximately what percentage of the total sales was from CDs?

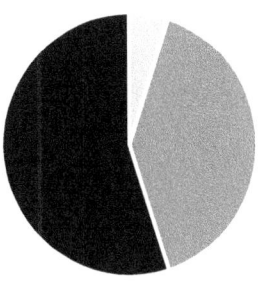

Total Sales of Vinyl Records, CDs, and MP3 Downloads (in millions)

Vinyl CD MP3

  a. 5%
  b. 25%
  c. 40%
  d. 55%

12. In 2015, it was estimated that there were 7,350,000,000 people living on Earth. Express this value in scientific notation.

  a. 7.35×10^7
  b. 7.35×10^9
  c. 73.5×10^8
  d. 73.5×10^9

13. A school's faculty consists of 15 teachers and 20 teaching assistants. They have 200 students. What is the ratio of faculty to students?

  a. $3:20$
  b. $4:17$
  c. $11:54$
  d. $7:40$

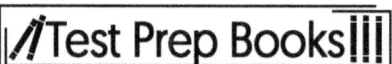

14. The total perimeter of a rectangle is 36 cm. If the length is 12 cm, what is the width?
    a. 3 cm
    b. 6 cm
    c. 9 cm
    d. 12 cm

15. If h is a multiple of 5, which of the following must also be multiples of 5?
    a. $5h - 3$
    b. $4h + 1$
    c. $10h + 20$
    d. $h^3 + 6$

16. If $4x - 3 = 5$, what is the value of x?
    a. 1
    b. 2
    c. 3
    d. 4

17. On Monday, Robert mopped the floor in 4 hours. On Tuesday, he did it in 3 hours. If on Monday, his average rate of mopping was p sq. ft. per hour, what was his average rate on Tuesday?
    a. $\frac{1}{3}p$ sq. ft. per hour
    b. $\frac{3}{4}p$ sq. ft. per hour
    c. $\frac{5}{4}p$ sq. ft. per hour
    d. $\frac{4}{3}p$ sq. ft. per hour

18. A rectangle was formed out of pipe cleaner. Its length was 3 in, and its width was 8 inches. What is its area in square inches?
    a. 16 in²
    b. 22 in²
    c. 24 in²
    d. 32 in²

Practice Test #2

19. If $6t + 4 = 16$, what is t?
    a. 1
    b. 2
    c. 3
    d. 4

20. Suppose $\frac{x+2}{x} = 2$. What is x?
    a. -1
    b. 0
    c. 2
    d. 4

21. If the sides of a cube are 3 inches long, what is its volume?
    a. 3 in^3
    b. 6 in^3
    c. 18 in^3
    d. 27 in^3

Quantitative Comparisons

For questions 22–37, compare Quantity A to Quantity B, using additional information presented above the two quantities if provided:

22. An octagon has a perimeter equaling 17.6 inches.

Quantity A	Quantity B
The length of 6 of its sides	13.4 inches

    a. Quantity A is greater.
    b. Quantity B is greater.
    c. The two quantities are equal.
    d. The relationship cannot be determined from the information given.

23.

Quantity A	Quantity B
$(5.25)^{-4}$	$\left(\frac{1}{5.25}\right)^4$

    a. Quantity A is greater.
    b. Quantity B is greater.
    c. The two quantities are equal.
    d. The relationship cannot be determined from the information given.

24.

Quantity A	Quantity B
5% of 0.55	4% of 0.44

    a. Quantity A is greater.
    b. Quantity B is greater.
    c. The two quantities are equal.
    d. The relationship cannot be determined from the information given.

25.

Quantity A	Quantity B
$(x + 2y)(x^2 - 2xy + 4y^2)$	$x^3 + 8y^3$

a. Quantity A is greater.
b. Quantity B is greater.
c. The two quantities are equal.
d. The relationship cannot be determined from the information given.

26.

Quantity A	Quantity B
$2x$	$\sqrt{4x^2}$

a. Quantity A is greater.
b. Quantity B is greater.
c. The two quantities are equal.
d. The relationship cannot be determined from the information given.

27. Let $h(x) = 8x^2 + 2x$

Quantity A	Quantity B
$h(-3)$	$h(3)$

a. Quantity A is greater.
b. Quantity B is greater.
c. The two quantities are equal.
d. The relationship cannot be determined from the information given.

28.

Quantity A	Quantity B
The slope of the line $2x + 3y = 8$	The slope of the line $-2x + 3y = -8$

a. Quantity A is greater.
b. Quantity B is greater.
c. The two quantities are equal.
d. The relationship cannot be determined from the information given.

29. Calculate the slope of the lines that connect the points in each quantity.

Quantity A	Quantity B
(-1,1) and (2,2)	(1,-1) and (-2,-2)

a. Quantity A is greater.
b. Quantity B is greater.
c. The two quantities are equal.
d. The relationship cannot be determined from the information given.

Practice Test #2

30. The area of a circle with radius r is πr^2.

Quantity A	Quantity B
The area of a circle with a radius of 9 ft	The area of a circle with a diameter of 18 ft

   a. Quantity A is greater.
   b. Quantity B is greater.
   c. The two quantities are equal.
   d. The relationship cannot be determined from the information given.

31.

Quantity A	Quantity B
$(a-b)^2$	$a^2 - 2ab + b^2$

   a. Quantity A is greater.
   b. Quantity B is greater.
   c. The two quantities are equal.
   d. The relationship cannot be determined from the information given.

32.

Quantity A	Quantity B
The y-intercept of the line $-3x + 6y = 9$	The y-intercept of the line $3x + 4y = -10$

   a. Quantity A is greater.
   b. Quantity B is greater.
   c. The two quantities are equal.
   d. The relationship cannot be determined from the information given.

33. Consider the following data set: {1, 3, 5, 7, 9, 11, 13}

Quantity A	Quantity B
The mean of the data set	The median of the data set

   a. Quantity A is greater.
   b. Quantity B is greater.
   c. The two quantities are equal.
   d. The relationship cannot be determined from the information given.

34.

Quantity A	Quantity B
The largest prime factor of 98	The largest prime factor of 51

   a. Quantity A is greater.
   b. Quantity B is greater.
   c. The two quantities are equal.
   d. The relationship cannot be determined from the information given.

35.

Quantity A	Quantity B
$4x^2 + 2x - 10x - 5$	$(2x-5)(2x+1)$

   a. Quantity A is greater.
   b. Quantity B is greater.
   c. The two quantities are equal.
   d. The relationship cannot be determined from the information given.

36.

Quantity A	Quantity B
The standard deviation of the data set {100, 100, 100, 100, 100}	The standard deviation of the data set {1, 2, 3, 4, 5}

   a. Quantity A is greater.
   b. Quantity B is greater.
   c. The two quantities are equal.
   d. The relationship cannot be determined from the information given.

37. Michael mows lawns twice as fast as Jay. Together, they mowed 22 lawns.

Quantity A	Quantity B
The number of lawns mowed by Michael	The number of lawns mowed by Jay

   a. Quantity A is greater.
   b. Quantity B is greater.
   c. The two quantities are equal.
   d. The relationship cannot be determined from the information given.

Reading Comprehension

Passage 1

[1] George Washington emerged out of the American Revolution as an unlikely champion of liberty. On June 14, 1775, the Second Continental Congress created the Continental [3]Army, and John Adams, serving in the Congress, nominated Washington to be its first commander. Washington had fought under the British during the French and Indian [5]War, and his experience and prestige proved instrumental to the American war effort. Washington provided invaluable leadership, training, and strategy during the [7]Revolutionary War. He emerged from the war as the embodiment of liberty and freedom from tyranny.

[9]After vanquishing the heavily favored British forces, Washington could have pronounced himself the autocratic leader of the former colonies without any [11]opposition, but he famously refused and returned to his Mount Vernon plantation. His restraint proved his commitment to the fledgling state's republicanism. Washington was [13]later unanimously elected as the first American president. But it is Washington's farewell address that cemented his legacy as a visionary worthy of study.

[15]In 1796, President Washington issued his farewell address by public letter. Washington enlisted his good friend, Alexander Hamilton, in drafting his most famous address. The [17]letter expressed Washington's faith in the Constitution and rule of law. He encouraged his fellow Americans to put aside partisan differences and establish a national union. [19]Washington warned Americans against meddling in foreign affairs and entering military alliances. Additionally, he stated his opposition to national political parties, [21]which he considered partisan and counterproductive.

Americans would be wise to remember Washington's farewell, especially during [23]presidential elections, when politics hit a fever pitch. They might want to question the political institutions that were not planned by the Founding Fathers, such as the [25]nomination process and political parties themselves.

Practice Test #2

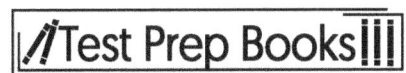

1. Which of the following statements could be inferred based on the informative in the passage?
    a. George Washington's background as a wealthy landholder directly led to his faith in equality, liberty, and democracy.
    b. George Washington would have opposed America's involvement in the Second World War.
    c. George Washington would not have been able to write as great a farewell address without the assistance of Alexander Hamilton.
    d. George Washington would probably not approve of modern political parties.

2. What is the purpose of this passage?
    a. To introduce George Washington to readers as a historical figure worthy of study
    b. To note that George Washington was more than a famous military hero
    c. To convince readers that George Washington is a hero of republicanism and liberty
    d. To inform American voters about a Founding Father's sage advice on a contemporary issue and explain its applicability to modern times

3. What is the tone of the passage?
    a. Informative
    b. Excited
    c. Bitter
    d. Comic

4. What does the word *meddling* mean in line 19?
    a. Supporting
    b. Speaking against
    c. Interfering
    d. Gathering

5. According to the passage, what did George Washington do when he was offered a role as leader of the former colonies?
    a. He refused the offer.
    b. He accepted the offer.
    c. He became angry at the offer.
    d. He accepted the offer then regretted it later.

6. What is the meaning of the word *hit* in line 23?
    a. Slapped
    b. Succeeded
    c. Caused
    d. Reached

Passage 2

¹Christopher Columbus is often credited with discovering America. This is incorrect. First, it is impossible to "discover" something where people already live; however, ³Christopher Columbus did explore places in the New World that were previously untouched by Europe, so the term "explorer" would be more accurate. Another ⁵correction must be made, as well: Christopher Columbus was not the first European explorer to reach the Americas! Rather, it was Leif Erikson who first came to the New ⁷World and contacted the natives, nearly five hundred years before Christopher Columbus.

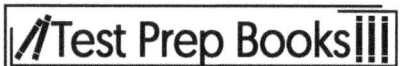

[9]Leif Erikson, the son of Erik the Red (a famous Viking outlaw and explorer in his own right), was born in either 970 or 980, depending on which historian you read. His own [11]family, though, did not raise Leif, which was a Viking tradition. Instead, one of Erik's prisoners taught Leif reading and writing, languages, sailing, and weaponry. At age 12, [13]Leif was considered a man and returned to his family. He killed a man during a dispute shortly after his return, and the council banished the Erikson clan to Greenland.

[15]In 999, Leif left Greenland and traveled to Norway, where he would serve as a guard to King Olaf Tryggvason. It was there that he became a convert to Christianity. Leif later [17]tried to return home with the intention of taking supplies and spreading Christianity to Greenland, but his ship was blown off course and he arrived in a strange new land: [19]present-day Newfoundland, Canada.

When he finally returned to his adopted homeland of Greenland, Leif consulted with a [21]merchant who had also seen the shores of this previously unknown land. The son of the legendary Viking explorer then gathered a crew of 35 men and set sail. Leif became [23]the first European to set foot in the New World as he explored present-day Baffin Island and Labrador, Canada. His crew called the land Vinland since it was plentiful with [25]grapes.

During their time in present-day Newfoundland, Leif's expedition made contact with the [27]natives, whom they referred to as Skraelings (which translates to "wretched ones" in Norse). There are several secondhand accounts of their meetings. Some contemporaries [29]described trade between the peoples. Other accounts describe clashes where the Skraelings defeated the Viking explorers with long spears, while still others claim the [31]Vikings dominated the natives. Regardless of the circumstances, it seems that the Vikings made contact of some kind. This happened around 1000, nearly 500 years [33]before Columbus famously sailed the ocean blue.

Eventually, in 1003, Leif set sail for home and arrived at Greenland with a ship full of [35]timber.

In 1020, 17 years later, the legendary Viking died. Many believe that Leif Erikson should [37]receive more credit for his contributions in exploring the New World.

7. Which of the following best describes how the author generally presents the information?
    a. Chronological order
    b. Comparison-contrast
    c. Cause-effect
    d. Conclusion-premises

8. Which of the following is an opinion, rather than a historical fact, expressed by the author?
    a. Leif Erikson was definitely the son of Erik the Red; however, historians debate the year of his birth.
    b. Leif Erikson's crew called the land Vinland since it was plentiful with grapes.
    c. Leif Erikson deserves more credit for his contributions in exploring the New World.
    d. Leif Erikson explored the Americas nearly 500 years before Christopher Columbus.

9. Which of the following most accurately describes the main idea of the passage?
    a. Leif Erikson is a legendary Viking explorer.
    b. Leif Erikson deserves more credit for exploring America hundreds of years before Columbus.
    c. Spreading Christianity motivated Leif Erikson's expeditions more than any other factor.
    d. Leif Erikson contacted the natives nearly five hundred years before Columbus.

10. Which of the following best describes the author's intent in the passage?
    a. To entertain
    b. To inform
    c. To alert
    d. To suggest

11. Which of the following can be logically inferred from the passage?
    a. The Vikings disliked exploring the New World.
    b. Leif Erikson's banishment from Iceland led to his exploration of present-day Canada.
    c. Leif Erikson never shared his stories of exploration with the King of Norway.
    d. Historians have difficulty definitively pinpointing events in the Vikings' history.

12. What can be inferred from the information in the passage?
    a. In addition to grapes, Erikson found trees to be plentiful in Vinland.
    b. Erikson spread Christianity among the Skraelings.
    c. Erikson's crew traded weapons with the natives in Vinland.
    d. Leif Erikson was born in Norway.

Passage 3

The Myth of Head Heat Loss

[1]It has recently been brought to my attention that most people believe that 75% of your body heat is lost through your head. I had certainly heard this before, and I'm not going [3]to attempt to say I didn't believe it when I first heard it. It is natural to be gullible to anything said with enough authority. But the "fact" that the majority of your body heat [5]is lost through your head is a lie.

Let me explain. Heat loss is proportional to surface area exposed. An elephant loses a [7]great deal more heat than an anteater because it has a much greater surface area than an anteater. Each cell has mitochondria that produce energy in the form of heat, and it [9]takes a lot more energy to run an elephant than an anteater.

So, each part of your body loses its proportional amount of heat in accordance with its [11]surface area. The human torso probably loses the most heat, though the legs lose a significant amount as well. Some people have asked, "Why does it feel so much warmer [13]when you cover your head than when you don't?" Well, that's because your head loses a lot of heat when it is not clothed, while the clothing on the rest of your body [15]provides insulation. If you went outside with a hat and pants but no shirt, not only would you look silly, but your heat loss would be significantly greater because so much [17]more of you would be exposed. So, if given the choice to cover your chest or your head in the cold, choose the chest. It could save your life.

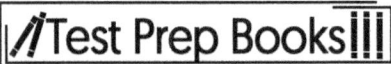

13. Why does the author compare elephants and anteaters?
    a. To express an opinion
    b. To give an example that helps clarify the main point
    c. To show the differences between the two
    d. To persuade why one is better than the other

14. Which of the following best describes the tone of the passage?
    a. Harsh
    b. Angry
    c. Casual
    d. Indifferent

15. According to the passage, which of the following probably loses the most heat?
    a. Head
    b. Leg
    c. Feet
    d. Torso

16. What does the word *gullible* mean in line 3?
    a. To be angry toward
    b. To distrust something
    c. To believe something easily
    d. To be happy toward

17. What is the main idea of the passage?
    a. To illustrate how people can easily believe anything they are told
    b. To prove that you have to have a hat to survive in the cold
    c. To persuade the audience that anteaters are better than elephants
    d. To debunk the myth that heat loss comes mostly from the head

18. Which of the following can be inferred based on the information in the passage?
    a. To cool down, taking your hat off will work better than taking your shirt off.
    b. To cool down, taking your shirt off will work better than taking your hat off.
    c. Removing your hat to cool down will only work if cool air is blowing toward your head.
    d. If you insulate your torso enough, your head does need to be covered in order to keep warm.

Passage 4

[1]People who argue that William Shakespeare is not responsible for the plays attributed to his name are known as anti-Stratfordians (from the name of Shakespeare's [3]birthplace, Stratford-upon-Avon). The most common anti-Stratfordian claim is that William Shakespeare simply was not educated enough or from a high enough social [5]class to have written plays overflowing with references to such a wide range of subjects like history, the classics, religion, and international culture. William Shakespeare was the [7]son of a glove-maker, he only had a basic grade-school education, and he never set foot outside of England—so how could he have produced plays of such sophistication and [9]imagination? How could he have written in such detail about historical figures and events, or about different cultures and locations around Europe? According to anti-[11]Stratfordians, the depth of knowledge contained in Shakespeare's plays suggests a well-traveled writer from a wealthy background with a university education, not a [13]countryside writer like Shakespeare. But in fact, there is not much substance to such speculation, and most anti-

Stratfordian arguments can be refuted with a little [15]background about Shakespeare's time and upbringing.

First of all, those who doubt Shakespeare's authorship often point to his common birth [17]and brief education as stumbling blocks to his writerly genius. Although it is true that Shakespeare did not come from a noble class, his father was a very successful glove-[19]maker and his mother was from a very wealthy landowning family—so while Shakespeare may have had a country upbringing, he was certainly from a well-off family [21]and would have been educated accordingly. Also, even though he did not attend university, grade-school education in Shakespeare's time was actually quite rigorous and [23]exposed students to classic drama through writers like Seneca and Ovid. It is not unreasonable to believe that Shakespeare received a very solid foundation in poetry and [25]literature from his early schooling.

Next, anti-Stratfordians tend to question how Shakespeare could write so extensively [27]about countries and cultures he had never visited before. For instance, several of his most famous works like *Romeo and Juliet* and *The Merchant of Venice* were set in Italy, [29]which is located on the opposite side of Europe from England. But again, this criticism does not hold up under scrutiny. For one thing, Shakespeare was living in London, a [31]bustling metropolis of international trade, the most populous city in England, and a political and cultural hub of Europe. In the daily crowds of people, Shakespeare would [33]certainly have been able to meet travelers from other countries and hear firsthand accounts of life in their home country. And, in addition to the influx of information from [35]world travelers, this was also the age of the printing press. This jump in technology made it possible to print and circulate books much more easily than in the past. This [37]also facilitated a freer flow of information across different countries, allowing people to read about life and ideas from all over Europe. One needn't travel the continent in [39]order to learn and write about its different cultures.

19. Which sentence contains the author's thesis?
    a. People who argue that William Shakespeare is not responsible for the plays attributed to his name are known as anti-Stratfordians.
    b. It is not unreasonable to believe that Shakespeare received a very solid foundation in poetry and literature from his early schooling.
    c. Next, anti-Stratfordians tend to question how Shakespeare could write so extensively about countries and cultures he had never visited before.
    d. But in fact, there is not much substance to such speculation, and most anti-Stratfordian arguments can be refuted with a little background about Shakespeare's time and upbringing.

20. In the first paragraph, "How could he have written in such detail about historical figures and events, or about different cultures and locations around Europe?" is an example of which of the following?
    a. Hyperbole
    b. Onomatopoeia
    c. Rhetorical question
    d. Appeal to authority

21. How does the author respond to the claim that Shakespeare was not well-educated because he did not attend university?
    a. By insisting upon Shakespeare's natural genius
    b. By explaining grade-school curriculum in Shakespeare's time
    c. By pointing out that Shakespeare's wealthy parents probably paid for private tutors
    d. By discussing Shakespeare's upbringing in London which was a political and cultural hub of Europe

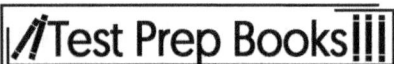

22. The word *bustling* in line 31 most nearly means which of the following?
    a. Busy
    b. Foreign
    c. Expensive
    d. Undeveloped

23. According to the passage, what did Shakespeare's father do to make a living?
    a. He was a king's guard.
    b. He acted in plays.
    c. He was a glove-maker.
    d. He was a cobbler.

24. Which of the following best describes the organization of the passage?
    a. A problem is presented and followed by two solutions.
    b. An argument is presented and followed by counterarguments.
    c. A chronological biography is given.
    d. A subject is presented and followed by facts and then opinions.

Passage 5

¹Do you want to vacation at a Caribbean island destination? We chose to go to St. Lucia, and it was the best vacation we ever had. We lounged in crystal blue waters, swam with ³dolphins, and enjoyed a family-friendly resort and activities. One of the activities we did was free diving in the ocean. We put our snorkels on, waded into the ocean, and swam ⁵down to the ocean floor. The water was clear all the way down—the greens and blues were so beautiful. We saw a stingray, some conches, and a Caribbean Reef Shark. The ⁷shark was so scary, I came up to the surface after that! But the rest of the day was spent lying on the beach, getting massages, and watching other kids play with a Frisbee ⁹in front of the water.

Towards the end of our vacation, I was reluctant to go home. We started to pack our ¹¹things, and then I realized I wanted to take one more walk with my mom and dad. Our resort was between the ocean and some mountains, so we decided to hike up a ¹³mountain and enjoy the view of the beach from way up high! We trekked for what seemed like miles, observing the vegetation along the way; it was so lush with reds and ¹⁵greens and blues. Finally, we got up to the top of the mountain and observed the wonderful ocean that stretched on for hundreds of miles. On our way back down, I felt ¹⁷totally at peace to be leaving the island, although I would miss it very much and would want to visit the island again soon. You should visit St. Lucia, or pick another island in ¹⁹the Caribbean! Every island offers a unique and dazzling vacation destination.

Practice Test #2

25. What island did the family stay on?
    a. St. Lucia
    b. Barbados
    c. Antigua
    d. Saint Kitts

26. What is/are the supporting detail(s) of this passage?
    a. Cruising to the Caribbean
    b. Local events
    c. Family activities
    d. Exotic cuisine

27. What was the last activity the speaker did?
    a. Swam with the sharks
    b. Went for a hike up a mountain
    c. Lounged on the beach
    d. Surfed in the waves

28. Which of the following is the best definition for the word *trekked* in line 13?
    a. Drove
    b. Ran
    c. Swam
    d. Walked

29. Which of the following words best describes the author's attitude toward the topic?
    a. Worried
    b. Resigned
    c. Objective
    d. Enthusiastic

30. Which of the following best states the author's purpose?
    a. To compare the ocean to the mountains on a Caribbean island
    b. To warn of the dangers of snorkeling
    c. To describe and encourage a Caribbean vacation
    d. To describe the wildlife and scenery of St. Lucia

Passage 6

[1]There are few people who haven't heard of the ancient city of Pompeii. It's the Roman city that was buried under nearly 19 feet of ash and debris after a two-day eruption [3]event at Mount Vesuvius. Many of the citizens were killed quickly, first by heat, and then others by ash suffocation. The ash preserved the area, providing a peek at daily life [5]in a Roman city. Initial excavations occurred early on, and the city was likely plundered. Further excavations by research and archaeological teams were banned after 1960 [7]when preceding expeditions left the city largely in decay. However, Pompeii would still have much more to reveal.

[9]After the eruption, it's believed that survivors as well as thieves visited the city to remove valuables, both personal and public. In fact, there was clear evidence, from [11]graffiti to actual dig holes, that homes were excavated and searched for prior to official or sanctioned explorations. The

city was largely undisturbed and remained [13]buried for a long time after this initial period. Then, in the 1500s and 1600s, there were two encounters with the ruins, although nothing major came of it.

[15]In the 1700s, the first major excavations were initiated after nearby Herculaneum was discovered. These led to several subsequent expeditions and major discoveries and a [17]greater understanding of the techniques and strategies that would best maintain the integrity of the site and reflect the moment when Pompeii was covered.

[19]For example, one archaeologist determined that air pockets under the ash were likely the result of decomposed organic remains and that if they injected the void with plaster, [21]they could re-create the body shapes. These advances were, unfortunately, matched by mistakes.

[23]In the 1920s and later in the 1950s, excavations were made that nearly uncovered whole sections in their entirety. However, these excavations and subsequent attempted [25]restorations were haphazard at best, and poor records were kept. As a result, further excavations were halted for several decades.

[27]Eventually, additional exploration was permitted but only in previously unexplored areas or other designated regions. Still, these new expeditions, with more modern [29]techniques and strategies, in part based on what we have already learned, are focused more on documenting and preserving than uncovering. That doesn't mean they haven't [31]come without their own amazing discoveries.

For example, in 2018, a well-preserved harnessed horse was unearthed in the Villa of [33]the Mysteries, a villa known for amazing frescoes. Subsequent discoveries in 2020 and 2021 have included slaves' quarters, a wealthy man and his slave, a ceremonial chariot, [35]an inn that revealed much about the fare being served, a dog's skeleton, and a fully intact tomb with mummified remains thought to belong to a freed slave.

[37]With so much left to be discovered, there's been a marked shift in strategies focused on preservation and conservation rather than continued digs. While buried, the city [39]remained fairly well preserved because it was protected from the elements. Once digging started, it was exposed to all sorts of vulnerabilities from the natural world, [41]including earthquakes, weather, erosion, water, and so forth. Similarly, it exposed the city and its treasures to humans. From poor excavation methods to vandalism and [43]human traffic, the city has further deteriorated.

There was a time when it was believed the preservation attempts were not enough, but [45]in the last few years, several buildings have reopened after restoration, giving some hope that both re-creation and restoration may be enough to show visitors the real [47]Pompeii.

31. What is the main idea of the passage?
    a. Roman life was captured by the eruption of Vesuvius.
    b. Preservation is more important than excavation in Pompeii.
    c. Excavations of Pompeii are revealing but must be done properly.
    d. Digging in Pompeii has been damaging to the ruins.

32. The discovery of a horse at the Villa of the Mysteries supports what claim in paragraph 1?
    a. Ash from the eruption preserved the area.
    b. Pompeii would have more to reveal.
    c. Many were killed quickly from heat.
    d. The city was left in decay.

Practice Test #2

33. Based on the passage, how does the writer feel about Pompeii?
    a. Disinterested
    b. Intrigued
    c. Protective
    d. Hopeful

34. What is meant by *frescoes* in line 33?
    a. Murals created using a special technique
    b. Horses of a particular breed
    c. Roman architectural designs
    d. Community parks

35. Based on the information in the passage, which of the following can be inferred?
    a. That more digs are needed in order to show what Pompeii was really like before it was covered in ash
    b. Making new discoveries in Pompeii is the main goal of researchers and archeologists
    c. Most of the citizens of Pompeii were slaves
    d. The city of Pompeii in its entirety may never be fully revealed

36. What method did researchers use to reveal body shapes?
    a. Finding mummified remains
    b. Filling voids with plaster
    c. Discovering remains preserved in ash
    d. Finding intact skeletons

Mathematics Achievement

1. The formula for the volume of a cylinder is $\pi r^2 h$, where r is the radius and h is the height. A truck is carrying three cylindrical barrels. Each barrel has a diameter of 2 feet and a height of 3 feet. What is the total volume of the three barrels in cubic feet?
    a. 3π
    b. 9π
    c. 12π
    d. 15π

2. In triangle DEF, the measure of angle D is less than or equal to 90° and greater than or equal 2°. Angles E and F are equal. Which of the following is a possible measure for angle F?
    a. 30°
    b. 44°
    c. 68°
    d. 91°

3. A pizzeria owner regularly creates jumbo pizzas, each with a radius of 9 inches. She is mathematically inclined, and wants to know the area of the pizza to purchase the correct boxes and know how much she is feeding her customers. The formula for the area of a circle *is* $A = \pi r^2$. What is the area of a circle with a radius of 9 inches, in terms of π?
    a. 9π in^2
    b. 18π in^2
    c. 81π in^2
    d. 90π in^2

4. Terri needs to slice a pie to share with her department at work. Terri knows that she needs to divide the pie into slices that are 0.20 of the total pie. How should Terri slice the pie so everyone gets an equal share?
   a. 5 slices
   b. 10 slices
   c. 15 slices
   d. 20 slices

5. The width of a rectangular house is 22 feet. What is the perimeter of this house if it has the same area as a house that is 33 feet wide and 50 feet long?
   a. 184 feet
   b. 194 feet
   c. 200 feet
   d. 206 feet

6. Which of the following expressions represents the length of side x?

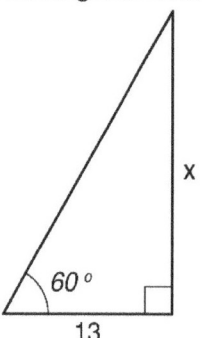

   a. $13 \tan 60°$
   b. $13 \sin 60°$
   c. $13 \cos 60°$
   d. $60 \tan 13°$

7. Subtract and express in reduced form: $\frac{23}{24} - \frac{1}{6}$.
   a. $\frac{19}{24}$
   b. $\frac{4}{5}$
   c. $\frac{22}{18}$
   d. $\frac{11}{9}$

8. What is the simplified quotient of $\frac{5x^3}{3x^2y} \div \frac{25}{3y^9}$?
   a. $\frac{125x}{9y^{10}}$
   b. $\frac{x}{5y^8}$
   c. $\frac{5}{xy^8}$
   d. $\frac{xy^8}{5}$

9. For the following similar triangles, what are the values of x and y (rounded to one decimal place)?

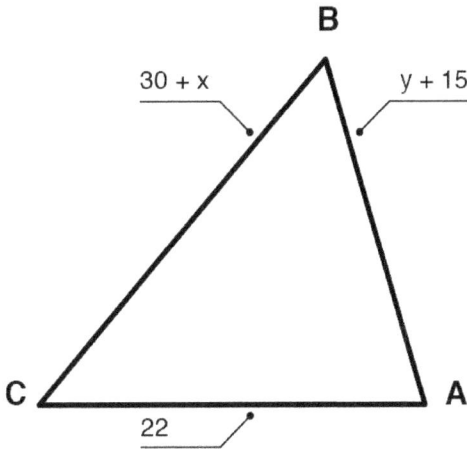
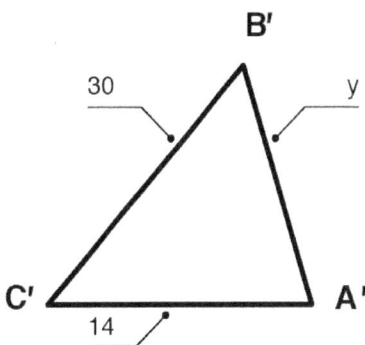

a. $x = 16.5, y = 25.1$
b. $x = 17.1, y = 26.3$
c. $x = 19.5, y = 24.1$
d. $x = 26.3, y = 17.1$

10. There are $4x + 1$ treats in each party favor bag. If a total of $60x + 15$ treats are distributed, how many bags are given out?
    a. 15 bags
    b. 16 bags
    c. 20 bags
    d. 22 bags

11. What is the volume of a cone, in terms of π, with a radius of 10 centimeters and height of 12 centimeters?
    a. 120π cm³
    b. 140π cm³
    c. 200π cm³
    d. 400π cm³

12. For which of the following are $x = 4$ and $x = -4$ solutions?
    a. $x^2 - 16 = 0$
    b. $x^2 - 2x - 2 = 0$
    c. $x^2 + 16 = 0$
    d. $x^2 + 4x - 4 = 0$

13. The Cross family is planning a trip to Florida. They will be taking two cars for the trip. One car gets 18 miles to the gallon of gas. The other car gets 25 miles to the gallon. If the total trip to Florida is 450 miles, and the cost of gas is $2.49 per gallon, how much will the gas cost for both cars to complete the trip?
    a. $32.33
    b. $43.00
    c. $44.82
    d. $107.07

14. The ratio of 5 angles in a pentagon is 2:2:2:2:1. What is the size of the smallest angle?
    a. 30°
    b. 60°
    c. 90°
    d. 120°

15. Gary is driving home to see his parents for Christmas. He travels at a constant speed of 60 miles per hour for a total of 350 miles. How many minutes will it take him to travel home if he takes a break for 10 minutes every 100 miles?
    a. 320 minutes
    b. 360 minutes
    c. 380 minutes
    d. 390 minutes

16. What is the value of the expression: $7^2 - 3 \times (4 + 2) + 15 \div 5$?
    a. 12.2
    b. 34
    c. 40.2
    d. 58.2

17. Simplify: $(5x^2 - 3x + 4) - (2x^2 - 7)$?
    a. $x - 3$
    b. x^5
    c. $3x^2 - 3x - 3$
    d. $3x^2 - 3x + 11$

18. The formula for finding the area of a regular polygon is $A = \frac{1}{2} \times a \times P$ where a is the length of the apothem (the distance from the center to any side at a right angle), and P is the perimeter of the figure. What is the area of the regular hexagon shown below?

    a. 72
    b. 124.68
    c. 374.04
    d. 748.08

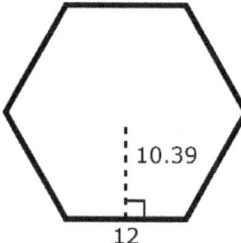

19. The area of a given rectangle is 24 cm². If the measure of each side is multiplied by 3, what is the area of the new figure?
    a. 48 cm²
    b. 72 cm²
    c. 111 cm²
    d. 216 cm²

20. Chris walks $\frac{4}{7}$ of a mile to school and Tina walks $\frac{5}{9}$ of a mile. Which student covers more distance on the walk to school?
    a. Chris, because $\frac{4}{7} < \frac{5}{9}$
    b. Chris, because $\frac{4}{7} > \frac{5}{9}$
    c. Tina, because $\frac{5}{9} < \frac{4}{7}$
    d. Tina, because $\frac{5}{9} > \frac{4}{7}$

21. Dwayne has received the following scores on his math tests: 78, 92, 83, 97. What score must Dwayne get on his next math test to have an overall average of 90?
    a. 89
    b. 95
    c. 98
    d. 100

22. Evaluate:

$$(\sqrt{36} \times \sqrt{16}) - 3^2$$

    a. 13
    b. 15
    c. 21
    d. 30

23. In Jim's school, there are a total of 650 students. There are three girls for every two boys. How many students are girls?
    a. 130 girls
    b. 260 girls
    c. 390 girls
    d. 410 girls

24. Kimberley earns $10 an hour babysitting, and after 10 p.m., she earns $12 an hour. The time she works is rounded to the nearest hour for pay purposes. On her last job, she worked from 5:30 p.m. to 11:00 p.m. In total, how much did Kimberley earn on her last job?
    a. $42
    b. $45
    c. $57
    d. $62

25. Keith's bakery had 252 customers go through its doors last week. This week, that number increased to 378. Express this increase as a percentage.
    a. 50%
    b. 35%
    c. 26%
    d. 12%

26. A ball is drawn at random from a ball pit containing 8 red balls, 7 yellow balls, 6 green balls, and 5 purple balls. What's the probability that the ball drawn is yellow?
    a. $\frac{1}{26}$
    b. $\frac{7}{26}$
    c. $\frac{19}{26}$
    d. 1

27. Let $f(x) = 2x + 1, g(x) = \frac{x-1}{4}$. Find $g(f(x))$.
    a. $\frac{x}{2}$
    b. $\frac{x+1}{2}$
    c. $\frac{2x^2-x-1}{4}$
    d. $3x$

28. The following rectangle in the second quadrant is translated 7 units to the right and 10 units down. Which of the following describes this transformation?

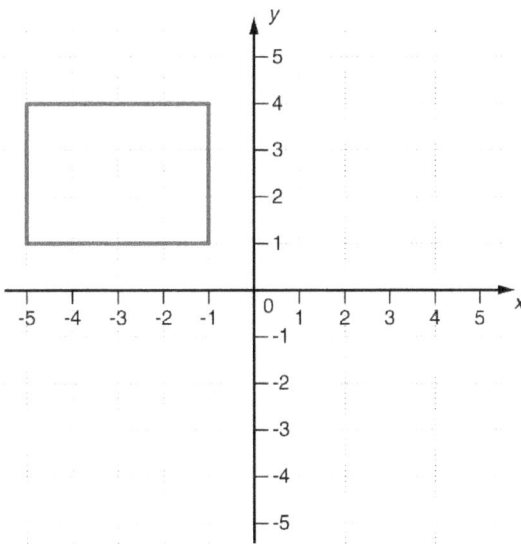

a. $(x, y) \Rightarrow (x + 7, y + 10)$
b. $(x, y) \Rightarrow (x - 7, y + 10)$
c. $(x, y) \Rightarrow (x + 7, y - 10)$
d. $(x, y) \Rightarrow (x - 7, y - 10)$

29. What is the product of the following expression?
$$(3 + 2i)(5 - 4i).$$

a. $15 - 8i$
b. $15 - 10i$
c. $15 - 8i^2$
d. $23 - 2i$

30. How many different ways can 7 textbooks be arranged on a bookshelf?
a. 21
b. 720
c. 5,040
d. 82,3543

31. A line passes through the origin and through the point (-3, 4). What is the slope of the line?
a. $-\frac{4}{3}$
b. $-\frac{3}{4}$
c. $\frac{3}{4}$
d. $\frac{4}{3}$

32. A bag contains 5 red marbles, 10 blue marbles, and 15 green marbles. What is the probability of picking a green marble out of the bag in a single try?
    a. $\frac{1}{6}$
    b. $\frac{1}{3}$
    c. $\frac{2}{5}$
    d. $\frac{1}{2}$

33. For which real numbers, x, is $-3x^2 + x - 8 > 0$?
    a. All real numbers x
    b. $-2\sqrt{\frac{2}{3}} < x < 2\sqrt{\frac{2}{3}}$
    c. $1 - 2\sqrt{\frac{2}{3}} < x < 1 + 2\sqrt{\frac{2}{3}}$
    d. For no real numbers x

34. What is the measurement of angle f in the following picture? Assume the lines are parallel.

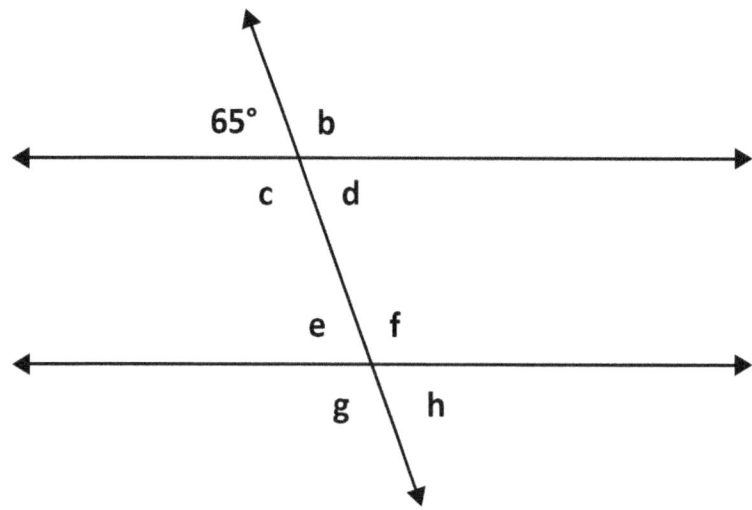

    a. 55 degrees
    b. 65 degrees
    c. 115 degrees
    d. 125 degrees

35. A data set is comprised of the following values: 30, 33, 33, 26, 27, 32, 33, 35, 29, 27. Which of the following has the greatest value?
    a. Mean
    b. Median
    c. Mode
    d. Range

Practice Test #2

36. What is the inverse of the function $f(x) = 3x - 5$?
    a. $f^{-1}(x) = \frac{x}{3} + 5$
    b. $f^{-1}(x) = \frac{5x}{3}$
    c. $f^{-1}(x) = 3x + 5$
    d. $f^{-1}(x) = \frac{x+5}{3}$

37. The height, in feet, of a baseball falling t seconds after it has reached its peak after being hit by a bat can be found by $-16t^2 + 170$. What is the baseball's altitude 1.5 seconds after it has reached its peak?
    a. 134 ft
    b. 154 ft
    c. 184 ft
    d. 206 ft

38. If $x > 3$, then $\frac{x^2 - 6x + 9}{x^2 - x - 6} =$
    a. $\frac{x+2}{x-3}$
    b. $\frac{x-2}{x-3}$
    c. $\frac{x-3}{x+3}$
    d. $\frac{x-3}{x+2}$

39. If the sides of a cube are 5 centimeters long, what is its volume?
    a. $10 \, cm^3$
    b. $15 \, cm^3$
    c. $50 \, cm^3$
    d. $125 \, cm^3$

40. Given the sets $A = \{1, 2, 3, 4, 5, 6, 7, 8, 9, 10\}$ and $B = \{1, 2, 3, 4, 5\}$, what is $A - (A \cap B)$?
    a. $\emptyset$
    b. $\{1, 2, 3, 4, 5\}$
    c. $\{1, 2, 3, 4, 5, 6, 7, 8, 9, 10\}$
    d. $\{6, 7, 8, 9, 10\}$

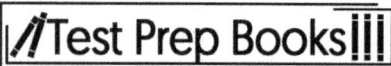

41. What value of x would solve the following equation?

$$20x + x - 6 = 11 + 3x$$

a. $x = \frac{17}{16}$
b. $x = \frac{17}{18}$
c. $x = \frac{17}{24}$
d. $x = \frac{5}{24}$

42. What is the product of the following expressions?

$$(4x - 8)(5x^2 + x + 6)$$

a. $2x^3 - 11x^2 - 32x + 20$
b. $6x^3 - 41x^2 + 12x + 15$
c. $20x^3 + 11x^2 - 37x - 12$
d. $20x^3 - 36x^2 + 16x - 48$

43. Which graph will be a line parallel to the graph of $y = 3x - 2$?
a. $6x - 2y = -2$
b. $4x - y = -4$
c. $3y = x - 2$
d. $2x - 2y = 2$

44. If $-3(x + 4) \geq x + 8$, what is the value of x?
a. $x \leq -5$
b. $x \geq -5$
c. $x \geq 2$
d. $x = 4$

45. Solve for x: $\frac{2x}{5} - 1 = 59$.
a. 60
b. 115
c. 145
d. 150

46. What is the probability of rolling a 6 exactly once in two rolls of a die?
a. $\frac{1}{36}$
b. $\frac{1}{6}$
c. $\frac{11}{36}$
d. $\frac{1}{3}$

47. A sample data set contains the following values: 1, 3, 5, 7. What's the standard deviation of the set?
a. 1.1
b. 2.58
c. 4
d. 6.23

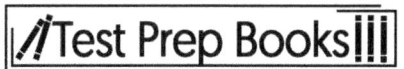

Essay

You have 30 minutes to plan and write your essay. Do not worry too much about length; it's most important to focus on the content and quality of your writing.

Where in the world would you most like to have a pen pal and why?

Answer Explanations #2

Verbal Reasoning

Synonyms

1. D: An *orchard* is most like a *grove* because both are areas like plantations that grow different kinds of fruit. Choice *A, farm,* may have an *orchard* or *grove* on the property, but they are not the same thing, and many farms do not grow fruit trees.

2. B: *Textile* is another word for *fabric.* The most confusing alternative choice in this case is *knit,* because some *textiles* are *knit* but *textile* and *knit* are not synonyms, and plenty of textiles are not knit.

3. B: *Offspring* are the *children* of parents. The other answer choice, *parent,* may be somewhat tricky because *parents* have *offspring*, but they are not synonyms.

4. A: *Permit* can be a verb or a noun. As a verb, it means to *allow* or *give authorization* for something. As a noun, it generally refers to a document or something that has been authorized like a parking permit or driving permit, allowing the authorized individual to park or drive under the rules of the document.

5. B: *Taut* means tight or rigid. The test taker might confuse *taut* with *taught* and believe that *instruct* is the best choice, but this is incorrect. One clue that this is incorrect is that *instruct* is in the wrong tense to be exactly synonymous with *taught*. Another possibility for confusion is mistaking *taut* with *tart* and choosing *sour* as the word with the closest meaning.

6. C: *Rotation* means to spin or turn, such as a wheel rotating on a car, although *wheel* does not mean rotation.

7. A: Something that is *consistent* is *steady, predictable, reliable,* or *constant*. The tricky one here is that the word *consistency* comes from the word *consistent*, and may describe something that is sticky.

8. A: A *principle* is a *foundation* or a *guiding law, code, or belief*. Someone with good moral character is described as having strong *principles*. Test takers must be careful not to get confused with the homonym's *principle* and *principal*, because these words have very different meanings. A principal is the leader of a school, and the word *principal* also refers to the main or most important idea or thing.

9. C: *Perimeter* refers to the outline or borders of an object. Test takers may recognize that word from math class, where *perimeter* refers to the edges or distance around an enclosed shape. Some of the other answer choices refer to other math vocabulary encountered in geometry lessons, but they do not have the same meaning as *perimeter*.

10. C: A *symbol* is an *object, picture,* or *sign* that is used to represent something. For example, a pink ribbon is a *symbol* for breast-cancer awareness, and a flag can be a *symbol* for a country. The tricky part of this question was also knowing the meaning of *emblem,* which typically describes a design that represents a group or concept, much like a *symbol*. *Emblems* often appear on flags or a coat of arms.

11. A: *Germinate* means to *develop* or *grow* and most often refers to sprouting seeds as a new plant first breaks through the seed coat. It can also refer to the development of an idea. Choice *C* may be an attractive choice since plants germinate, but *germinate* does not mean *plant*.

12. D: *Loquacious* means talkative. It does not refer to volume, so *quiet* and *loud* are incorrect.

Answer Explanations #2

13. B: *Facetious* means lighthearted or in a joking manner. Facetious comments may be, but are not always, annoying.

14. A: *Profuse* means copious or abundant. *Scarce* means little and is the opposite of profuse.

15. C: *Assimilate* means integrate; it does not mean to give up, hide, or limit, which are synonyms for the other answer choices.

16. D: *Incredulous* means unbelieving or doubtful.

17. C: *Schism* means separation, usually based on opposing beliefs or philosophies. *Laceration* means wound, which could refer to a split, or separation, in the skin, but *separation* is the best synonym for *schism* as *laceration* specifically refers to an injury to the skin.

18. C: *Dexterity* means deftness or skill.

19. B: *Dilapidated* means deteriorated or run-down.

Sentence Completion

20. A: Choice *A* is the correct answer because *ambitious* means having a desire for success, which accurately describes the volunteers who are eager to participate in the dog training program. *Munificent* means very generous, which fits the context of a wealthy benefactor who made a significant donation to fund the program. Choice *B* is incorrect because *diligent* describes hard-working volunteers, but *diminutive* means small, and that doesn't fit the context of a large donation. Choice *C* is incorrect because *indolent* means lazy, which contradicts the statement about the volunteers being hard-working. *Benevolent* does mean generous and would otherwise be correct. Choice *D* is incorrect because *inspiring* might describe the volunteers but doesn't capture their hard-working spirit. *Paltry* means insignificant, which is not accurate for describing a large donation.

21. B: Choice *B* is the correct answer because *frugal* means economical and conscious with money. Since Harry did not have a job any longer, it was necessary for him to be careful with his spending. Choice *A* is incorrect because *conventional* means traditional. This does not relate to Harry's financial decisions. Choice *C* is incorrect because *mundane* means dull. Harry not buying unnecessary items does not make him dull. Choice *D* is incorrect because *reclusive* means avoiding other people. There is no mention of other people in this sentence.

22. B: Choice *B* is the correct answer because *dilapidated* means in a state of disrepair, which fits the description of the school needing repairs. *Prohibitive* means restrictive, which explains why the repairs cannot be completed with a small budget. Choice *A* is incorrect because *deteriorate* is a verb and the adjective *deteriorated* is needed. *Impractical,* or not feasible, would fit otherwise. Choice *C* is incorrect because *tenable* means capable of being maintained, which does not fit the prohibitive costs. *Ruinous,* meaning in ruins, may otherwise work to describe the school. Choice *D* is incorrect because the words need to be switched in order to work. *Decaying* works as it means actively falling into despair. *Unreasonable,* or beyond acceptable limits, fits as a descriptor for the costs. However, the words are in the wrong positions.

23. C: Choice *C* is the correct answer because *patiently* means calm and unrushed, which fits the professor's approach to answering students' questions in a way that makes them feel comfortable. *Emboldened* means to be more confident, which accurately describes how the students would feel after the professor treats them with patience during questions. Choice *A* is incorrect because *hastily* means rushed, which contradicts the idea of making students feel comfortable. *Encouraged* fits but doesn't work with *hastily.* Choice *B* is incorrect because although *kindly* fits the context, the students being *hesitant* or cautious does not make sense if the teacher is kind. Choice *D* is incorrect because *vaguely* means unclearly, which would make students feel uncertain. *Inquisitive* means curious

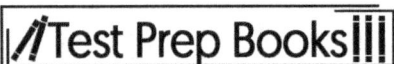

and would make sense if the students asked questions, but this does not match the description of the student's feeling comfortable sharing their thoughts.

24. A: Choice A is the correct answer because to be *anguished* means to show a great deal of pain. This fits the scenario of an archaeologist seeing a priceless artifact destroyed. Choice B is incorrect because *defiant* means showing disobedience. This does not fit the scenario as there is nobody that the archaeologist is resisting. Choice C is incorrect because *ecstatic* means extremely happy. This is the opposite of how we expect the archaeologist to feel. Choice D is incorrect because *nonchalant* suggests calmness or lack of care. The archaeologist crying out suggests that they are not calm or without care.

25. B: Choice B is the correct answer because *frantic* means panicked, which is how someone would feel when they realize they are trapped in a cave. *Methodical* means with planned care, which would have been useful when Marvin was packing as he might have included equipment that would save him. Choice A is incorrect because the words would need to be swapped in order to work. *Agitated* is a valid feeling for being trapped in a cave and *diligent* means showing care in one's duties which would fit. However, they are in the wrong positions. Choice C is incorrect because *morose* means gloomy, which does not capture the urgency of the situation, and does not work as well as *frantic* even if Marvin did feel morose. *Fortified* means strengthened and does not fit the sentence. Choice D is incorrect because although *panicked* works, *haphazard* means lacking organization which is the opposite of what Marvin needed in his packing.

26. B: Choice B is the correct answer because *elusive* means difficult to find, which fits the description of the panda located in a hard-to-reach place. *Inaccessible* fits the sentence because the forest is high altitude, making it is difficult to navigate and find animals within. Choice A is incorrect because *coveted* means greatly desired, which doesn't exactly fit the sentence since there is no indication that people want the pandas. *Laborious,* which means requiring great effort, doesn't quite make sense with the sentence. Although it may be laborious to travel in the forest, it does not make sense to call the forest itself laborious. Choice C is incorrect because *prevalent* would mean that the red pandas are common and easy to find, which does not fit Jeremy's mission to find one for a video. *Unattainable,* which means impossible to attain, does not quite make sense because a forest is not something that is attained. Choice D is incorrect; *secretive* almost makes sense since red pandas are hard to find, but the pandas do not hold secrets themselves. *Treacherous* means hazardous, which would otherwise make sense when describing a hard-to-navigate forest.

27. B: Choice B is the correct answer because *exemplary* means an excellent model. This fits the scenario described, in which the teacher uses the paper as a model for years. Choice A is incorrect because *austere* means severe or harsh. This does not fit the explanation of the teacher using the paper as a model. Choice C is incorrect because *intrepid* means brave. This is unrelated to an academic paper. Choice D is incorrect because *pedantic* would mean that the paper is overly academic and detailed. The paper would not be a model for success in that case.

28. B: Choice B is the correct answer because *devastated* means destroyed, which fits the assumption that Marianne is deeply unhappy about not being able to afford tickets to her favorite band. She is so keen on seeing the band that she cries to her mother for help buying tickets, showing that she truly wants this experience. *Implored* means pleaded with, which fits the context of her asking her mother for money to buy tickets. Choice A is incorrect because *apathetic* means without care, which does not fit the context since Marianne was distressed about not seeing her favorite band. *Pleaded,* which means begged, would otherwise work. Choice C is incorrect because *envious* means jealous, which doesn't fit the context of the sentence because there is nobody that Marianne would be jealous of. *Belittled* means demeaned, which does not fit the context since that is not a way to ask a person for money. Choice D is incorrect because *exasperation* is in the wrong form for this sentence and should read *exasperated*. *Beseeched,* which means asked passionately, would fit otherwise.

Answer Explanations #2

29. D: Choice *D* is the correct choice because the cakes being *inadequate* means that they were not up to the standard Penelope wants for her wedding. This explains the disappointment. Choice *A* is incorrect because *ambitious* means striving for greatness above what is expected. The cakes were disappointing, so it is unlikely that they were ambitious. Choice *B* is incorrect because *delectable* means that something tastes delicious. This is not the case in this scenario as Penelope dislikes the cakes. Choice *C* is incorrect because *dubious* would mean that the cakes are suspicious or of questionable value. Although it may be accurate to say that the cakes are of questionable value, it is better to say that they were *inadequate* since we are unsure why Penelope did not like them.

30. B: Choice *B* is the correct answer because *distraught* means deeply upset, which fits the context of Carlos doing poorly on an important exam. *Anticipated* means predicted, which fits since the context is Carlos not living up to his predicted performance. Choice *A* is incorrect because although *detached* means disconnected, which would work given the context, *foreseen* is in the incorrect form for the sentence structure. Choice *C* is incorrect because *jubilant* means joyful, which does not make sense considering that Carlos got a lower grade than expected. *Dreaded* does not work in this context because the sentence is setting up a contrast between the low grade and Carlos's higher expectation. Choice *D* is incorrect because *lethargic* means exhausted and it does not make sense that a grade would make someone feel that way. *Expectation* is in the wrong form and should read *expected* for the past tense.

31. D: Choice *D* is the correct answer because *unwavering* means without faltering, which fits the context of classmates providing support to someone who is ill. *Incapacitating* means preventing function, which fits the description of an illness that leaves someone bedbound. Choice *A* is incorrect because *reluctant,* meaning hesitant, does not make sense in this context. The sentence states that the classmates are happily providing support, so there is no reason to believe it is reluctant. *Manageable,* meaning able to be controlled, does not fit the sentence either as the illness leaves Cynthia bedbound. Choice *B* is incorrect because *debilitate* is the wrong form of the word; it should read *debilitating* instead. *Steadfast,* which means without faltering, would otherwise fit, but not with *debilitate. Unconditional* means not conditional, which would fit. *Temperate*, which means showing moderation, does not fit the context of the sentence; therefore, Choice *C* is incorrect.

32. C: Choice *C* is the correct answer because *gratitude* refers to feelings of appreciation, which fits the concept of Thanksgiving. *Delectable*, or delicious, works because it explains why some people are excited about the holiday food. Choice *A* is incorrect because *clemency* means forgiveness and it does not make sense to practice forgiveness for what you're thankful for. *Palatable* means pleasant to taste, which makes sense but does not work with *clemency*. Choice *B* is incorrect because *compassion,* which means showing or feeling sensitive concern, is usually associated with sad situations and wouldn't be expressed to show thankfulness. *Unappetizing,* meaning not appealing, does not work well since it does not explain why people enjoy the food. Choice *D* is incorrect because *pondering* means thinking carefully, which doesn't fit the context of the sentence and does not work well with its structure. *Abundant,* meaning plentiful, works here, but not with *pondering*.

33. A: Choice *A* is the correct answer because *complacent* means to be overly pleased with yourself and to ignore potential room for improvement. This would accurately describe the situation that led to Meghan being fired. Choice *B* is incorrect because *diligent* would mean that Meghan was working hard and being detail oriented. If this were the case, she would not be fired. Choice *C* is incorrect because *overzealous* means to have too much enthusiasm. Meghan's subpar performance suggests that she was not enthusiastic about the work that she was doing. Choice *D* is incorrect because *punctual* means to be on time. This is unrelated to Meghan's work performance issues.

34. B: Choice *B* is the correct answer because the word *convoluted* means to be unnecessarily complex and hard to follow. This would explain why Tiffany struggled to follow the instructions for building the model train as well as why an expert would also struggle. Choice *A* is incorrect because if the instructions were *adequate,* they would be satisfactory for Tiffany's needs. Choice *C* is incorrect because if the instructions were *pragmatic,* they would be sensible and practical. It is unlikely that Tiffany or an expert would struggle in that case. Choice *D* is incorrect

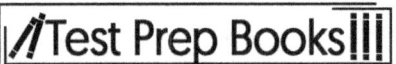

because *precarious* means that something is likely to collapse or that it is uncertain. This does not apply to a set of instructions or to this scenario.

35. B: Choice *B* is the correct answer because the word *lethargic* means that someone is feeling sluggish and lacking in energy, which fits being sick with the flu. Choice *A* is incorrect because *fervent* means passionate. This does not apply to someone who is sick with the flu. Choice *C* is incorrect because *melancholic* means depressed. Although someone who is sick may feel sad, the assumption that they are physically tired is more reasonable. Choice *D* is incorrect because *nostalgic* means wistfully happy about the past. There is no connection between illness and nostalgia.

36. C: Choice *C* is the correct answer because the word *relinquish* means to voluntarily give something up. This is fitting for the scenario in which the retiring CEO must pass on his role to someone else. Choice *A* is incorrect because to *assimilate* means to understand something fully. The CEO has been in his role for twenty-five years and is retiring; there is nothing for him to understand. Choice *B* is incorrect because to *condescend* means to act superior. There is nothing suggesting that the CEO would assume an air of superiority about his role since he is looking to retire after a long time. Choice *D* is incorrect because to *sustain* means to give support or to continue. The CEO is not looking to continue his role; he is looking to retire from it.

37. D: Choice *D* is the correct answer because *superfluous* means unnecessary. Since Cathy already has so many mugs, buying another one would be excessive. Choice *A* is incorrect because *affluent* means wealthy. This is generally not an appropriate adjective for an inanimate object, so Choice *A* is incorrect. Choice *B* is incorrect because *insentient* means incapable of feeling. Although the mug is incapable of feeling, it does not fit the context as to why Cathy feels regret about the mug when she clearly enjoys buying them. Choice *C* is incorrect because *obsolete* means that something is no longer used. This does not apply to the pretty mug, since it is a new object that Cathy has not used before.

38. C: Choice *C* is the correct answer because the word *incendiary* means likely to cause anger and conflict. This fits the context of the sentence since Janet caused her husband's feelings of rage during an argument. The words she said to him must have been inflammatory. Choice *A* is incorrect because *ambiguous* means that something is vague and unclear. If Janet's words were vague, it is unlikely that her husband would have such a strong anger response. Choice *B* is incorrect because *formidable* means to inspire respect through power. Although Janet's words may have been powerful, her husband's response of anger does not suggest that they spurred on feelings of respect. Choice *D* is incorrect because *trivial* means of little importance. The husband's strong reaction shows that the words had meaning or importance to his emotions.

39. C: Choice *C* is the correct answer because *meticulously* means with attention to detail. This matches Carrie's scenario of paying attention to every single stitch to prevent mistakes. Choice *A* is incorrect because *abnormally* means that out of the norm or unusual. Carrie does not want unusual stitches. Choice *B* is incorrect because *hastily* means quickly and without care. That is the opposite of what Carrie wants to do. Choice *D* is incorrect because *valiantly* means with bravery. This does not relate to Carrie's need for a detail-oriented approach.

40. B: Choice *B* is the correct answer because *conciliatory* means an attempt to calm down a person or situation. This aligns with the situation described in the sentence, as the principal is attempting to calm down an emotional student. Choice *A* is incorrect because *cautious* means careful to avoid problems, which almost works but does not capture the attempt to calm the student down like the word *conciliatory* does. Choice *C* is incorrect because *neutral* means without bias, which may be a good thing in this scenario but does not capture the principal's attempt to calm the student down. Choice *D* is incorrect because *skeptical* means to have doubt regarding something. The principal is attempting to put the student at ease, not determine the truth of the situation.

Answer Explanations #2

Quantitative Reasoning

Word Problems

1. C: This problem involved setting up an algebraic equation to solve for x, or the number of flower trays Carly purchased. The equation is as follows:

$$6x + 8x = 84$$

So,

$$14x = 84$$

Then divide each side by 14 to solve for x:

$$x = \frac{84}{14} = 6 \text{ trays}$$

2. D: We are given $t = 3$ and $r = 60$, so using the formula $d = r \times t$, we get $d = 60 \times 3 = 180$.

3. B: In this scenario, the variables are the number of sales and Karen's weekly pay. The weekly pay depends on the number of sales. Therefore, weekly pay is the dependent variable (y), and the number of sales is the independent variable (x). All four answer choices are in slope-intercept form, $y = mx + b$, so we just need to find m (the slope) and b (the y-intercept). We can calculate both by picking any two points, for example, (2, 380) and (4, 460).

The slope is given by $m = \frac{y_2 - y_1}{x_2 - x_1}$, so $m = \frac{460 - 380}{4 - 2} = 40$. This gives us the equation $y = 40x + b$. Now we can plug in the x and y values from our first point to find b. Since $380 = 40(2) + b$, we find $b = 300$. This means the equation is $y = 40x + 300$.

4. A: The core of the pattern consists of 4 items: ▲○○□. Therefore, the core repeats in multiples of 4, with the pattern starting over on the next step. The highest multiple of 4 that's below 42 is 40. Step 40 is the end of the core (□), so step 41 will start the core over (▲) and step 42 is ○.

5. D: Parallel lines will never intersect. Therefore, the lines are not parallel. Perpendicular lines intersect to form a right angle (90°). Although the lines intersect, they do not form a right angle, which is usually indicated with a box at the intersection point. Therefore, the lines are not perpendicular.

6. D: A cone is a three-dimensional figure and is classified as a solid. A polygon is a closed two-dimensional figure consisting of three or more sides. A pentagon is a polygon with five sides. A triangle is a polygon with three sides. A rhombus is a type of polygon with 4 sides.

7. D: The coordinates of a point are written as an ordered pair (x, y). To determine the x-coordinate, a line is traced directly above or below the point until reaching the x-axis. This step notes the value on the x-axis. In this case, the x-coordinate is -3. To determine the y-coordinate, a line is traced directly to the right or left of the point until reaching the y-axis, which notes the value on the y-axis. In this case, the y-coordinate is 2. Therefore, the ordered pair is written (-3, 2).

8. D: The perimeter is found by calculating the sum of all sides of the polygon:

$$9 + 9 + 9 + 8 + 8 + s = 56$$

Let s be the missing side length. Therefore, $43 + s = 56$. The missing side length is 13 cm.

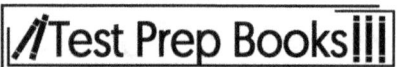

Answer Explanations #2

9. D: $\frac{1}{3}$ of the shirts sold were patterned. Therefore, $1 - \frac{1}{3}$ (that is, $\frac{2}{3}$) of the shirts sold were solid. A fraction of something is calculated with multiplication, so $192 \times (1 - \frac{1}{3})$ solid shirts were sold. We could calculate that this equals 128, but that's not necessary for this question.

10. B: The probability of picking the winner of the race is $\frac{1}{4}$, or $\left(\frac{\text{number of favorable outcomes}}{\text{number of total outcomes}}\right)$. Assuming the winner was picked on the first selection, three horses remain from which to choose the runner-up (these are dependent events). Therefore, the probability of picking the runner-up is $\frac{1}{3}$. To determine the probability that multiple events all happen, multiply the probabilities of the events:

$$\frac{1}{4} \times \frac{1}{3} = \frac{1}{12}$$

11. C: The total percentage of a pie chart equals 100%. We can see that CD sales make up less than half of the chart (50%) but more than a quarter (25%), and the only answer choice that meets these criteria is Choice C, 40%.

12. B: Scientific notation takes the form $a \times 10^n$, where a is any decimal number between 1 and 10 and n is the number of decimal places it takes to reach the first digit. In this case, take the first digit 7, add a decimal point, and then include each non-zero digit after that to determine the value of a as 7.35. Next, count the place values from the position of the decimal point in standard form to the position in scientific notation in order to determine the value of n, which would be 9. Therefore, this number expressed in scientific notation would be 7.35×10^9.

13. D: The total faculty is $15 + 20 = 35$. So, the ratio is 35:200. Then, divide both of these numbers by 5, since 5 is a common factor to both, with a result of 7:40.

14. B: The formula for the perimeter of a rectangle is $P = 2L + 2W$, where P is the perimeter, L is the length, and W is the width. The first step is to substitute all of the data into the formula:

$$36 = 2(12) + 2W$$

Simplify by multiplying 2×12:

$$36 = 24 + 2W$$

Simplifying this further by subtracting 24 on each side, which gives:

$$36 - 24 = 24 - 24 + 2W$$

$$12 = 2W$$

Divide by 2:

$$6 = W$$

The width is 6 cm. Remember to test this answer by substituting this value into the original formula:

$$36 = 2(12) + 2(6)$$

15. C: For $10h + 20$, both the number multiplied by h and the number added to h are divisible by 5. The result will always be divisible by 5. For $5h - 3$, multiplying h by 5 yields a multiple of 5, but subtracting 3 means the final answer will no longer be a multiple of 5. For $4h + 1$, multiplying h by 4 yields a multiple of 5, but adding 1 means

Answer Explanations #2

the final answer will no longer be a multiple of 5. For the final expression, $h^3 + 6$, h cubed yields an answer divisible by 5, but the addition of 6 means the answer is no longer divisible by 5.

16. B: When solving for x, add 3 to both sides to get $4x = 8$. Then, divide both sides by 4 to get $x = 2$.

17. D: If s is the size of the floor in square feet and r is the rate on Tuesday, then, based on the information given, $p = \frac{s}{4}$ and $r = \frac{s}{3}$. Solve the Monday rate for s, $s = 4p$, and then substitute that in the expression for Tuesday.

18. C: $Area = length \times width$. Therefore, the area of the rectangle is equal to 3 in $\times$ 8 in $= 24$ in^2.

19. B: First, subtract 4 from each side:

$$6t + 4 = 16$$
$$6t + 4 - 4 = 16 - 4$$
$$6t = 12$$

Now, divide both sides by 6:

$$\frac{6t}{6} = \frac{12}{6}$$
$$t = 2$$

20. C: Multiply both sides by x to get $x + 2 = 2x$, which simplifies to $-x = -2$, or $x = 2$.

21. D: The formula for the volume of a cube is $V = s^3$, where V is the volume and s is the side length. Here, $s = 3$ in, so $V = (3 \text{ in})^3 = 27 \text{ in}^3$.

Quantitative Comparisons

22. B: An octagon has 8 equal sides. Therefore, the perimeter is equal to the sum of these 8 sides. Divide 17.6 by 8 to obtain 2.2 inches. This is the length of 1 side. Multiply this quantity by 6, resulting in 13.2 inches. This is the length of 6 of its sides. Therefore, Quantity B is greater.

23. C: We know that a^{-b} is equal to $\frac{1}{a^b}$. Therefore, $(5.25)^{-4} = \frac{1}{5.25^4}$, which is the same as $\left(\frac{1}{5.25}\right)^4$. The two quantities are equal.

24. A: 5% of 0.55 is equal to $0.05(.55) = 0.0275$. 4% of 0.44 is equal to $0.04(.44) = 0.0176$. Therefore, Quantity A is larger.

25. C: The formula for a sum of cubes is $(a^3 + b^3) = (a + b)(a^2 - ab + b^2)$. In this example, $a = x$ and $b = 2y$. Therefore, we have that $x^3 + 8y^3 = (x + 2y)(x^2 - 2xy + 4y^2)$. The two quantities are equal.

26. D: If $x > 0$, the two quantities are equal because $\sqrt{4x^2} = 2|x| = 2x$. However, if $x < 0$, $\sqrt{4x^2}$ is greater because $\sqrt{4x^2} = 2|x|$, which is positive, and $2x$ would be negative. Therefore, there is not enough information to determine which quantity is greater.

27. B: $h(-3) = 8(-3)^2 + 2(-3) = 8(9) - 6 = 66$. $h(3) = 8(3)^2 + 2(3) = 8(9) + 6 = 78$. Therefore, Quantity B is greater.

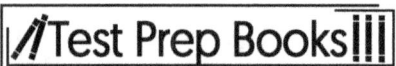

28. B: We need to place both equations into slope intercept form $y = mx + b$. Subtract $2x$ from both sides and divide by 3 in the equation in Quantity A to obtain $y = -\frac{2}{3}x + \frac{8}{3}$. The slope of this line is $-\frac{2}{3}$. Add $2x$ onto both sides and divide by 3 in the equation in Quantity B to obtain $y = \frac{2}{3}x - \frac{8}{3}$. The slope of this line is $\frac{2}{3}$. Therefore, Quantity B is greater.

29. C: The slope of the line in Quantity A is $m = \frac{2-1}{2-(-1)} = \frac{1}{3}$. The slope of the line in Quantity B is $m = \frac{-2-(-1)}{-2-1} = \frac{-1}{-3} = \frac{1}{3}$. The two quantities are equal.

30. C: The area of the circle in Quantity A is $\pi(9)^2 = 81\pi \ ft^2$. The circle in Quantity B has a diameter of 18ft. The radius is half the diameter, so the circle in Quantity B has a radius of 9ft. Therefore, the area of the circle in Quantity B is $\pi(9)^2 = 81\pi \ ft^2$. The two quantities are equal.

30. C: The area of the circle in Quantity A is $\pi(9)^2 = 81\pi \ ft^2$. The circle in Quantity B has a diameter of 18ft. The radius is half the diameter, so the circle in Quantity B has a radius of 9ft. Therefore, the area of the circle in Quantity B is $\pi(9)^2 = 81\pi \ ft^2$. The two quantities are equal.

31. C: If we multiply out Quantity A by foiling, we obtain $a^2 - 2ab - b^2$. This is the square of a binomial. The two quantities are equal.

32. A: We need to place both equations of lines into slope-intercept form $y = mx + b$, where b is the y-intercept. For the line in Quantity A, add $3x$ to both sides and divide through by 6 to obtain $y = \frac{1}{2}x + \frac{3}{2}$. For the line in Quantity B, subtract $3x$ from both sides and divide through by 4 to obtain $y = -\frac{3}{4}x - \frac{5}{2}$. The y-intercept $\frac{3}{2}$ is larger than $-\frac{5}{2}$.

33. C: The mean of the data set is $\frac{1+3+5+7+9+11+13}{7} = 7$. The median of the data set is the center value, which is 7. The 2 values are equal.

34. B: The number 98 can be factored into the prime factorization $7 \cdot 7 \cdot 2$. The number 51 is equal to $17 \cdot 3$. The largest prime factor of 51 is 17, which is greater than the largest prime factor of 49, which is 7.

35. C: The polynomial in Quantity A can be factored by grouping. Factor a $2x$ out of the first set of 2 terms and a -5 out of the second set of two terms to obtain $2x(2x + 1) - 5(2x + 1)$. Then, factor the binomial $2x + 1$ out of both terms to obtain $(2x - 5)(x + 1)$, which is the same as Quantity B.

36. B: The standard deviation of a data set measures the spread of the data, which describes how far away the data values are from the mean. The standard deviation of Quantity A is 0 because all of the values are the same. The standard deviation of Quantity B is larger than 0 because the data values do vary from the mean.

37. D: We are not given a time frame, so we do not know how many each person mowed. For example, Michael could have mowed 2 lawns, and Jay could have mowed 20 lawns—or the opposite could have happened.

Reading Comprehension

Passage 1

1. D: Although Washington was from a wealthy background, the passage does not say that his wealth led to his republican ideals, so Choice *A* is not supported. Choice *B* also does not follow from the passage. Washington's warning against meddling in foreign affairs does not mean that he would oppose wars of every kind, so Choice *B* is

Answer Explanations #2

incorrect. Choice C is also unjustified since the author does not indicate that Alexander Hamilton's assistance was absolutely necessary. Choice D is correct because the passage states that Washington's farewell address clearly opposes political parties and partisanship. The author then notes that presidential elections often hit a fever pitch of partisanship. Thus, it follows that George Washington would probably not approve of modern political parties and their involvement in presidential elections.

2. D: The author finishes the passage by applying Washington's farewell address to modern politics, so the purpose probably includes this application. Choice A is incorrect because George Washington is already a well-established historical figure; furthermore, the passage does not seek to introduce him. Choice B is incorrect because the author is not fighting a common perception that Washington was merely a military hero. Choice C is incorrect because the author is not convincing readers. Persuasion does not correspond to the passage. Choice D states the primary purpose.

3. A: The tone in this passage is informative. Choice B, excited, is incorrect, because there are not many word choices used that would indicate excitement from the author. Choice C, bitter, is incorrect. Although the author does make a suggestion in the last paragraph to Americans, the statement is not necessarily bitter, but based on the preceding information. Choice D, comic, is incorrect, as the author does not try to make the audience laugh, nor do they make light of the situation in any way.

4. C: *Meddling* means to interfere in something. Choice A is incorrect. One helpful thing would be to use the word in the sentence: "Washington warned Americans against 'supporting' in foreign affairs" does not make that much sense, so we can mark it off. Choice B, *speaking against*, is incorrect. This phrase would make sense in the sentence, but it goes against the meaning that is intended. George Washington warned against interference in foreign affairs, not speaking *against* foreign affairs. Choice D is also incorrect, because "gathering in foreign affairs" does not sound quite right. Choice C, *interfering*, is therefore the best choice for this question.

5. A: When Washington was offered a role as leader of the former colonies, he refused the offer. This is explained in the first sentence of the second paragraph. All of the other answer choices are incorrect and not mentioned in the passage.

6. D: In the context of the sentence, the best choice is *reached*, making Choice D correct. The phrase "hit a fever pitch" is best interpreted as "reached a state of extreme excitement." The word *hit* can also mean to slap, and something that is a hit is a success, but Choices A and B do not work in the sentence in the passage. Choice C might be a little harder to eliminate because the reader might think that it makes sense that politics would "cause" a state of extreme excitement or a fever pitch. However, if we use substitution, considering that something can "reach" a certain point or "hit" a certain point but something can "cause" something else to happen but NOT "hit" something else to happen, we can definitely eliminate Choice C.

Passage 2

7. D: The passage does not proceed in chronological order since it begins by pointing out Christopher Columbus's explorations in America, so Choice A does not work. Although the author compares and contrasts Erikson with Columbus, this is not the main way the information is presented; therefore, Choice B does not work. Choice C is also incorrect because there is no mention of or reference to cause and effect in the passage. However, the passage does offer a conclusion (Leif Erikson deserves more credit) and premises (first European to set foot in the New World and first to contact the natives) to substantiate Erikson's historical importance. Thus, Choice D is correct.

8. C: Choice A is incorrect because it describes facts: Leif Erikson was the son of Erik the Red and historians debate Leif's date of birth. These are not opinions. Choice B is incorrect; Erikson calling the land Vinland is a verifiable fact, as is Choice D, because he did contact the natives almost 500 years before Columbus. Choice C is the correct answer

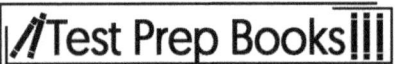

Answer Explanations #2

because it is the author's opinion that Erikson deserves more credit. Another person could argue that Columbus or another explorer deserves more credit, which makes it an opinion rather than a historical fact.

9. B: Choice A is incorrect because the author aims to go beyond describing Erikson as merely a legendary Viking. Choice C is incorrect because the author does not focus on Erikson's motivations, let alone name the spreading of Christianity as his primary objective. Choice D is incorrect because it is a premise that Erikson contacted the natives 500 years before Columbus, which is simply a part of supporting the author's conclusion. Choice B is correct because it accurately identifies the author's statement that Erikson deserves more credit than he has received for being the first European to explore the New World.

10. B: Choice B is correct because the author wants the reader to be informed about Leif Erikson's contribution to exploring the new world. While several other answers are possible options, Choice B is the strongest. Choice A is incorrect because the author is not in any way trying to entertain the reader. Choice C is incorrect because the nature of the writing does not indicate the author would be satisfied with the reader merely being alerted to Erikson's exploration; instead, the author is making an argument about the credit he should receive. Choice D is incorrect because the author goes beyond merely a suggestion; "suggest" is too vague.

11. D: Choice A is incorrect because the author never addresses the Vikings' state of mind or emotions. Choice B is incorrect because the author does not elaborate on Erikson's exile and whether he would have become an explorer if not for his banishment. Choice C is incorrect because there is not enough information to support this premise. It is unclear whether Erikson informed the King of Norway of his findings. Although it is true that the king did not send a follow-up expedition, he could have simply chosen not to expend the resources after receiving Erikson's news. It is not possible to logically infer whether Erikson told him. Choice D is correct because the uncertainty about Leif Erikson's birth year is an example of how historians have trouble pinning down important details in Viking history.

12. A: Choice A is correct because Leif Erikson "arrived at Greenland with a ship full of timber." It can be inferred that he found plenty of trees in Greenland. Erikson planned to spread Christianity to Greenland, but there is no indication in the passage that he converted any of the Skraelings to Christianity, making Choice B incorrect. Choice C is incorrect because although trade and weapons are mentioned in the passaged, nothing in the passage would lead the reader to assume that weapons were traded. Choice D is also incorrect. Erikson's birthplace is unknown. All that is known is that he was not born in Greenland because that is where he was banished to. There is not enough information in the passage to infer that Norway was his place of birth.

Passage 3

13. B: Choice B is correct because the author is trying to demonstrate the main idea, which is that heat loss is proportional to surface area, so they compare two animals with different surface areas to clarify the main point. Choice A is incorrect because the author uses elephants and anteaters to prove a point, that heat loss is proportional to surface area, not to express an opinion. Choice C is incorrect because though the author does use them to show differences, they do so in order to give examples that prove the above points. Choice D is incorrect because there is no language to indicate favoritism between the two animals.

14. C: Because of the way the author addresses the reader and the colloquial language the author uses (e.g., "let me explain," "so," "well," "didn't," "you would look stupid"), Choice C is the best answer because it has a much more casual tone than the usual informative article. Choice A may be a tempting choice because the author says the "fact" that most of one's heat is lost through their head is a "lie" and that someone who does not wear a shirt in the cold looks stupid. However, this only happens twice within the passage, and the passage does not give an overall tone of harshness. Choice B is incorrect because again, while not necessarily nice, the language does not carry an angry charge. The author is clearly not indifferent to the subject because of the passionate language that they use, so Choice D is incorrect.

Answer Explanations #2

15. D: The passage states that while the legs do lose a significant amount of heat, the torso probably loses more, so Choice *D* is correct and Choice *B* is incorrect. The author says that the amount of heat lost is in proportion with the surface area of the particular body part. The head and feet have smaller surface areas than the torso, so Choices *A* and *C* are not correct.

16. C: *Gullible* means to believe something easily. The other answer choices could fit easily within the context of the passage: you can be angry toward, distrustful toward, or frightened by authority. For this answer choice and the surrounding context, however, the author talks about a myth that people believe easily, so *gullible* would be the word that fits best in this context.

17. D: The whole passage is dedicated to debunking the head heat loss myth. The passage says that "each part of your body loses its proportional amount of heat in accordance with its surface area," which means an area such as the chest would lose more heat than the head because it's bigger.

18. B: Choice *B* is correct because the passage explains that more heat is lost in areas that have more surface area; therefore, is can be inferred that to cool down, the better option would be to remove a shirt because it covers more surface area. Choice A is incorrect because by removing the hat, a smaller area would be cooled down. Choice *C* is incorrect. This inference cannot be made based on the details in the passage. The inference made in Choice *D* cannot be supported by the details in the passage. A person might need to cover their head even if the torso is covered well. The passage merely states that a larger surface area loses more heat than a smaller surface area, therefore covering large areas works better than covering small areas.

Passage 4

19. D: The thesis is a statement that contains the author's topic and main idea. The main purpose of this article is to use historical evidence to provide counterarguments to anti-Stratfordians. Choice *A* is simply a definition; Choice *B* is a supporting detail, not a main idea; and Choice *C* represents an idea of anti-Stratfordians, not the author's opinion.

20. C: This requires readers to be familiar with different types of rhetorical devices. A rhetorical question is a question that is asked not to obtain an answer but to encourage readers to more deeply consider an issue.

21. B: This particular detail can be found in lines 18–19 where the author says, "even though he did not attend university, grade-school education in Shakespeare's time was actually quite rigorous."

22. A: This is a vocabulary question that can be answered using context clues. Other sentences in the paragraph describe London as "the most populous city in England" filled with "crowds of people," giving an image of a busy city full of people. Choice *B* is incorrect because London was in Shakespeare's home country, not a foreign one. Choice *C* is not mentioned in the passage. Choice *D* is not a good answer choice because the passage describes how London was a popular and important city, not an undeveloped one.

23. C: The passage states this fact in line 15, where it says "his father was a very successful glove-maker."

24. B: Choice *B* best describes the organization of the passage. The argument that William Shakespeare is not responsible for the plays he supposedly wrote is the main topic of the first paragraph. The next two paragraphs give reasons why the argument may not be valid. Choices *A* and *C* do not describe the organization of the passage because there is not a problem to solve but rather an argument to counter and there is not a chronological account of Shakespeare's life but rather a chronological presentation of counterarguments. Choice *D* is incorrect because the subject presented in the first paragraph is specifically an argument, and the paragraphs that follow present counterarguments, not facts and then opinions. Choice *B* gives the best description of how the passage is organized.

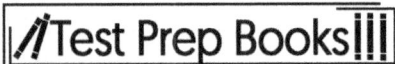

Answer Explanations #2

Passage 5

25. A: The author mentions St. Lucia a couple times throughout the passage.

26. C: Remember that supporting details help readers find out the main idea by answering questions like *who, what, where, when, why,* and *how*. In this question, cruises, local events, and cuisine are not talked about in the passage. However, family resorts and activities are talked about.

27. B: The last activity the author did was go for a hike up a mountain. The author "wanted to take one more walk" before the family left. The author did do Choices *A* and *C*—swam with the sharks and lounged on the beach—, but those weren't the last activities they did. They never said anything about surfing in the waves, so Choice *D* is incorrect.

28. D: To trek means to hike or walk, so Choice *D* is the best answer here. The other choices (drove, ran, and swam) are incorrect because they do not reflect the hike mentioned earlier in the passage.

29. D: The author's attitude towards the topic is enthusiastic. The author's enthusiasm is seen in the word choices such as *best vacation, enjoyed, beautiful,* and *peace*. The author also uses multiple exclamation marks, which denotes excitement. Therefore, the best answer is Choice *D*. The author doesn't demonstrate any worry or resignation, except maybe a bit in the part where they have to go home soon, but the enthusiasm overrides these feelings in the rest of the passage. Choice *C*, objective, means to be fair and based in fact, and the author is far too enthusiastic toward St. Lucia, which creates some bias towards the topic.

30. C: Choice *C* is correct because the author gives a description of their vacation to St. Lucia, a Caribbean island. At the end of the passage the author says, "You should visit St. Lucia, or pick another island in the Caribbean!" This is clearly encouragement for others to enjoy a Caribbean vacation. Choice *A* is incorrect because the author discusses the ocean and the mountains to provide descriptions, not to make a comparison of the two. Choice *B* is also incorrect. The author mentions seeing a scary shark while snorkeling and returning to the surface after seeing it, but they do not give a warning or discourage others from snorkeling. In fact, they give a lovely description of the other things they saw while snorkeling. Choice *D* is incorrect as well. Although the author mentions the wildlife and scenery in St. Lucia, these are only a part of the overall description of the author's vacation in St. Lucia, not the main point.

Passage 6

31. C: A good portion of the passage discusses errors in excavation and efforts to both preserve what is there and be more mindful regarding future excavations. Choice *A* is incorrect. Roman life was captured in the ash, but the focus of the paragraph goes well beyond that fact. Choice *B* is incorrect. According to the passage and the author, both are important, but the focus is mostly on excavation efforts. Choice *D* is incorrect. This fact is true, but the focus is too narrow. The passage discusses excavation successes, goals, and so forth.

32. B: Paragraph 1 claims that Pompeii has more to reveal, and discoveries in the last five years, such as the horse, prove that to be true. Choice *A* is incorrect. This fact is true, and Paragraph 1 discusses the preservation, but the horse demonstrates more than preservation. Choice *C* is incorrect. The fact is established in Paragraph 1, but there is no indicator that the horse died from the heat. Choice *D* is incorrect. The ability for researchers to make new discoveries suggests that the entire city is not in decay.

33. C: Throughout the passage, the author stresses both the mistakes made and efforts to protect the site and its value. Therefore, it can be inferred that the author feels protective toward Pompeii. Choice *A* is incorrect. The level of detail and concern in the author's tone does not suggest disinterest. Choice *B* is incorrect. The author does seem intrigued, but there's a greater focus on preservation and protection. Choice *D* is incorrect. The end of the passage suggests hope regarding better effort to preserve and protect. In other words, the overwhelming feeling is still protective.

34. A: Choice A is correct. Frescoes are murals that are made using fresh lime plaster. The other choices are incorrect.

35. D: Throughout the passage the author explains that various excavations were attempted and then halted. Later the author says that strategies have changed to preservation. Then they mention that there was a time when it was believed that preservation would not be enough but that now restoration might be enough to show the real Pompeii to visitors. All of this leads to the inference that future excavations may never happen, but that what has been uncovered up to this point may be enough, if restored, to present an accurate representation to visitors of what Pompeii had been like. Therefore, this proves Choice D to be correct and Choice A to be incorrect. Choice B is incorrect due to the fact that the strategies have shifted from making new discoveries to restoring and preserving what has already been uncovered. There is nothing in the passage that supports the inference suggested in Choice C.

36. B: Researchers used plaster to fill voids and re-create body shapes. Choice A is incorrect. Mummified remains were found elsewhere. Choice C is incorrect. Most of the city was preserved in ash, so this method would have been unnecessary. Choice D is incorrect. Skeletal remains were found, but they were not used to help re-create body shapes.

Mathematics Achievement

1. B: The formula for the volume of a cylinder is $\pi r^2 h$, where r is the radius and h is the height. The diameter is twice the radius, so these barrels have a radius of 1 foot. That means each barrel has a volume of:

$$\pi \times 1\, ft^2 \times 3\, ft = 3\pi\, ft^3$$

Since there are three of them, the total is:

$$3 \times 3\pi\, ft = 9\pi\, ft^3$$

2. C: The sum of 3 angles in a triangle is 180°. The maximum value that angles E and F can be is 89° since angle D is greater than or equal to 2° and they must be equal. The minimum value that angles E and F can be is 45° since angle D is less than or equal to 45°. Only 68° is an appropriate choice.

3. C: The formula for the area of a circle is $A = \pi r^2$. Here, $r = 9$, so we calculate $A = \pi(9^2) = 81\pi$.

4. A: 0.20 can be converted into the fraction $\frac{20}{100}$, which can then be reduced to $\frac{1}{5}$. Terri needs to slice the pie into five pieces; everyone will get $\frac{1}{5}$ of the pie.

5. B: First, find the area of the second house. The area is:

$$A = l \times w = 33 \times 50 = 1{,}650 \text{ square feet}$$

Then, use the area formula to determine what length gives the first house an area of 1,650 square feet. So:

$$1{,}650 = 22 \times l, l = \frac{1{,}650}{22} = 75 \text{ feet}$$

Then, use the formula for perimeter ($A = l + l + w + w$) to get:

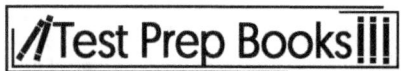

Answer Explanations #2

$$75 + 75 + 22 + 22 = 194 \text{ feet}$$

6. A: The side adjacent to the 60-degree angle. We are seeking to find the side opposite. We can use SOHCAHTOA to find this missing side length.

$$\tan 60° = \frac{opp}{adj} = \frac{x}{13}$$

Therefore, $x = 13 \tan 60°$.

7. A: To find a common denominator, look for a number that has both denominators (24 and 6) as factors. 24 works. Multiply the top and bottom of each fraction by whatever number will make the denominator 24:

$$\frac{23}{24} \times \frac{1}{1} = \frac{23}{24} \text{ and } \frac{1}{6} \times \frac{4}{4} = \frac{4}{24}$$

Now that we have a common denominator, subtract the numerators:

$$\frac{23}{24} - \frac{4}{24} = \frac{23 - 4}{24} = \frac{19}{24}$$

Since 19 and 24 have no common factors except 1, this fraction can't be reduced.

8. D: Dividing rational expressions follows the same rule as dividing fractions. The division is changed to multiplication by the reciprocal of the second fraction. This turns the expression into:

$$\frac{5x^3}{3x^2y} \times \frac{3y^9}{25}$$

This can be simplified by finding common factors in the numerators and denominators of the two fractions.

$$\frac{x^3}{x^2y} \times \frac{y^9}{5}$$

Multiplying across creates:

$$\frac{x^3 y^9}{5x^2 y}$$

Simplifying leads to the final expression of $\frac{xy^8}{5}$.

9. B: Because the triangles are similar, the lengths of the corresponding sides are proportional. Therefore:

$$\frac{30 + x}{30} = \frac{22}{14} = \frac{y + 15}{y}$$

This results in the equation:

$$14(30 + x) = 22 \times 30$$

When solved, this gives $x = 17.1$. The proportion also results in the equation:

$$14(y + 15) = 22y$$

Answer Explanations #2

When solved, this gives $y = 26.3$.

10. A: The total number of treats distributed will be the number of treats per bag $(4x + 1)$ times the number of bags given out, which can be represented by the variable n. This expression is $n(4x + 1)$. Since this is the amount of treats distributed, set it equal to $60x + 15$.

$$n(4x + 1) = 60x + 15$$

In order to figure out what n is, determine what number times 4 results in 60 ($4n = 60$) and what number times 1 results in 15 ($1n = 15$). In both cases, $n = 15$. Therefore, 15 bags are given out.

11. D: The volume of a cone is $(\pi r^2 h)/3$, and $(\pi \times 10^2 \times 12)/3 = 400$ cm³. Choice A is incorrect because it is 10×12. Choice B is also incorrect because that is $10^2 + 40$. Choice C is $10^2 \times 2$.

12. A: One approach is to simply try substituting each value of x into each equation.

Choice B can be eliminated since:

$$4^2 - 2 \times 4 - 2 = 6$$

Choice C can be eliminated since:

$$4^2 + 16 = 32$$

Choice D can be eliminated since:

$$4^2 + 4 \times 4 - 4 = 28$$

But, plugging in either value into $x^2 - 16$ gives the following:

$$(\pm 4)^2 - 16 = 16 - 16 = 0$$

13. D: For the first car, the trip will be 450 miles at 18 miles to the gallon. The total gallons needed for this car will be:

$$450 \div 18 = 25$$

For the second car, the trip will be 450 miles at 25 miles to the gallon, or $450 \div 25 = 18$, which will require 18 gallons of gas. Adding these two amounts of gas gives a total of 43 gallons of gas. If the gas costs $2.49 per gallon, the cost of the trip for both cars is:

$$43 \times \$2.49 = \$107.07$$

14. B: The interior angles inside a pentagon have sum of 540°. The sum of the given ratios is $2 + 2 + 2 + 2 + 1 = 9$. Therefore, the smallest angle has $\frac{1}{9}$ of the angle sum. $\frac{1}{9}(540) = 60°$.

15. C: To find the total driving time, the total distance of 350 miles can be divided by the constant speed of 60 miles per hour. This yields a time of 5.8333 hours, which is then rounded. Once the driving time is computed, the break times need to be found. If Gary takes a break for 10 minutes every 100 miles, he will take 3 breaks on his trip. This will yield a total of 30 minutes of break time. Since the answer is needed in minutes, 5.8333 hours can be converted to minutes by multiplying by 60, giving a driving time of 350 minutes. Adding the break time of 30 minutes to the driving time of 350 minutes gives a total travel time of 380 minutes.

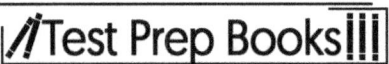

16. B: When performing calculations consisting of more than one operation, the order of operations should be followed: parentheses, exponents, multiplication & division, addition & subtraction.

Parentheses:

$$7^2 - 3 \times (4 + 2) + 15 \div 5$$

$$7^2 - 3 \times (6) + 15 \div 5$$

Exponents:

$$49 - 3 \times 6 + 15 \div 5$$

Multiplication & division (from left to right):

$$49 - 18 + 3$$

Addition & subtraction (from left to right):

$$49 - 18 + 3 = 34$$

17. D: By distributing the implied 1 in front of the first set of parentheses and the negative one in front of the second set of parentheses, the parentheses can be eliminated:

$$1(5x^2 - 3x + 4) - 1(2x^2 - 7)$$

$$5x^2 - 3x + 4 - 2x^2 + 7$$

Next, like terms are combined by adding the coefficients of the same variables with the same exponents, while keeping the variables and their powers unchanged:

$$5x^2 - 3x + 4 - 2x^2 + 7$$

$$3x^2 - 3x + 11$$

18. C: The formula for finding the area of a regular polygon is $A = \frac{1}{2} \times a \times P$ where a is the length of the apothem (the distance from the center to any side at a right angle), and P is the perimeter of the figure. The apothem a is given as 10.39, and the perimeter can be found by multiplying the length of one side by the number of sides (since the polygon is regular):

$$P = 12 \times 6 \rightarrow P = 72$$

To find the area, substitute the values for a and P into the formula:

$$A = \frac{1}{2} \times a \times P$$

$$A = \frac{1}{2} \times (10.39) \times (72)$$

$$A = 374.04$$

19. D: The area of a rectangle is $A = lw$. We don't know the length or width of this rectangle, but the area is 24, so we can say that $lw = 24$. Length and width are each multiplied by 3, so the area of our new rectangle is $3l \times 3w$, or $9lw$. Since we know that $lw = 24$, the area of the new rectangle is $9lw = 9 \times 24 = 216 \text{ cm}^2$.

20. B: In order to compare the fractions $\frac{4}{7}$ and $\frac{5}{9}$, a common denominator must be used. The least common denominator is 63, which is found by multiplying the two denominators together (7×9). The conversions are as follows:

$$\frac{4}{7} \times \frac{9}{9} = \frac{36}{63}$$
$$\frac{5}{9} \times \frac{7}{7} = \frac{35}{63}$$

Although they walk nearly the same distance, $\frac{4}{7}$ is slightly more than $\frac{5}{9}$ because $\frac{36}{63} > \frac{35}{63}$. Remember, the sign > means "is greater than." Therefore, Chris walks further than Tina, and Choice *B* correctly shows this expression in mathematical terms.

21. D: To find the average of a set of values, add the values together and then divide by the total number of values. In this case, include the unknown value, x, of what Dwayne needs to score on his next test. The average must equal 90. Set up the equation and solve:

First, combine like terms:

$$\frac{78 + 92 + 83 + 97 + x}{5} = 90$$

Next, divide both sides by 5:

$$\frac{350 + x}{5} = 90$$

Lastly, subtract 350 from both sides:

$$350 + x = 450$$

$$x = 100$$

22. B: Follow the order of operations in order to solve this problem. Evaluate inside the parentheses first, being sure to follow the order of operations inside the parentheses as well. First, simplify the square roots:

$$(6 \times 4) - 3^2$$

Then, multiply inside the parentheses:

$$24 - 3^2$$

Next, simplify the exponents:

$$24 - 9$$

Finally, subtract to get 15, Choice *B*.

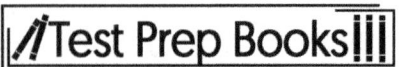

Answer Explanations #2

23. C: Three girls for every two boys can be expressed as a ratio: 3∶2. This can be visualized as splitting the school into five groups: three girl groups and two boy groups. The number of students that are in each group can be found by dividing the total number of students by five:

$$\frac{650 \text{ students}}{5 \text{ groups}} = \frac{130 \text{ students}}{\text{group}}$$

To find the total number of girls, multiply the number of students per group (130) by the number of girl groups in the school (3). This equals 390, Choice *C*.

24. D: Kimberley worked 4.5 hours at the rate of $10/h and 1 hour at the rate of $12/h. The problem states that her time is rounded to the nearest hour, so the 4.5 hours would round up to 5 hours at the rate of $10/h.

$$(5 \text{ h}) \times \left(\frac{\$10}{\text{h}}\right) + (1 \text{ h}) \times \left(\frac{\$12}{\text{h}}\right) = \$50 + \$12 = \$62$$

25. A: First, calculate the difference between the larger value and the smaller value.

$$378 - 252 = 126$$

To calculate this difference as a percentage of the original value, and thus calculate the percentage *increase*, divide 126 by 252 to get 0.5, then multiply by 100 to reach the percentage 50%, Choice *A*.

26. B: The sample space is made up of $8 + 7 + 6 + 5 = 26$ balls. The probability of pulling each individual ball is $\frac{1}{26}$. Since there are 7 yellow balls, the probability of pulling a yellow ball is $\frac{7}{26}$.

27. A: To compose these functions (that is, to find g of f), start with $g(x) = \frac{x-1}{4}$ and replace x with $f(x)$. So:

$$g(f(x)) = \frac{f(x) - 1}{4} = \frac{2x + 1 - 1}{4} = \frac{2x}{4} = \frac{x}{2}$$

28. C: The *x*-coordinates are shifted to the right 7 units, so 7 is added to the first coordinate. The *y*-coordinates are shifted down 10 units, so 10 is subtracted from the second coordinate. $(x, y) \Rightarrow (x + 7, y - 10)$ is the correct choice.

29. D: The notation i stands for an imaginary number. The value of i is equal to $\sqrt{-1}$. When performing calculations with imaginary numbers, treat i as a variable, and simplify when possible. Multiplying the binomials by the FOIL method produces:

$$15 - 12i + 10i - 8i^2$$

Combining like terms yields $15 - 2i - 8i^2$. Since:

$$i = \sqrt{-1}, i^2 = (\sqrt{-1})^2 = -1$$

Therefore, substitute -1 for i^2:

$$15 - 2i - 8(-1)$$

Simplifying results in:

$$15 - 2i + 8 \rightarrow 23 - 2i$$

Answer Explanations #2

30. C: This is a permutation because it is an arrangement of 7 objects where order matters. The first spot on the bookshelf has 7 options, and once the first textbook is selected, there are 6 options, etc. Therefore, there are $7 \times 6 \times 5 \times 4 \times 3 \times 2 \times 1 = 7! = 5,040$ ways to arrange the textbooks.

31. A: The slope is given by:

$$m = \frac{y_2 - y_1}{x_2 - x_1} = \frac{0 - 4}{0 - (-3)} = -\frac{4}{3}$$

32. D: The total number of marbles is 5 + 10 + 15 = 30. Of these, 15 are green. All marbles have an equal probability of getting picked, so the probability is $\frac{15}{30} = \frac{1}{2}$.

33. D: Because the coefficient of x^2 is negative, this function has a graph that is a parabola that opens downward. Therefore, it will be greater than 0 between its real roots, if it has any. Checking the discriminant, the result is:
$$1^2 - 4(-3)(-8) = 1 - 96 = -95$$

Since the discriminant is negative, this equation has no real solutions. Since this has no real roots, it must be always positive or always negative. Its graph opens downward, so it has at least some negative values. That means it is always negative. Thus, it is greater than zero for no real numbers.

34. C: Because the 65-degree angle and angle b sum to 180 degrees, the measurement of angle b is 115 degrees. Because of corresponding angles, angle b is equal to angle f. Therefore, angle f measures 115 degrees.

35. C: Each value can be calculated so that they can be compared to find which one is the greatest. The mean is equal to:

$$\frac{26 + 27 + 27 + 29 + 30 + 32 + 33 + 33 + 33 + 35}{10} = 30.5$$

The median is equal to:

$$\frac{30 + 32}{2} = 31$$

The mode is equal to 33 because that number occurs 3 times in the data set. The range is equal to:

$$35 - 26 = 9$$

Therefore, the mode is the greatest value of the answer choices.

36. D: The inverse of a function is found by following these steps:

1. Change $f(x)$ to y.

2. Switch the x and y in the equation.

3. Solve for y. In the given equation, solving for y is done by adding 5 to both sides, then dividing both sides by 3.

This answer can be checked on the graph by verifying the lines are reflected over $y = x$.

37. A: This amount can be found by plugging $t = 1.5$ into the expression. Therefore, the baseball's altitude is equal to $-16(1.5^2) + 170 = -16(2.25) + 170 = -36 + 170 = 134$ ft.

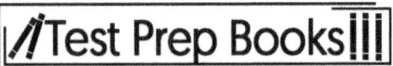

38. D: Factor the numerator into $x^2 - 6x + 9 = (x-3)^2$, since:

$$-3 - 3 = -6$$
$$(-3)(-3) = 9$$

Factor the denominator into $x^2 - x - 6 = (x-3)(x+2)$, since:

$$-3 + 2 = -1,$$
$$(-3)(2) = -6$$

This means the rational function can be rewritten as:

$$\frac{x^2 - 6x + 9}{x^2 - x - 6} = \frac{(x-3)^2}{(x-3)(x+2)}$$

Using the restriction of $x > 3$, do not worry about any of these terms being 0, and cancel an $x - 3$ from the numerator and the denominator, leaving $\frac{x-3}{x+2}$.

39. D: The volume of a cube with sides of length s is $V = s^3$. Here, $s = 5$, so $V = 5^3 = 125$.

40. D: $(A \cap B)$ is equal to the intersection of the two sets A and B, which is $\{1, 2, 3, 4, 5\}$. $A - (A \cap B)$ is equal to the elements of A that are *not* included in the set $(A \cap B)$. Therefore, $A - (A \cap B) = \{6, 7, 8, 9, 10\}$.

41. B:

$20x + x - 6 = 11 + 3x$	Combine $20x$ and x.
$21x - 6 = 11 + 3x$	
$21x - 6 + 6 = 11 + 3x + 6$	Add 6 to both sides to remove -6.
$21x = 17 + 3x$	
$21x - 3x = 17 + 3x - 3x$	Subtract $3x$ from both sides to move it to the other side of the equation.
$18x = 17$	
$\frac{18x}{18} = \frac{17}{18}$	Divide by 18 to get x by itself.
$x = \frac{17}{18}$	

42. D: Finding the product means distributing one polynomial to the other so that each term in the first is multiplied by each term in the second. Then, like terms can be collected. Multiplying the factors yields the expression:

$$20x^3 + 4x^2 + 24x - 40x^2 - 8x - 48$$

Collecting like terms means adding the x^2 terms and adding the x terms. The final answer after simplifying the expression is:

$$20x^3 - 36x^2 + 16x - 48$$

Answer Explanations #2

43. A: Parallel lines have the same slope. The slope of the given equation is 3. The slope of Choice C can be seen to be $\frac{1}{3}$ by dividing both sides by 3. The other choices are in standard form $Ax + By = C$, for which the slope is given by $\frac{-A}{B}$. For Choice A, the equation can be written as $6x - 2y = -2$. Therefore, the slope is:

$$\frac{-A}{B} = \frac{-6}{-2} = 3$$

This is the same as the given equation.

The slope of Choice B is 4:

$$\frac{-A}{B} = \frac{-4}{-1} = 4$$

The slope of Choice D is 1:

$$\frac{-A}{B} = \frac{-2}{-2} = 1$$

Therefore, the only equation with a parallel slope of 3 is $6x - 2y = -2$.

44. A: Solve a linear inequality in a similar way to solving a linear equation. First, start by distributing the –3 on the left side of the inequality.

$$-3x - 12 \geq x + 8$$

Then, add 12 to both sides.

$$-3x \geq x + 20$$

Next, subtract x from both sides.

$$-4x \geq 20$$

Finally, divide both sides of the inequality by –4. Don't forget to flip the inequality sign because you are dividing by a negative number.

$$x \leq -5$$

45. D: Set up the initial equation.

$$\frac{2x}{5} - 1 = 59$$

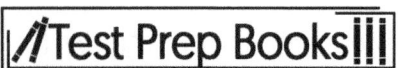

Add 1 to both sides.

$$\frac{2x}{5} - 1 + 1 = 59 + 1$$

$$\frac{2x}{5} = 60$$

Multiply both sides by $\frac{5}{2}$.

$$\frac{2x}{5} \times \frac{5}{2} = \frac{60}{1} \times \frac{5}{2}$$

$$x = 150$$

46. C: The addition rule is necessary to determine the probability because a 6 can be rolled on either roll of the die but not both. The rule used is:

$$P(A \text{ or } B) = P(A) + P(B) - P(A \text{ and } B)$$

The probability of a 6 being individually rolled is $\frac{1}{6}$ and the probability of a 6 being rolled twice is:

$$\frac{1}{6} \times \frac{1}{6} = \frac{1}{36}$$

Therefore, the probability that a 6 is rolled at least once is:

$$\frac{1}{6} + \frac{1}{6} - \frac{1}{36} = \frac{11}{36}$$

47. B: First, the sample mean must be calculated. $\bar{x} = \frac{1}{4}(1 + 3 + 5 + 7) = 4$. The sample standard deviation of the data set is:

$$s = \sqrt{\frac{\sum(x - \bar{x})^2}{n - 1}}$$

$n = 4$ represents the number of data points.

Therefore, the sample standard deviation is:

$$s = \sqrt{\frac{1}{3}[(1 - 4)^2 + (3 - 4)^2 + (5 - 4)^2 + (7 - 4)^2]}$$

$$s = \sqrt{\frac{1}{3}(9 + 1 + 1 + 9)} = 2.58$$

ISEE Upper Practice Tests #3 & #4

To keep the size of this book manageable, save paper, and provide a digital test-taking experience, the 3rd and 4th practice tests can be found online. Scan the QR code or go to this link to access it:

testprepbooks.com/online387/isee-upper

The first time you access the tests, you will need to register as a "new user" and verify your email address.

If you have any issues, please email support@testprepbooks.com.

Dear ISEE Upper Test Taker,

Thank you for purchasing this study guide for your ISEE Upper exam. We hope that we exceeded your expectations.

Our goal in creating this study guide was to cover all of the topics that you will see on the test. We also strove to make our practice questions as similar as possible to what you will encounter on test day. With that being said, if you found something that you feel was not up to your standards, please send us an email and let us know.

We would also like to let you know about other books in our catalog that may interest you.

SSAT Upper

This can be found on Amazon: amazon.com/dp/1637750749

PSAT

amazon.com/dp/1637757026

SAT

amazon.com/dp/1637754051

ACT

amazon.com/dp/1637758596

We have study guides in a wide variety of fields. If the one you are looking for isn't listed above, then try searching for it on Amazon or send us an email.

Thanks Again and Happy Testing!
Product Development Team
support@testprepbooks.com

Online Resources

Included with your purchase are multiple online resources. This includes the practice tests in an interactive format and a convenient study timer to help you manage your time.

Scan the QR code or go to this link to access this content:

testprepbooks.com/online387/isee-upper

The first time you access the tests, you will need to register as a "new user" and verify your email address.

If you have any issues, please email support@testprepbooks.com.
Thank you for allowing us to be a part of your studying journey.

www.ingramcontent.com/pod-product-compliance
Lightning Source LLC
Chambersburg PA
CBHW080546230426
43663CB00015B/2725